Venus versus Virus III

ヴィーナス ヴァーサス ヴァイアラス

Illustrated by Atsushi Suzumi

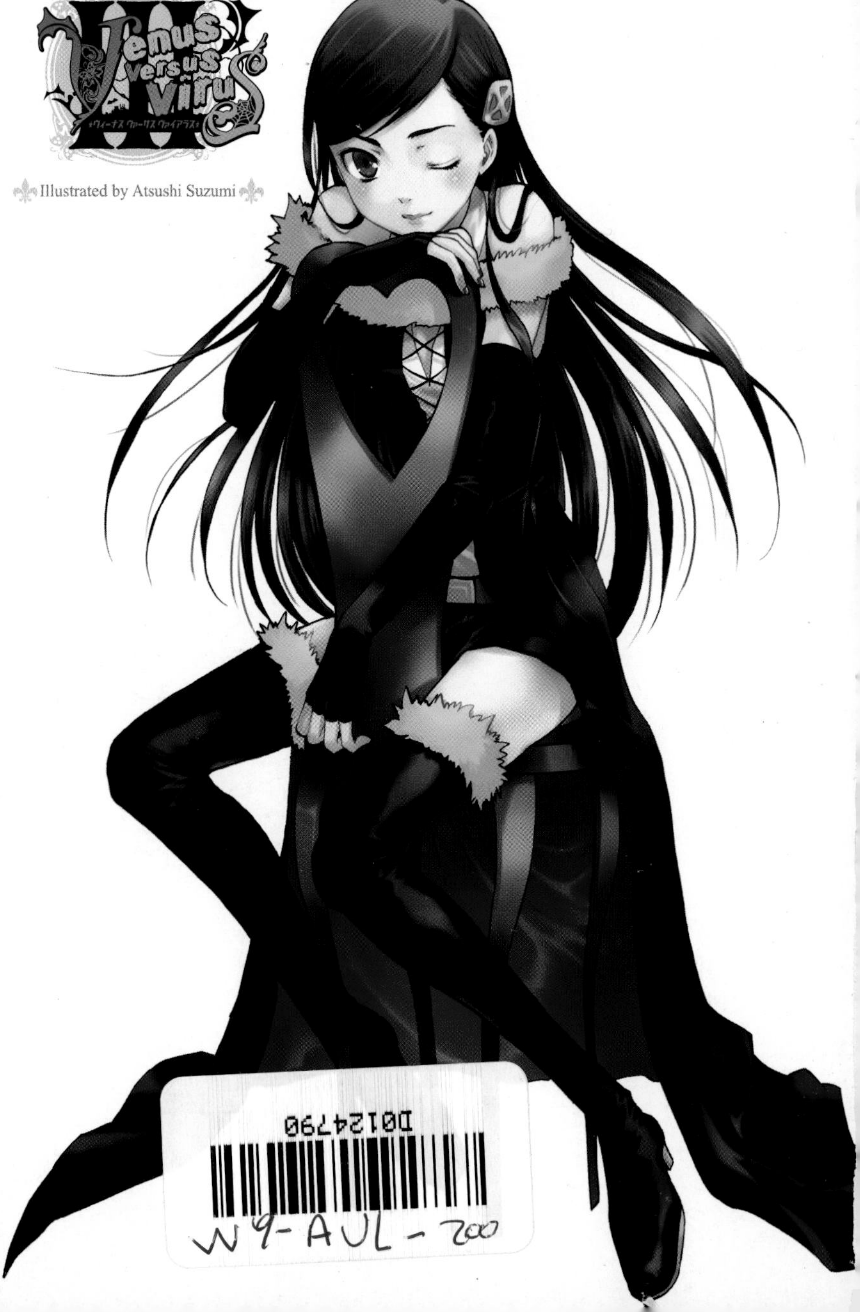

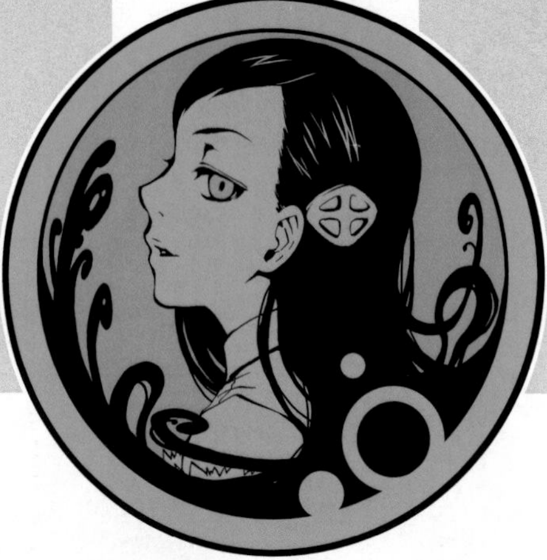

Venus Versus Virus

ヴィーナス ヴァーサス ヴァイアラス

VOLUME 3

CONTENTS

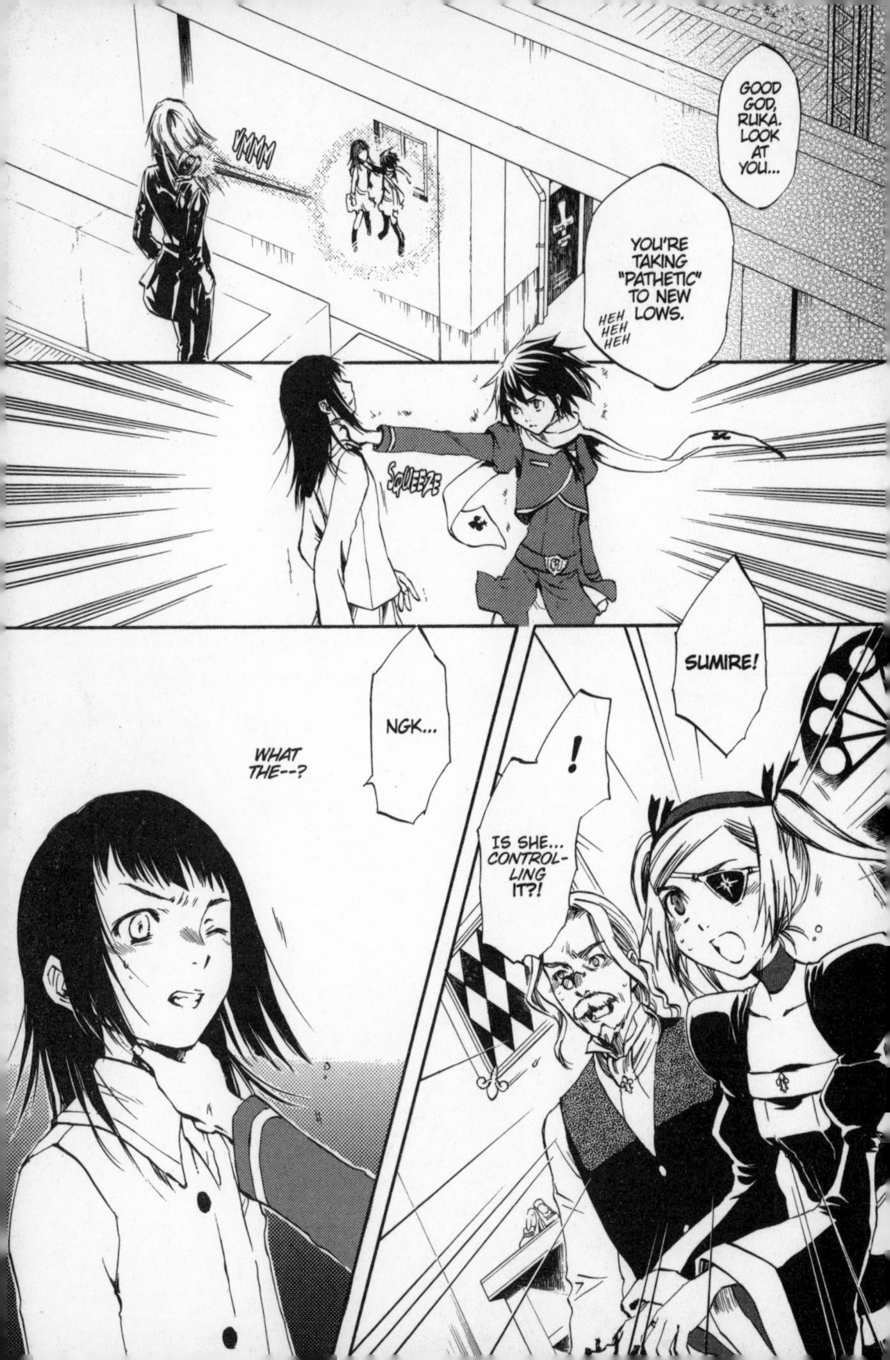
GOOD GOD, RUKA. LOOK AT YOU...
YOU'RE TAKING "PATHETIC" TO NEW LOWS.
HEH HEH HEH
VMMM
SQUEEZE
SUMIRE!
!
IS SHE... CONTROL-LING IT?!
NGK...
WHAT THE--?

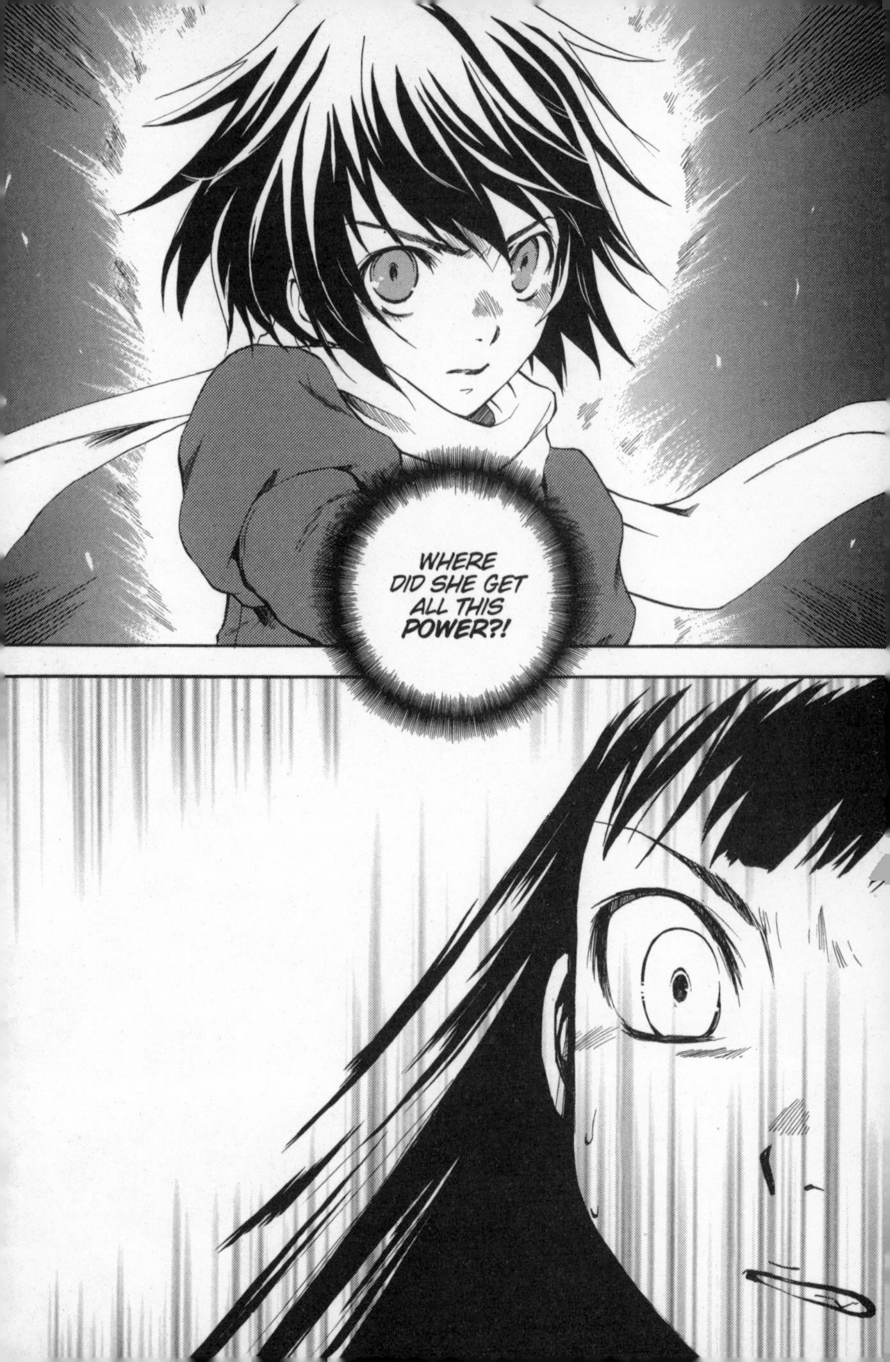
WHERE DID SHE GET ALL THIS POWER?!

Piece 11: DISTANT. MESSENGER.

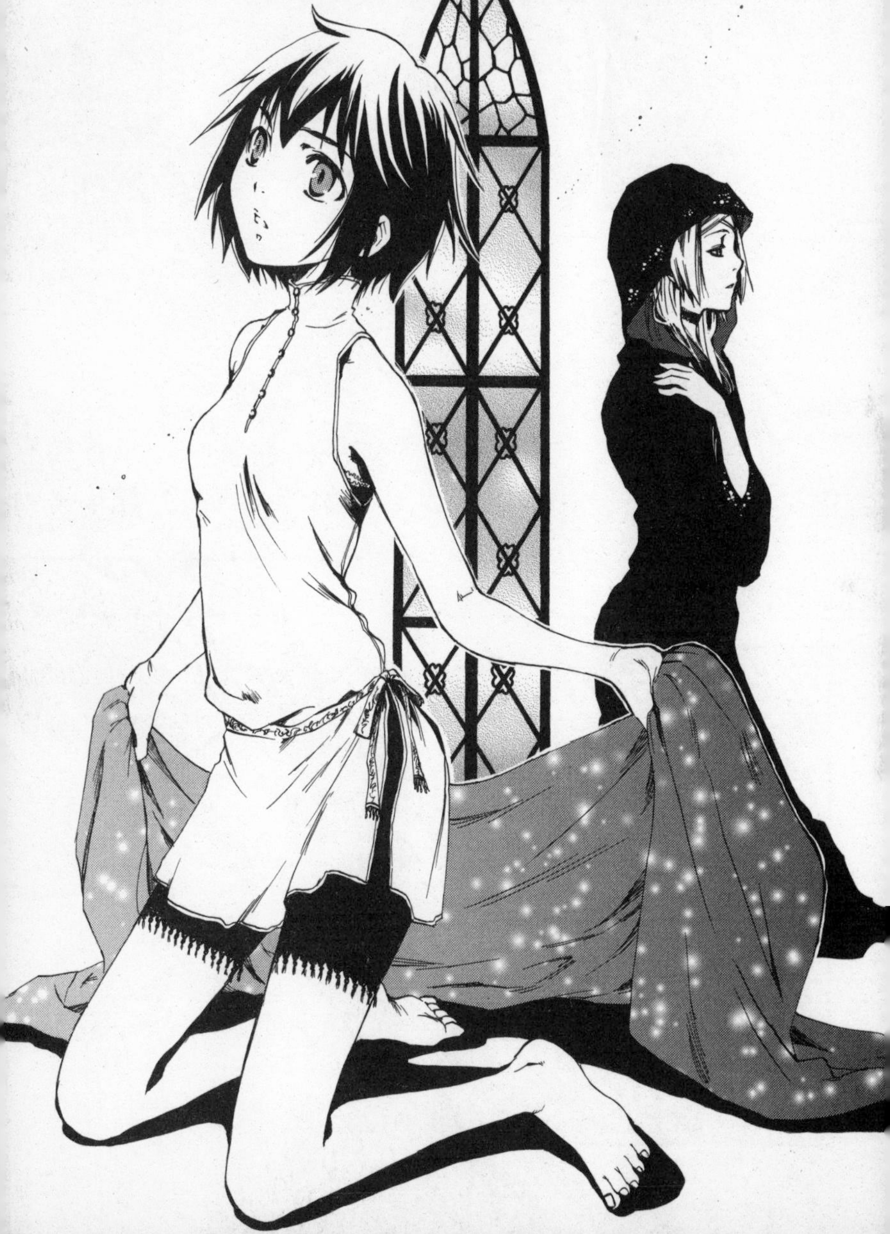

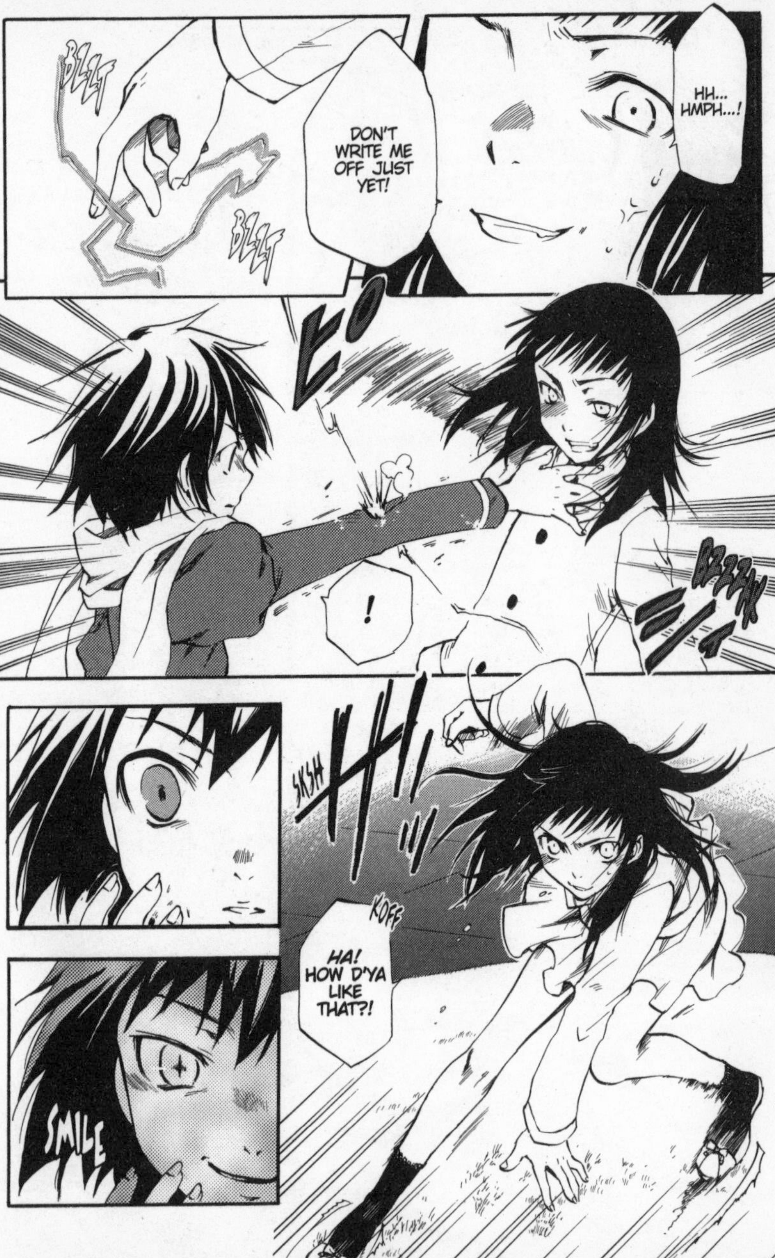
HH... HMPH...!
DON'T WRITE ME OFF JUST YET!
BZZT
BZZT
BZZZK
!
SKSH
KOFF
HA! HOW D'YA LIKE THAT?!
SMILE

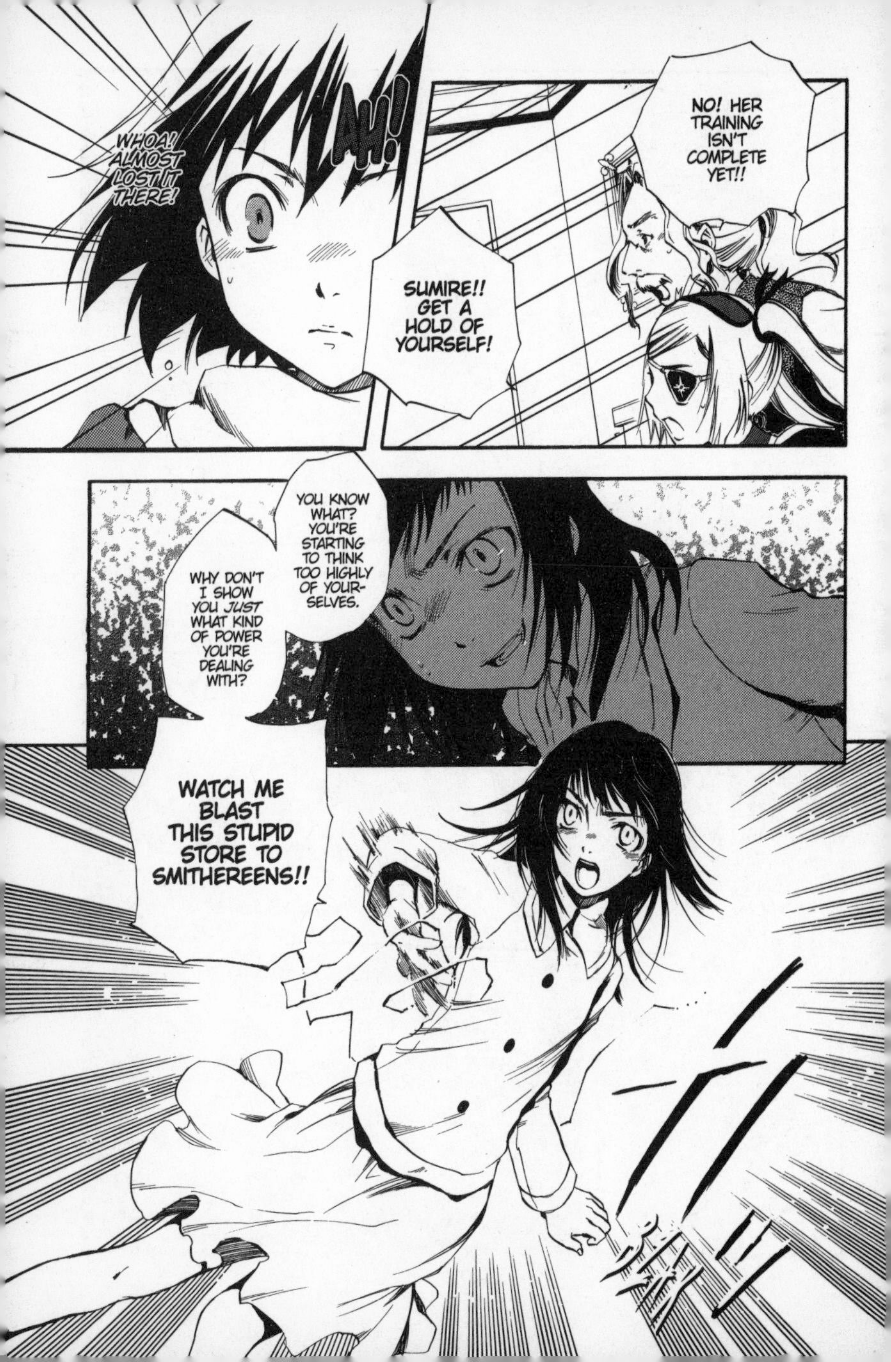
NO! HER TRAINING ISN'T COMPLETE YET!!
AH!
SUMIRE!! GET A HOLD OF YOURSELF!
WHOA! ALMOST LOST IT THERE!
YOU KNOW WHAT? YOU'RE STARTING TO THINK TOO HIGHLY OF YOUR-SELVES.
WHY DON'T I SHOW YOU *JUST* WHAT KIND OF POWER YOU'RE DEALING WITH?
WATCH ME BLAST THIS STUPID STORE TO SMITHEREENS!!

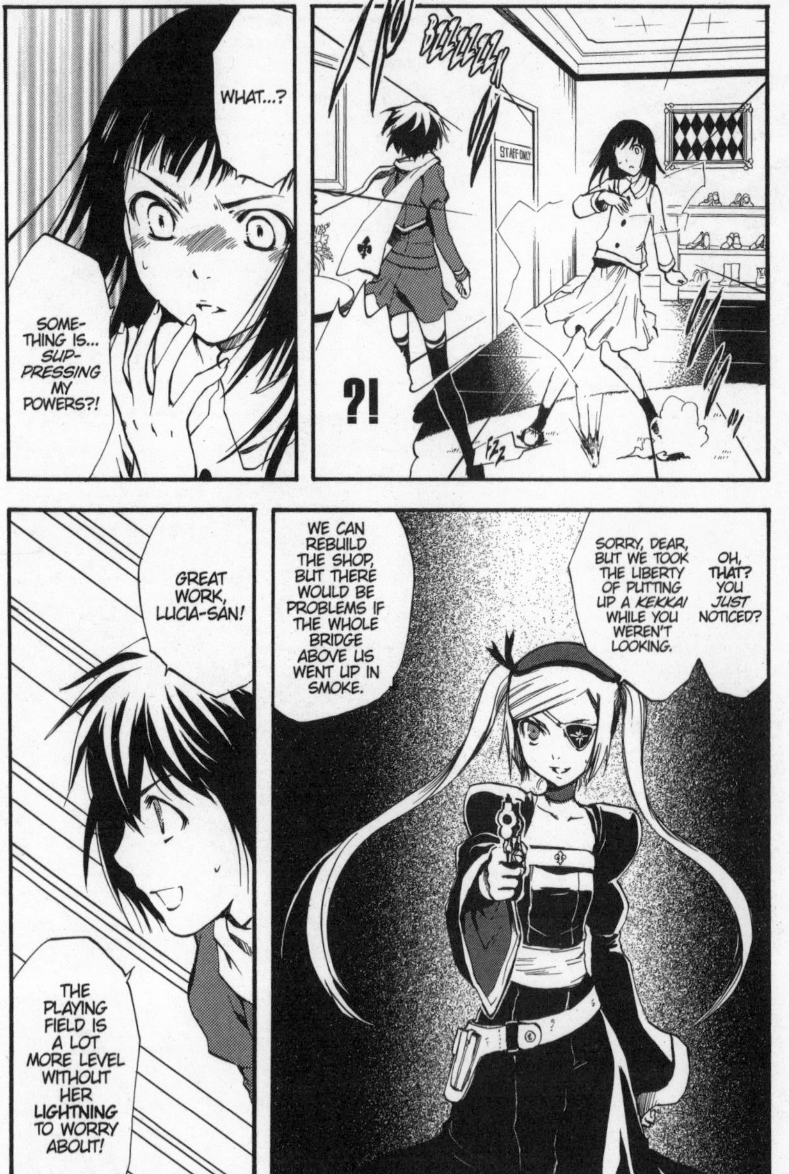
STAFF ONLY
?!
WHAT...?
SOME-THING IS... SUP-PRESSING MY POWERS?!
OH, THAT? YOU JUST NOTICED?
SORRY, DEAR, BUT WE TOOK THE LIBERTY OF PUTTING UP A KEKKAI WHILE YOU WEREN'T LOOKING.
WE CAN REBUILD THE SHOP, BUT THERE WOULD BE PROBLEMS IF THE WHOLE BRIDGE ABOVE US WENT UP IN SMOKE.
GREAT WORK, LUCIA-SAN!
THE PLAYING FIELD IS A LOT MORE LEVEL WITHOUT HER LIGHTNING TO WORRY ABOUT!

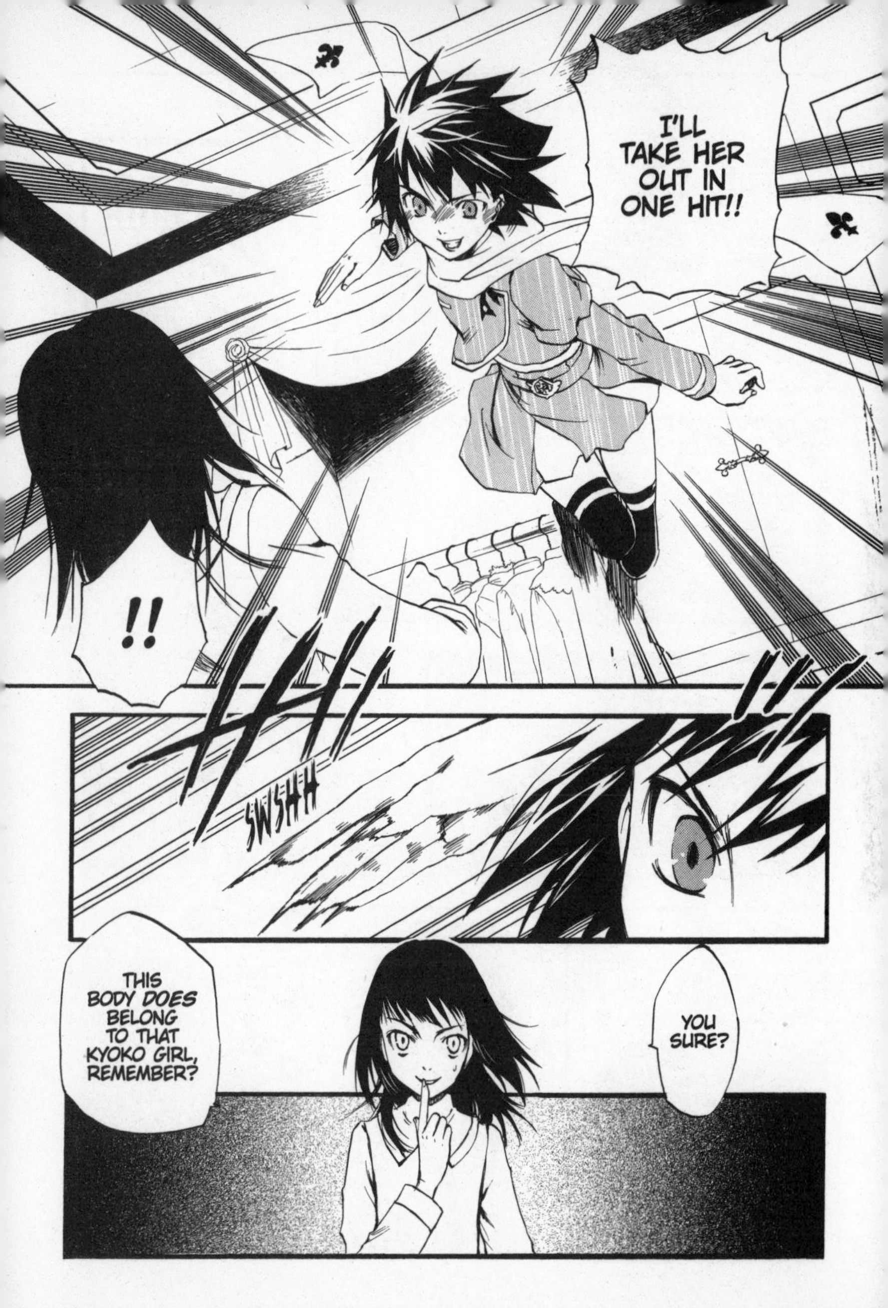
I'LL TAKE HER OUT IN ONE HIT!!
!!
SWSHH
YOU SURE?
THIS BODY *DOES* BELONG TO THAT KYOKO GIRL, REMEMBER?

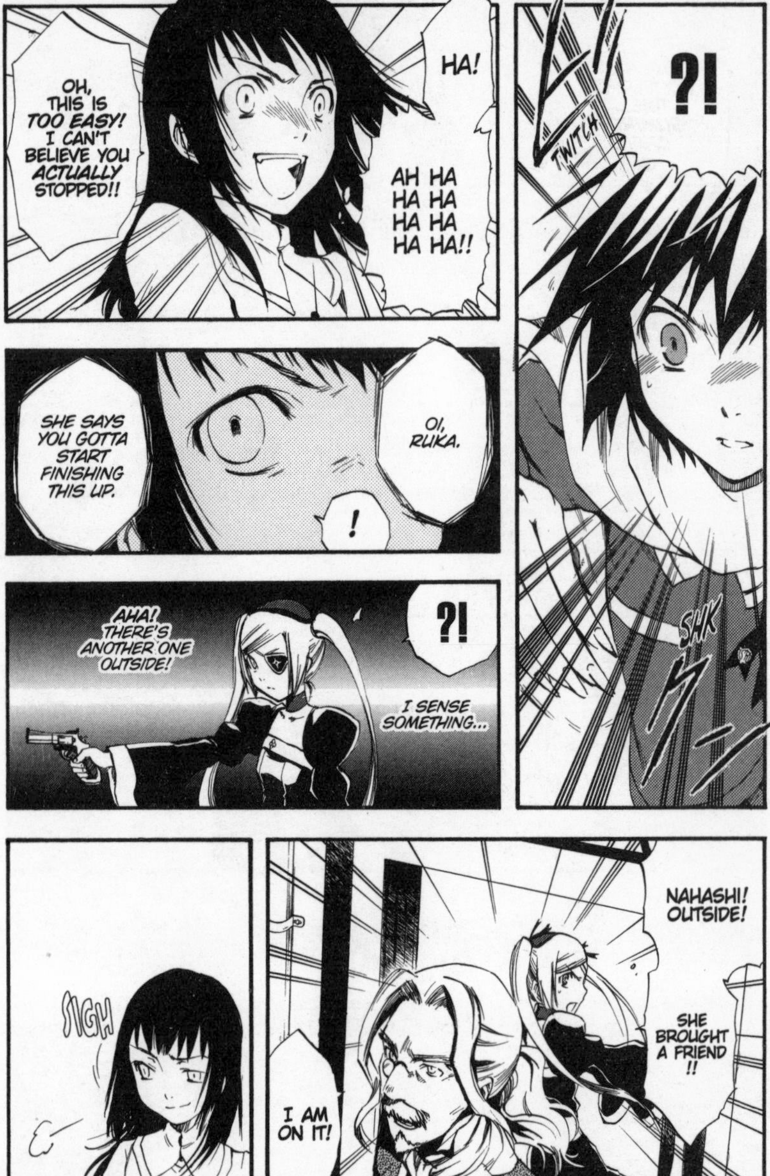
?!
TWITCH
SHK
HA!
AH HA HA HA HA HA HA HA!!
OH, THIS IS TOO EASY! I CAN'T BELIEVE YOU ACTUALLY STOPPED!!
OI, RUKA.
!
SHE SAYS YOU GOTTA START FINISHING THIS UP.
?!
I SENSE SOMETHING...
AHA! THERE'S ANOTHER ONE OUTSIDE!
NAHASHI! OUTSIDE!
SHE BROUGHT A FRIEND !!
I AM ON IT!
SIGH

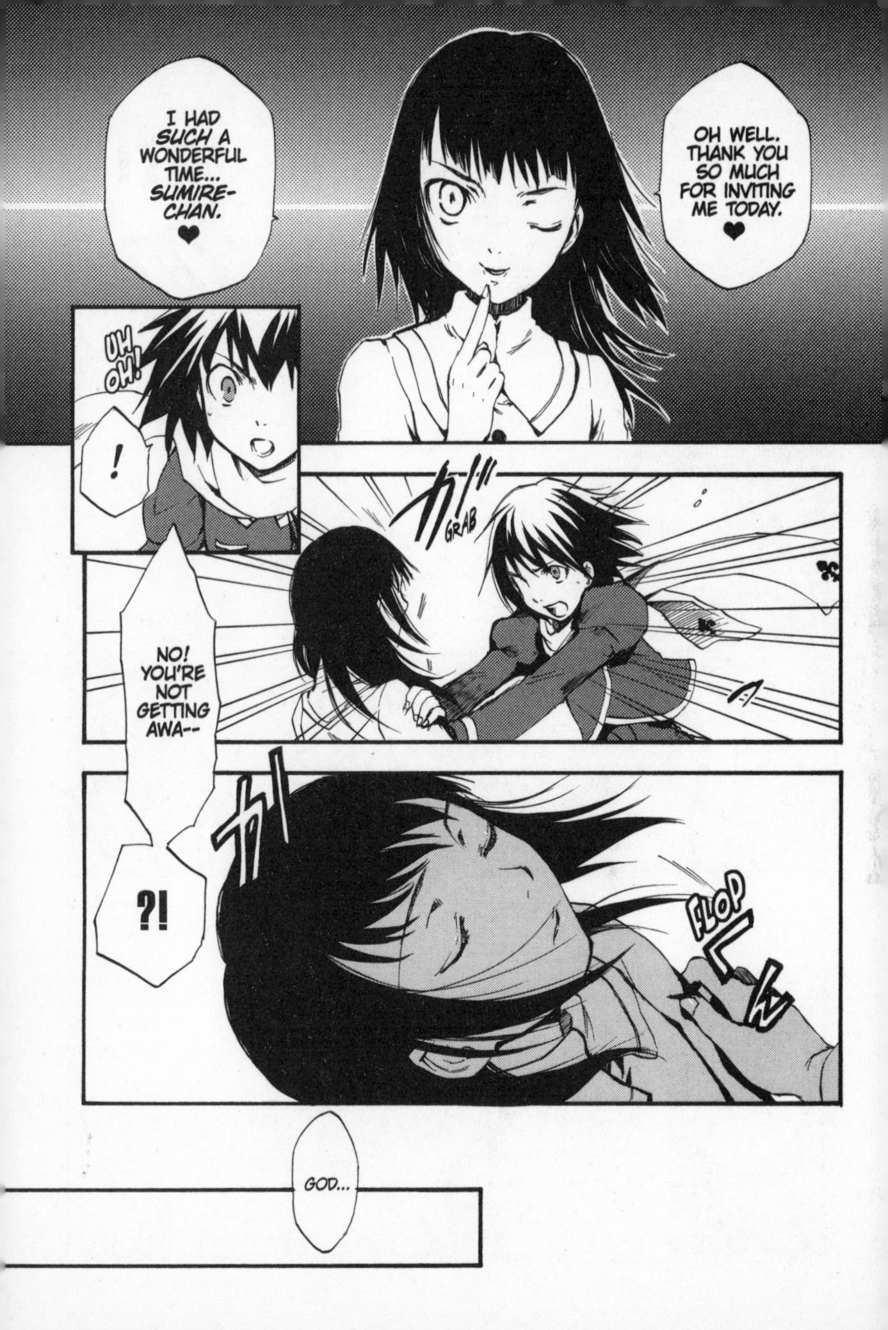

OH WELL. THANK YOU SO MUCH FOR INVITING ME TODAY. ❤
I HAD SUCH A WONDERFUL TIME... SUMIRE-CHAN. ❤
UH OH!
!
GRAB
NO! YOU'RE NOT GETTING AWA--
?!
FLOP
GOD...

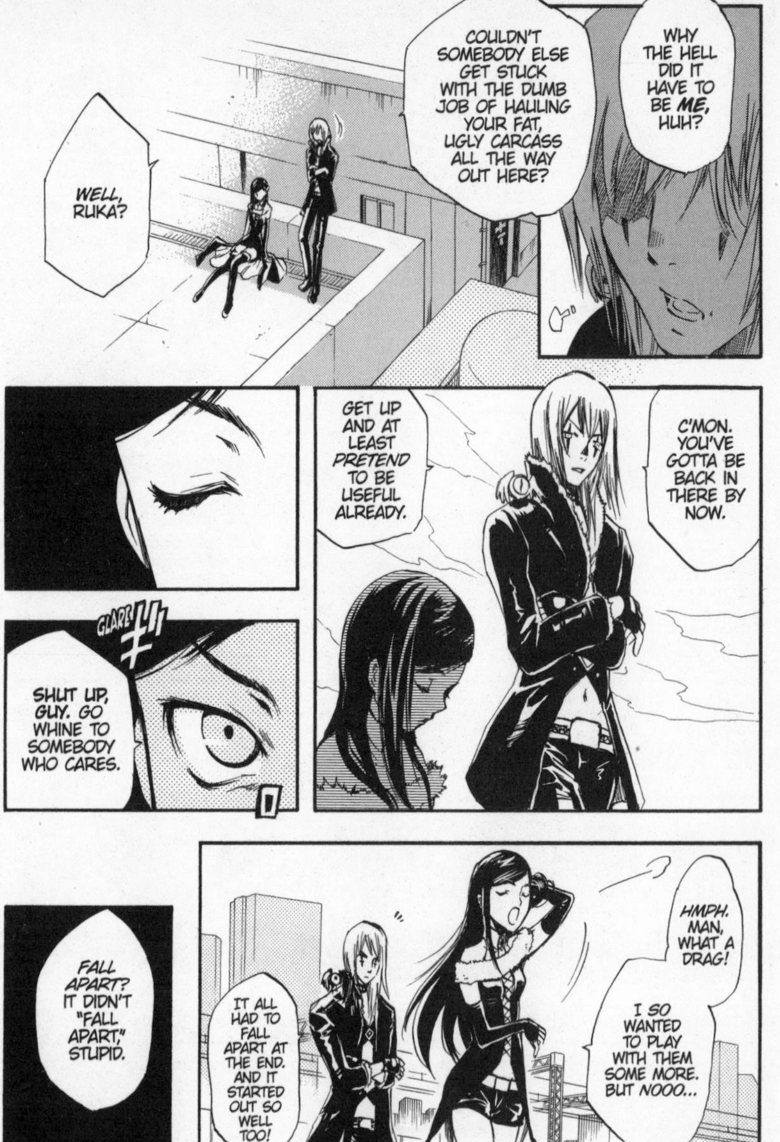
WHY THE HELL DID IT HAVE TO BE *ME*, HUH?
COULDN'T SOMEBODY ELSE GET STUCK WITH THE DUMB JOB OF HAULING YOUR FAT, UGLY CARCASS ALL THE WAY OUT HERE?
WELL, RUKA?
C'MON. YOU'VE GOTTA BE BACK IN THERE BY NOW.
GET UP AND AT LEAST *PRETEND* TO BE USEFUL ALREADY.
GLARE
SHUT UP, GUY. *GO* WHINE TO SOMEBODY WHO CARES.
HMPH. MAN, WHAT A DRAG!
I SO WANTED TO PLAY WITH THEM SOME MORE. BUT *NOOO...*
IT ALL HAD TO FALL APART AT THE END. AND IT STARTED OUT SO WELL TOO!
FALL APART? IT DIDN'T "FALL APART," STUPID.

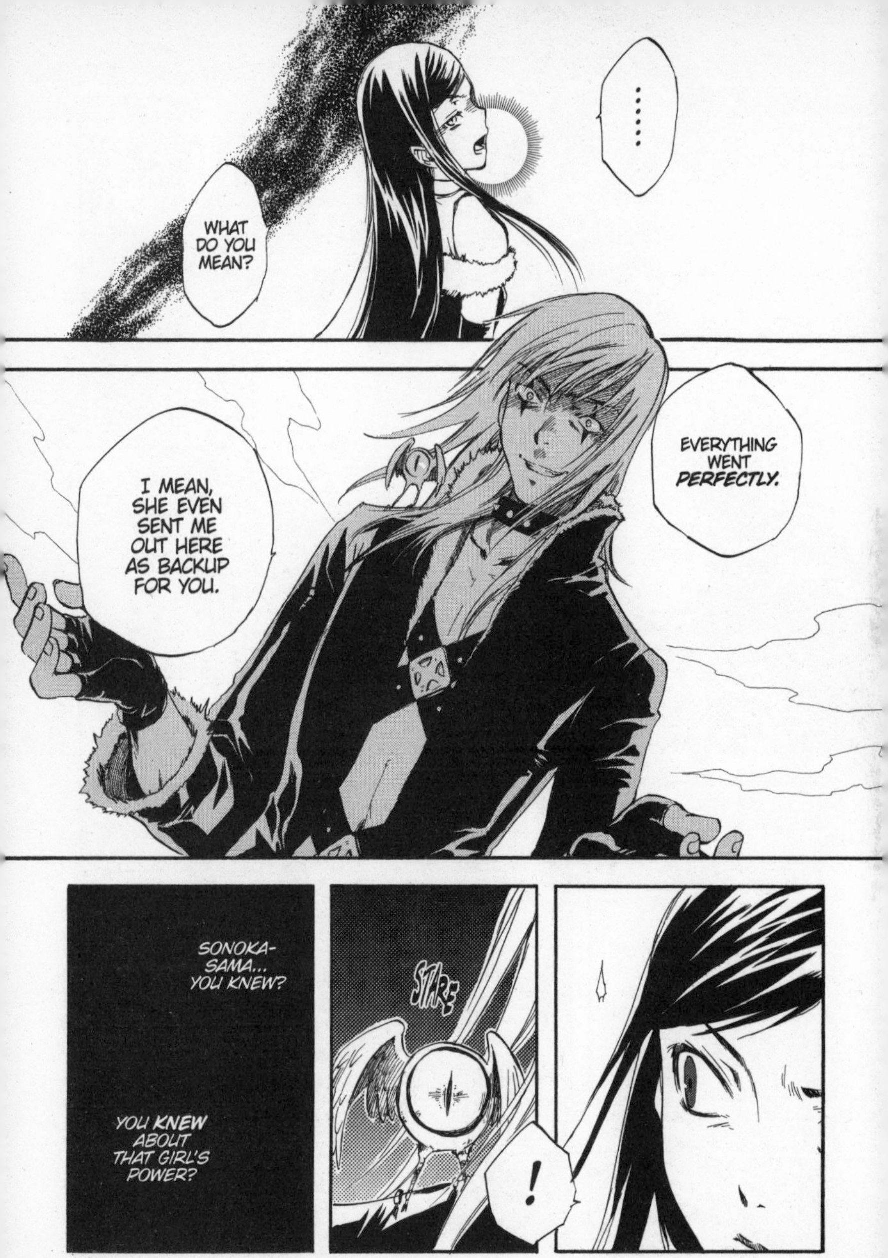
......
WHAT DO YOU MEAN?
EVERYTHING WENT *PERFECTLY.*
I MEAN, SHE EVEN SENT ME OUT HERE AS BACKUP FOR YOU.
STARE
!
SONOKA-SAMA... YOU KNEW?
*YOU **KNEW** ABOUT THAT GIRL'S POWER?*

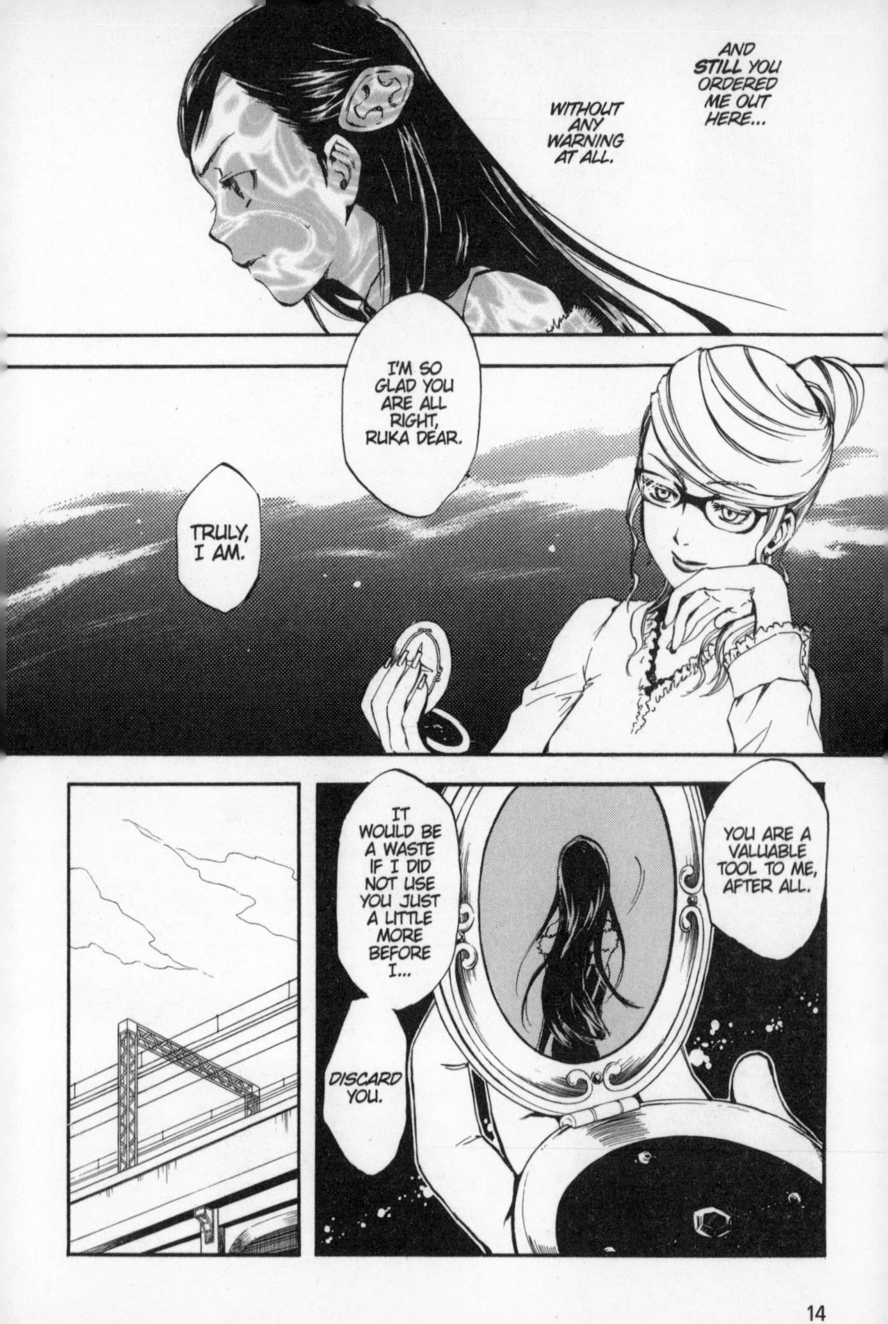
AND STILL YOU ORDERED ME OUT HERE...
WITHOUT ANY WARNING AT ALL.
I'M SO GLAD YOU ARE ALL RIGHT, RUKA DEAR.
TRULY, I AM.
YOU ARE A VALUABLE TOOL TO ME, AFTER ALL.
IT WOULD BE A WASTE IF I DID NOT USE YOU JUST A LITTLE MORE BEFORE I...
DISCARD YOU.

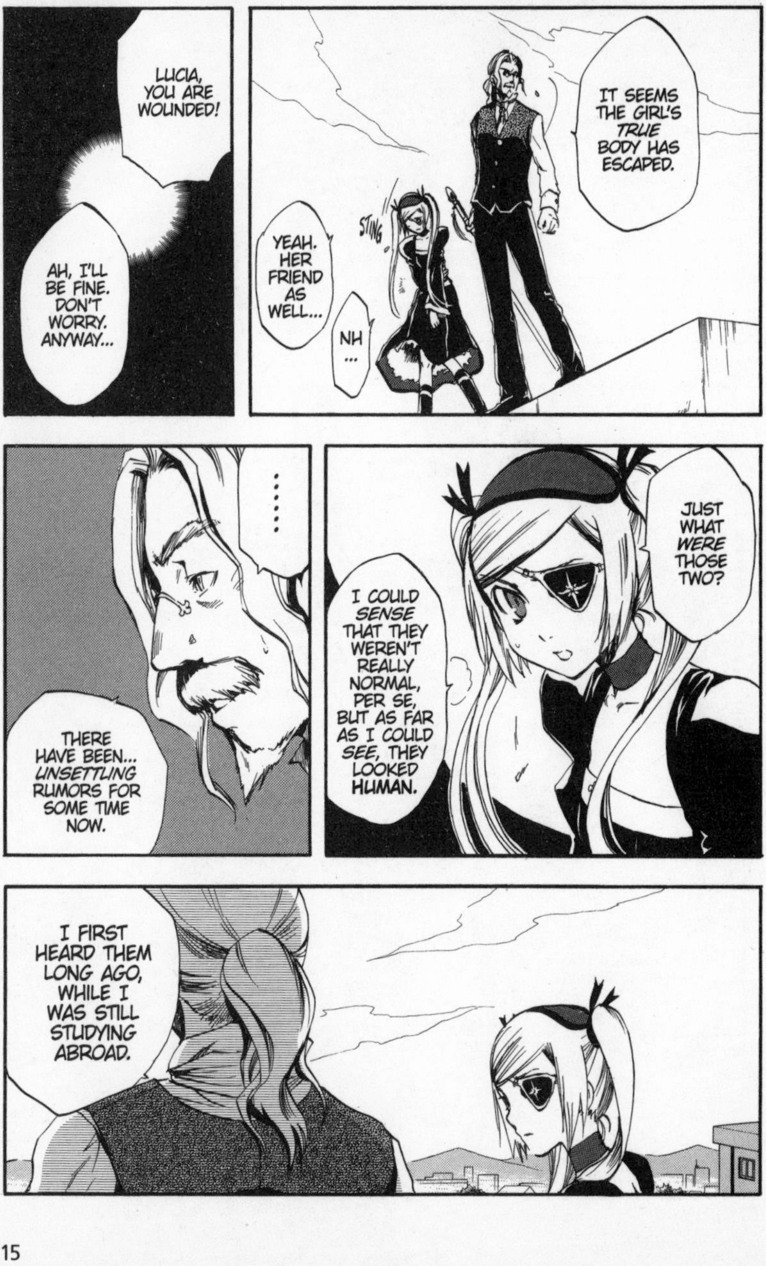
IT SEEMS THE GIRL'S TRUE BODY HAS ESCAPED.
STING
YEAH. HER FRIEND AS WELL...
NH...
LUCIA, YOU ARE WOUNDED!
AH, I'LL BE FINE. DON'T WORRY. ANYWAY...
JUST WHAT WERE THOSE TWO?
I COULD SENSE THAT THEY WEREN'T REALLY NORMAL, PER SE, BUT AS FAR AS I COULD SEE, THEY LOOKED HUMAN.
......
THERE HAVE BEEN... UNSETTLING RUMORS FOR SOME TIME NOW.
I FIRST HEARD THEM LONG AGO, WHILE I WAS STILL STUDYING ABROAD.

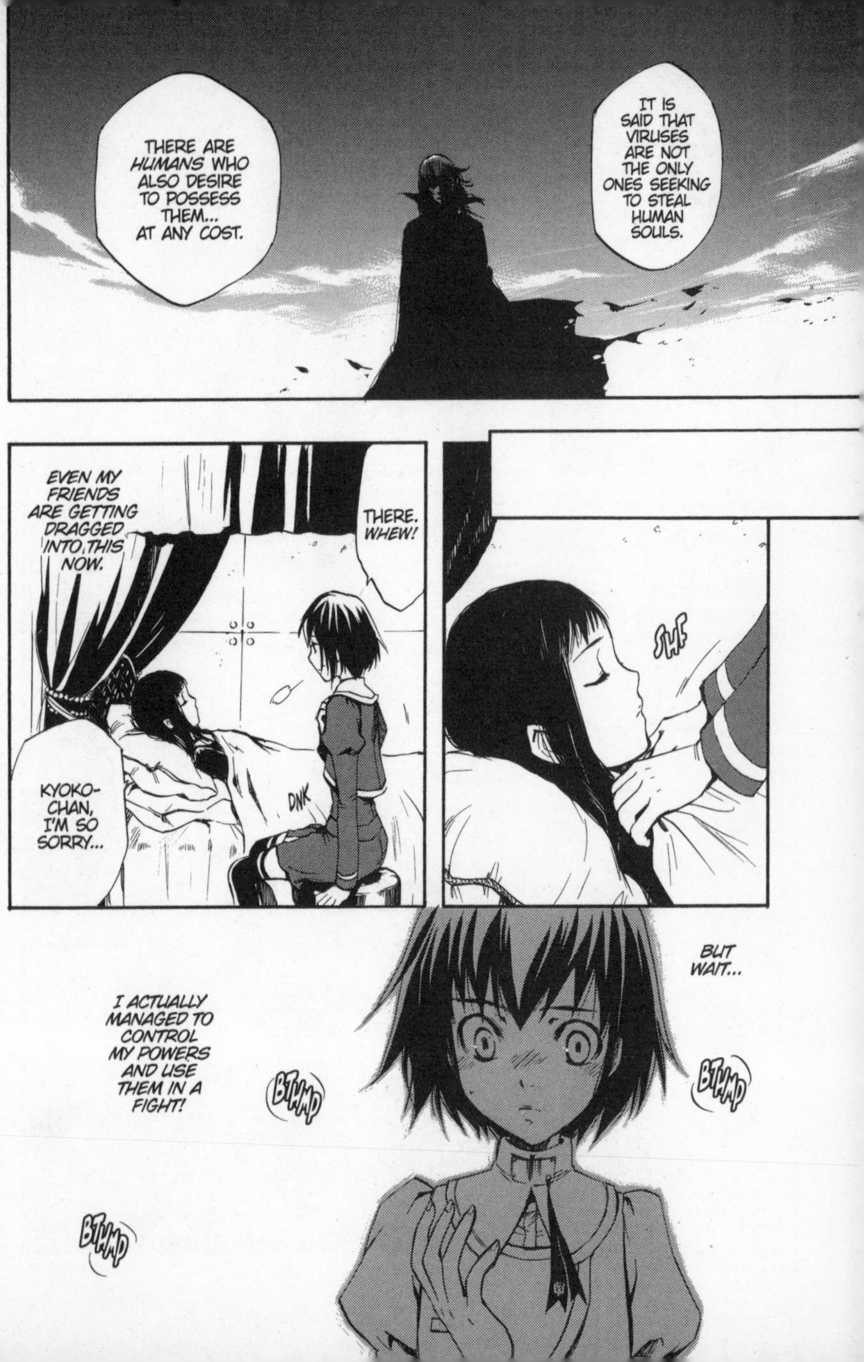
IT IS SAID THAT VIRUSES ARE NOT THE ONLY ONES SEEKING TO STEAL HUMAN SOULS.
THERE ARE HUMANS WHO ALSO DESIRE TO POSSESS THEM... AT ANY COST.
SHF
THERE. WHEW!
EVEN MY FRIENDS ARE GETTING DRAGGED INTO THIS NOW.
DNK
KYOKO-CHAN, I'M SO SORRY...
BUT WAIT...
BTHMP
I ACTUALLY MANAGED TO CONTROL MY POWERS AND USE THEM IN A FIGHT!
BTHMP
BTHMP

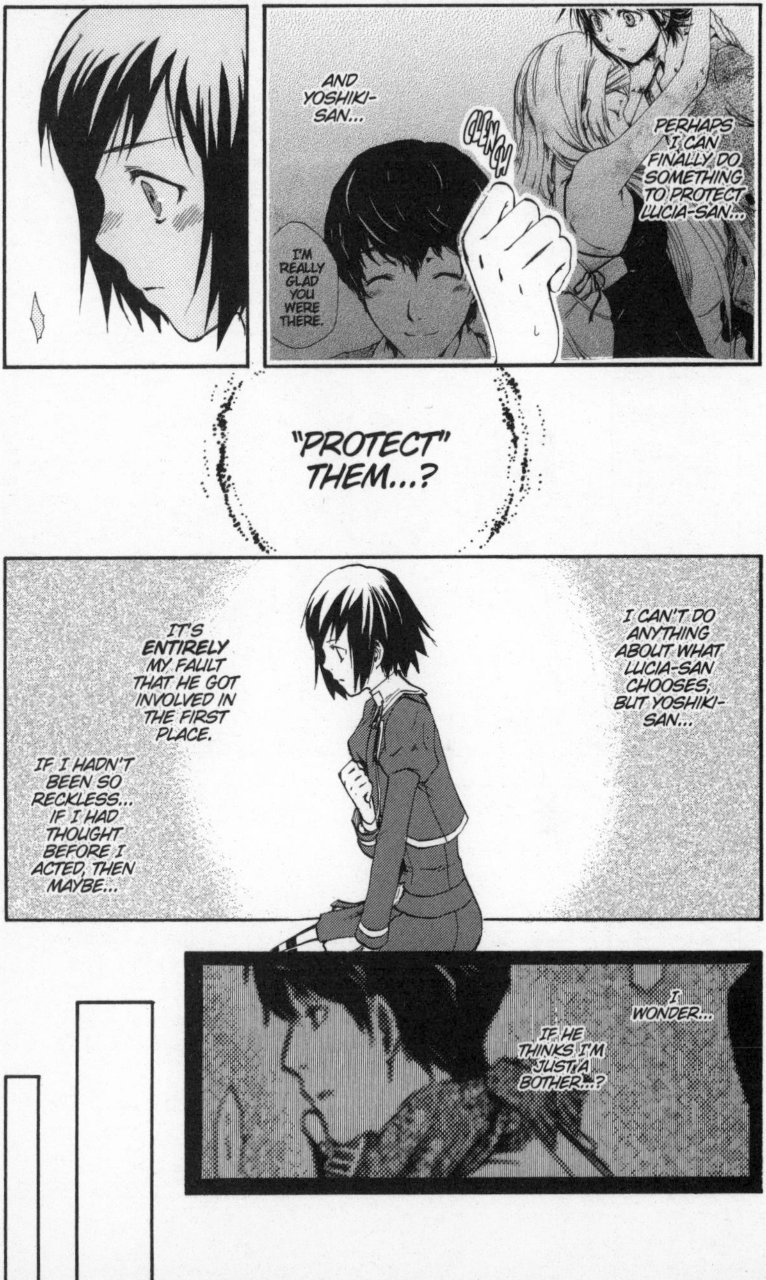
PERHAPS I CAN FINALLY DO SOMETHING TO PROTECT LUCIA-SAN...
CLENCH
AND YOSHIKI-SAN...
I'M REALLY GLAD YOU WERE THERE.
"PROTECT" THEM...?
I CAN'T DO ANYTHING ABOUT WHAT LUCIA-SAN CHOOSES, BUT YOSHIKI-SAN...
IT'S ENTIRELY MY FAULT THAT HE GOT INVOLVED IN THE FIRST PLACE.
IF I HADN'T BEEN SO RECKLESS... IF I HAD THOUGHT BEFORE I ACTED, THEN MAYBE...
I WONDER...
IF HE THINKS I'M JUST A BOTHER...?

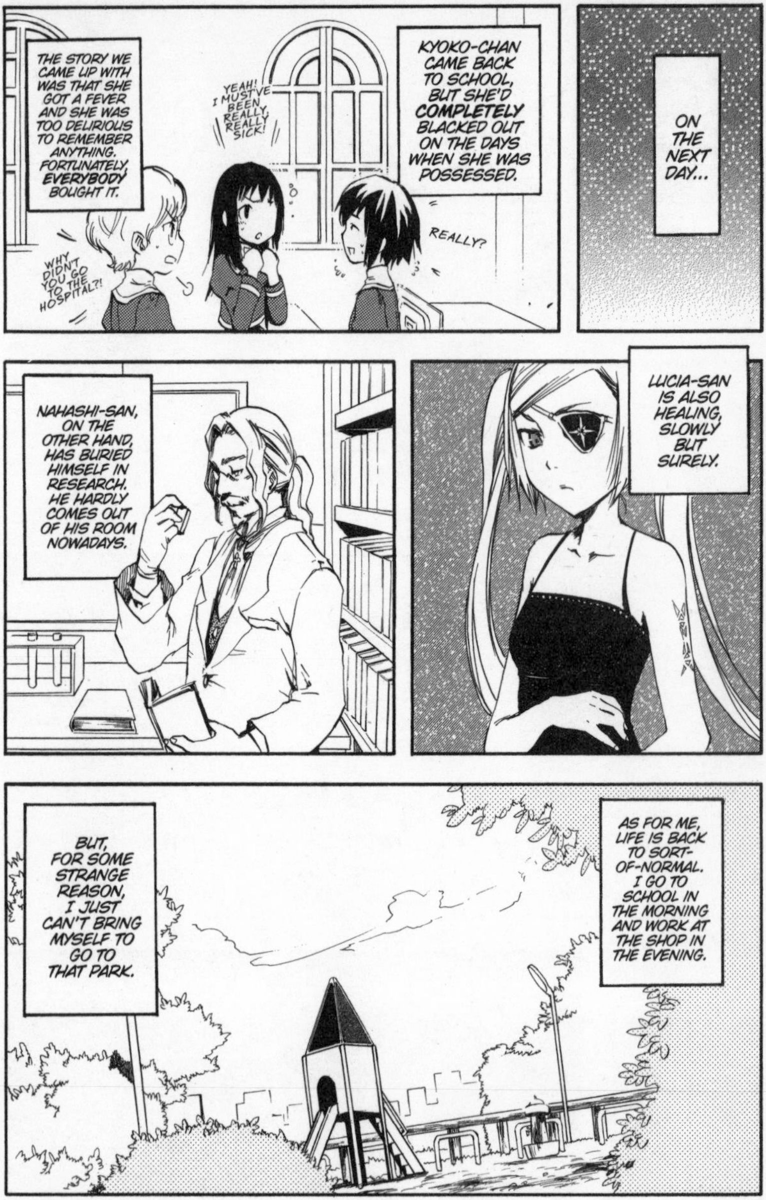
ON THE NEXT DAY...
KYOKO-CHAN CAME BACK TO SCHOOL, BUT SHE'D COMPLETELY BLACKED OUT ON THE DAYS WHEN SHE WAS POSSESSED.
YEAH! I MUST'VE BEEN REALLY, REALLY SICK!
THE STORY WE CAME UP WITH WAS THAT SHE GOT A FEVER AND SHE WAS TOO DELIRIOUS TO REMEMBER ANYTHING. FORTUNATELY, EVERYBODY BOUGHT IT.
REALLY?
WHY DIDN'T YOU GO TO THE HOSPITAL?!
LUCIA-SAN IS ALSO HEALING, SLOWLY BUT SURELY.
NAHASHI-SAN, ON THE OTHER HAND, HAS BURIED HIMSELF IN RESEARCH. HE HARDLY COMES OUT OF HIS ROOM NOWADAYS.
AS FOR ME, LIFE IS BACK TO SORT-OF-NORMAL. I GO TO SCHOOL IN THE MORNING AND WORK AT THE SHOP IN THE EVENING.
BUT, FOR SOME STRANGE REASON, I JUST CAN'T BRING MYSELF TO GO TO THAT PARK.

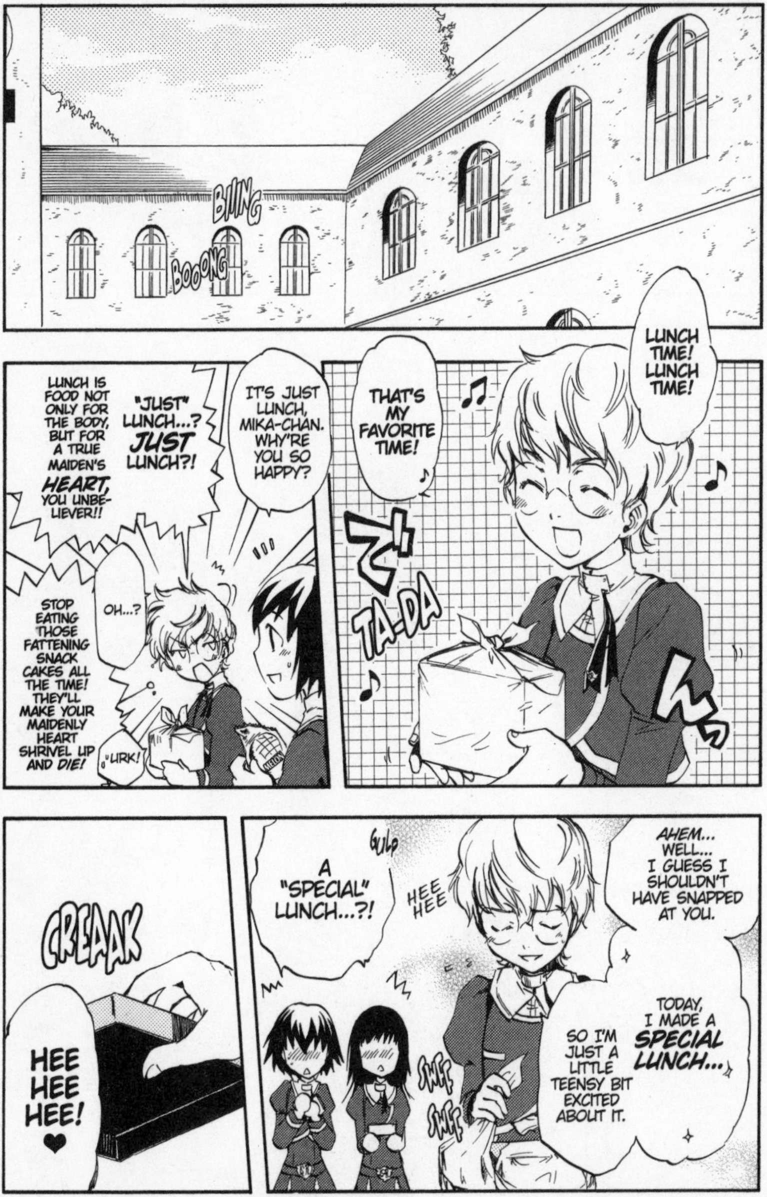
BIIING
BOOONG
LUNCH TIME! LUNCH TIME!
THAT'S MY FAVORITE TIME!
TA-DA
IT'S JUST LUNCH, MIKA-CHAN. WHY'RE YOU SO HAPPY?
"JUST" LUNCH...? JUST LUNCH?!
LUNCH IS FOOD NOT ONLY FOR THE BODY, BUT FOR A TRUE MAIDEN'S HEART, YOU UNBELIEVER!!
OH...?
STOP EATING THOSE FATTENING SNACK CAKES ALL THE TIME! THEY'LL MAKE YOUR MAIDENLY HEART SHRIVEL UP AND DIE!
URK!
AHEM... WELL... I GUESS I SHOULDN'T HAVE SNAPPED AT YOU.
TODAY, I MADE A SPECIAL LUNCH...
SO I'M JUST A LITTLE TEENSY BIT EXCITED ABOUT IT.
HEE HEE
A "SPECIAL" LUNCH...?!
GULP
SWFF
SWFF
CREAAK
HEE HEE HEE! ❤

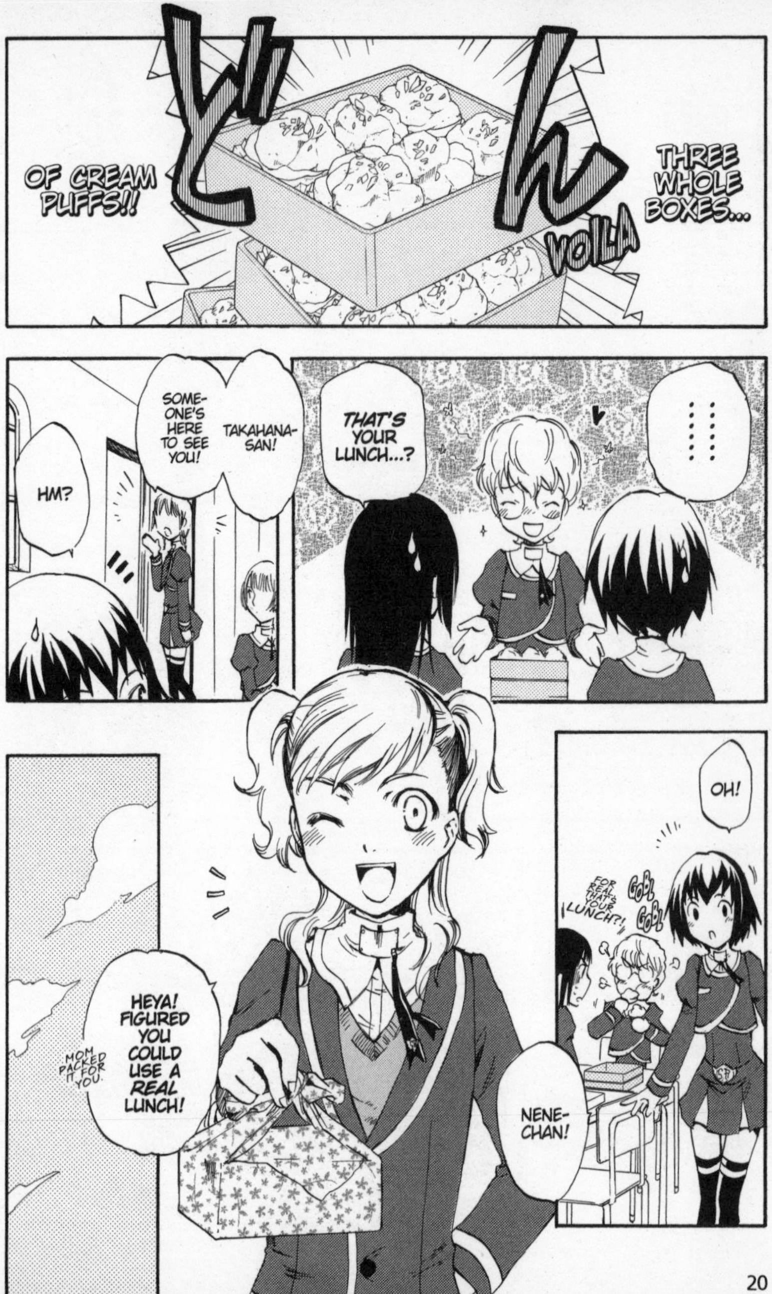
THREE WHOLE BOXES...
どん
VOILA
OF CREAM PUFFS!!
......!!
THAT'S YOUR LUNCH...?
TAKAHANA-SAN!
SOME-ONE'S HERE TO SEE YOU!
HM?
OH!
FOR REAL, THAT'S YOUR LUNCH?!
GOBL GOBL
NENE-CHAN!
HEYA! FIGURED YOU COULD USE A REAL LUNCH!
MOM PACKED IT FOR YOU.

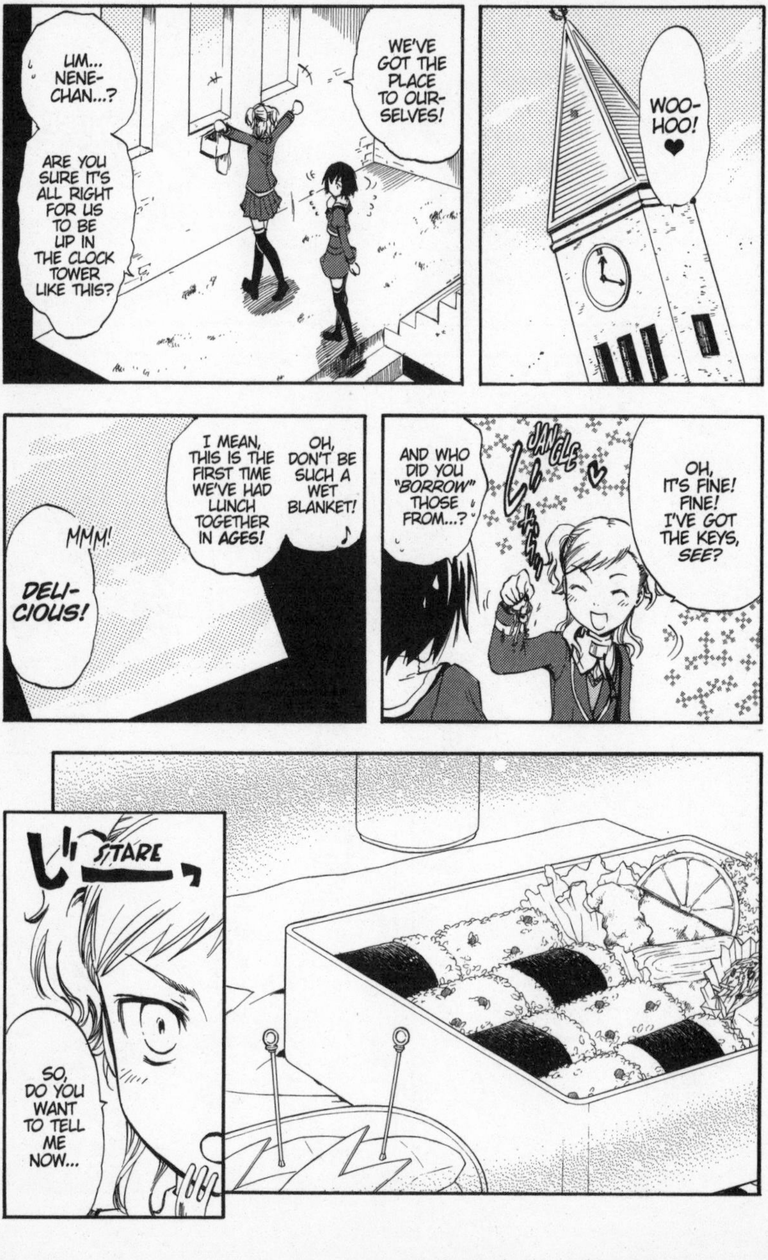
WOO-HOO! ❤
WE'VE GOT THE PLACE TO OUR-SELVES!
UM... NENE-CHAN...?
ARE YOU SURE IT'S ALL RIGHT FOR US TO BE UP IN THE CLOCK TOWER LIKE THIS?
OH, IT'S FINE! FINE! I'VE GOT THE KEYS, SEE?
JANGLE
AND WHO DID YOU "BORROW" THOSE FROM...?
OH, DON'T BE SUCH A WET BLANKET! ♪
I MEAN, THIS IS THE FIRST TIME WE'VE HAD LUNCH TOGETHER IN AGES!
MMM!
DELI-CIOUS!
STARE
SO, DO YOU WANT TO TELL ME NOW...

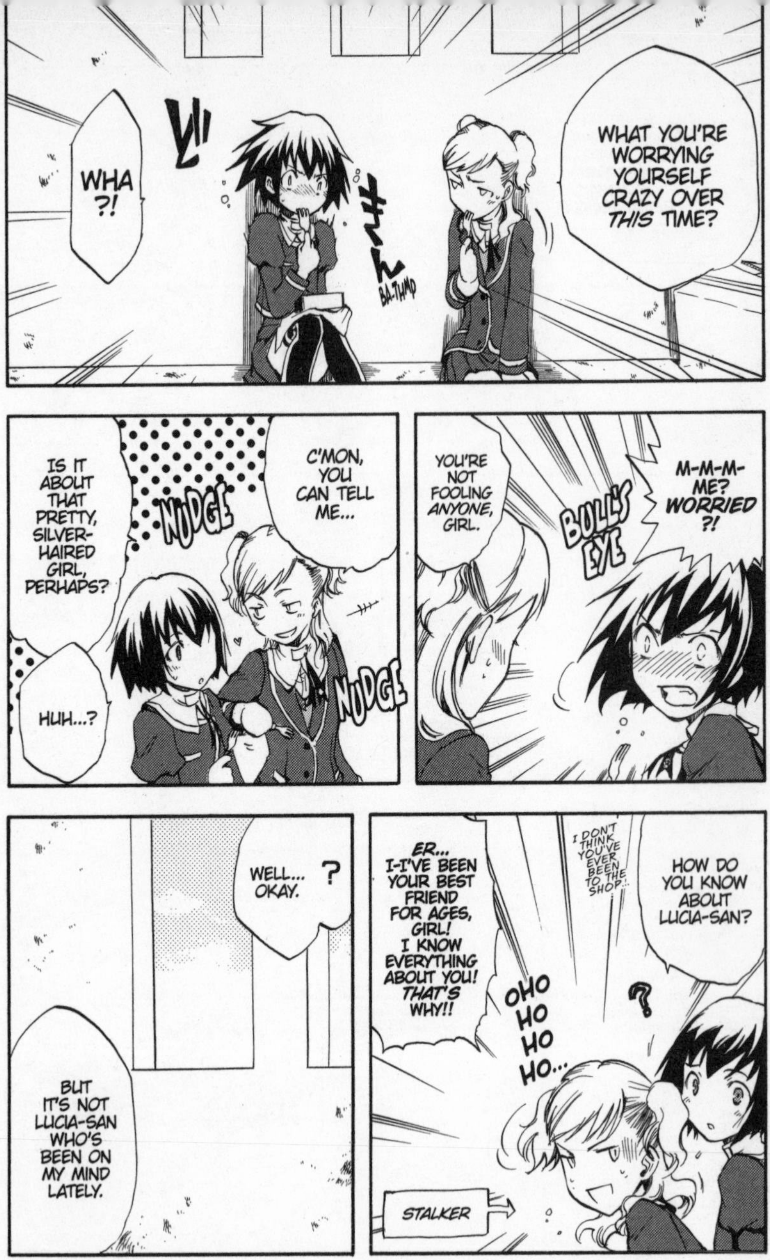
WHAT YOU'RE WORRYING YOURSELF CRAZY OVER THIS TIME?
BA-THUMP
WHA ?!
M-M-M-ME? WORRIED ?!
BULL'S EYE
YOU'RE NOT FOOLING ANYONE, GIRL.
C'MON, YOU CAN TELL ME...
IS IT ABOUT THAT PRETTY, SILVER-HAIRED GIRL, PERHAPS?
NUDGE
NUDGE
HUH...?
HOW DO YOU KNOW ABOUT LUCIA-SAN?
I DON'T THINK YOU'VE EVER BEEN TO THE SHOP...
ER... I-I'VE BEEN YOUR BEST FRIEND FOR AGES, GIRL! I KNOW EVERYTHING ABOUT YOU! THAT'S WHY!!
?
OHO HO HO HO...
STALKER
WELL... OKAY.
?
BUT IT'S NOT LUCIA-SAN WHO'S BEEN ON MY MIND LATELY.

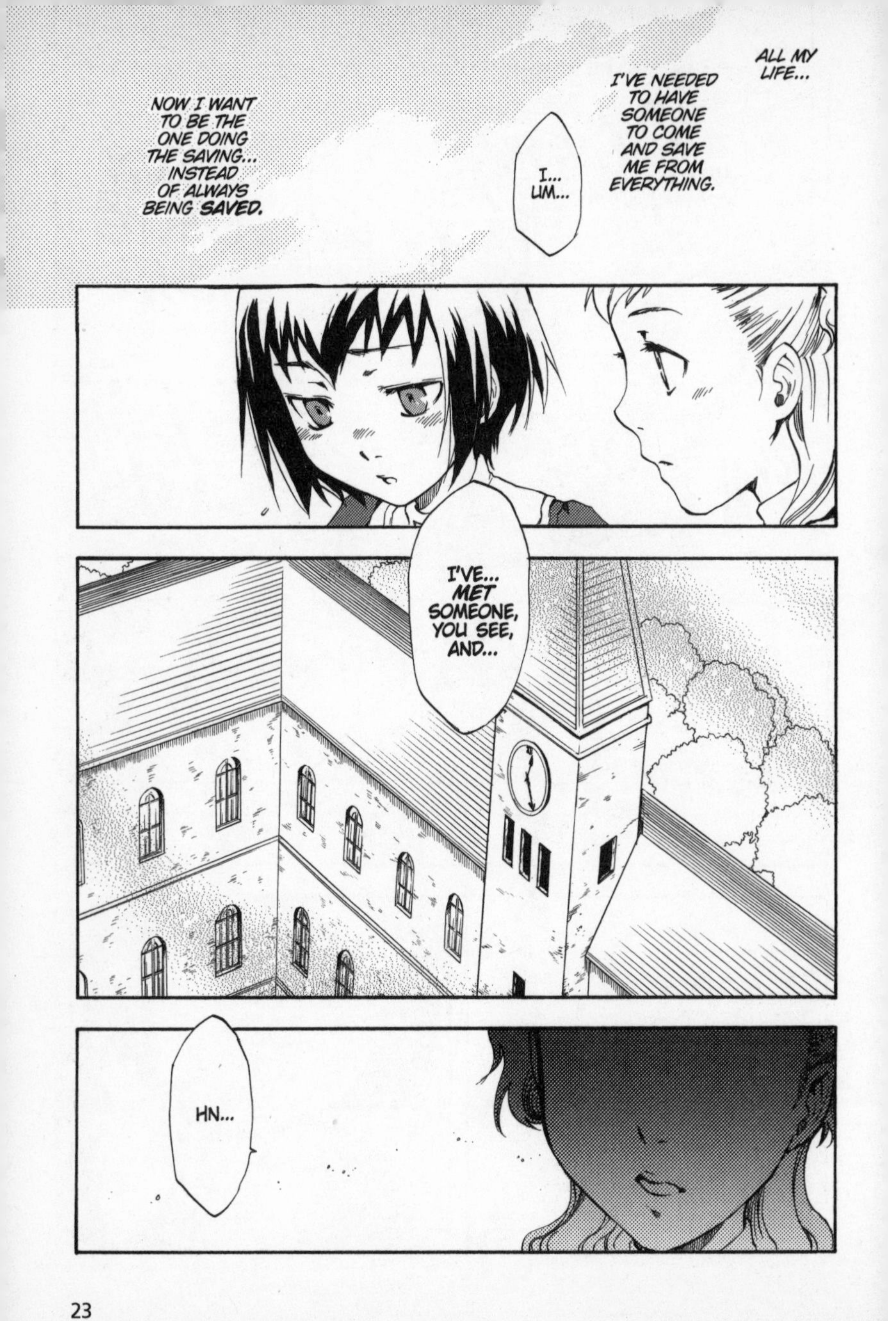
ALL MY LIFE...
I'VE NEEDED TO HAVE SOMEONE TO COME AND SAVE ME FROM EVERYTHING.
I... UM...
NOW I WANT TO BE THE ONE DOING THE SAVING... INSTEAD OF ALWAYS BEING SAVED.
I'VE... MET SOMEONE, YOU SEE, AND...
HN...

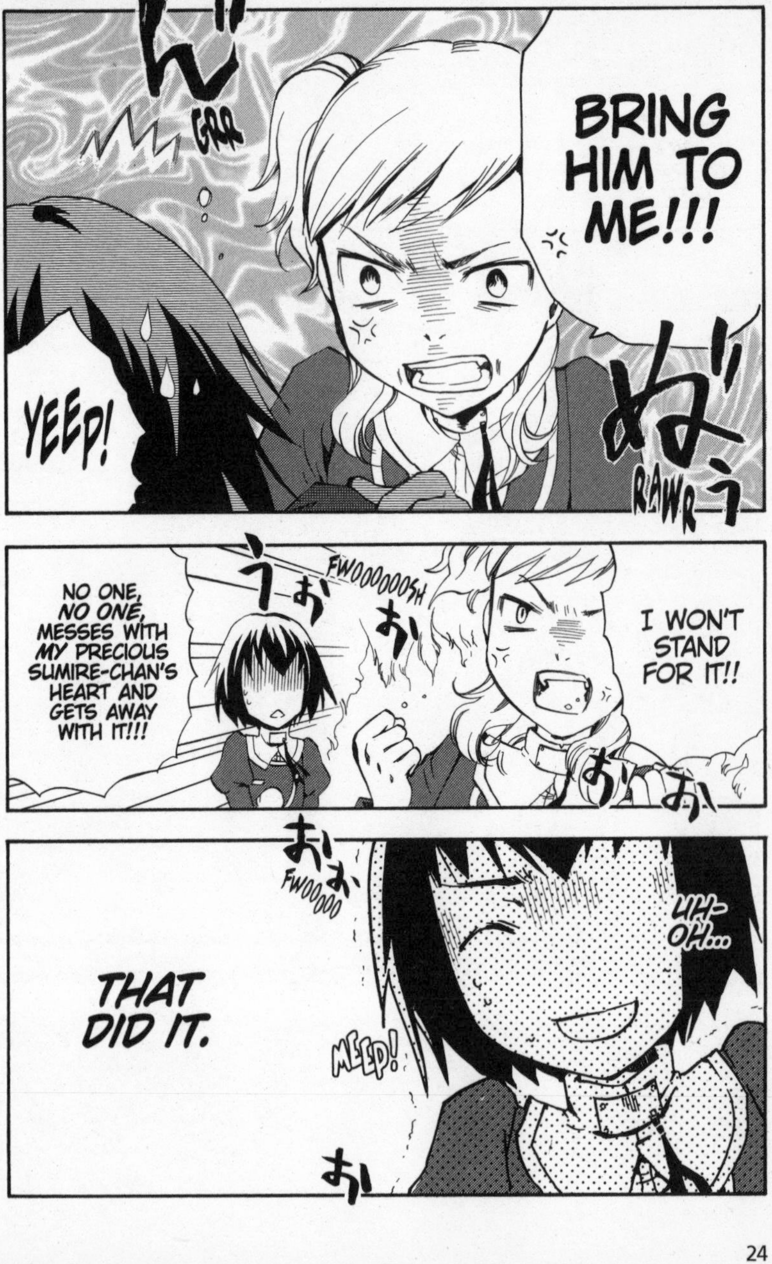
BRING HIM TO ME!!!
ぬ゛う
RAWR
ん゛
GRR
YEEP!
I WON'T STAND FOR IT!!
おぉおぉ
FWOOOOOOOSH
うぉお
NO ONE, *NO ONE*, MESSES WITH *MY* PRECIOUS SUMIRE-CHAN'S HEART AND GETS AWAY WITH IT!!!
UH-OH...
おぉ
FWOOOOO
MEEP!
おぃ
THAT DID IT.

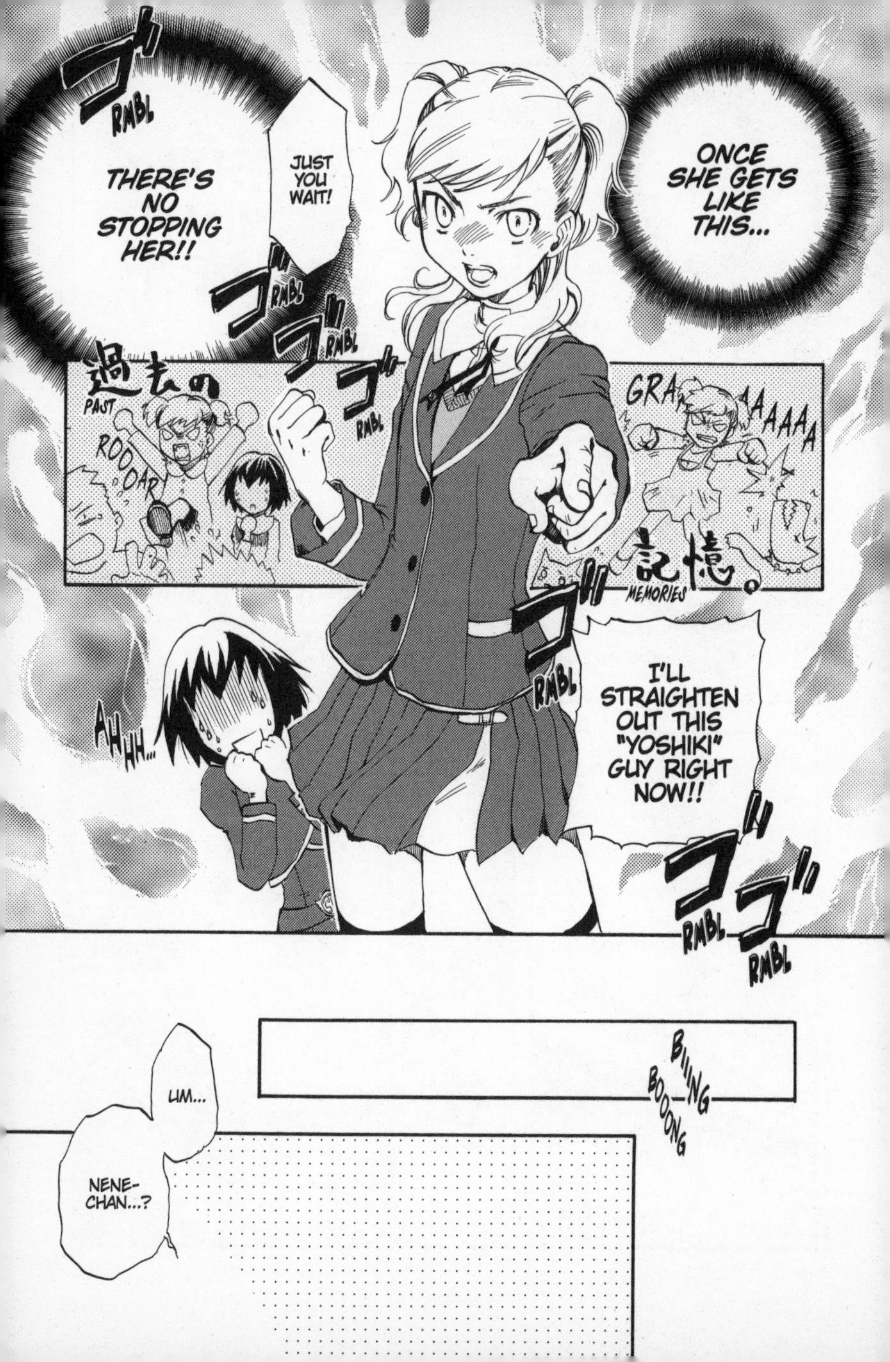
ONCE SHE GETS LIKE THIS...
JUST YOU WAIT!
THERE'S NO STOPPING HER!!
RMBL
RMBL
RMBL
RMBL
GRAAAAAAAA
記憶。
MEMORIES
過去の
PAST
ROOOAR
I'LL STRAIGHTEN OUT THIS "YOSHIKI" GUY RIGHT NOW!!
RMBL
AHHH...
RMBL
RMBL
BIIING
BOOONG
UM...
NENE-CHAN...?

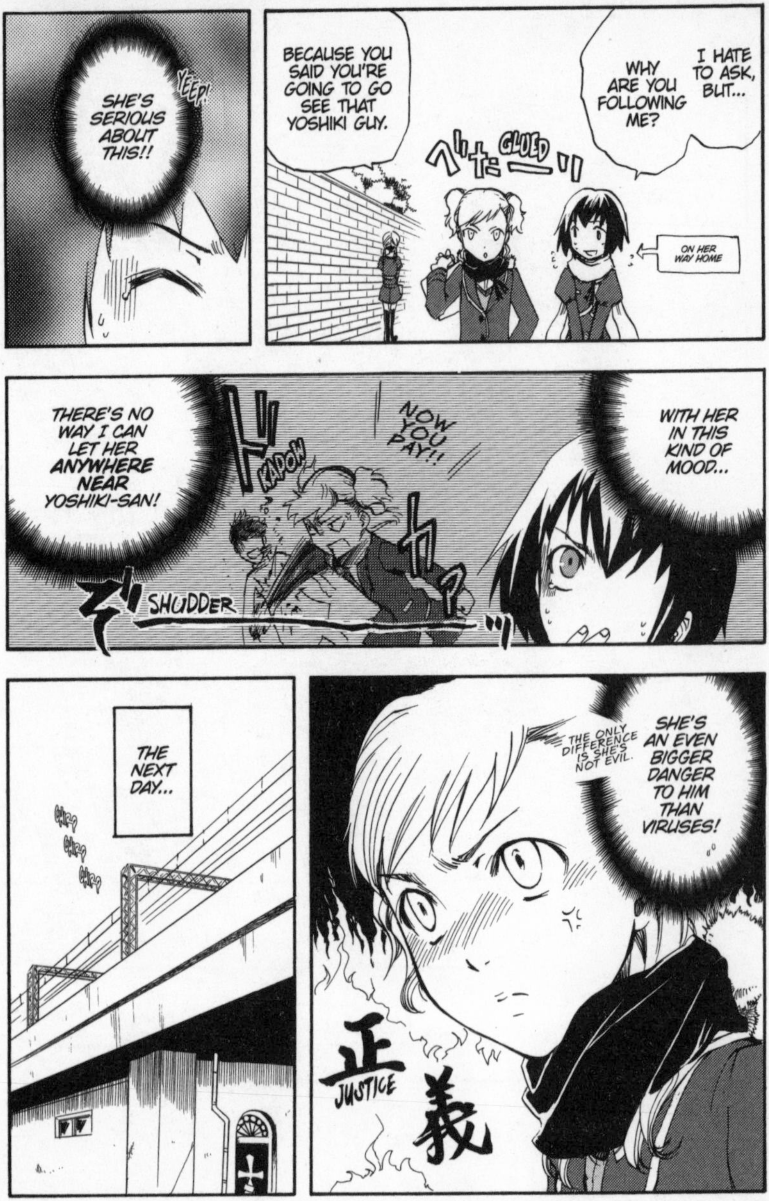
I HATE TO ASK, BUT...
WHY ARE YOU FOLLOWING ME?
GLUED
ON HER WAY HOME
BECAUSE YOU SAID YOU'RE GOING TO GO SEE THAT YOSHIKI GUY.
YEEP!
SHE'S SERIOUS ABOUT THIS!!
WITH HER IN THIS KIND OF MOOD...
NOW YOU PAY!!
KAPOW
SHUDDER
THERE'S NO WAY I CAN LET HER ANYWHERE NEAR YOSHIKI-SAN!
SHE'S AN EVEN BIGGER DANGER TO HIM THAN VIRUSES!
THE ONLY DIFFERENCE IS SHE'S NOT EVIL.
正義
JUSTICE
THE NEXT DAY...
CHIRP
CHIRP
CHIRP

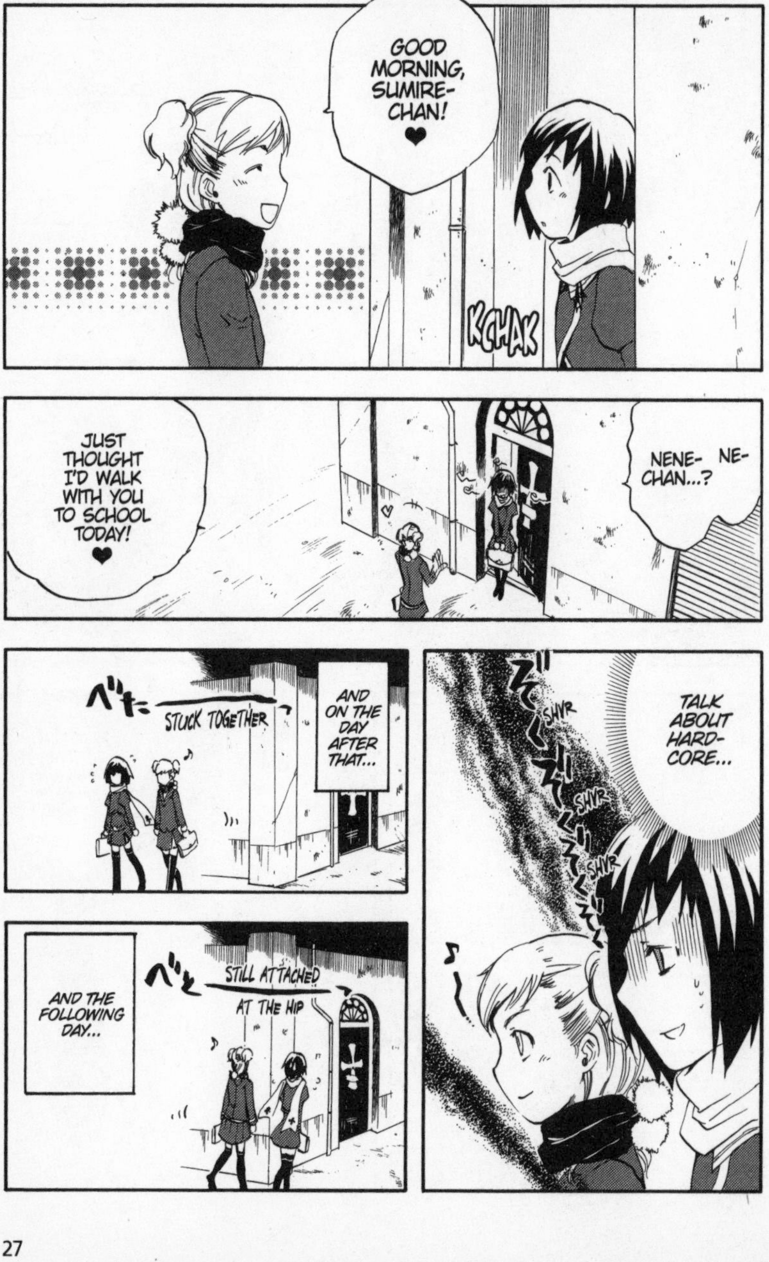
GOOD MORNING, SUMIRE-CHAN! ❤
KCHAK
NENE- NE-CHAN...?
JUST THOUGHT I'D WALK WITH YOU TO SCHOOL TODAY! ❤
TALK ABOUT HARD-CORE...
SHVR
SHVR
SHVR
AND ON THE DAY AFTER THAT...
べた
STUCK TOGETHER
AND THE FOLLOWING DAY...
べと
STILL ATTACHED AT THE HIP

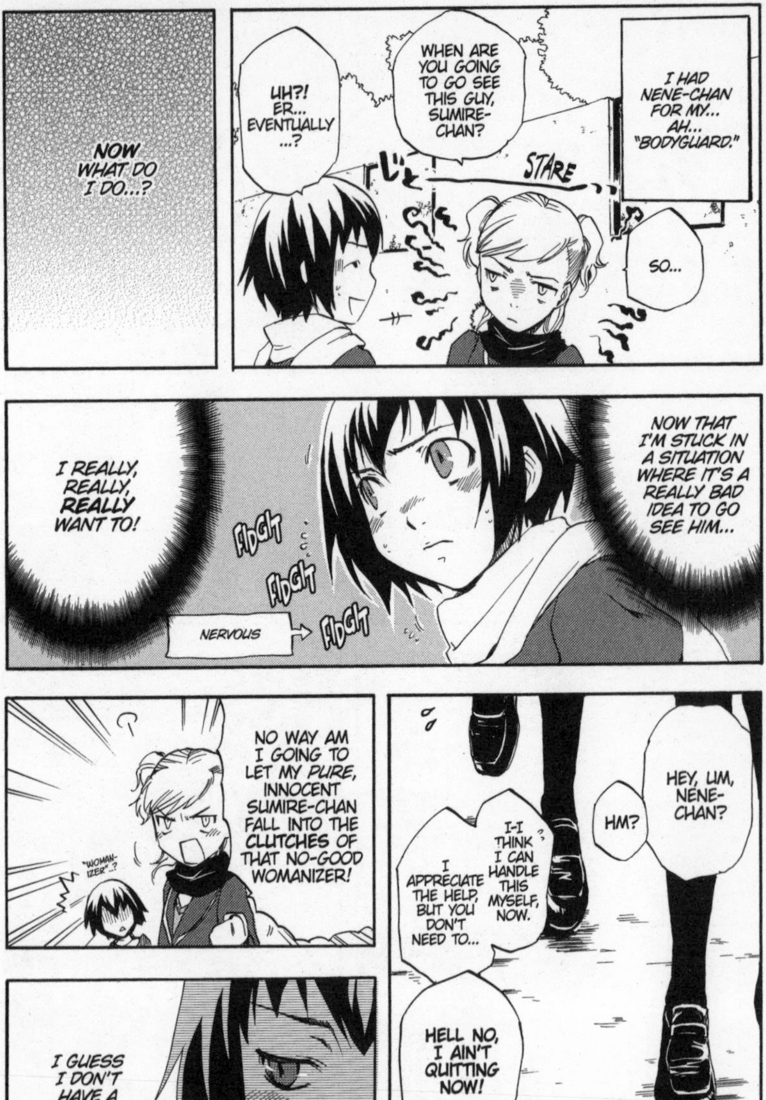
I HAD NENE-CHAN FOR MY... AH... "BODYGUARD."
SO...
STARE
WHEN ARE YOU GOING TO GO SEE THIS GUY, SUMIRE-CHAN?
UH?! ER... EVENTUALLY ...?
NOW WHAT DO I DO...?
NOW THAT I'M STUCK IN A SITUATION WHERE IT'S A REALLY BAD IDEA TO GO SEE HIM...
FIDGIT
FIDGIT
FIDGIT
NERVOUS
I REALLY, REALLY, **REALLY** WANT TO!
HEY, UM, NENE-CHAN?
HM?
I-I THINK I CAN HANDLE THIS MYSELF, NOW.
I APPRECIATE THE HELP, BUT YOU DON'T NEED TO...
HELL NO, I AIN'T QUITTING NOW!
NO WAY AM I GOING TO LET MY *PURE*, INNOCENT SUMIRE-CHAN FALL INTO THE **CLUTCHES** OF THAT NO-GOOD WOMANIZER!
"WOMAN-IZER"...?
I GUESS I DON'T HAVE A CHOICE...

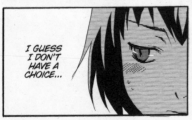

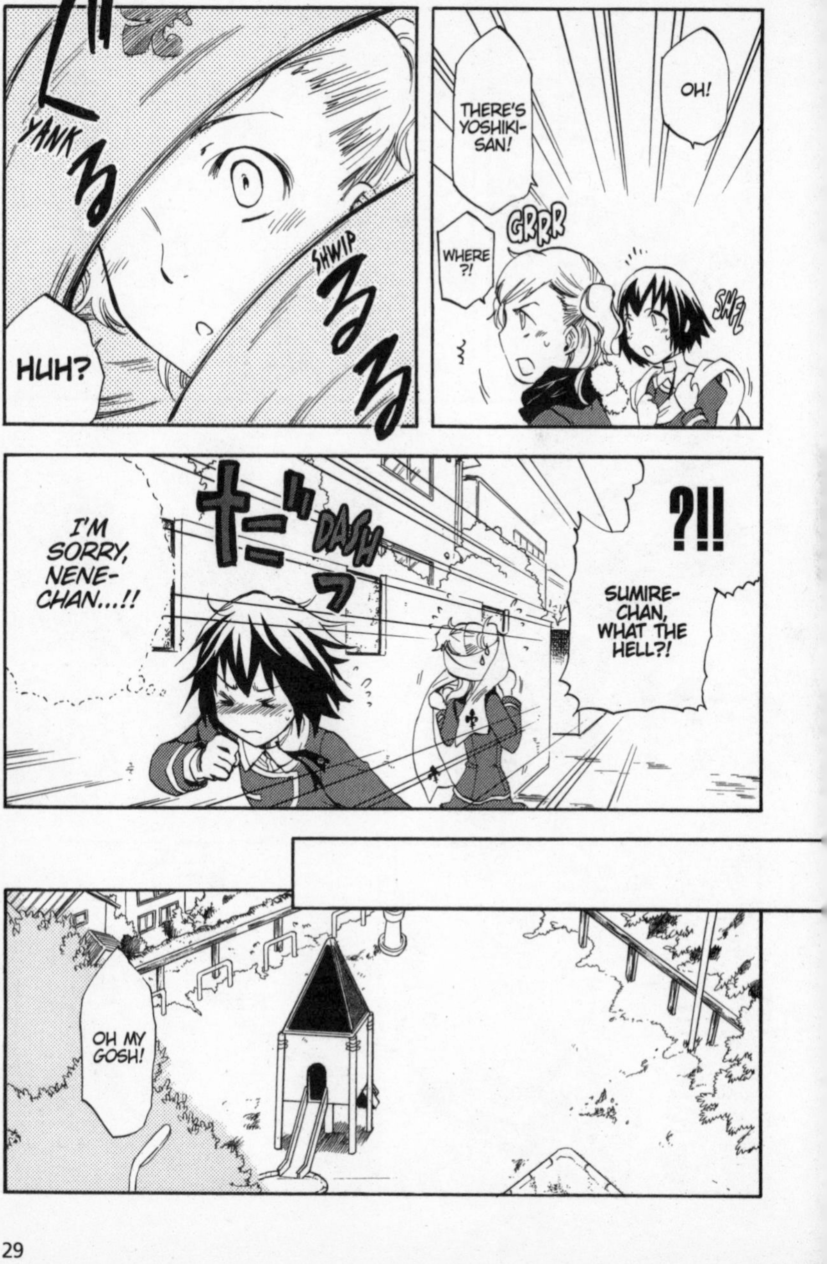
OH!
THERE'S YOSHIKI-SAN!
GRRR
WHERE ?!
SHFL
YANK
SHWIP
HUH?
?!!
SUMIRE-CHAN, WHAT THE HELL?!
DASH
I'M SORRY, NENE-CHAN...!!
OH MY GOSH!

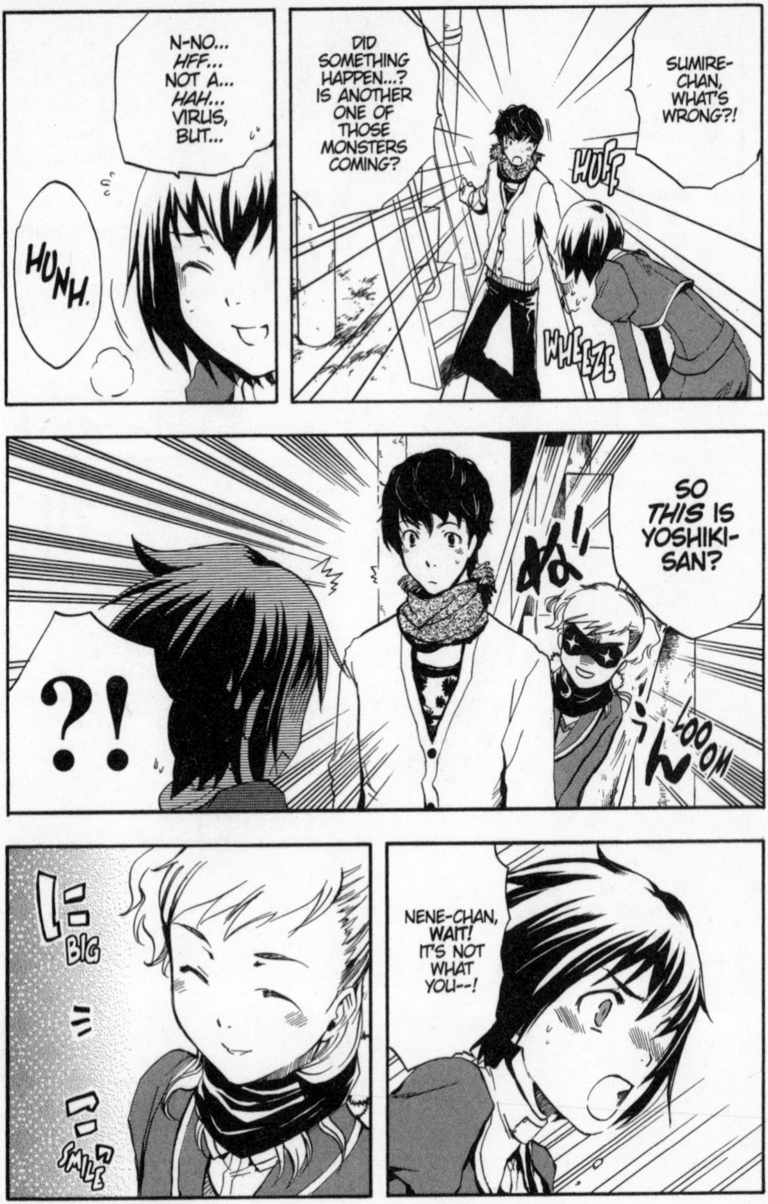
SUMIRE-CHAN, WHAT'S WRONG?!
HUFF
DID SOMETHING HAPPEN...? IS ANOTHER ONE OF THOSE MONSTERS COMING?
WHEEZE
N-NO... *HFF*... NOT A... *HAH*... VIRUS, BUT...
HUNH.
SO *THIS* IS YOSHIKI-SAN?
ぬ
LOOOM
?!
NENE-CHAN, WAIT! IT'S NOT WHAT YOU--!
BIG
SMILE

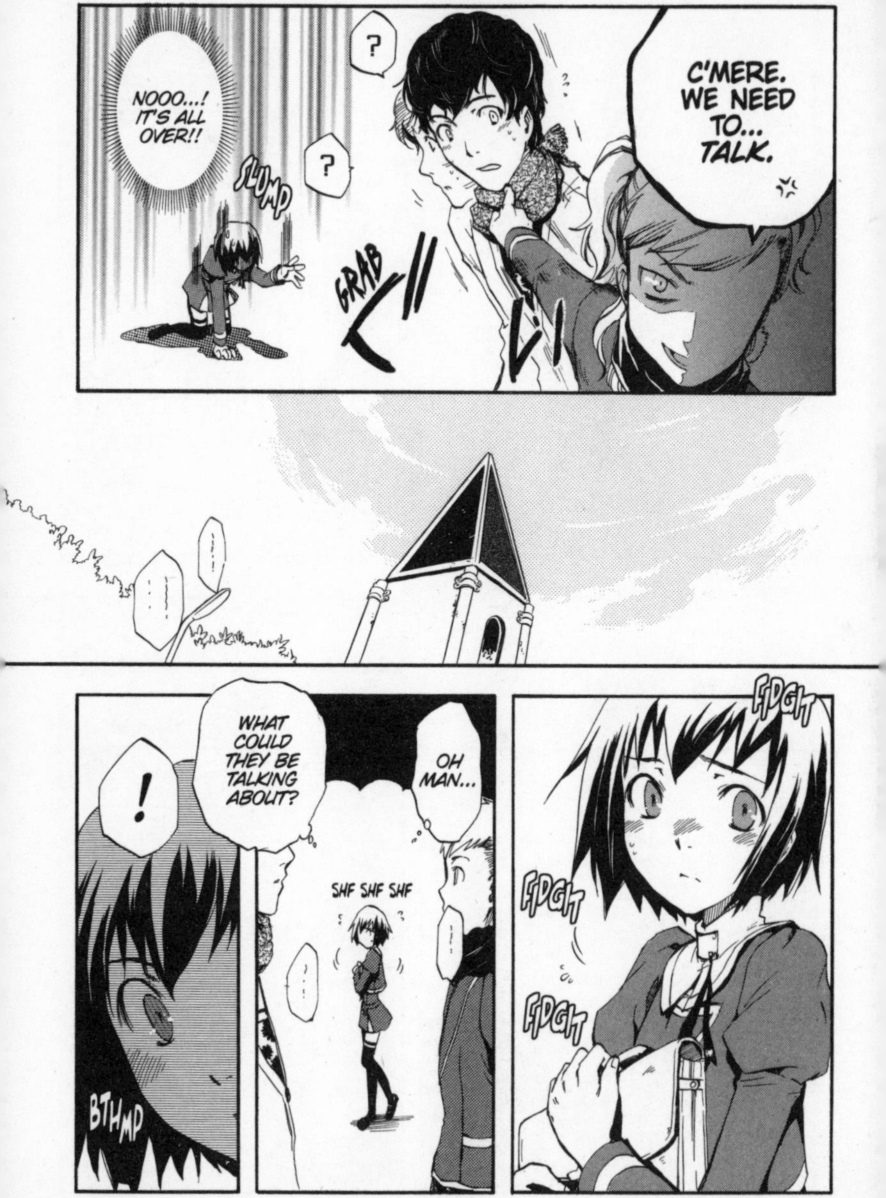

C'MERE. WE NEED TO... TALK.
?
?
GRAB
SLUMP
NOOO...! IT'S ALL OVER!!
FIDGIT
FIDGIT
FIDGIT
OH MAN...
WHAT COULD THEY BE TALKING ABOUT?
SHF SHF SHF
!
BTHMP

I....

I FEEL SO... GROGGY ALL OF A SUDDEN... THAT RUN MUST'VE TAKEN MORE OUT OF ME THAN I THOUGHT...

WH-WHA...?

SMILE

SUMIRE-CHAN!

CHAN...?

I HAD A GOOD LONG CHAT WITH YOSHIKI-SAN.

I'M SORRY, GIRL.

LOOKS LIKE I HAD THE TOTALLY WRONG IDEA ABOUT HIM.

SORRY TO MAKE YOU WAIT.

AH!

HUH?

WHA?

32

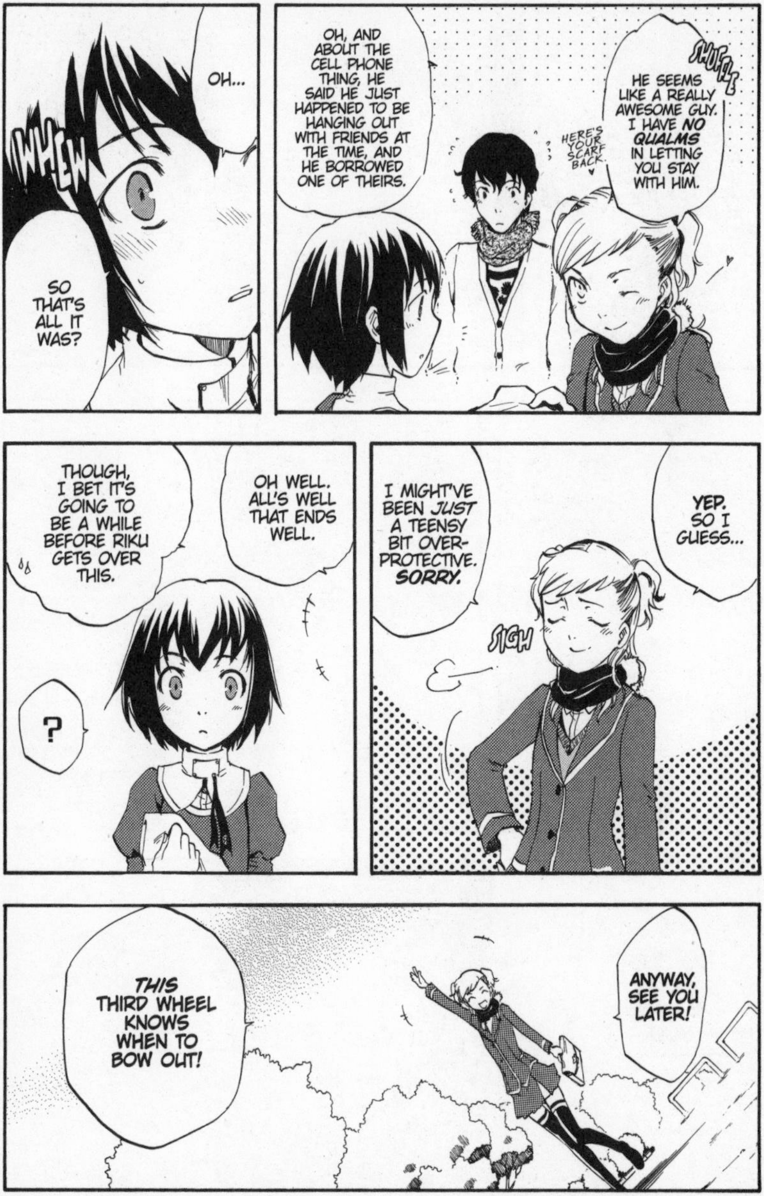
SHUFFLE
HE SEEMS LIKE A REALLY AWESOME GUY. I HAVE NO QUALMS IN LETTING YOU STAY WITH HIM.
HERE'S YOUR SCARF BACK.
OH, AND ABOUT THE CELL PHONE THING, HE SAID HE JUST HAPPENED TO BE HANGING OUT WITH FRIENDS AT THE TIME, AND HE BORROWED ONE OF THEIRS.
OH...
WHEW
SO THAT'S ALL IT WAS?
YEP. SO I GUESS...
I MIGHT'VE BEEN JUST A TEENSY BIT OVER-PROTECTIVE. SORRY.
SIGH
OH WELL. ALL'S WELL THAT ENDS WELL.
THOUGH, I BET IT'S GOING TO BE A WHILE BEFORE RIKU GETS OVER THIS.
?
ANYWAY, SEE YOU LATER!
THIS THIRD WHEEL KNOWS WHEN TO BOW OUT!

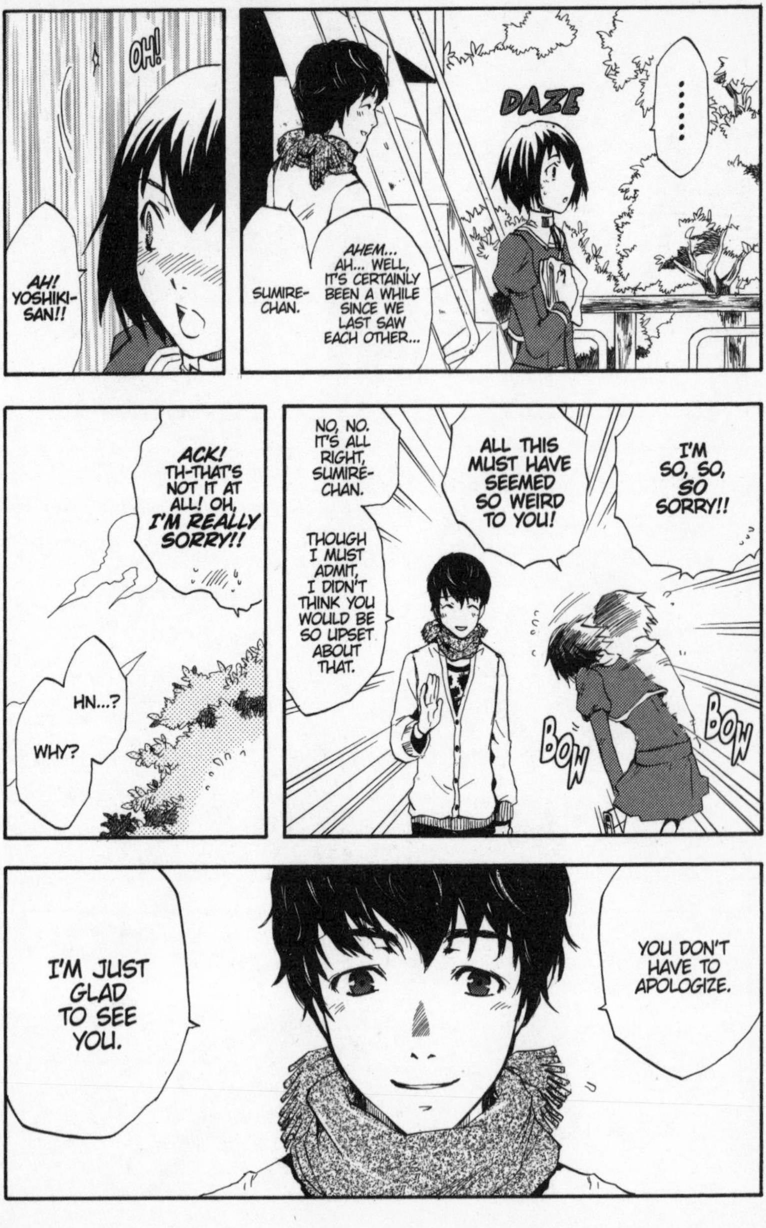
......
DAZE
AHEM... AH... WELL, IT'S CERTAINLY BEEN A WHILE SINCE WE LAST SAW EACH OTHER...
SUMIRE-CHAN.
OH!
AH! YOSHIKI-SAN!!
I'M SO, SO, SO SORRY!!
ALL THIS MUST HAVE SEEMED SO WEIRD TO YOU!
NO, NO. IT'S ALL RIGHT, SUMIRE-CHAN.
THOUGH I MUST ADMIT, I DIDN'T THINK YOU WOULD BE SO UPSET ABOUT THAT.
BOW
BOW
ACK! TH-THAT'S NOT IT AT ALL! OH, I'M REALLY SORRY!!
HN...?
WHY?
YOU DON'T HAVE TO APOLOGIZE.
I'M JUST GLAD TO SEE YOU.

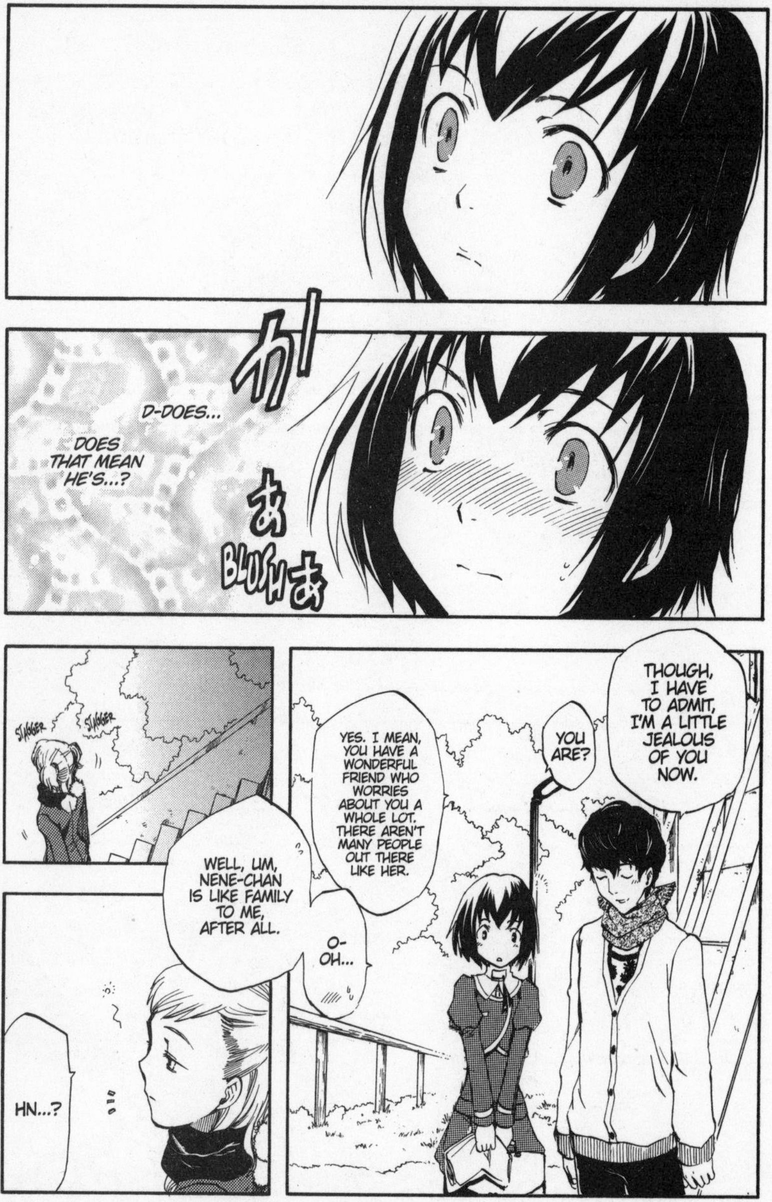

わ
あ
BLUSH あ
D-DOES...
DOES THAT MEAN HE'S...?
WELL, UM, NENE-CHAN IS LIKE FAMILY TO ME, AFTER ALL.
THOUGH, I HAVE TO ADMIT, I'M A LITTLE JEALOUS OF YOU NOW.
YOU ARE?
YES. I MEAN, YOU HAVE A WONDERFUL FRIEND WHO WORRIES ABOUT YOU A WHOLE LOT. THERE AREN'T MANY PEOPLE OUT THERE LIKE HER.
O-OH...
STAGGER
STAGGER
HN...?

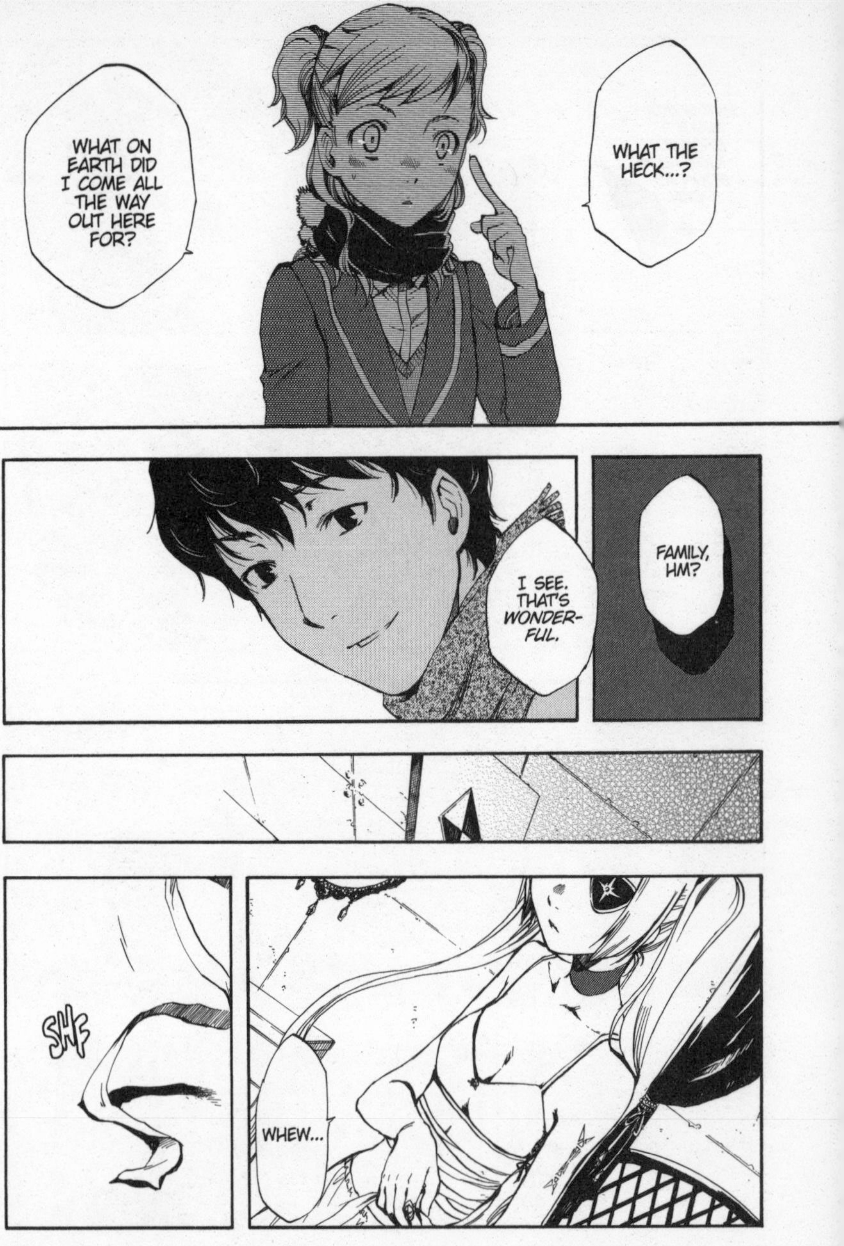
WHAT THE HECK...?
WHAT ON EARTH DID I COME ALL THE WAY OUT HERE FOR?
FAMILY, HM?
I SEE. THAT'S WONDERFUL.
WHEW...
SHF

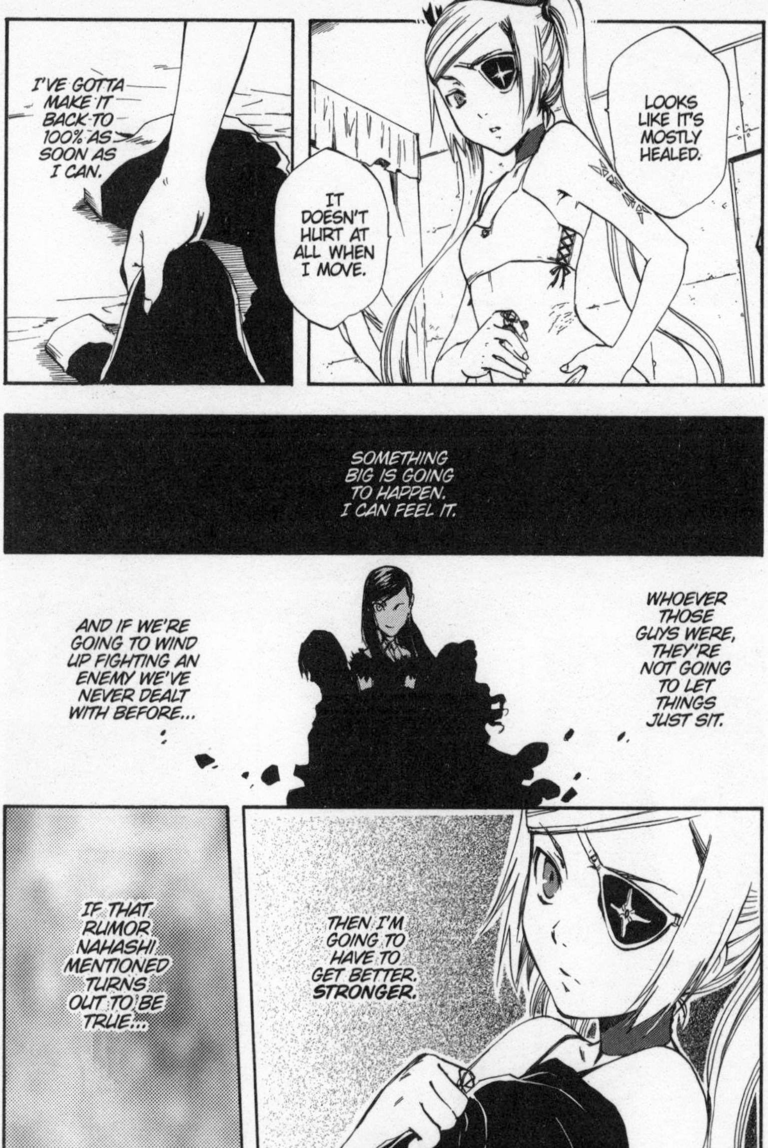
LOOKS LIKE IT'S MOSTLY HEALED.
IT DOESN'T HURT AT ALL WHEN I MOVE.
I'VE GOTTA MAKE IT BACK TO 100% AS SOON AS I CAN.
SOMETHING BIG IS GOING TO HAPPEN. I CAN FEEL IT.
WHOEVER THOSE GUYS WERE, THEY'RE NOT GOING TO LET THINGS JUST SIT.
AND IF WE'RE GOING TO WIND UP FIGHTING AN ENEMY WE'VE NEVER DEALT WITH BEFORE...
THEN I'M GOING TO HAVE TO GET BETTER. STRONGER.
IF THAT RUMOR NAHASHI MENTIONED TURNS OUT TO BE TRUE...

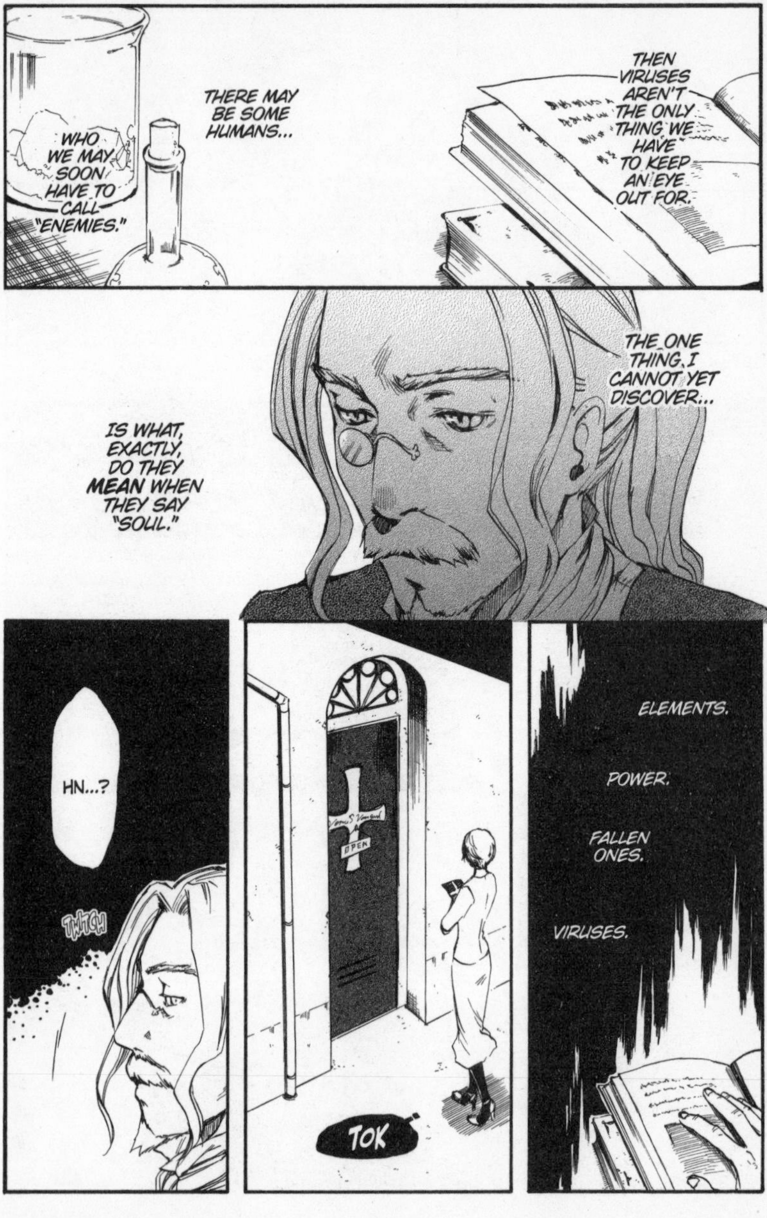
THEN VIRUSES AREN'T THE ONLY THING WE HAVE TO KEEP AN EYE OUT FOR.
THERE MAY BE SOME HUMANS...
WHO WE MAY SOON HAVE TO CALL "ENEMIES."
THE ONE THING I CANNOT YET DISCOVER...
IS WHAT, EXACTLY, DO THEY MEAN WHEN THEY SAY "SOUL."
ELEMENTS.
POWER.
FALLEN ONES.
VIRUSES.
OPEN
TOK
HN...?
TWITCH

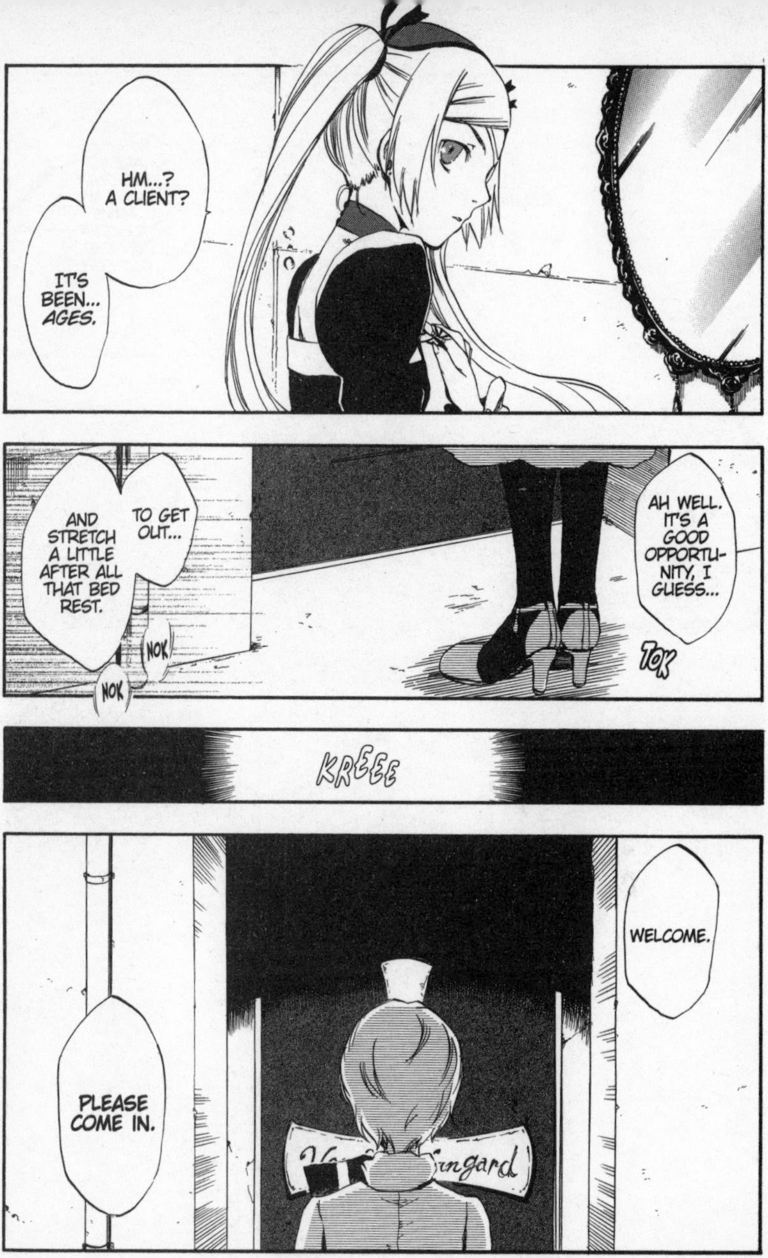
HM...? A CLIENT?
IT'S BEEN... AGES.
AH WELL. IT'S A GOOD OPPORTU-NITY, I GUESS...
TOK
TO GET OUT...
AND STRETCH A LITTLE AFTER ALL THAT BED REST.
NOK
NOK
KREEE
WELCOME.
PLEASE COME IN.

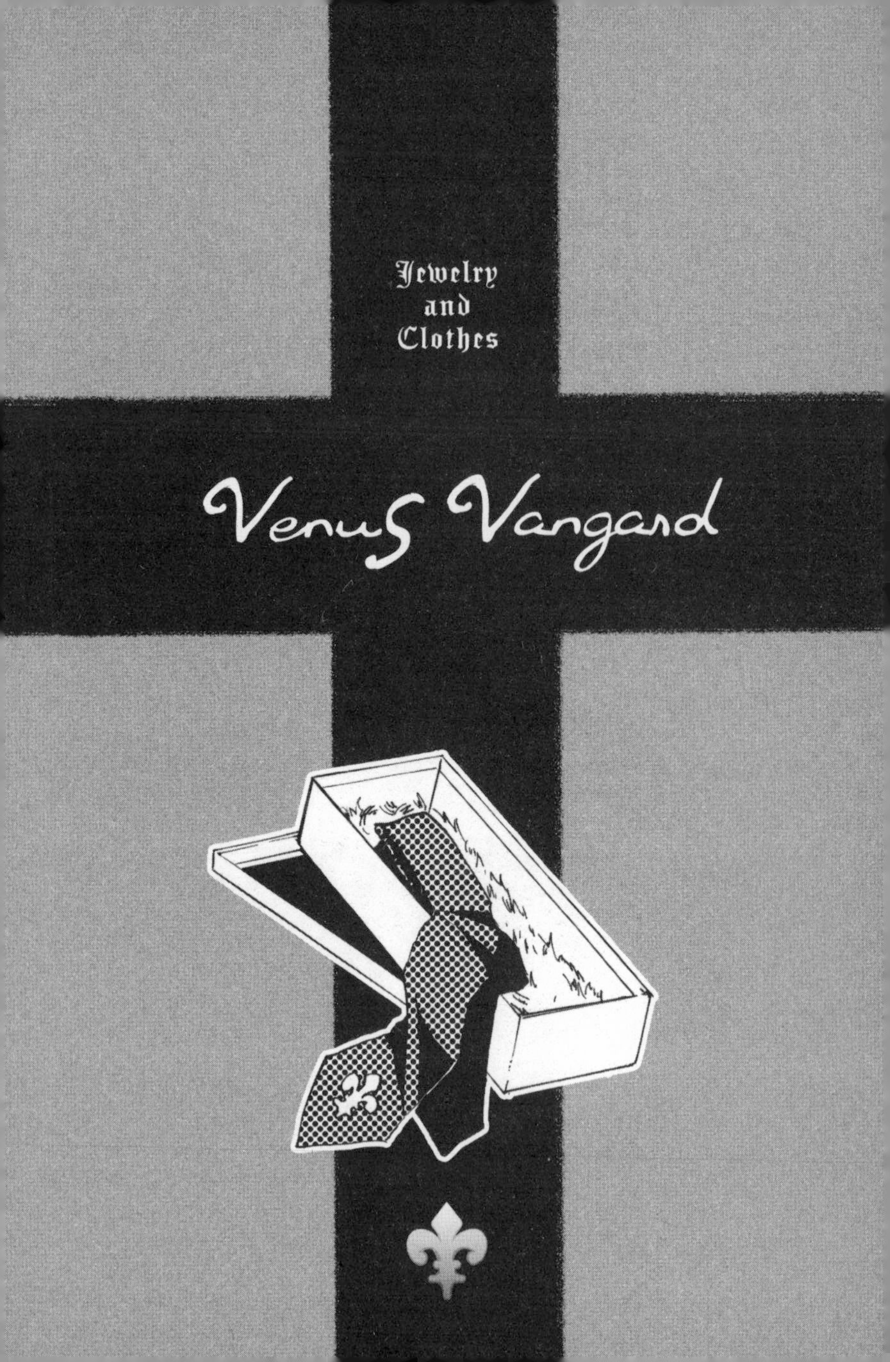
Jewelry
and
Clothes
Venus Vangard

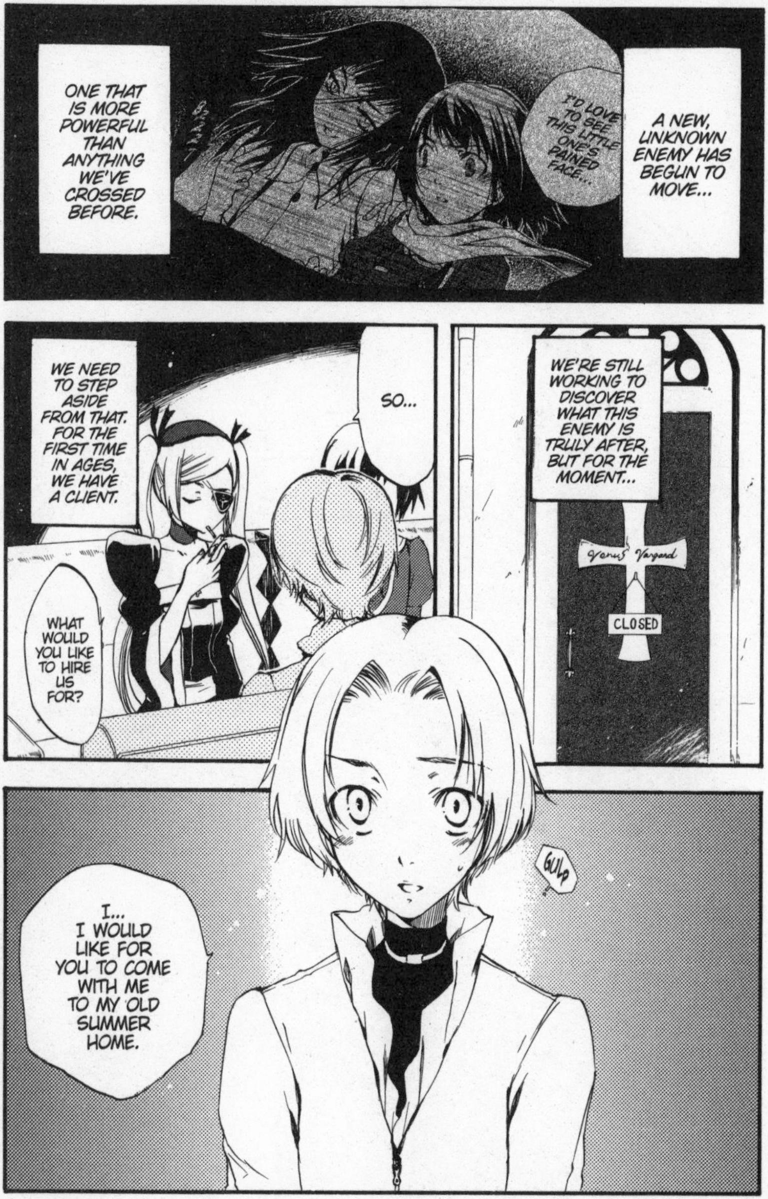
A NEW, UNKNOWN ENEMY HAS BEGUN TO MOVE...
I'D LOVE TO SEE THIS LITTLE ONE'S PAINED FACE...
ONE THAT IS MORE POWERFUL THAN ANYTHING WE'VE CROSSED BEFORE.
WE'RE STILL WORKING TO DISCOVER WHAT THIS ENEMY IS TRULY AFTER, BUT FOR THE MOMENT...
Venus Vangard
CLOSED
SO...
WE NEED TO STEP ASIDE FROM THAT. FOR THE FIRST TIME IN AGES, WE HAVE A CLIENT.
WHAT WOULD YOU LIKE TO HIRE US FOR?
GULP
I... I WOULD LIKE FOR YOU TO COME WITH ME TO MY OLD SUMMER HOME.

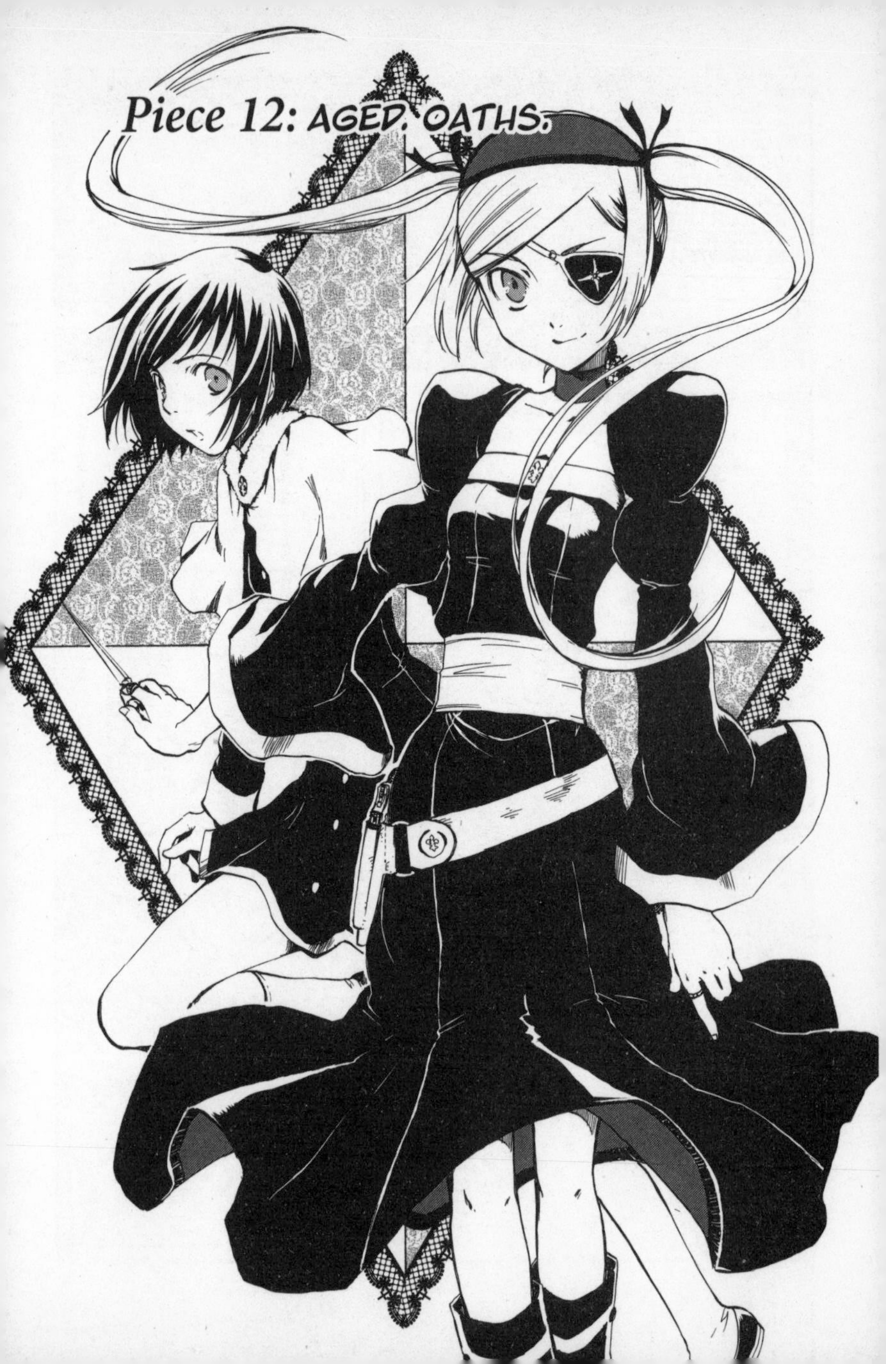
Piece 12: AGED. OATHS.

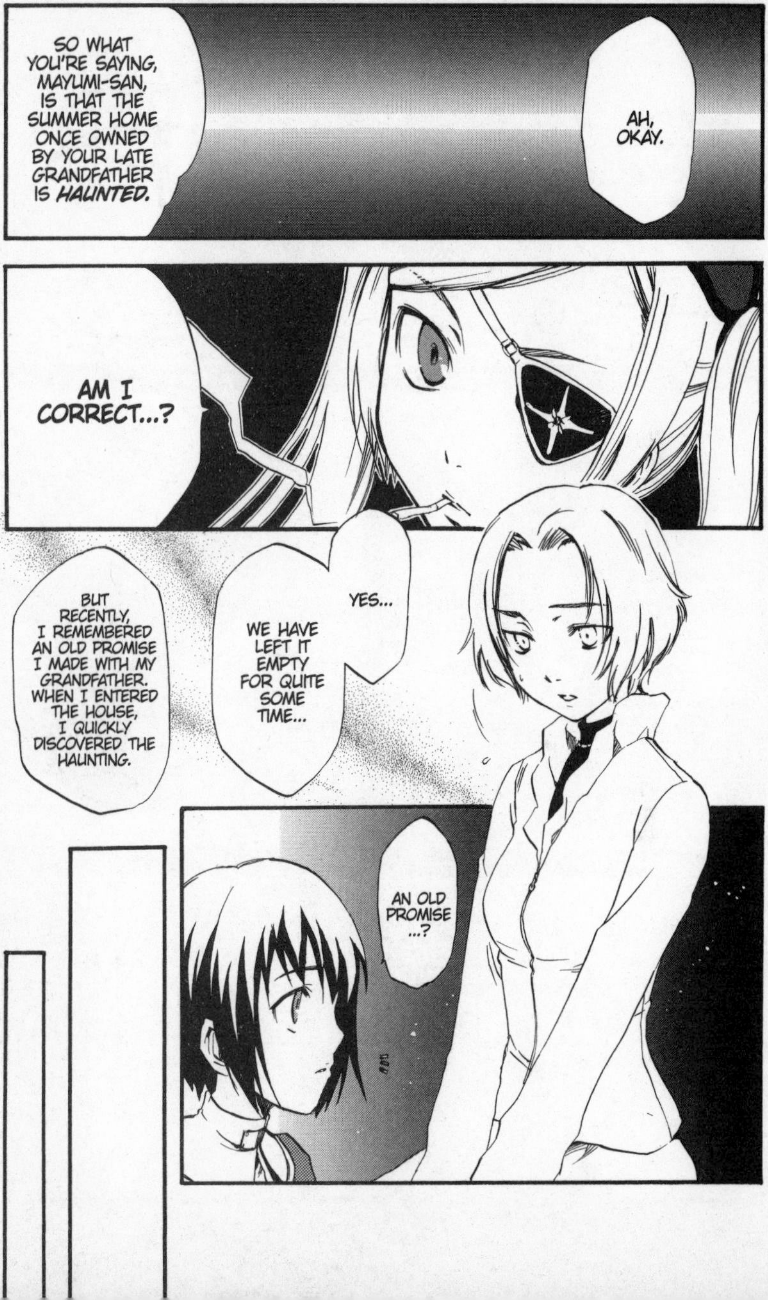
AH, OKAY.
SO WHAT YOU'RE SAYING, MAYUMI-SAN, IS THAT THE SUMMER HOME ONCE OWNED BY YOUR LATE GRANDFATHER IS *HAUNTED*.
AM I CORRECT...?
YES... WE HAVE LEFT IT EMPTY FOR QUITE SOME TIME...
BUT RECENTLY, I REMEMBERED AN OLD PROMISE I MADE WITH MY GRANDFATHER. WHEN I ENTERED THE HOUSE, I QUICKLY DISCOVERED THE HAUNTING.
AN OLD PROMISE ...?

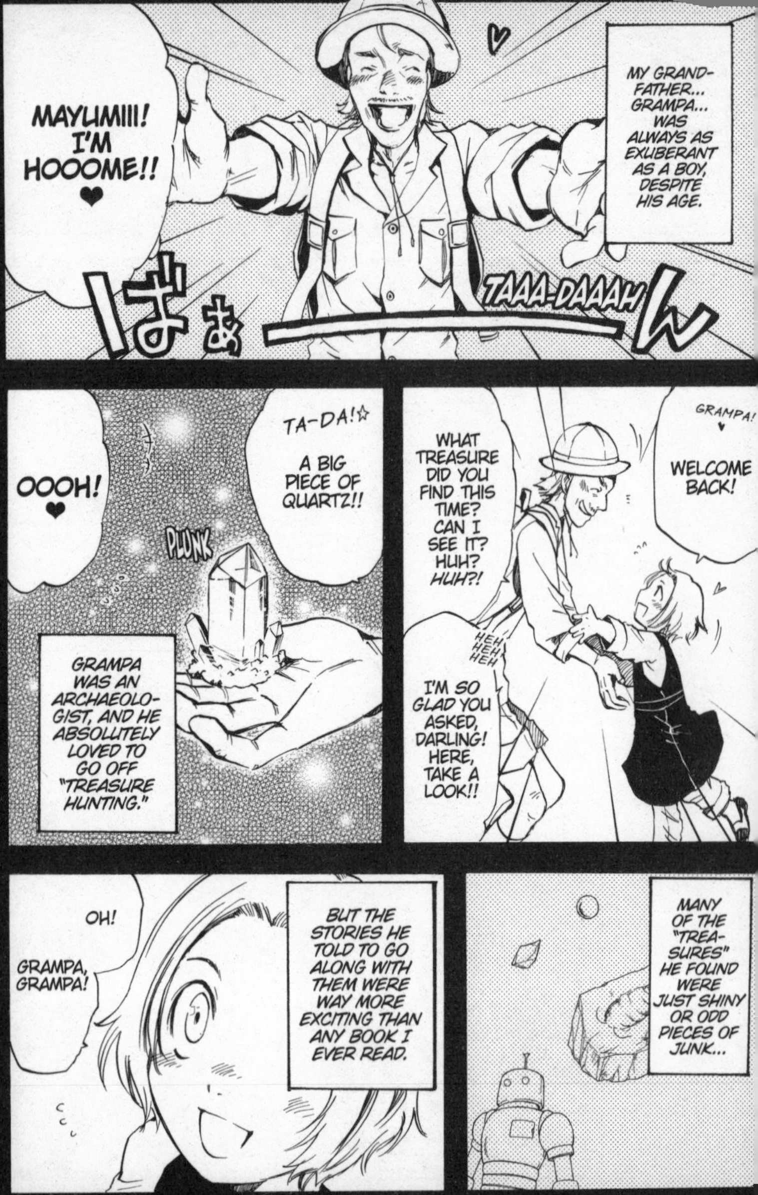
MY GRAND-FATHER... GRAMPA... WAS ALWAYS AS EXUBERANT AS A BOY, DESPITE HIS AGE.
MAYUMIIII! I'M HOOOME!! ❤
TAAA-DAAAH
GRAMPA! ♥ WELCOME BACK!
WHAT TREASURE DID YOU FIND THIS TIME? CAN I SEE IT? HUH? HUH?!
HEH HEH HEH
I'M SO GLAD YOU ASKED, DARLING! HERE, TAKE A LOOK!!
TA-DA!☆ A BIG PIECE OF QUARTZ!!
OOOH! ❤
PLUNK
GRAMPA WAS AN ARCHAEOLO-GIST, AND HE ABSOLUTELY LOVED TO GO OFF "TREASURE HUNTING."
MANY OF THE "TREA-SURES" HE FOUND WERE JUST SHINY OR ODD PIECES OF JUNK...
BUT THE STORIES HE TOLD TO GO ALONG WITH THEM WERE WAY MORE EXCITING THAN ANY BOOK I EVER READ.
OH!
GRAMPA, GRAMPA!

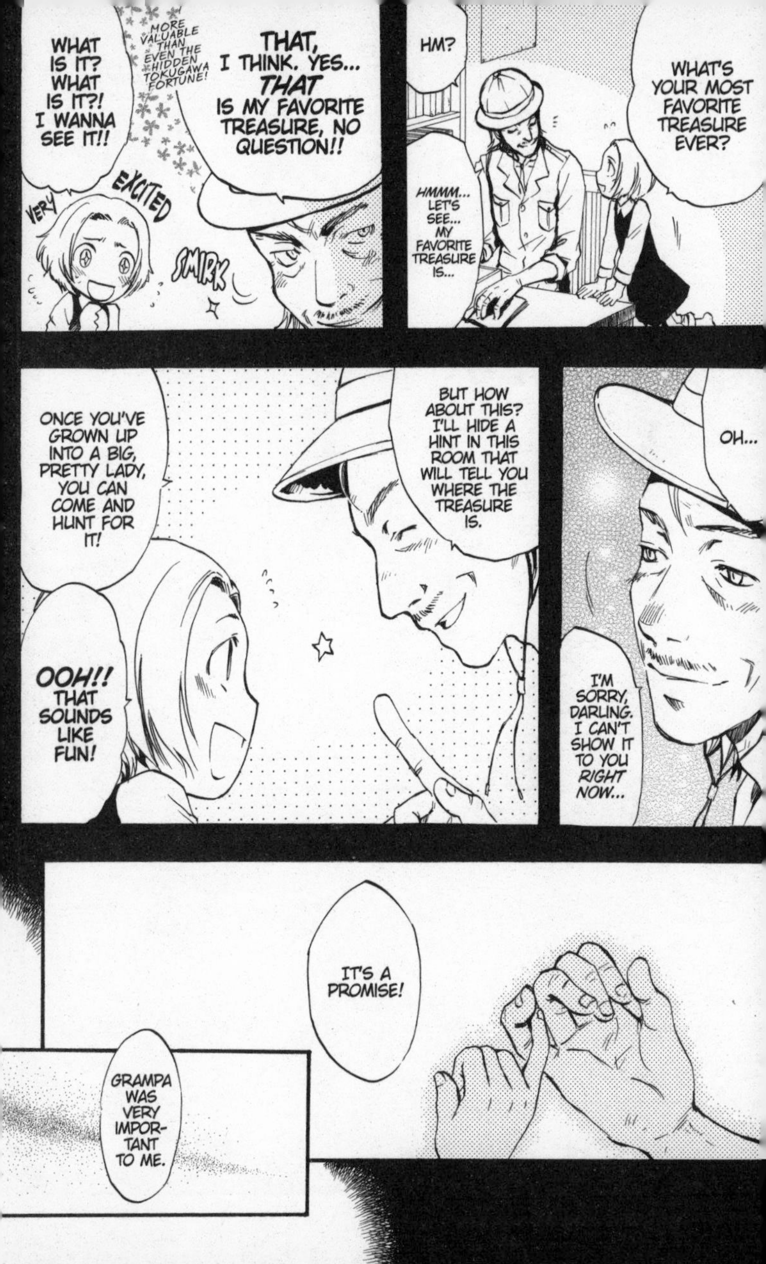
WHAT'S YOUR MOST FAVORITE TREASURE EVER?
HM?
HMMM... LET'S SEE... MY FAVORITE TREASURE IS...
THAT, I THINK. YES... THAT IS MY FAVORITE TREASURE, NO QUESTION!!
MORE VALUABLE THAN EVEN THE HIDDEN TOKUGAWA FORTUNE!
WHAT IS IT? WHAT IS IT?! I WANNA SEE IT!!
VERY EXCITED
SMIRK
OH...
I'M SORRY, DARLING. I CAN'T SHOW IT TO YOU RIGHT NOW...
BUT HOW ABOUT THIS? I'LL HIDE A HINT IN THIS ROOM THAT WILL TELL YOU WHERE THE TREASURE IS.
ONCE YOU'VE GROWN UP INTO A BIG, PRETTY LADY, YOU CAN COME AND HUNT FOR IT!
OOH!! THAT SOUNDS LIKE FUN!
IT'S A PROMISE!
GRAMPA WAS VERY IMPORTANT TO ME.

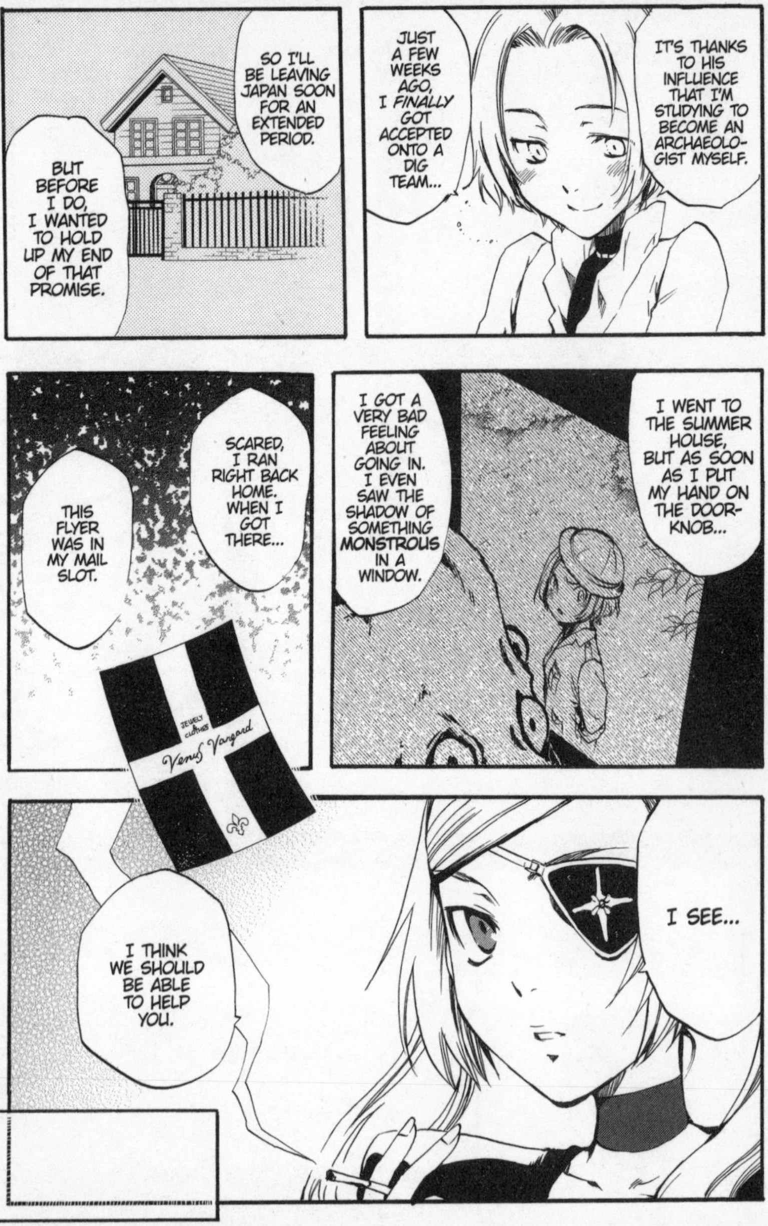
IT'S THANKS TO HIS INFLUENCE THAT I'M STUDYING TO BECOME AN ARCHAEOLOGIST MYSELF.
JUST A FEW WEEKS AGO, I *FINALLY* GOT ACCEPTED ONTO A DIG TEAM...
SO I'LL BE LEAVING JAPAN SOON FOR AN EXTENDED PERIOD.
BUT BEFORE I DO, I WANTED TO HOLD UP MY END OF THAT PROMISE.
I WENT TO THE SUMMER HOUSE, BUT AS SOON AS I PUT MY HAND ON THE DOORKNOB...
I GOT A VERY BAD FEELING ABOUT GOING IN. I EVEN SAW THE SHADOW OF SOMETHING **MONSTROUS** IN A WINDOW.
SCARED, I RAN RIGHT BACK HOME. WHEN I GOT THERE...
THIS FLYER WAS IN MY MAIL SLOT.
JEWELY CLOTHES
Venus Vangard
I SEE...
I THINK WE SHOULD BE ABLE TO HELP YOU.

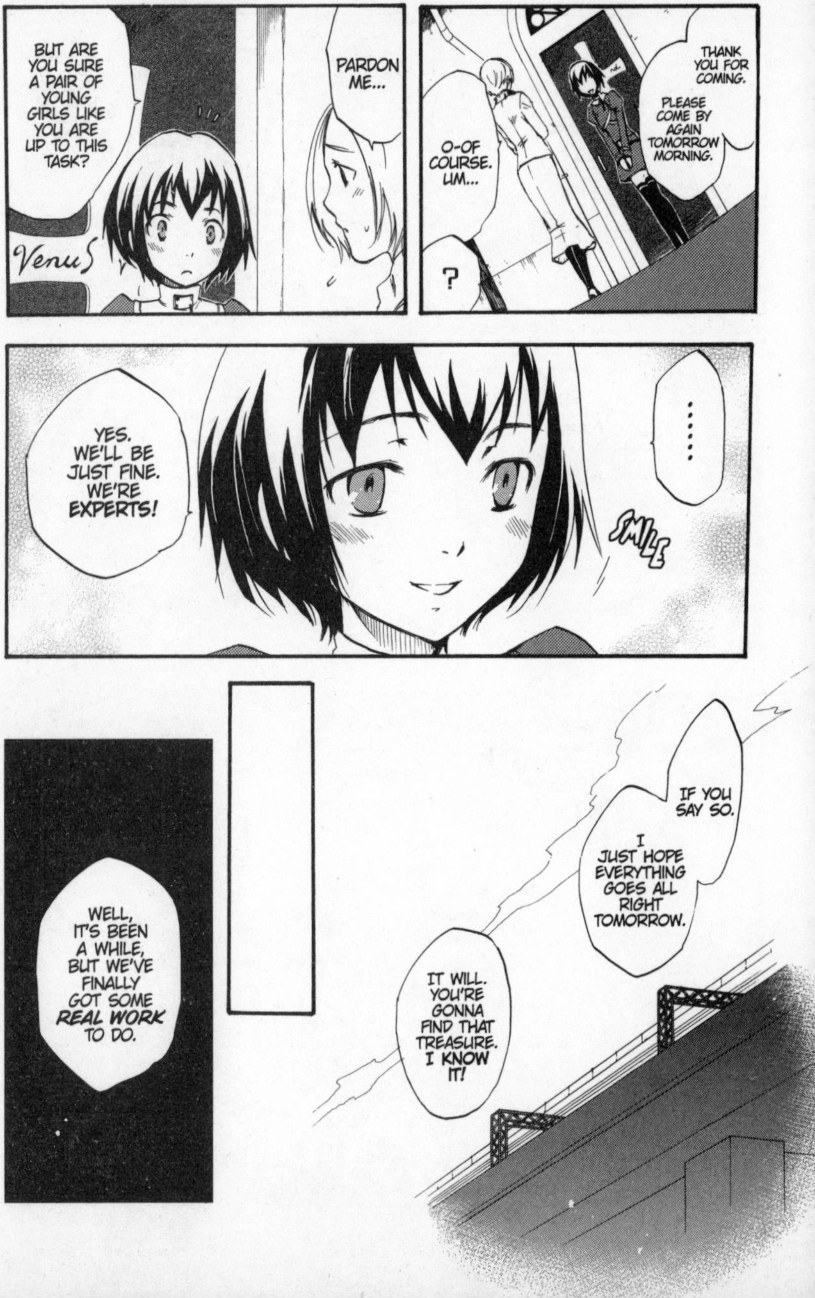
THANK YOU FOR COMING.
PLEASE COME BY AGAIN TOMORROW MORNING.
O-OF COURSE. UM...
?
PARDON ME...
BUT ARE YOU SURE A PAIR OF YOUNG GIRLS LIKE YOU ARE UP TO THIS TASK?
Venus
......
SMILE
YES. WE'LL BE JUST FINE. WE'RE EXPERTS!
IF YOU SAY SO.
I JUST HOPE EVERYTHING GOES ALL RIGHT TOMORROW.
IT WILL. YOU'RE GONNA FIND THAT TREASURE. I KNOW IT!
WELL, IT'S BEEN A WHILE, BUT WE'VE FINALLY GOT SOME REAL WORK TO DO.

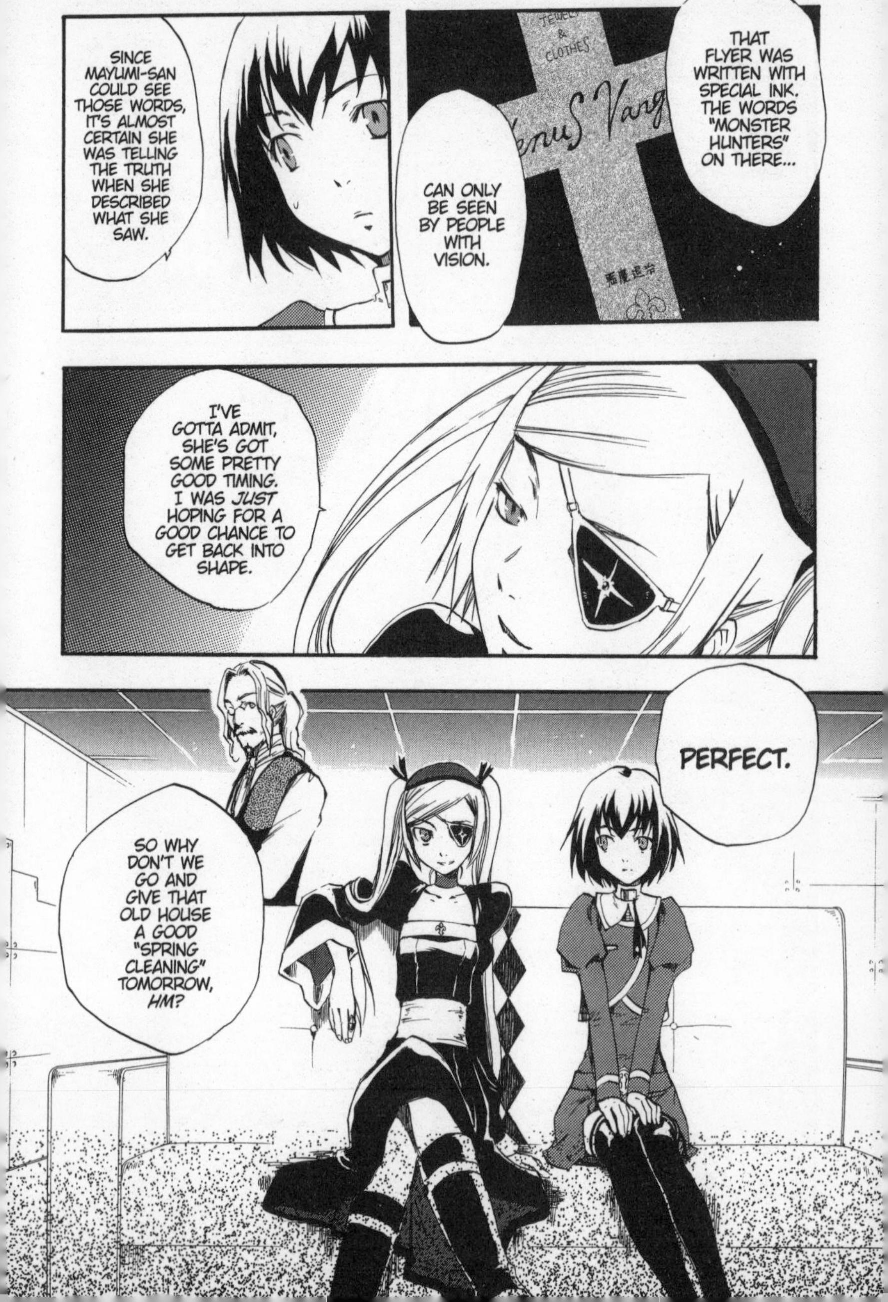
THAT FLYER WAS WRITTEN WITH SPECIAL INK. THE WORDS "MONSTER HUNTERS" ON THERE...
JEWEL & CLOTHES
CAN ONLY BE SEEN BY PEOPLE WITH VISION.
SINCE MAYUMI-SAN COULD SEE THOSE WORDS, IT'S ALMOST CERTAIN SHE WAS TELLING THE TRUTH WHEN SHE DESCRIBED WHAT SHE SAW.
I'VE GOTTA ADMIT, SHE'S GOT SOME PRETTY GOOD TIMING. I WAS *JUST* HOPING FOR A GOOD CHANCE TO GET BACK INTO SHAPE.
PERFECT.
SO WHY DON'T WE GO AND GIVE THAT OLD HOUSE A GOOD "SPRING CLEANING" TOMORROW, HM?

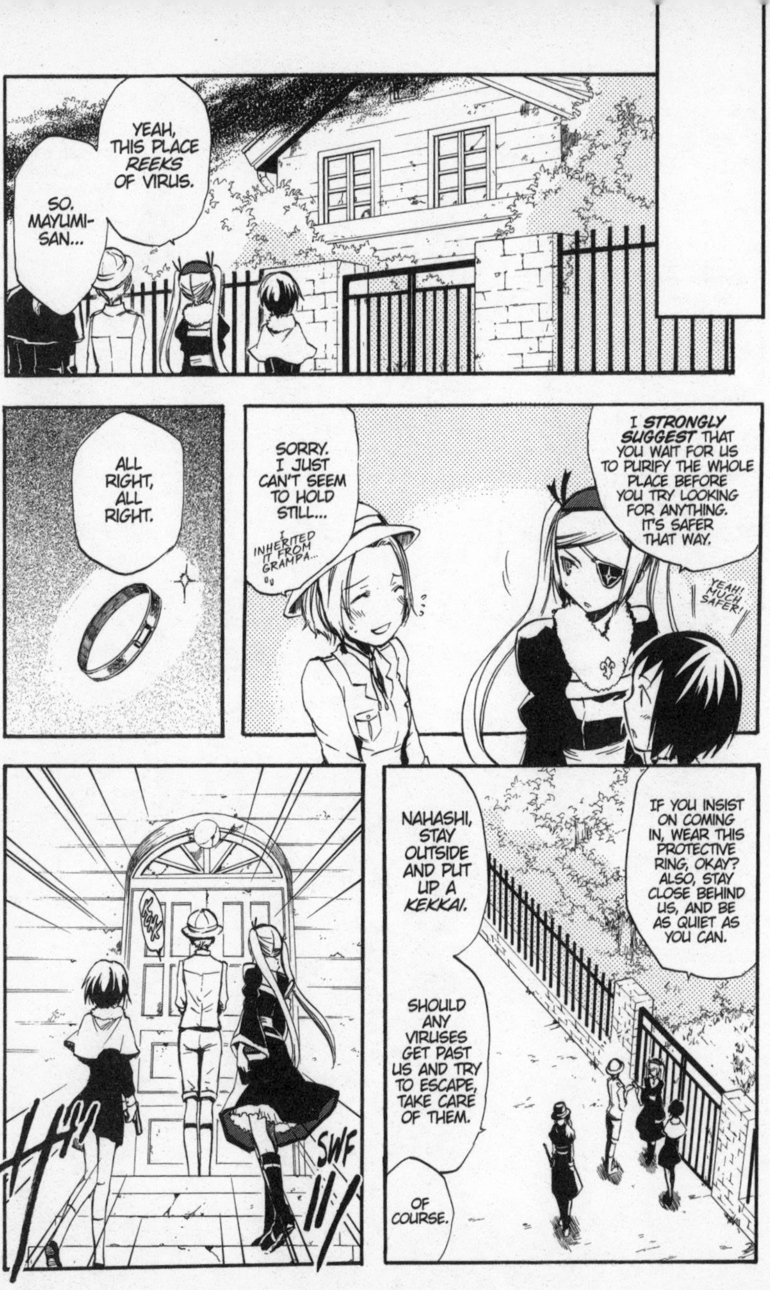
YEAH, THIS PLACE *REEKS* OF VIRUS.
SO. MAYUMI-SAN...
I ***STRONGLY SUGGEST*** THAT YOU WAIT FOR US TO PURIFY THE WHOLE PLACE BEFORE YOU TRY LOOKING FOR ANYTHING. IT'S SAFER THAT WAY.
YEAH! MUCH SAFER!
SORRY. I JUST CAN'T SEEM TO HOLD STILL...
I INHERITED IT FROM GRAMPA...
ALL RIGHT, ALL RIGHT.
IF YOU INSIST ON COMING IN, WEAR THIS PROTECTIVE RING, OKAY? ALSO, STAY CLOSE BEHIND US, AND BE AS QUIET AS YOU CAN.
NAHASHI, STAY OUTSIDE AND PUT UP A *KEKKAI.*
SHOULD ANY VIRUSES GET PAST US AND TRY TO ESCAPE, TAKE CARE OF THEM.
OF COURSE.
SWF

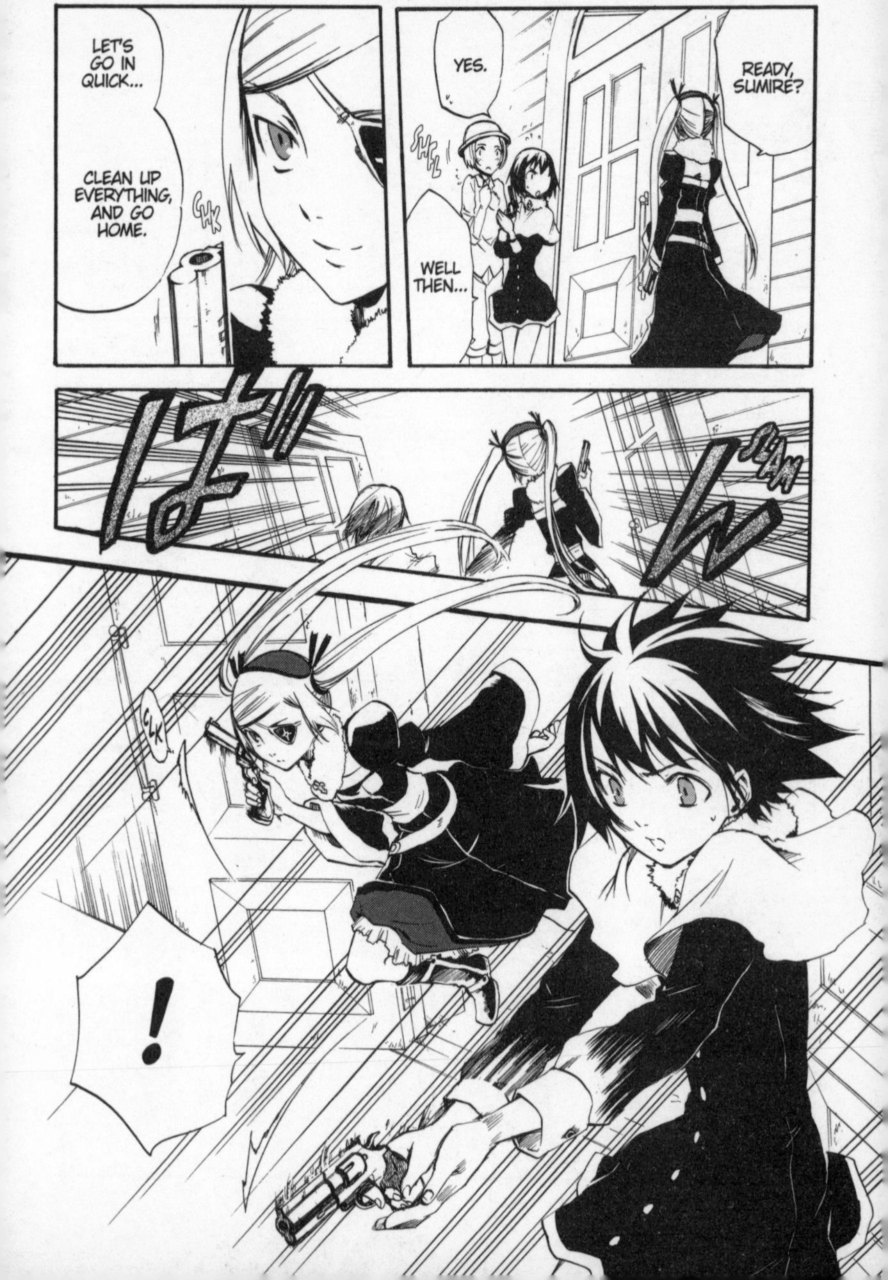
READY, SUMIRE?
YES.
WELL THEN...
LET'S GO IN QUICK...
CHK
CLEAN UP EVERYTHING, AND GO HOME.
SLAM
ば
ん
CLK
!

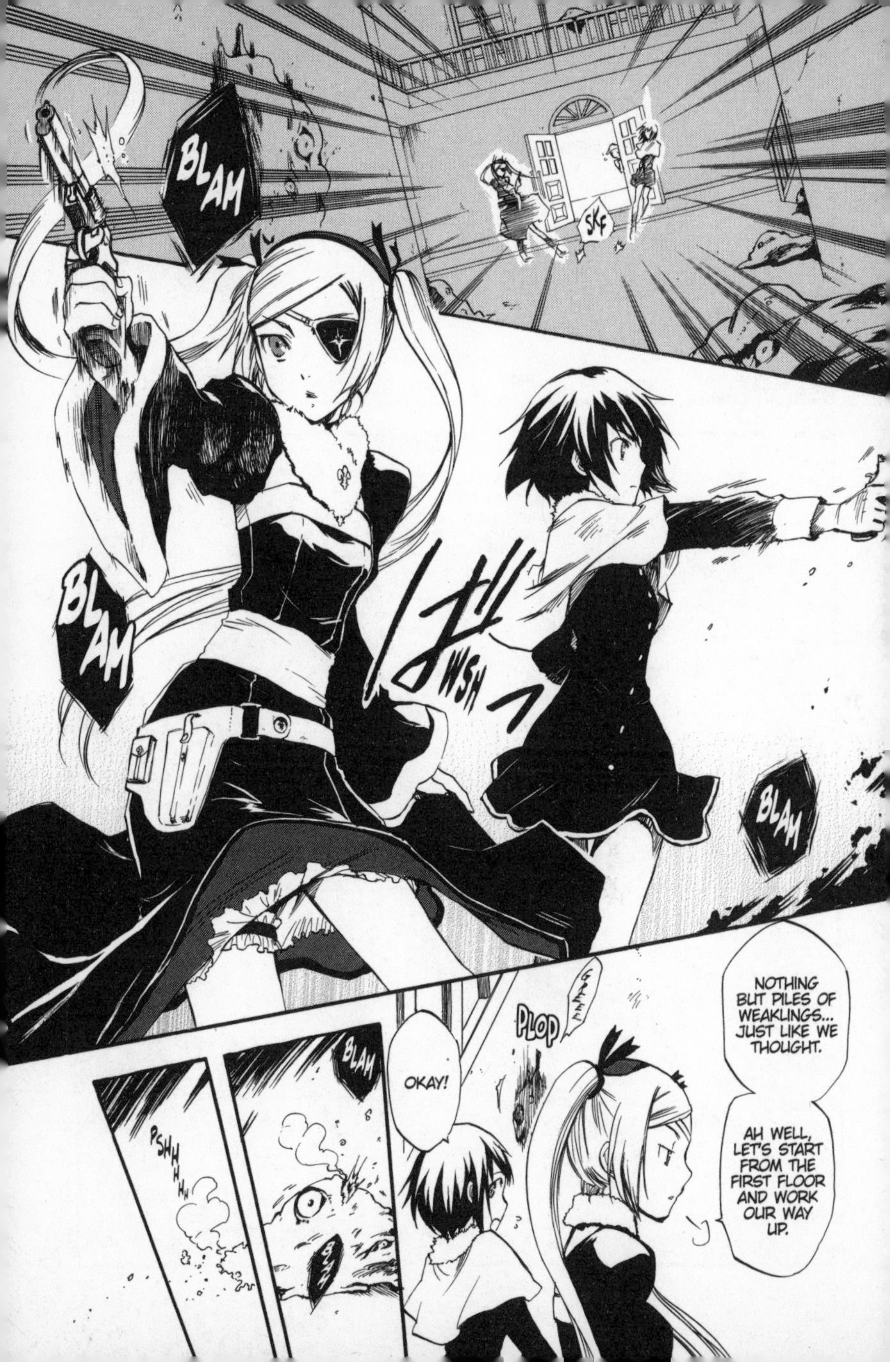
SKF
BLAM
BLAM
WSH
BLAM
NOTHING BUT PILES OF WEAKLINGS... JUST LIKE WE THOUGHT.
AH WELL, LET'S START FROM THE FIRST FLOOR AND WORK OUR WAY UP.
PLOP
OKAY!
BLAM
PSHHHHH

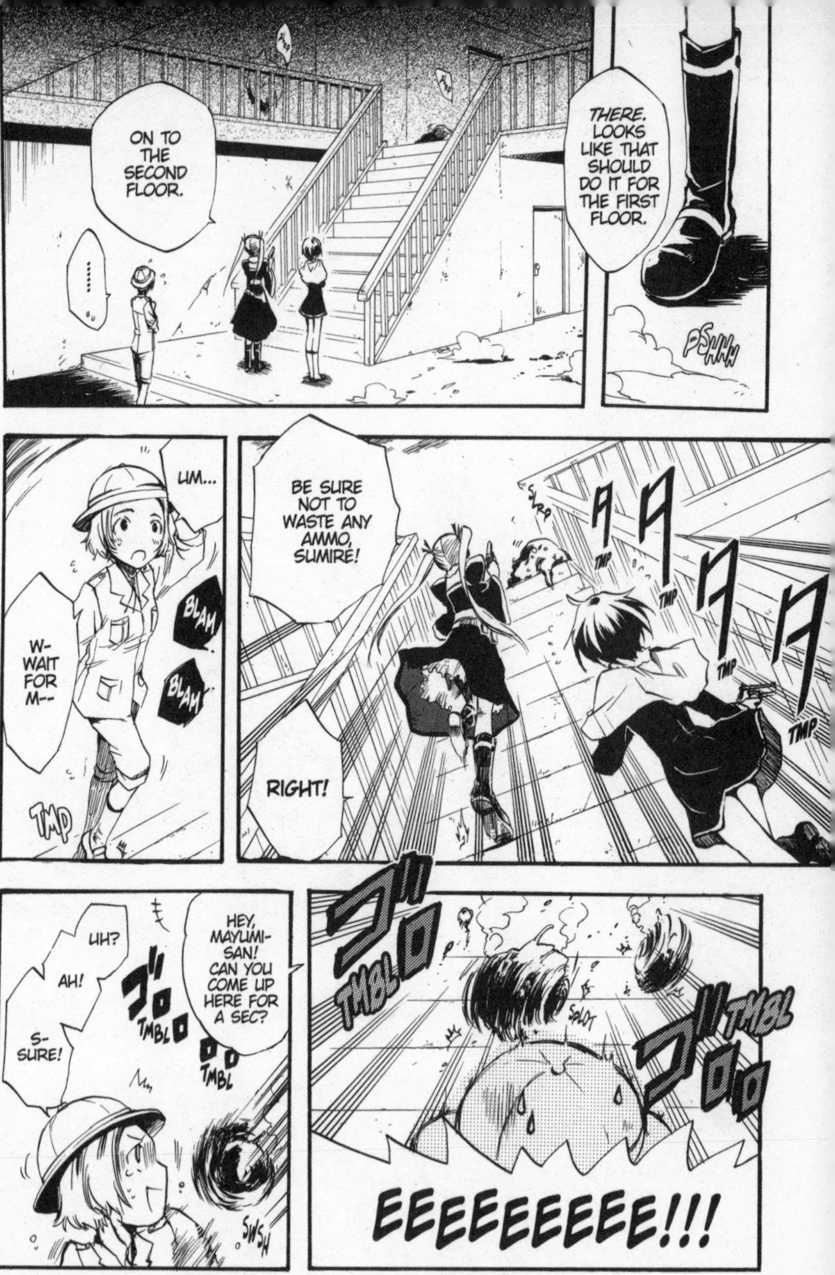
THERE. LOOKS LIKE THAT SHOULD DO IT FOR THE FIRST FLOOR.
PSHHH
ON TO THE SECOND FLOOR.
......
BE SURE NOT TO WASTE ANY AMMO, SUMIRE!
TMP
TMP
TMP
TMP
RIGHT!
UM...
BLAM
BLAM
W-WAIT FOR M--
TMP
TMBL
TMBL
SPLOT
EEEEEEEEEE!!!
HEY, MAYUMI-SAN! CAN YOU COME UP HERE FOR A SEC?
UH?
AH!
S-SURE!
TMBL
TMBL
SWSH

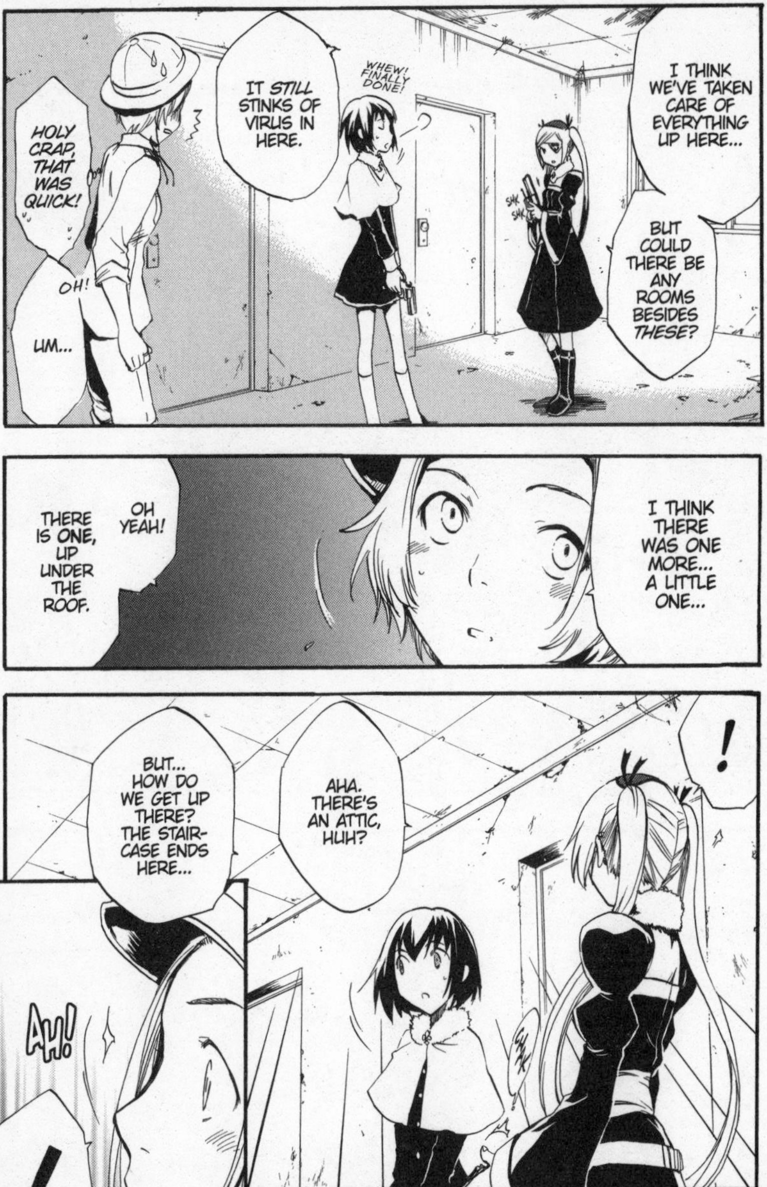
I THINK WE'VE TAKEN CARE OF EVERYTHING UP HERE...
BUT COULD THERE BE ANY ROOMS BESIDES THESE?
SHK SHK
WHEW! FINALLY DONE!
IT STILL STINKS OF VIRUS IN HERE.
HOLY CRAP, THAT WAS QUICK!
OH!
UM...
I THINK THERE WAS ONE MORE... A LITTLE ONE...
OH YEAH!
THERE IS ONE, UP UNDER THE ROOF.
!
AHA. THERE'S AN ATTIC, HUH?
BUT... HOW DO WE GET UP THERE? THE STAIR-CASE ENDS HERE...
AH!
!

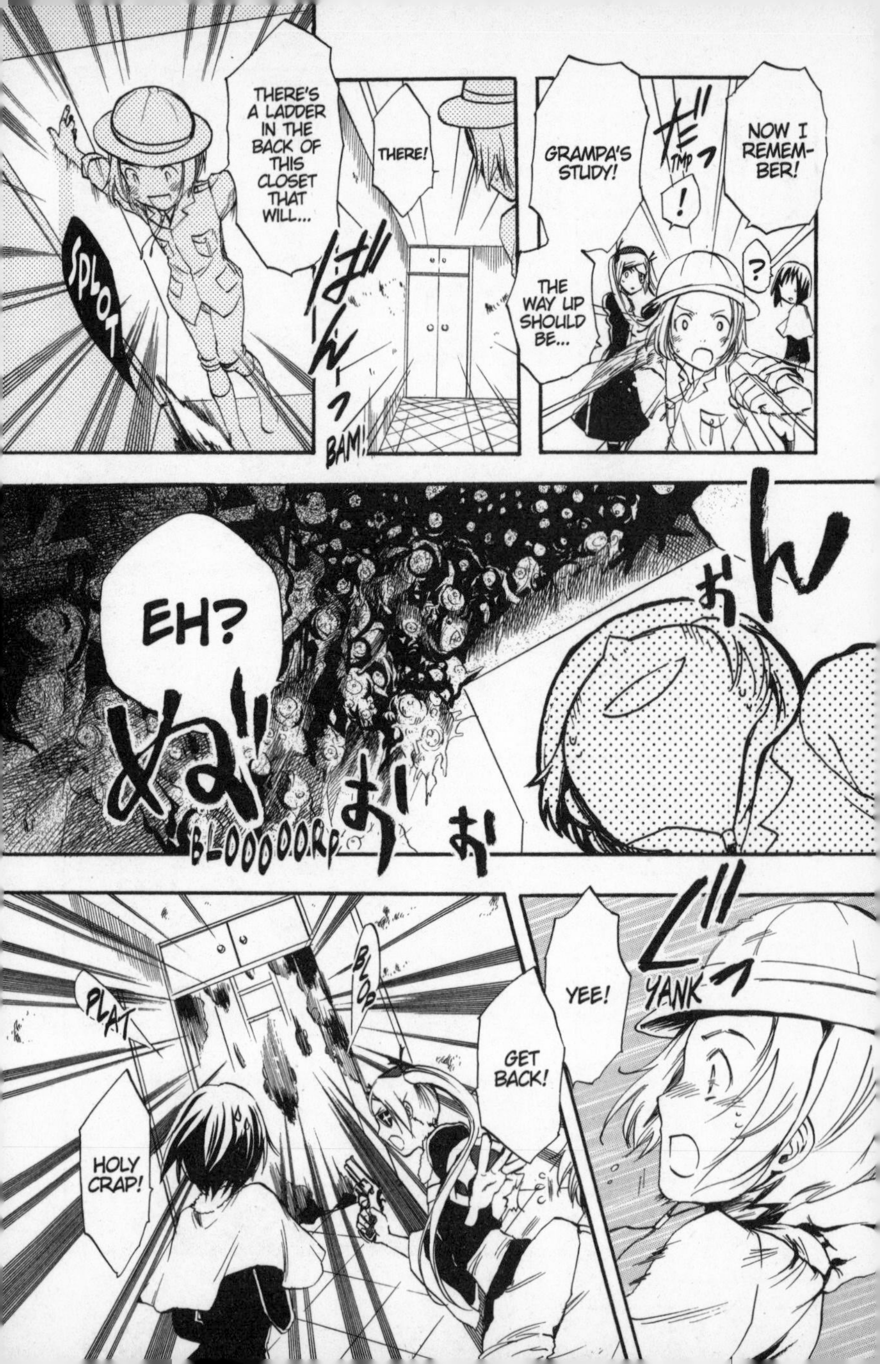
NOW I REMEMBER!
TMP
!
?
GRAMPA'S STUDY!
THE WAY UP SHOULD BE...
THERE!
BAM!
THERE'S A LADDER IN THE BACK OF THIS CLOSET THAT WILL...
SPLOT
EH?
BLOOOOORP
YANK
YEE!
GET BACK!
BLOP
PLAT
HOLY CRAP!

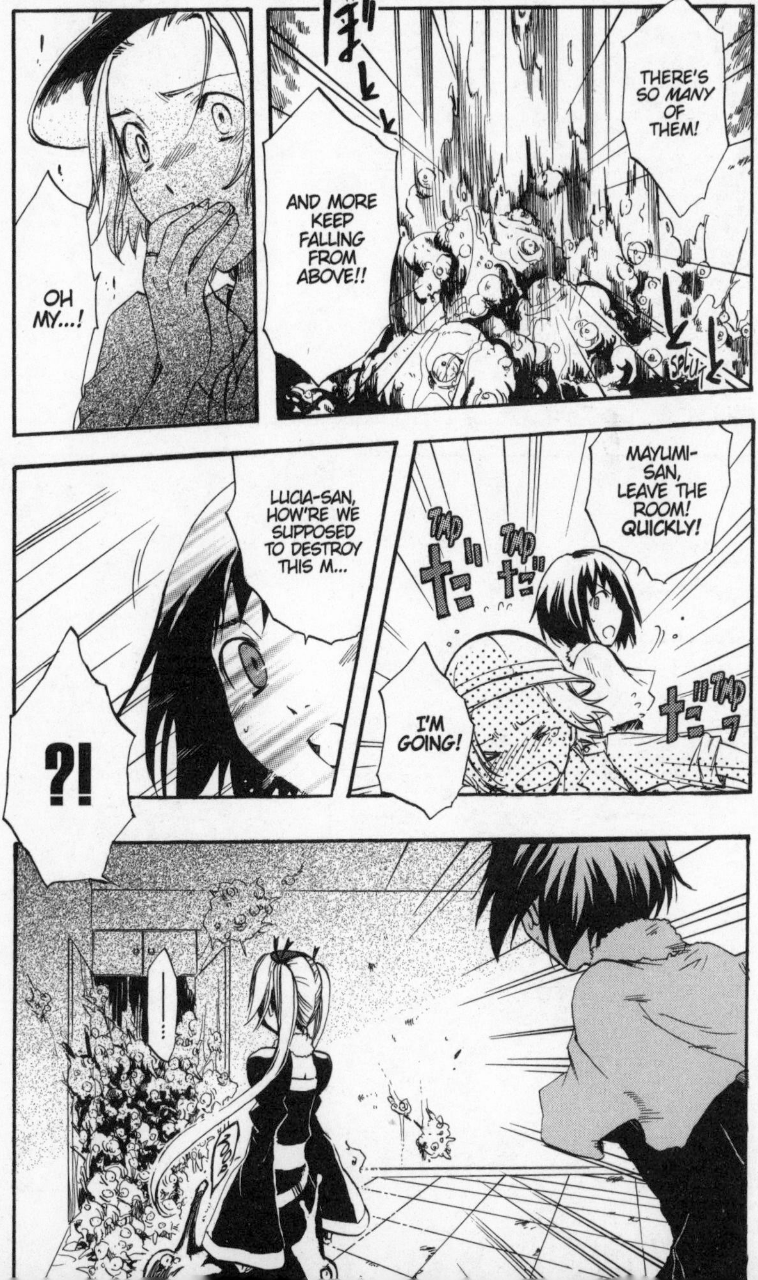

THERE'S SO MANY OF THEM!
SPLAK
AND MORE KEEP FALLING FROM ABOVE!!
SPLUT
!
OH MY...!
MAYUMI-SAN, LEAVE THE ROOM! QUICKLY!
TAP
TAP
I'M GOING!
TAP
LUCIA-SAN, HOW'RE WE SUPPOSED TO DESTROY THIS M...
?!
!...

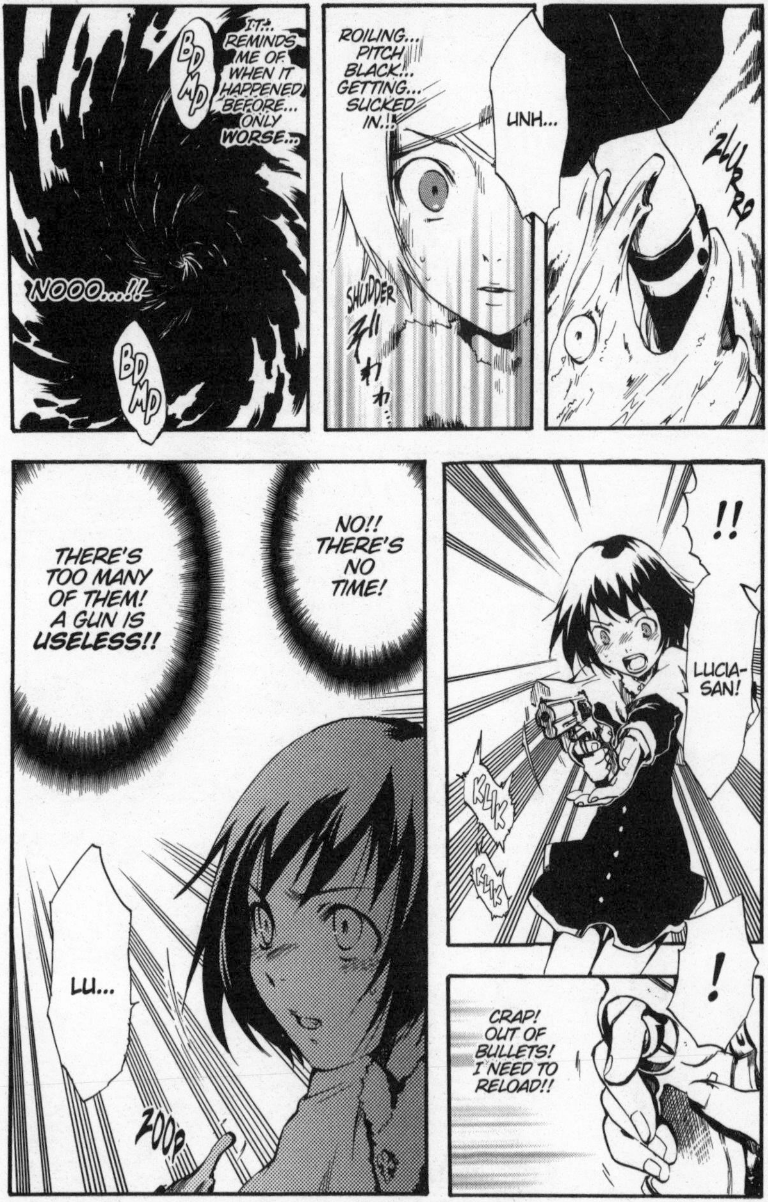
UNH...
...ZLURRG
ROILING... PITCH BLACK... GETTING... SUCKED IN..!!
SHUDDER
IT... REMINDS ME OF WHEN IT HAPPENED BEFORE... ONLY WORSE...
BDMP
NOOO...!!
BDMP
!!
LUCIA-SAN!
KLIK
KLIK
!
CRAP! OUT OF BULLETS! I NEED TO RELOAD!!
NO!! THERE'S NO TIME!
THERE'S TOO MANY OF THEM! A GUN IS USELESS!!
LU...
ZOOP

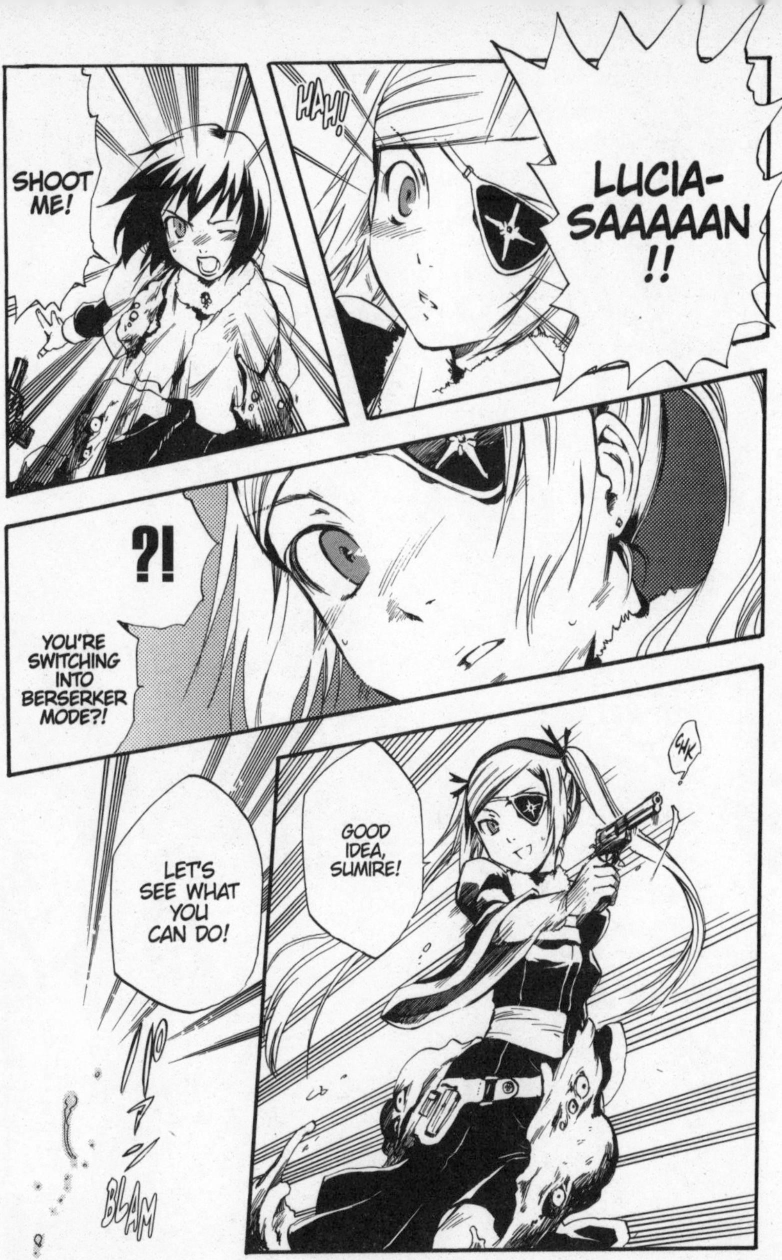
LUCIA-SAAAAAN!!
HAH!
SHOOT ME!
?!
YOU'RE SWITCHING INTO BERSERKER MODE?!
CHK
GOOD IDEA, SUMIRE!
LET'S SEE WHAT YOU CAN DO!
BLAM

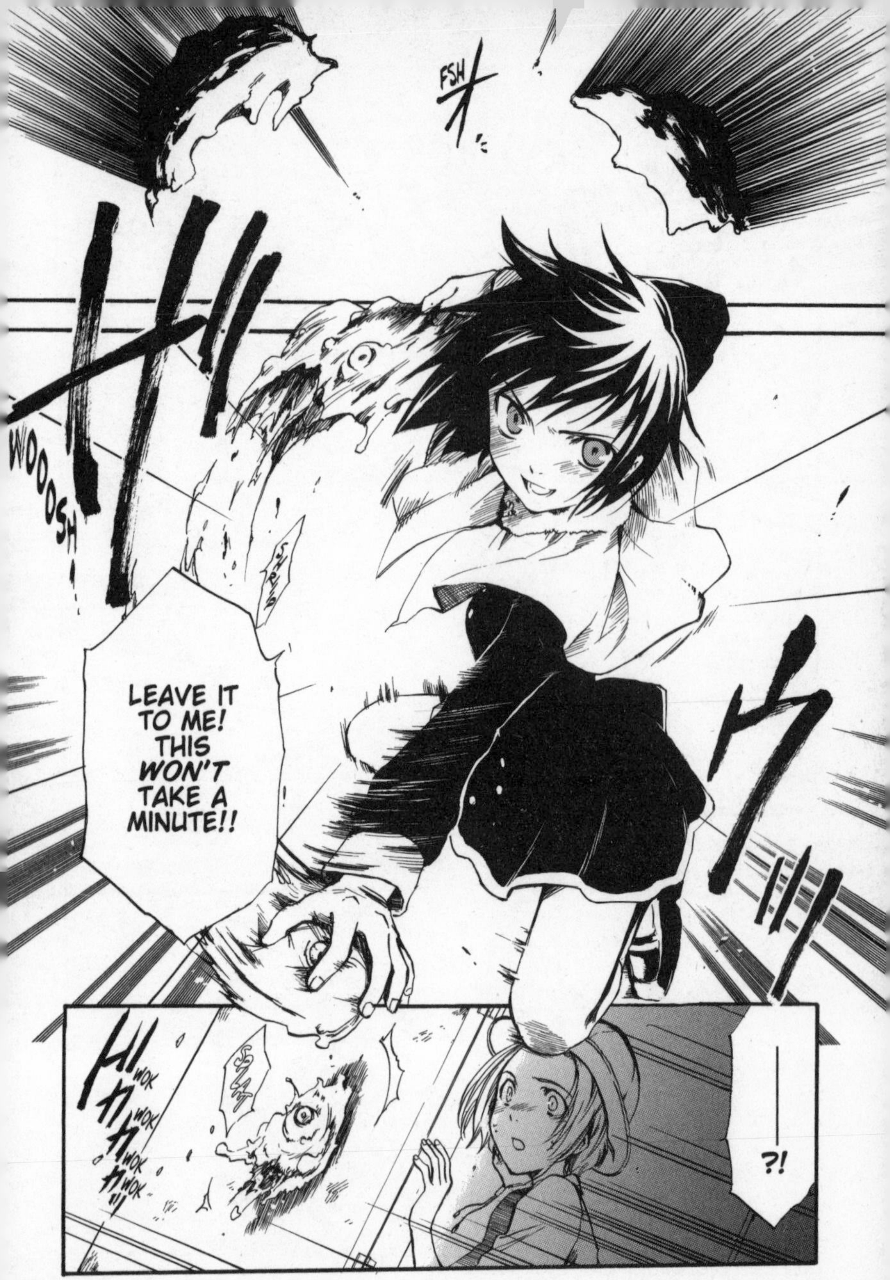
FSH
WOOOSH
LEAVE IT TO ME! THIS *WON'T* TAKE A MINUTE!!
—?!
WOK WOK WOK WOK

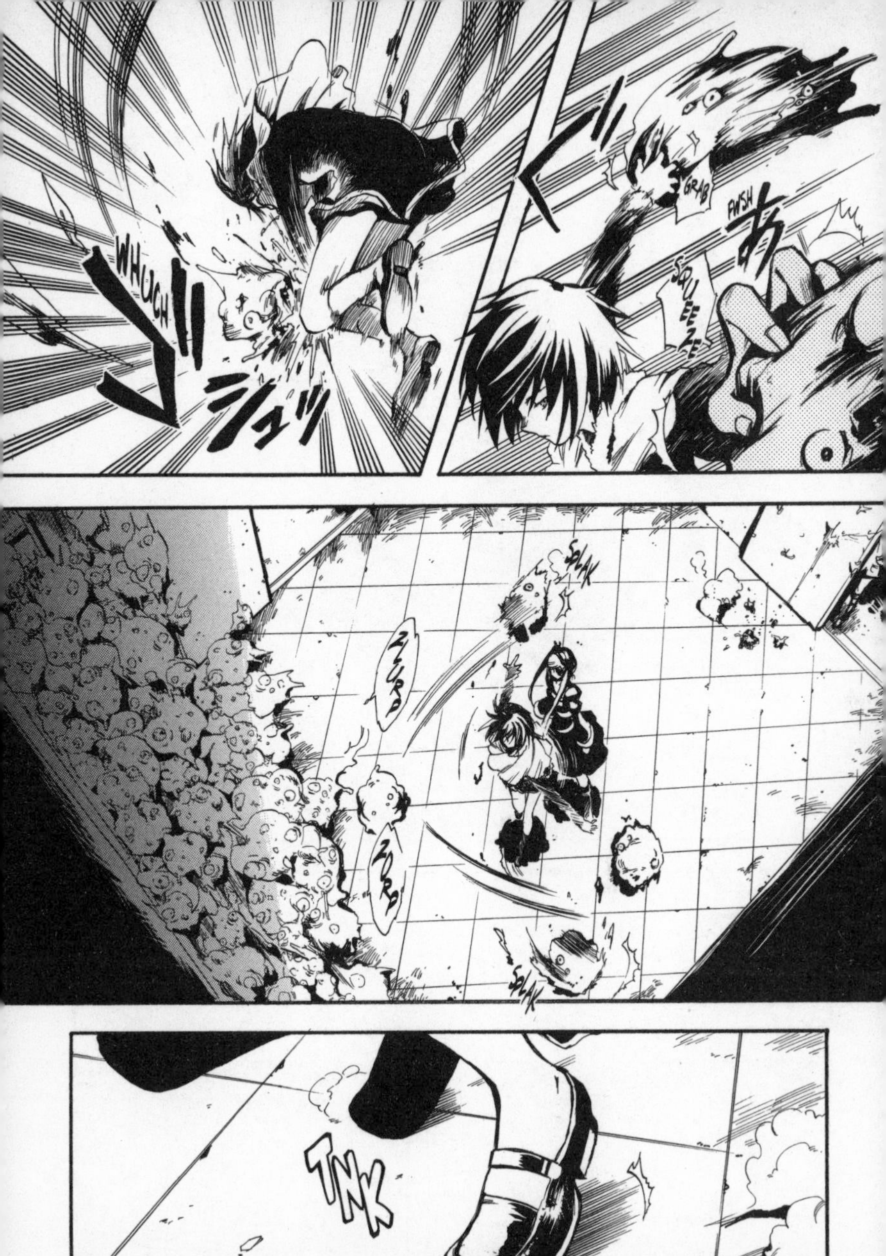
GRAB
FWSH
SQUEEZE
WHUCH
SPLAK
ZLURP
ZLRP
SPLAK
TNK

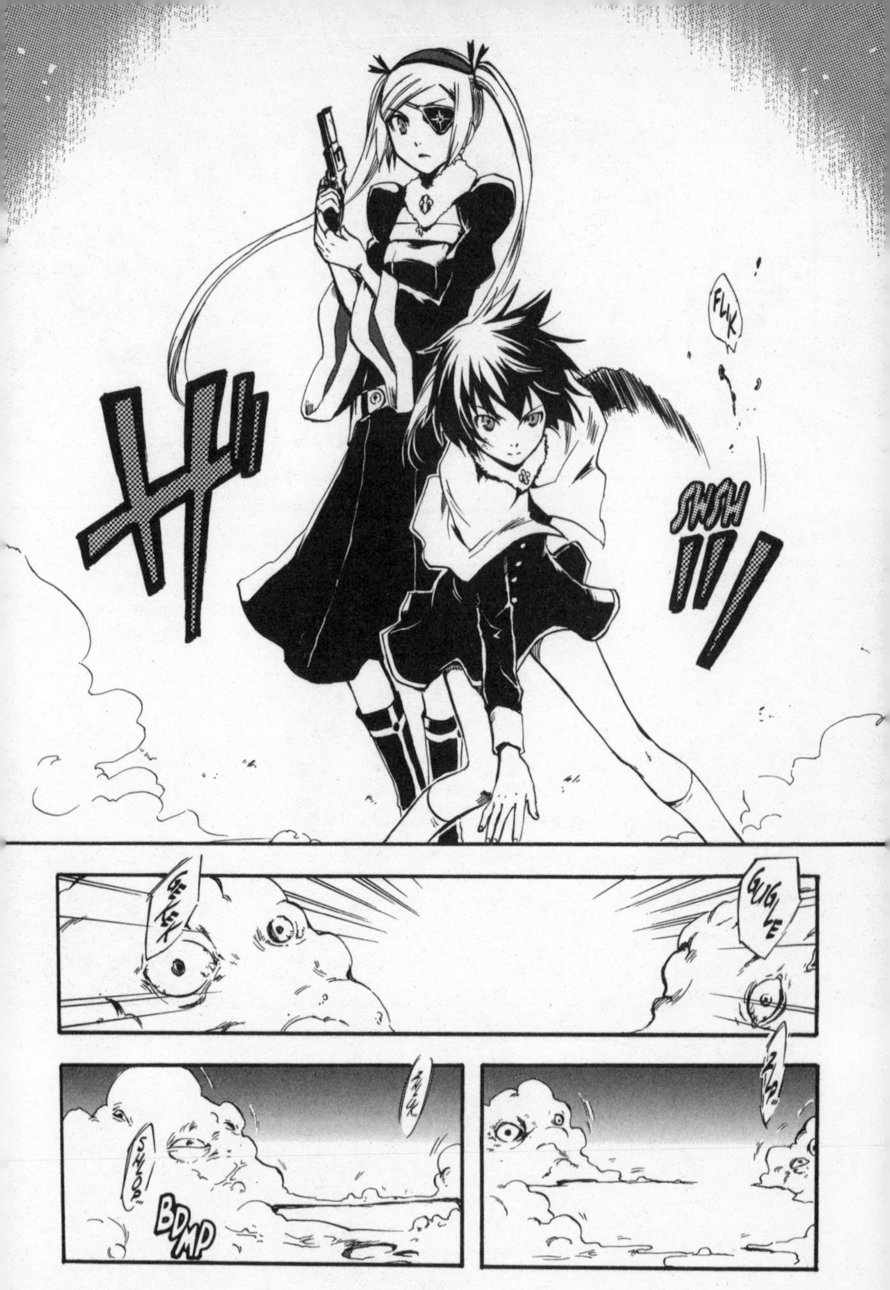
FLIK
SWISH
GUGLE
GEEK
ZLP
SHLOP
BDMP

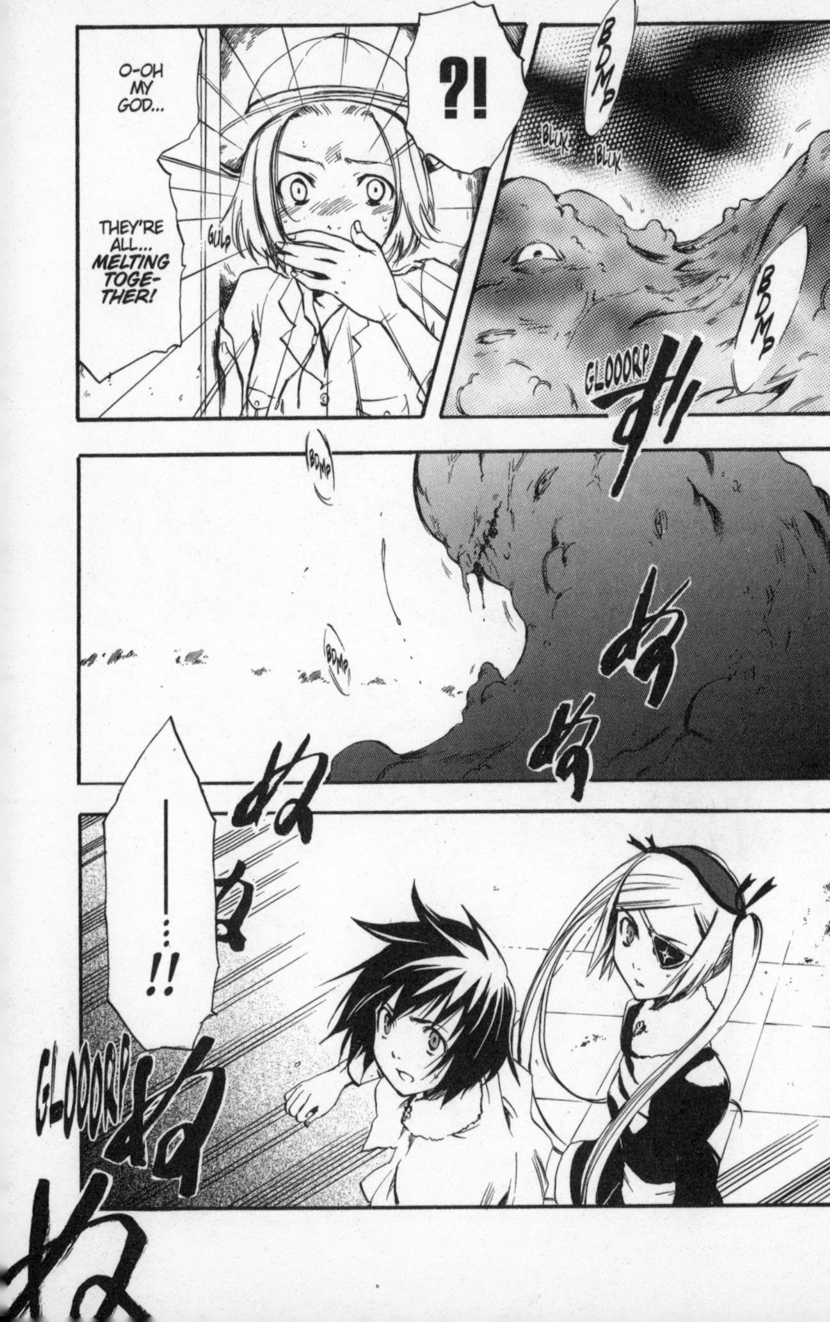
BDMP
BLUK
BLUK
BDMP
GLOOORP
?!
O-OH MY GOD...
THEY'RE ALL... MELTING TOGE-THER!
GULP
BDMP
BDMP
——...!!
GLOOORP

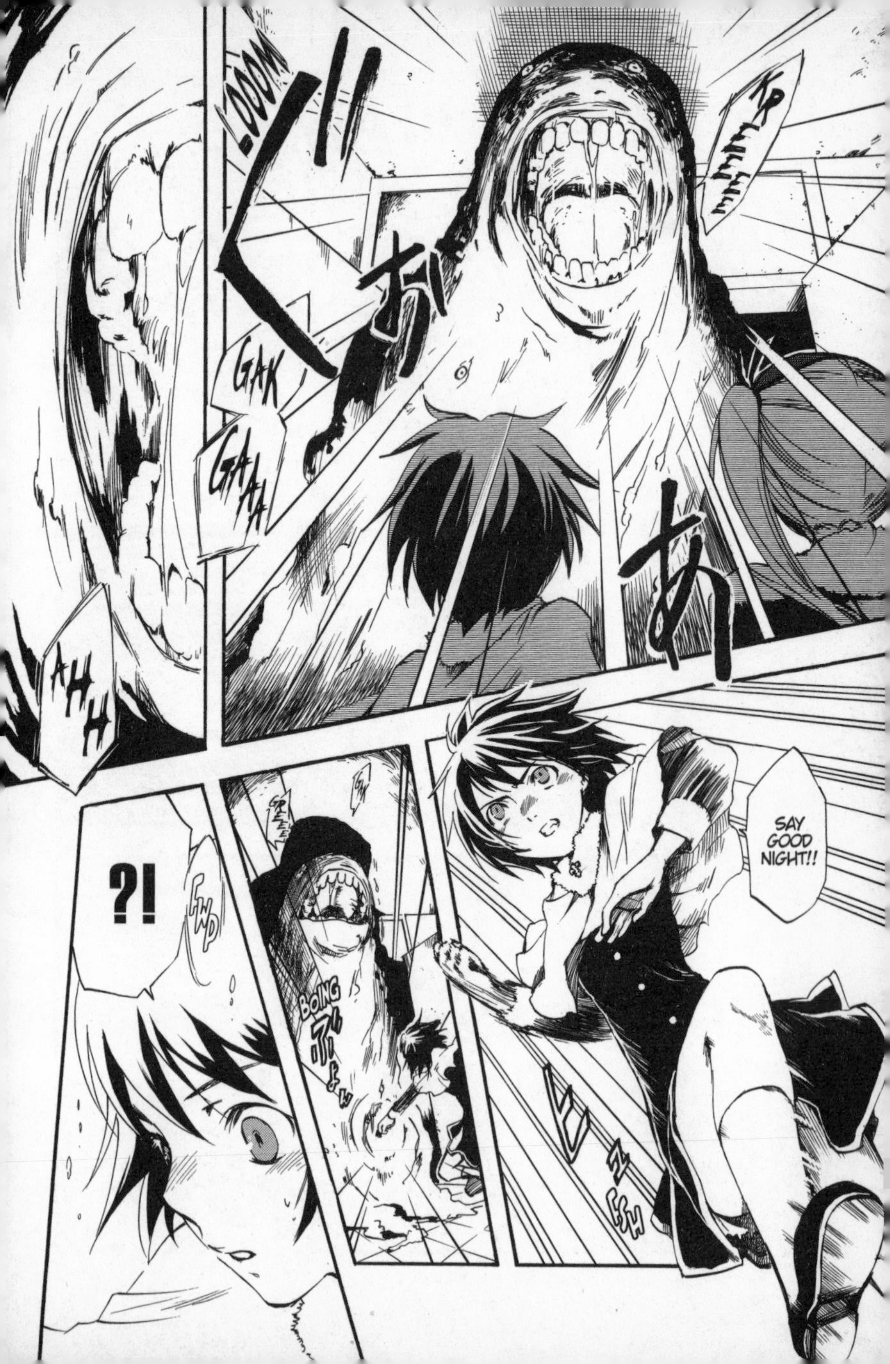
KREEEEEE
DOOM!
GAK
GAAAA
AHHH
SAY GOOD NIGHT!!
BOING
FWD
?!

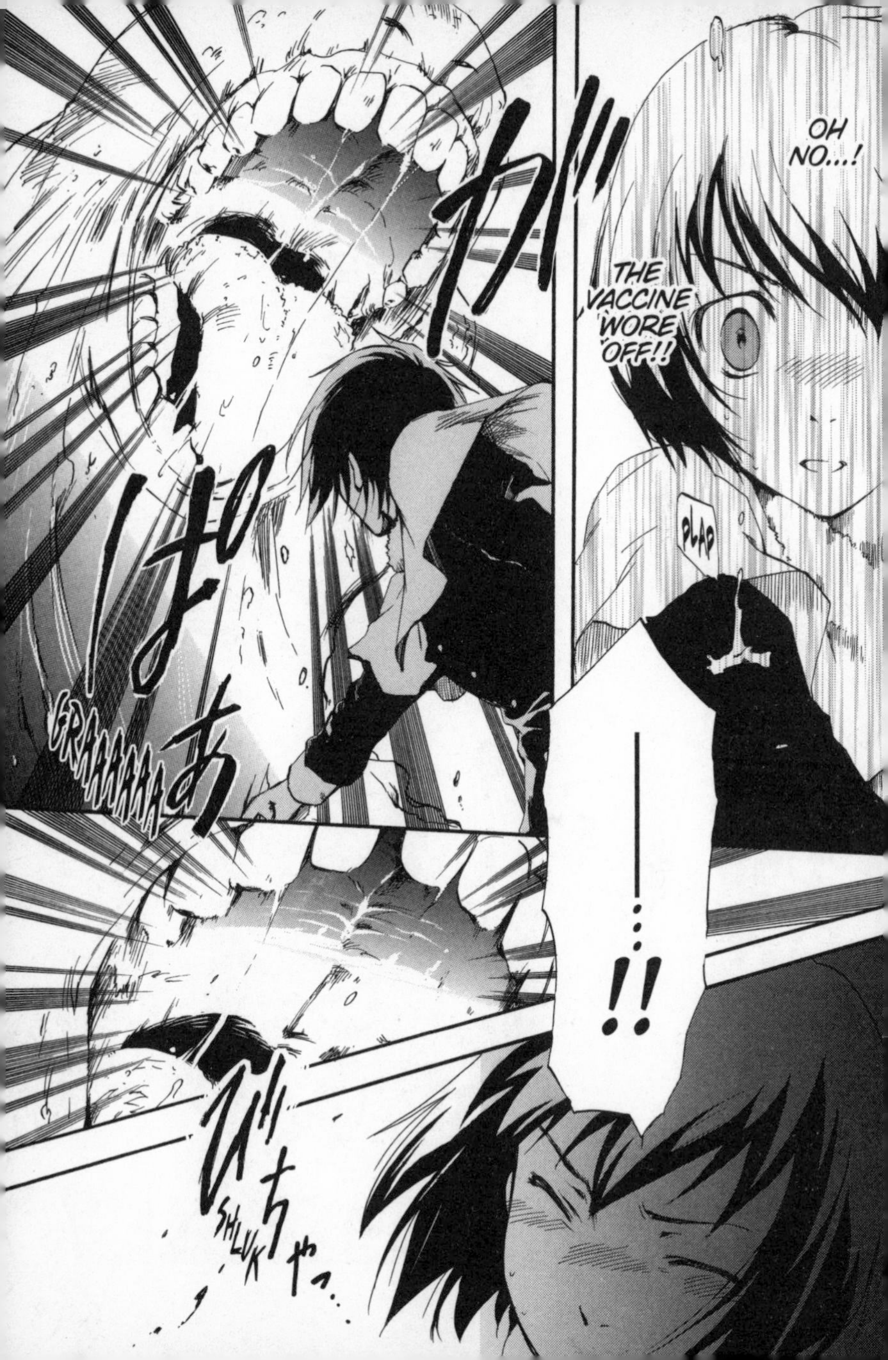

OH NO...!
THE VACCINE WORE OFF!!
PLAP
GRAAAAAAA
―……!!
SHLUK

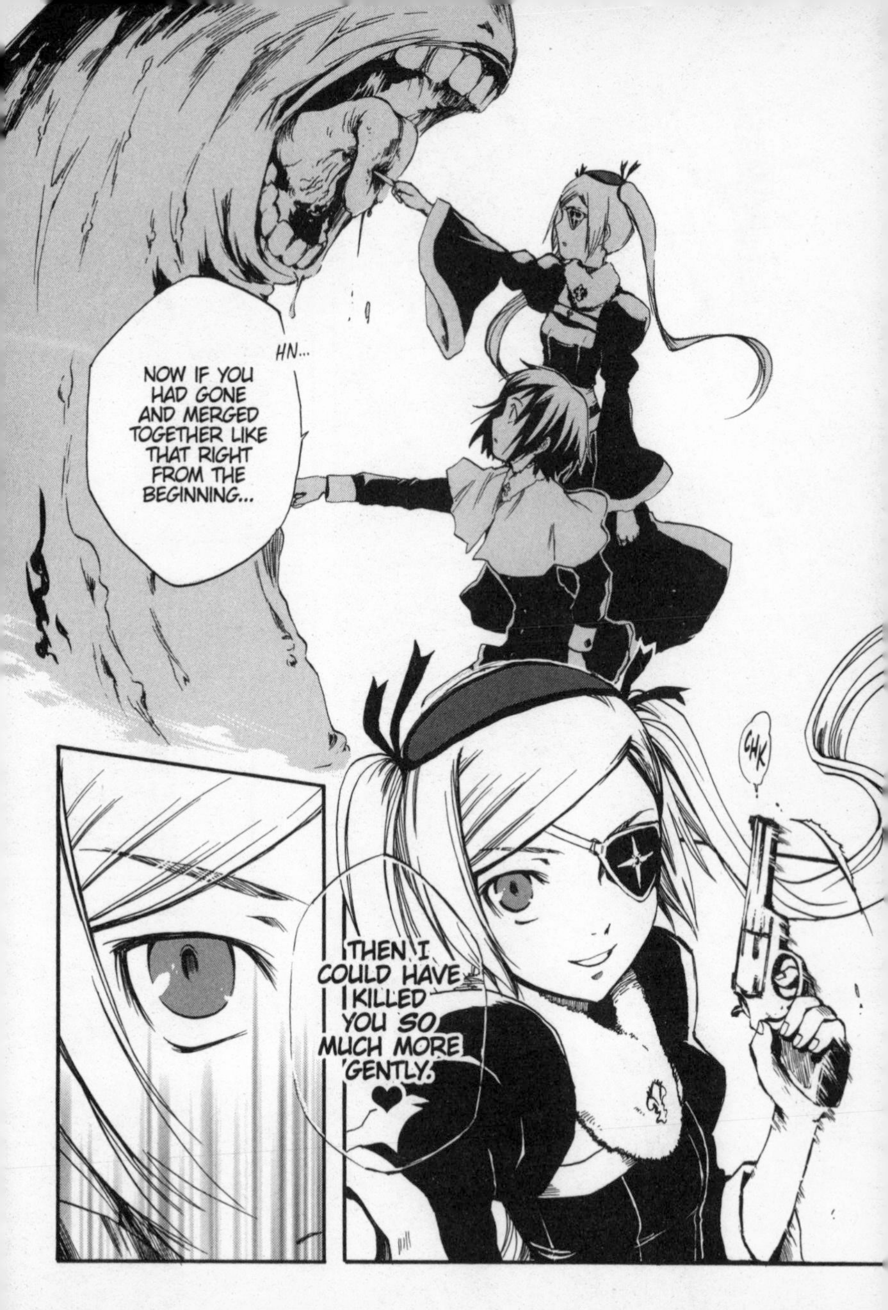
HN...
NOW IF YOU HAD GONE AND MERGED TOGETHER LIKE THAT RIGHT FROM THE BEGINNING...
CHK
THEN I COULD HAVE KILLED YOU SO MUCH MORE GENTLY. ♥

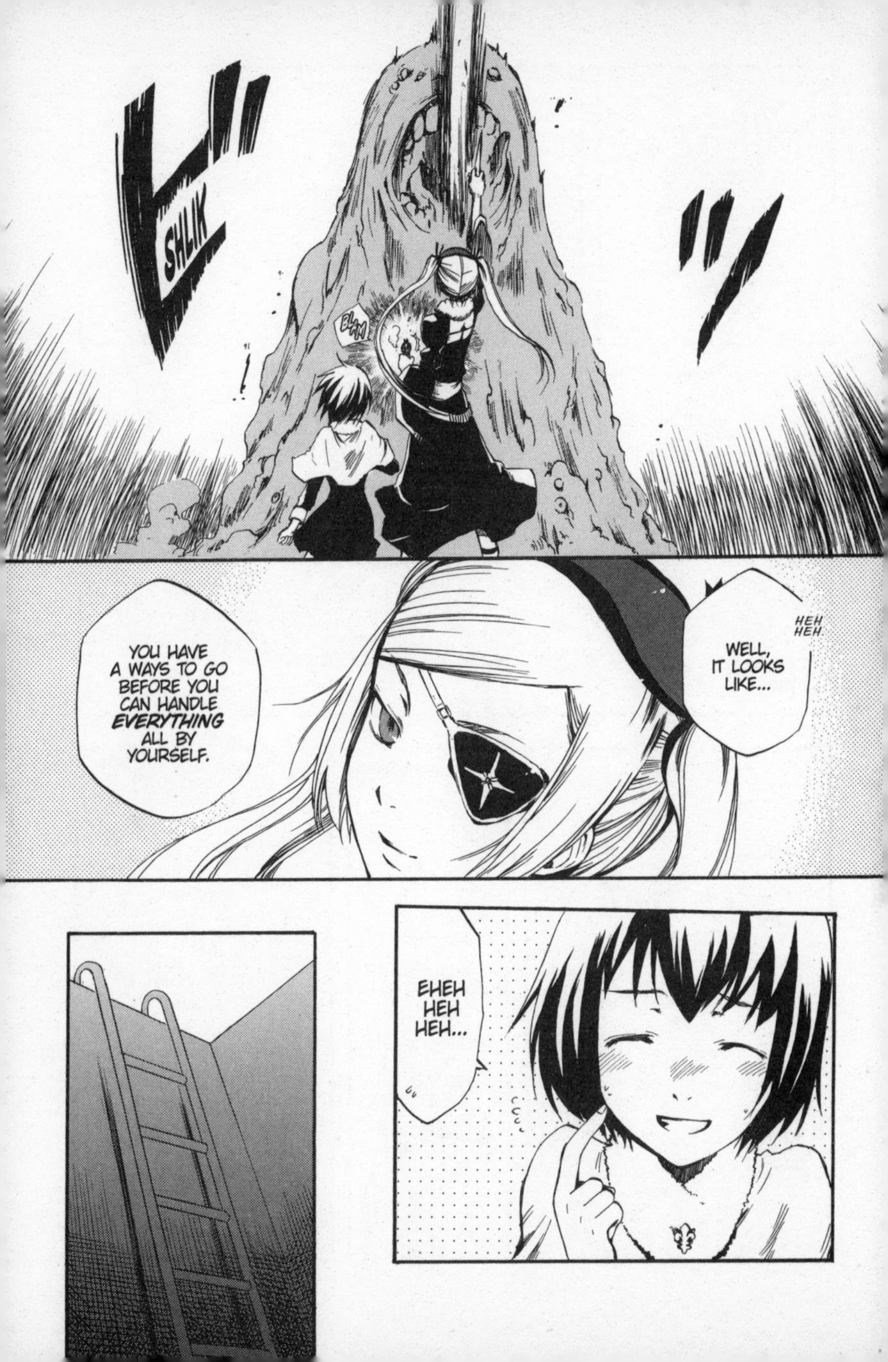
SHLIK
BLAM
HEH HEH.
WELL, IT LOOKS LIKE...
YOU HAVE A WAYS TO GO BEFORE YOU CAN HANDLE ***EVERYTHING*** ALL BY YOURSELF.
EHEH HEH HEH...

OH...

OOH! IT'S LIKE A SUPER-SECRET HIDDEN ROOM UP HERE! NEAT!

GISH

GRAMPA'S DESK...

IT'S...

IT'S A TREASURE MAP!

A TREASURE MAP OUT OF ONE OF MY FAVORITE STORIES!

!

I WONDER...

TP

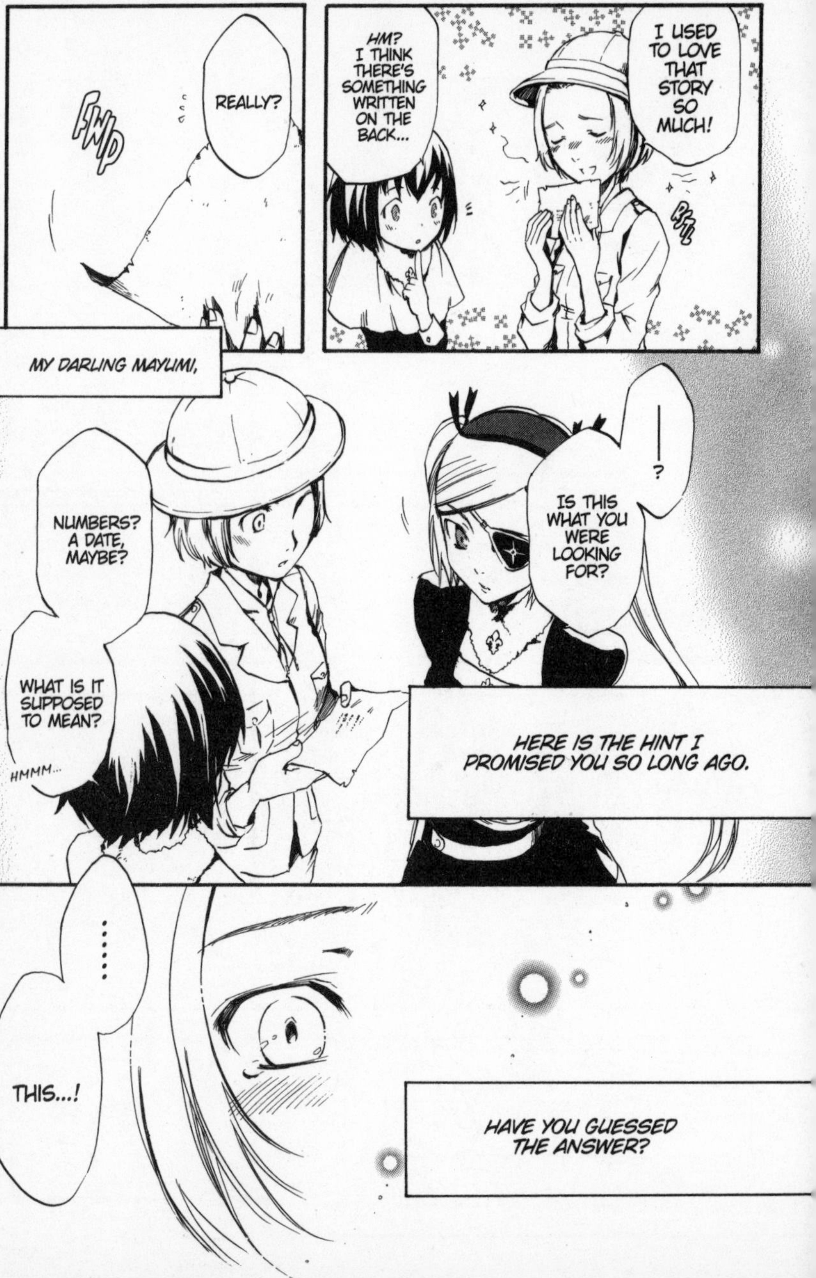
I USED TO LOVE THAT STORY SO MUCH!
RSTL
HM? I THINK THERE'S SOMETHING WRITTEN ON THE BACK...
REALLY?
FWIP
—?
IS THIS WHAT YOU WERE LOOKING FOR?
MY DARLING MAYUMI,
NUMBERS? A DATE, MAYBE?
HERE IS THE HINT I PROMISED YOU SO LONG AGO.
WHAT IS IT SUPPOSED TO MEAN?
HMMM...
HAVE YOU GUESSED THE ANSWER?
......
THIS...!

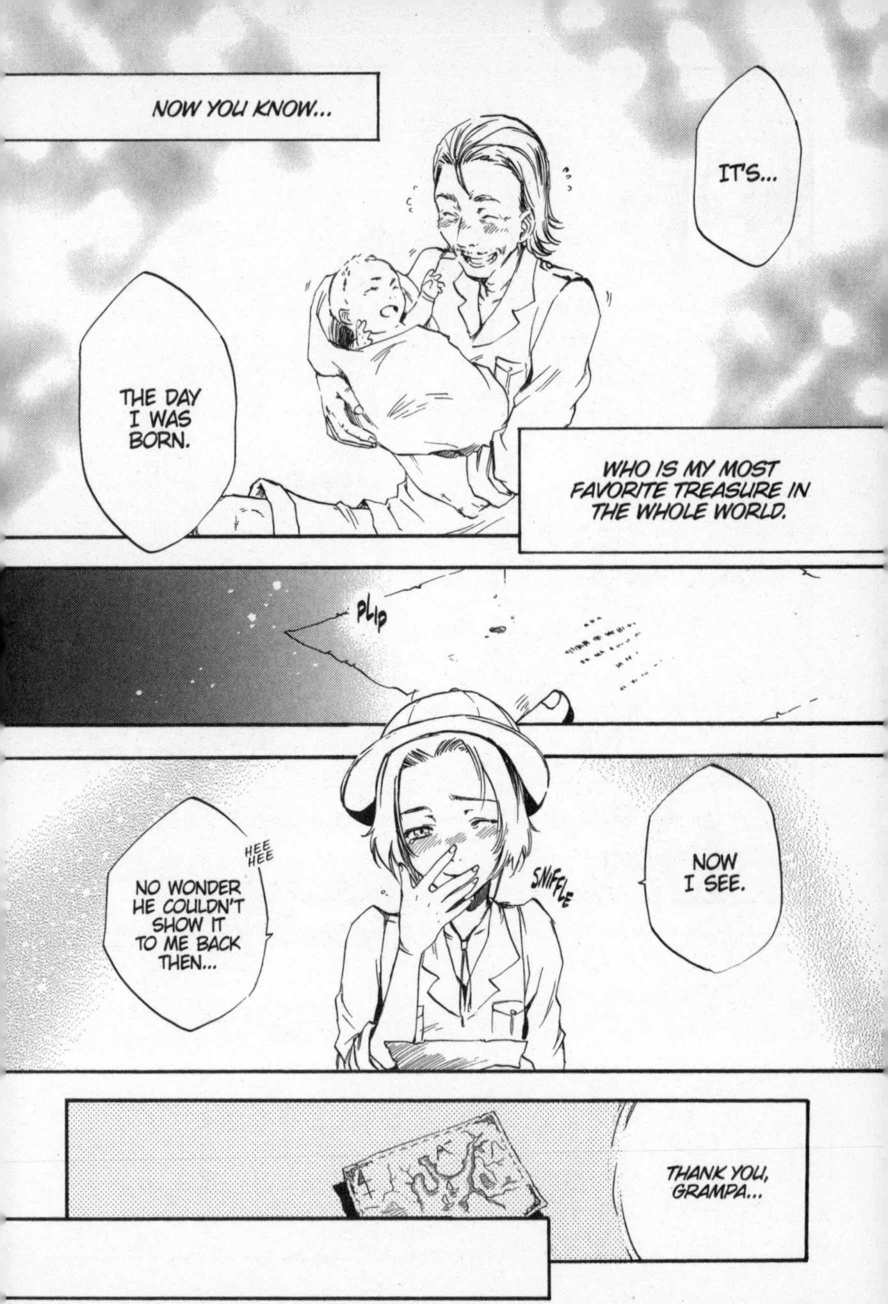
IT'S...
NOW YOU KNOW...
THE DAY I WAS BORN.
WHO IS MY MOST FAVORITE TREASURE IN THE WHOLE WORLD.
PLIP
NOW I SEE.
SNIFFLE
HEE HEE
NO WONDER HE COULDN'T SHOW IT TO ME BACK THEN...
THANK YOU, GRAMPA...

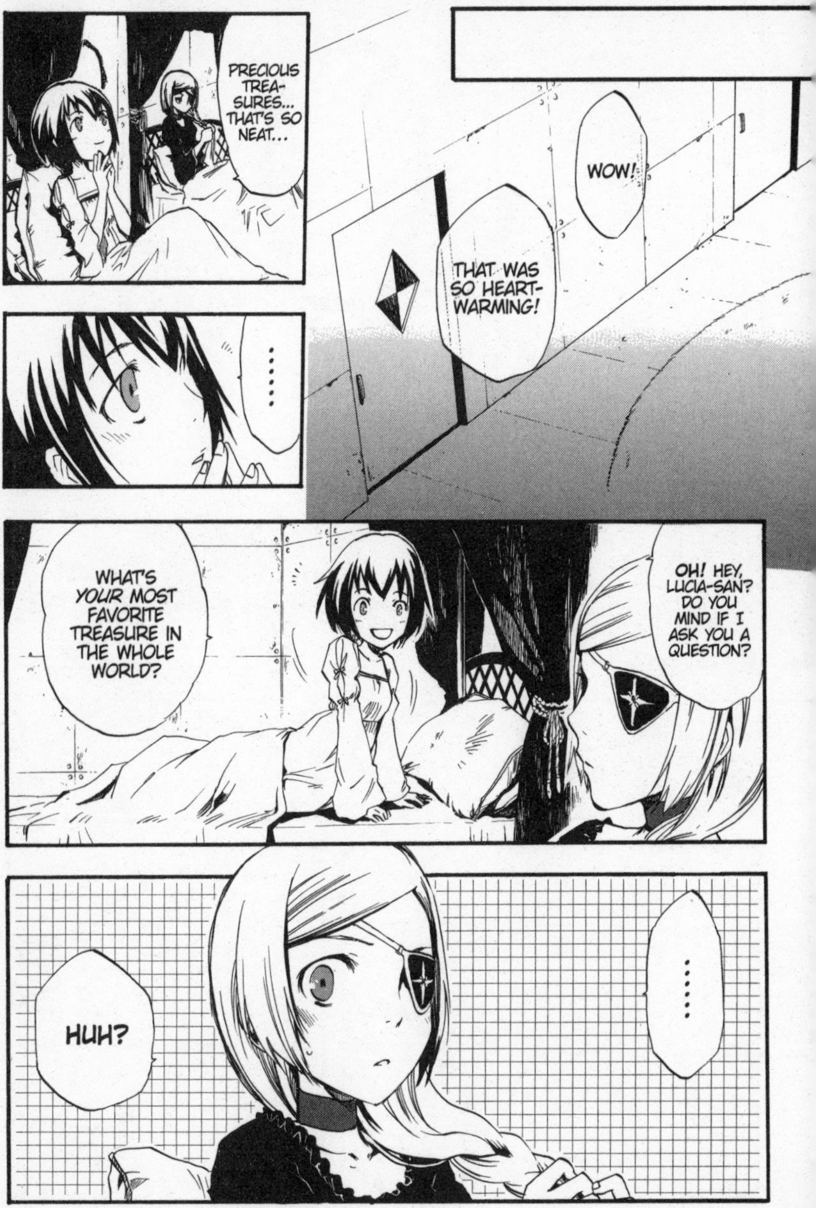
WOW!
THAT WAS SO HEART-WARMING!
PRECIOUS TREASURES... THAT'S SO NEAT...
......
OH! HEY, LUCIA-SAN? DO YOU MIND IF I ASK YOU A QUESTION?
WHAT'S *YOUR* MOST FAVORITE TREASURE IN THE WHOLE WORLD?
......
HUH?

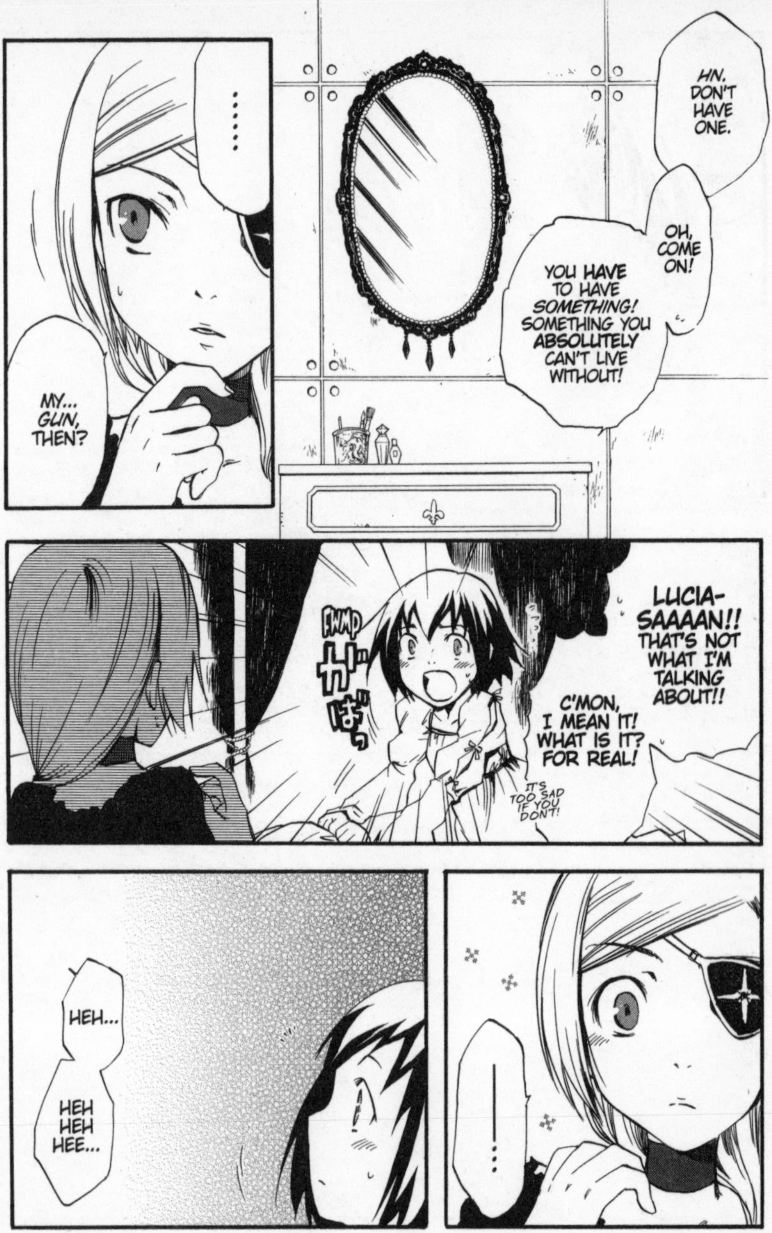
HN. DON'T HAVE ONE.
OH, COME ON!
YOU HAVE TO HAVE SOMETHING! SOMETHING YOU ABSOLUTELY CAN'T LIVE WITHOUT!
......
MY... GUN, THEN?
LUCIA-SAAAAN!! THAT'S NOT WHAT I'M TALKING ABOUT!!
C'MON, I MEAN IT! WHAT IS IT? FOR REAL!
IT'S TOO SAD IF YOU DON'T!
FWMP
......
HEH...
HEH HEH HEE...

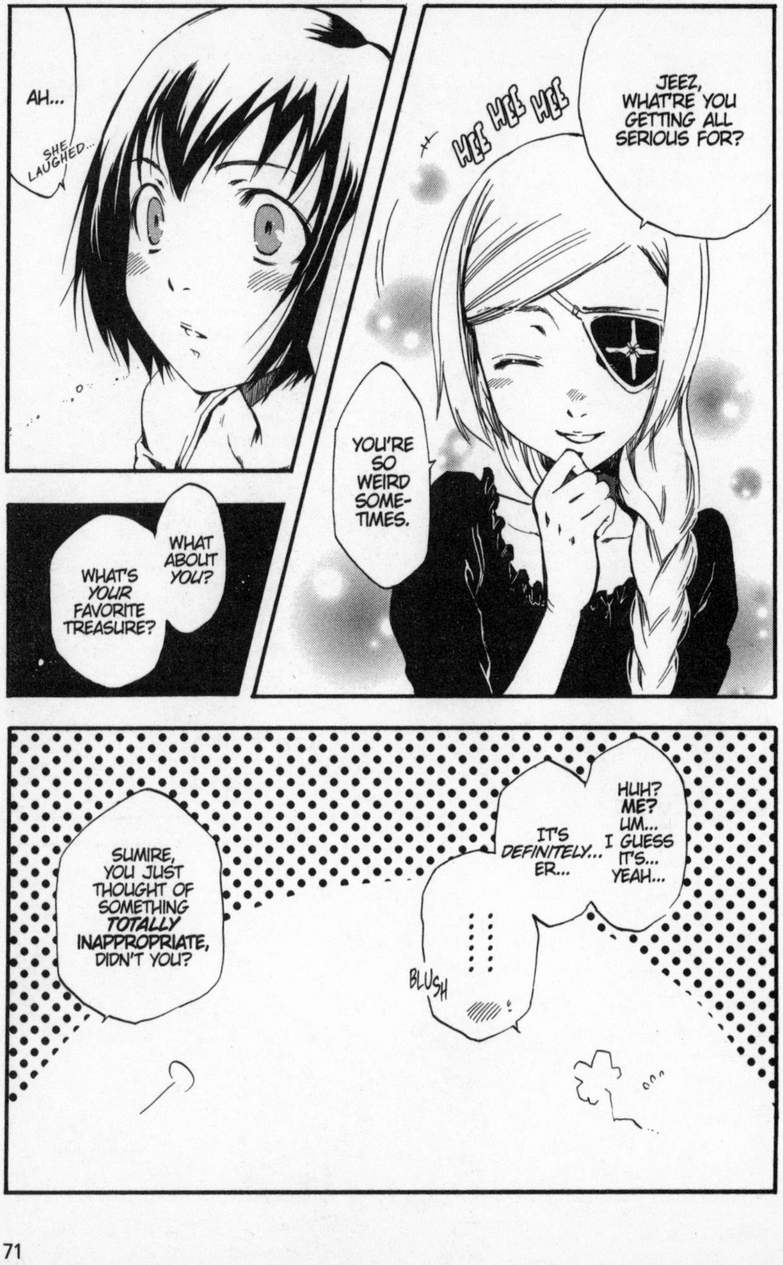
HEE HEE HEE
JEEZ, WHAT'RE YOU GETTING ALL SERIOUS FOR?
YOU'RE SO WEIRD SOME-TIMES.
AH...
SHE LAUGHED...
WHAT ABOUT *YOU*?
WHAT'S *YOUR* FAVORITE TREASURE?
HUH? ME? UM... I GUESS IT'S... YEAH...
IT'S *DEFINITELY*... ER...
BLUSH
SUMIRE, YOU JUST THOUGHT OF SOMETHING *TOTALLY* INAPPROPRIATE, DIDN'T YOU?

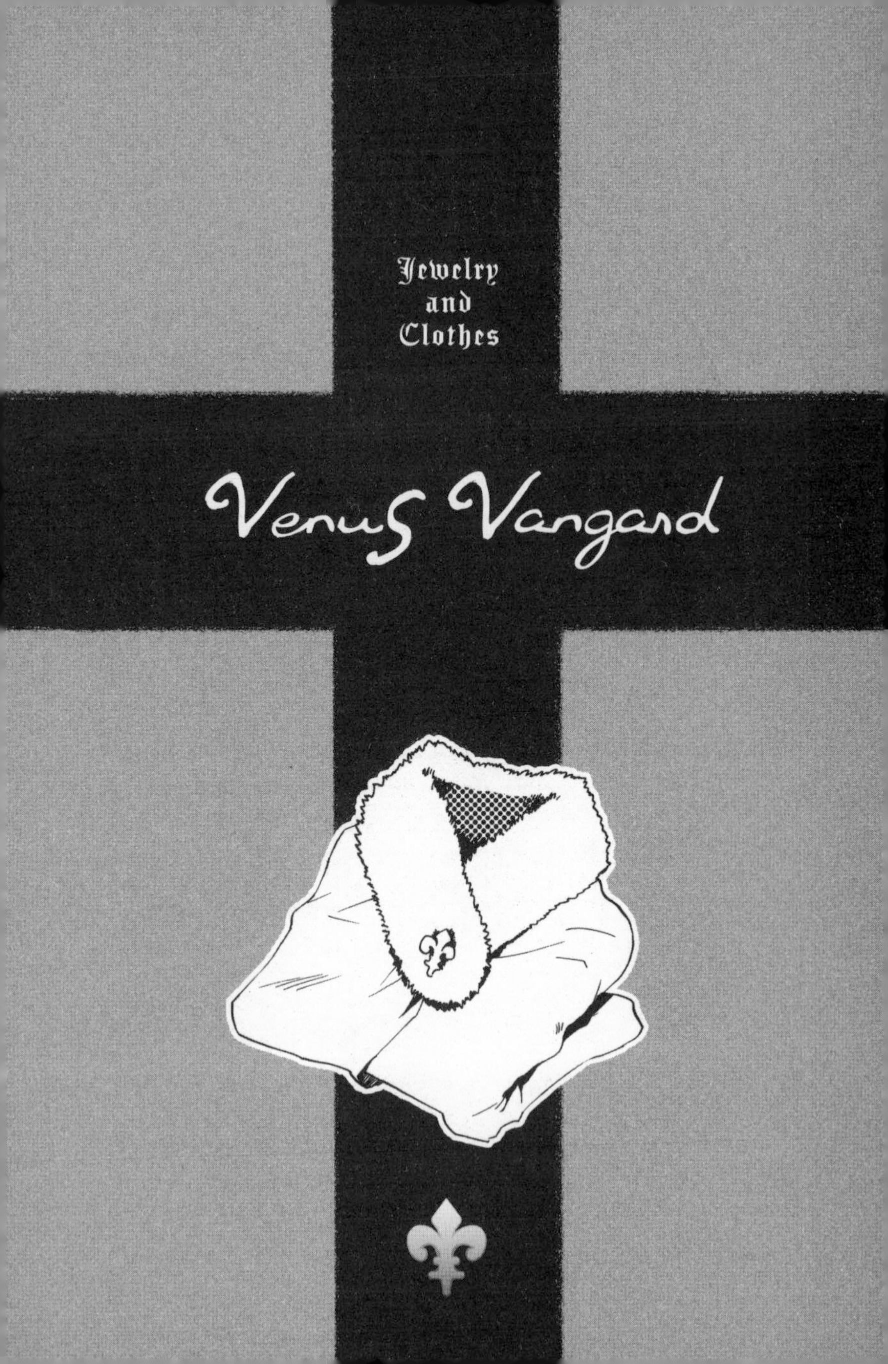
Jewelry
and
Clothes
Venus Vangard

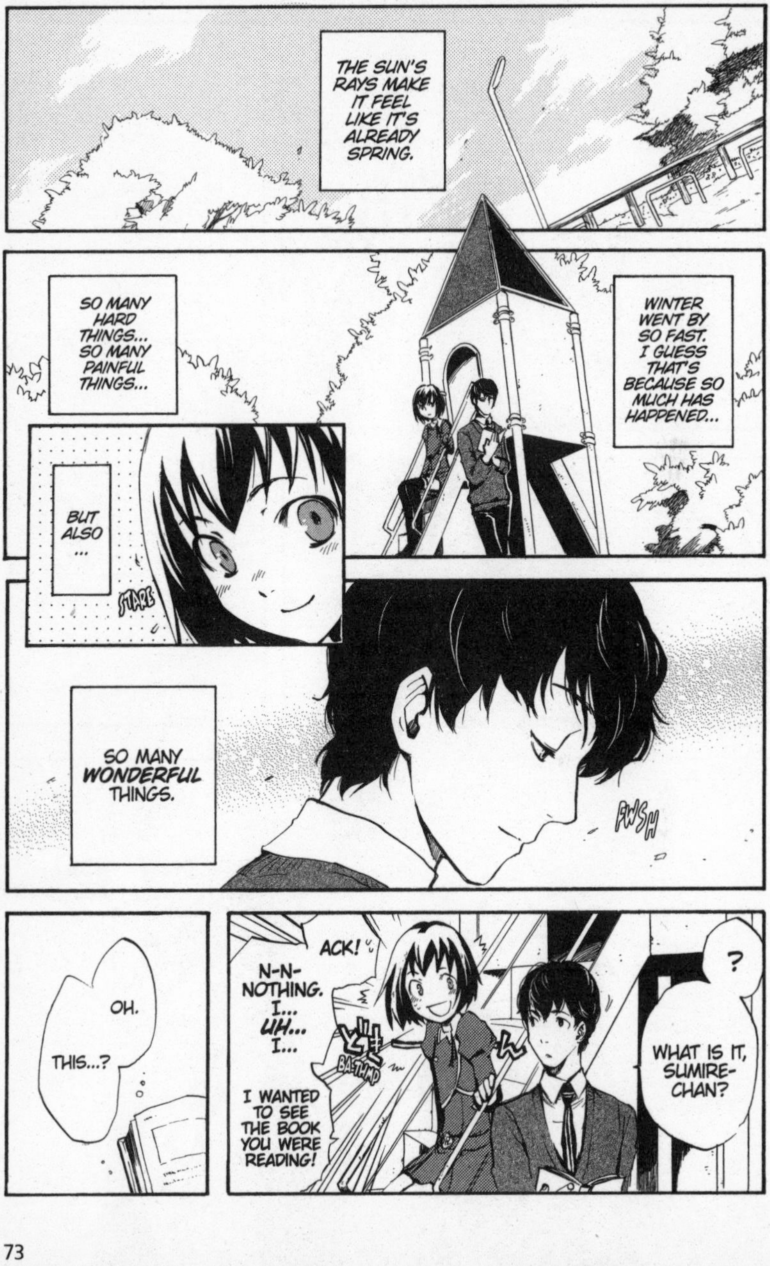
THE SUN'S RAYS MAKE IT FEEL LIKE IT'S ALREADY SPRING.
WINTER WENT BY SO FAST. I GUESS THAT'S BECAUSE SO MUCH HAS HAPPENED...
SO MANY HARD THINGS... SO MANY PAINFUL THINGS...
BUT ALSO ...
STARE
SO MANY WONDERFUL THINGS.
FWSH
?
WHAT IS IT, SUMIRE-CHAN?
ACK!
N-N-NOTHING. I... UH... I...
BA-THMP
I WANTED TO SEE THE BOOK YOU WERE READING!
OH.
THIS...?

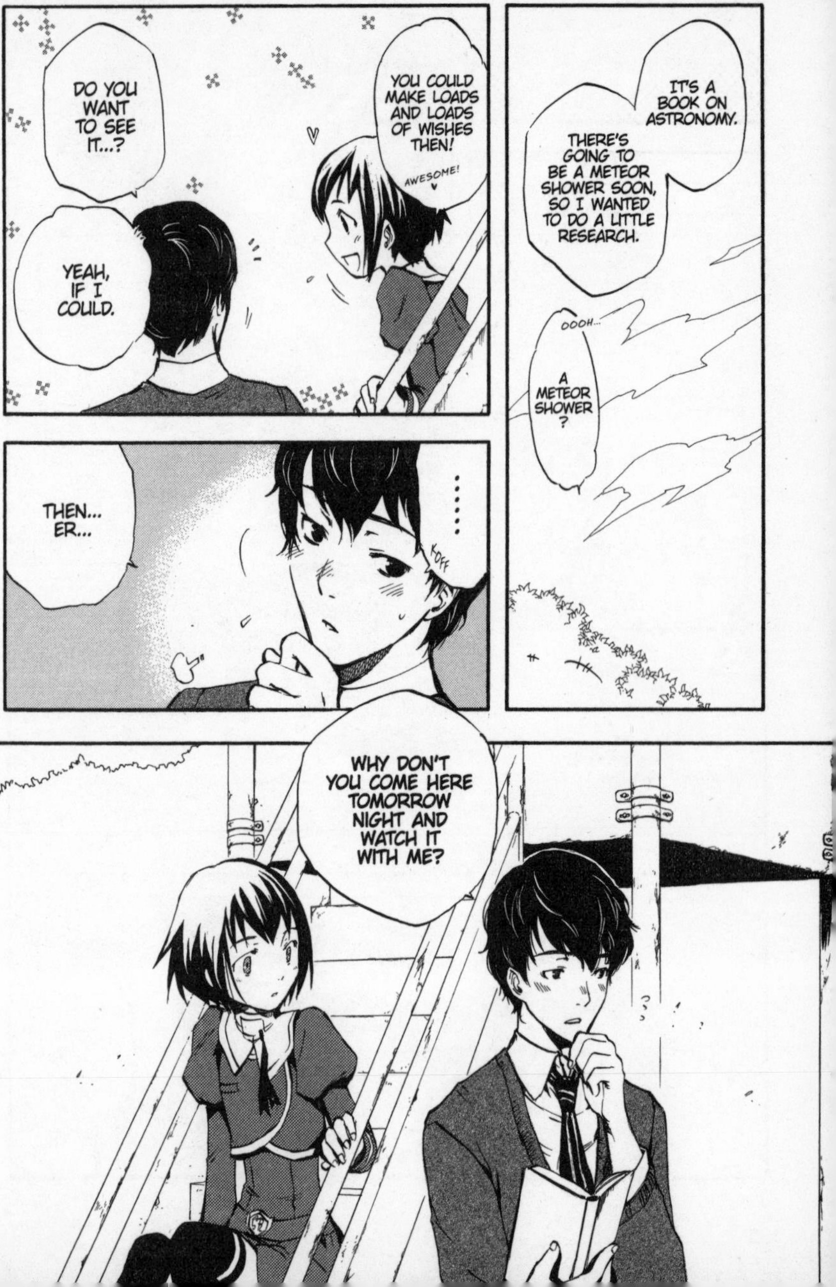
IT'S A BOOK ON ASTRONOMY.
THERE'S GOING TO BE A METEOR SHOWER SOON, SO I WANTED TO DO A LITTLE RESEARCH.
OOOH...
A METEOR SHOWER?
YOU COULD MAKE LOADS AND LOADS OF WISHES THEN!
AWESOME!
DO YOU WANT TO SEE IT...?
YEAH, IF I COULD.
......
KOFF
THEN... ER...
WHY DON'T YOU COME HERE TOMORROW NIGHT AND WATCH IT WITH ME?

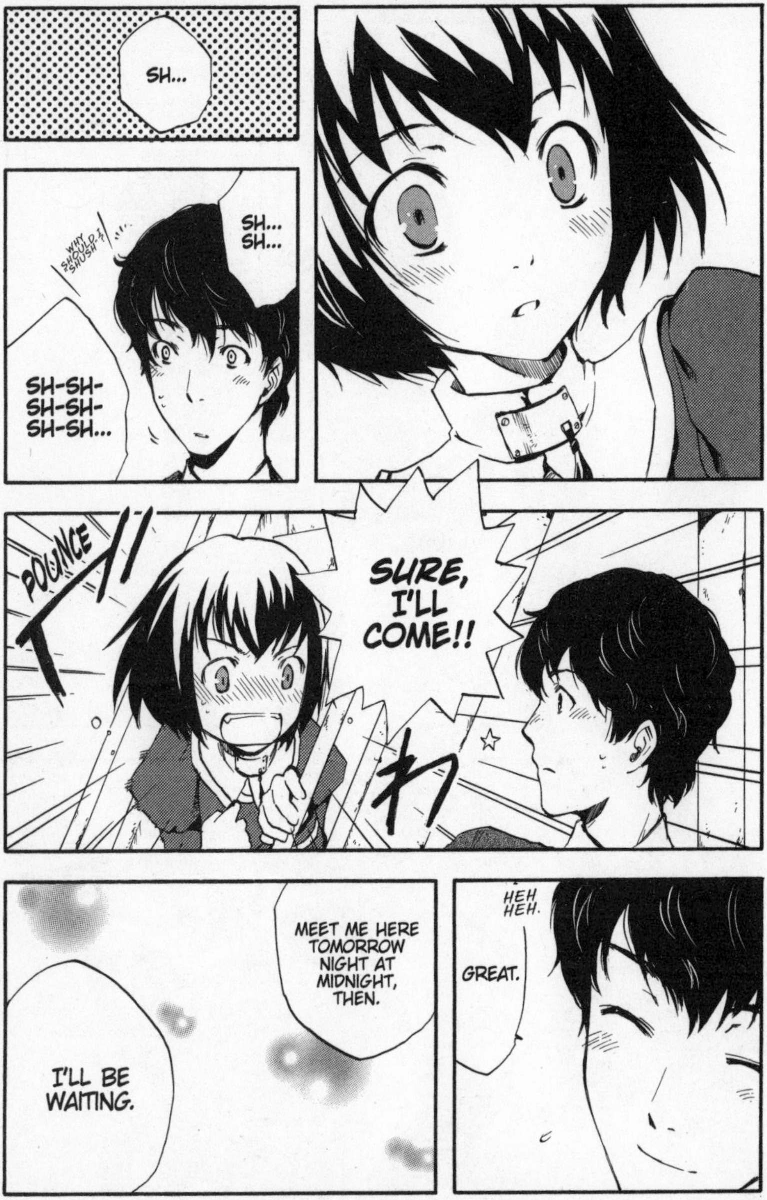
SH...
SH... SH...
WHY SHOULD I SHUSH?
SH-SH-SH-SH-SH-SH...
SURE, I'LL COME!!
POUNCE
わ
HEH HEH.
GREAT.
MEET ME HERE TOMORROW NIGHT AT MIDNIGHT, THEN.
I'LL BE WAITING.

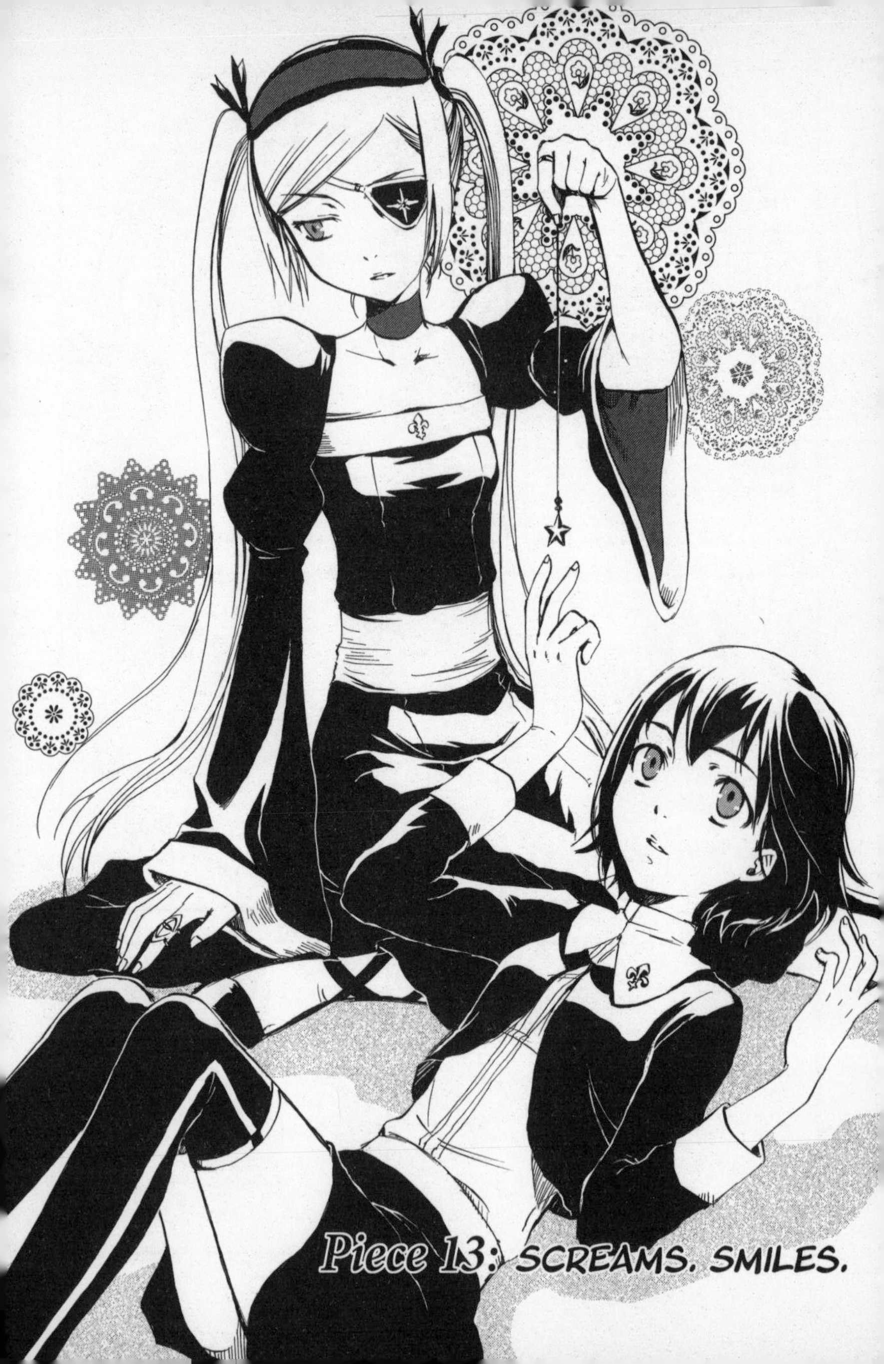
Piece 13: SCREAMS. SMILES.

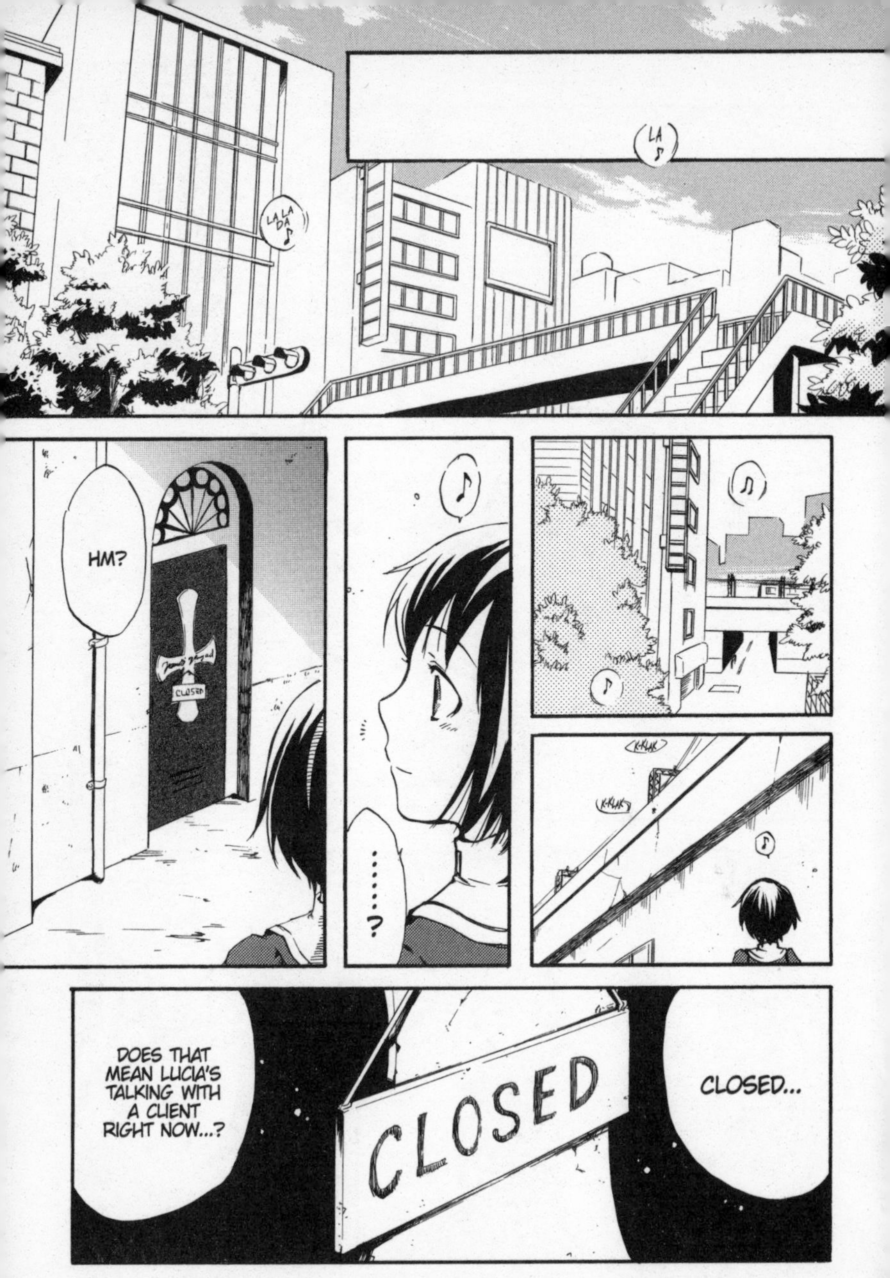
LA ♪
LA LA DA ♪
♫
♪
K-KLAK
K-KLAK
♪
♪
......?
HM?
CLOSED
CLOSED...
CLOSED
DOES THAT MEAN LUCIA'S TALKING WITH A CLIENT RIGHT NOW...?

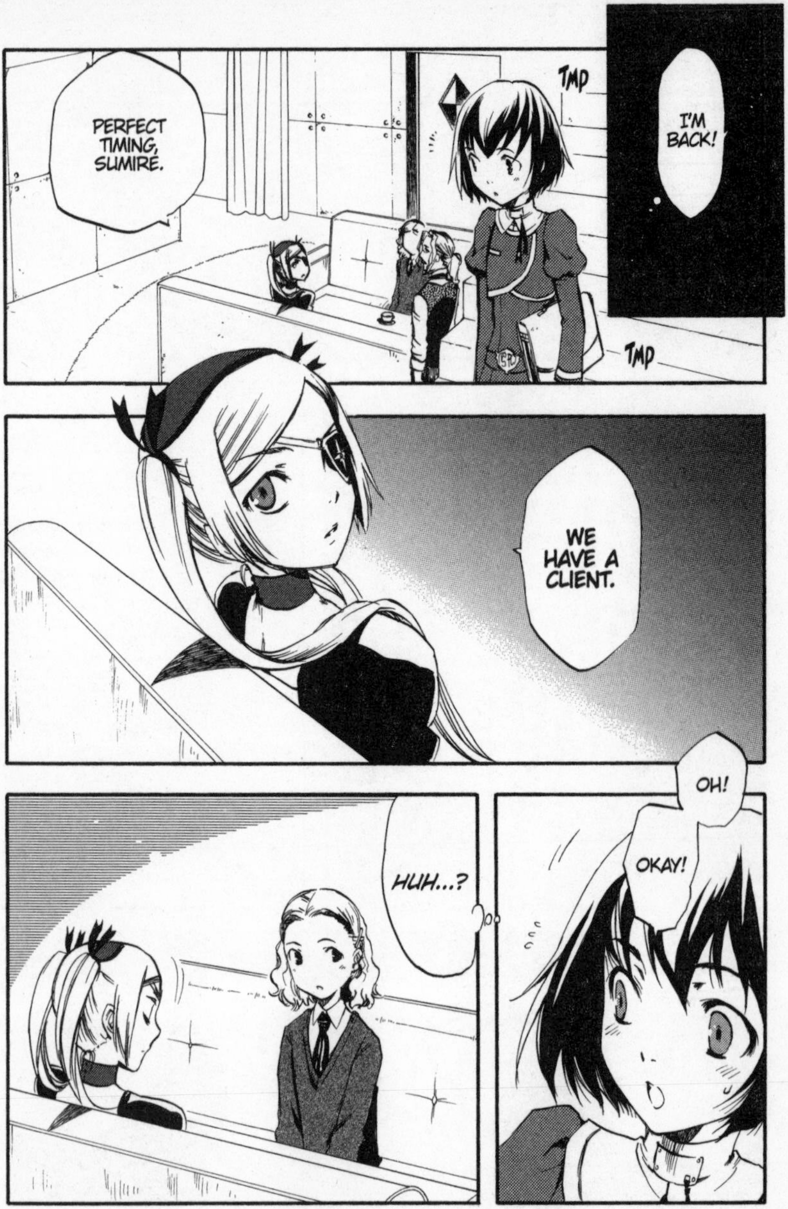
I'M BACK!
TMP
PERFECT TIMING, SUMIRE.
TMP
WE HAVE A CLIENT.
OH!
OKAY!
HUH...?

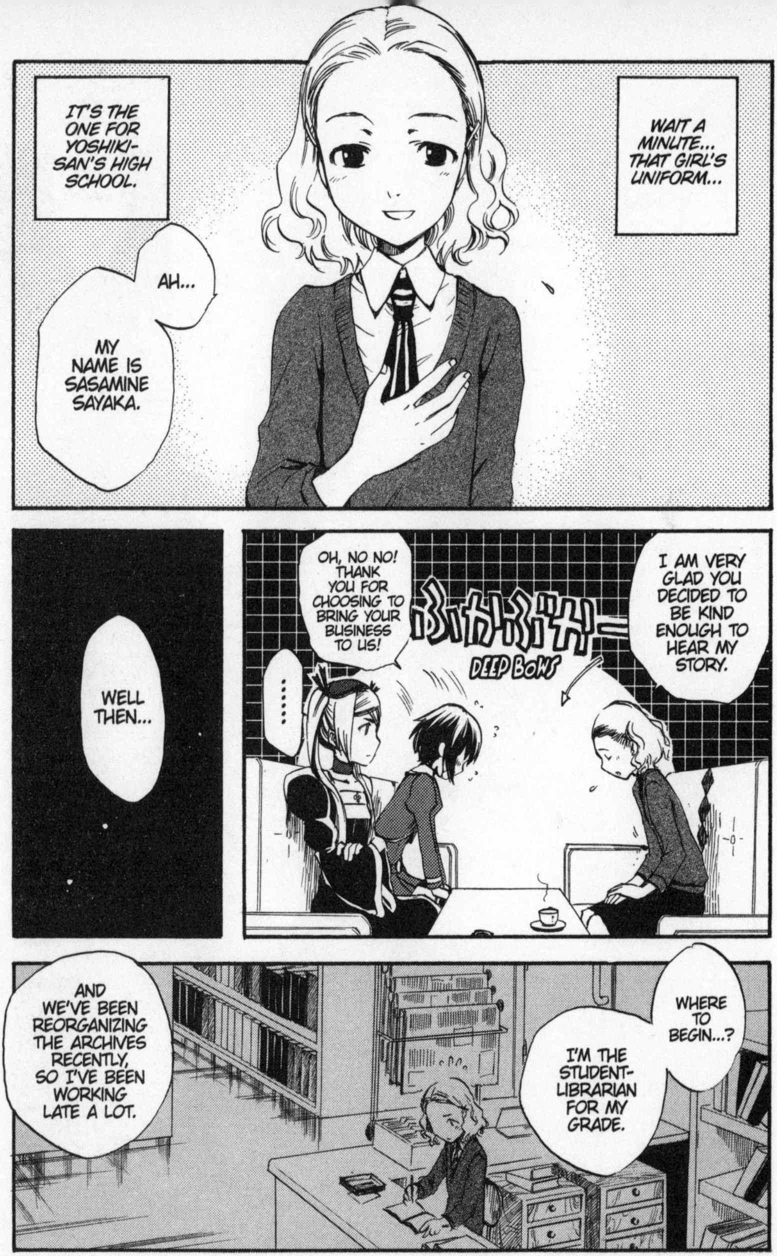
WAIT A MINUTE... THAT GIRL'S UNIFORM...
IT'S THE ONE FOR YOSHIKI-SAN'S HIGH SCHOOL.
AH...
MY NAME IS SASAMINE SAYAKA.
I AM VERY GLAD YOU DECIDED TO BE KIND ENOUGH TO HEAR MY STORY.
ふかぶかー
DEEP BOWS
OH, NO NO! THANK YOU FOR CHOOSING TO BRING YOUR BUSINESS TO US!
......
WELL THEN...
WHERE TO BEGIN...?
I'M THE STUDENT-LIBRARIAN FOR MY GRADE.
AND WE'VE BEEN REORGANIZING THE ARCHIVES RECENTLY, SO I'VE BEEN WORKING LATE A LOT.

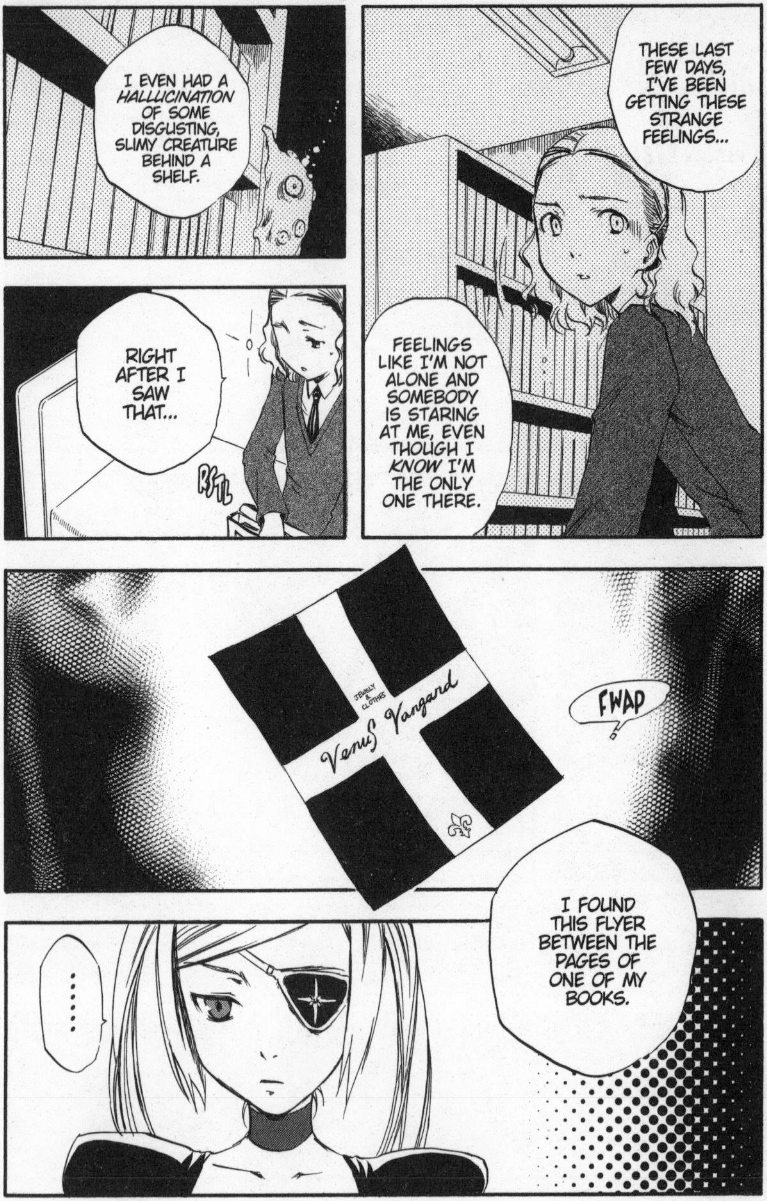
THESE LAST FEW DAYS, I'VE BEEN GETTING THESE STRANGE FEELINGS...
FEELINGS LIKE I'M NOT ALONE AND SOMEBODY IS STARING AT ME, EVEN THOUGH I *KNOW* I'M THE ONLY ONE THERE.
I EVEN HAD A *HALLUCINATION* OF SOME DISGUSTING, SLIMY CREATURE BEHIND A SHELF.
RIGHT AFTER I SAW THAT...
RSTL
JEWELY & CLOTHES
VenuS Vangard
FWAP
I FOUND THIS FLYER BETWEEN THE PAGES OF ONE OF MY BOOKS.
......

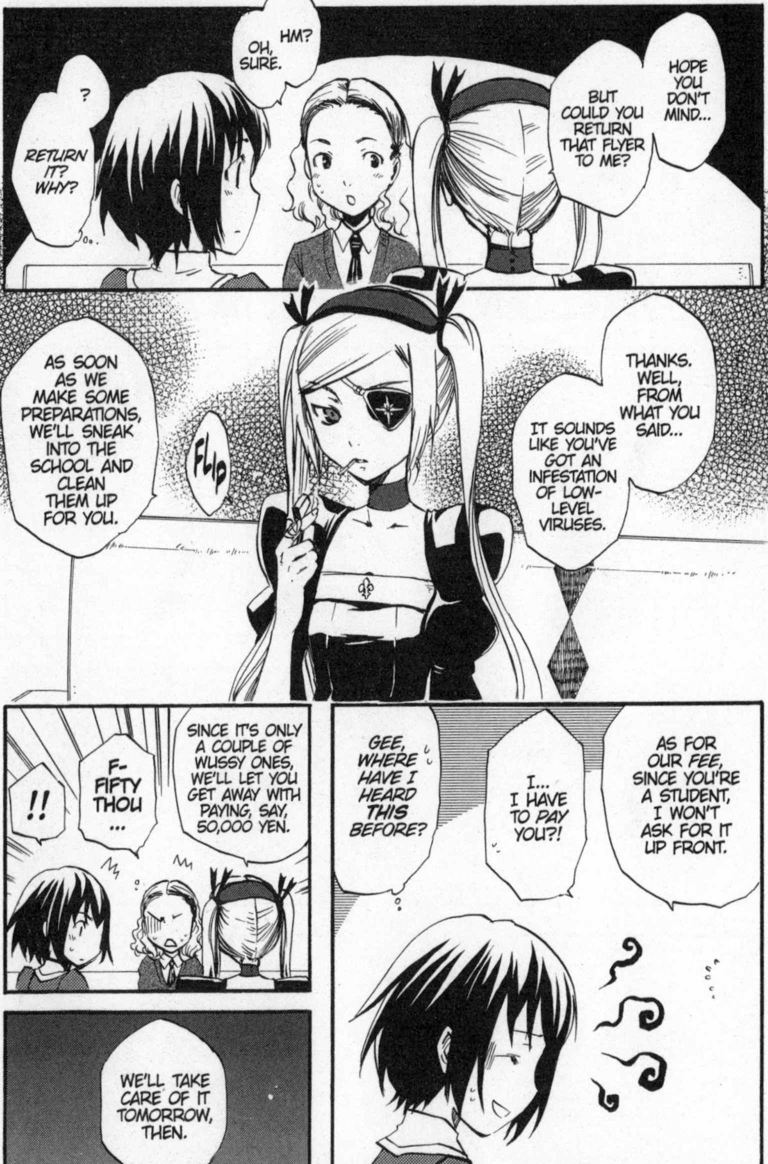
HOPE YOU DON'T MIND...
BUT COULD YOU RETURN THAT FLYER TO ME?
HM? OH, SURE.
?
RETURN IT? WHY?
THANKS. WELL, FROM WHAT YOU SAID...
IT SOUNDS LIKE YOU'VE GOT AN INFESTATION OF LOW-LEVEL VIRUSES.
FLIP
AS SOON AS WE MAKE SOME PREPARATIONS, WE'LL SNEAK INTO THE SCHOOL AND CLEAN THEM UP FOR YOU.
AS FOR OUR *FEE*, SINCE YOU'RE A STUDENT, I WON'T ASK FOR IT UP FRONT.
I... I HAVE TO *PAY* YOU?!
GEE, WHERE HAVE I HEARD **THIS** BEFORE?
SINCE IT'S ONLY A COUPLE OF WUSSY ONES, WE'LL LET YOU GET AWAY WITH PAYING, SAY, 50,000 YEN.
F- FIFTY THOU ...
!!
WE'LL TAKE CARE OF IT TOMORROW, THEN.

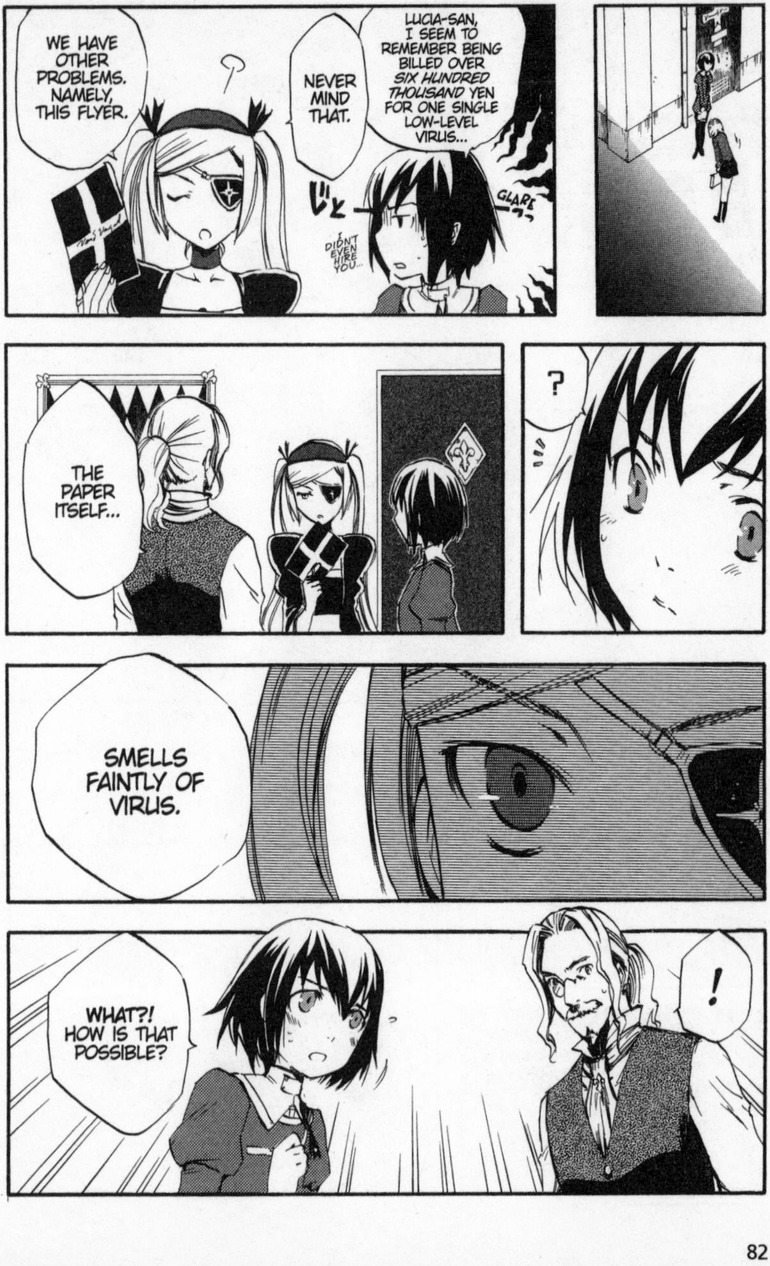
LUCIA-SAN, I SEEM TO REMEMBER BEING BILLED OVER SIX HUNDRED THOUSAND YEN FOR ONE SINGLE LOW-LEVEL VIRUS...
GLARE
NEVER MIND THAT.
じと
I DIDN'T EVEN HIRE YOU...
WE HAVE OTHER PROBLEMS. NAMELY, THIS FLYER.
?
THE PAPER ITSELF...
SMELLS FAINTLY OF VIRUS.
!
WHAT?! HOW IS THAT POSSIBLE?

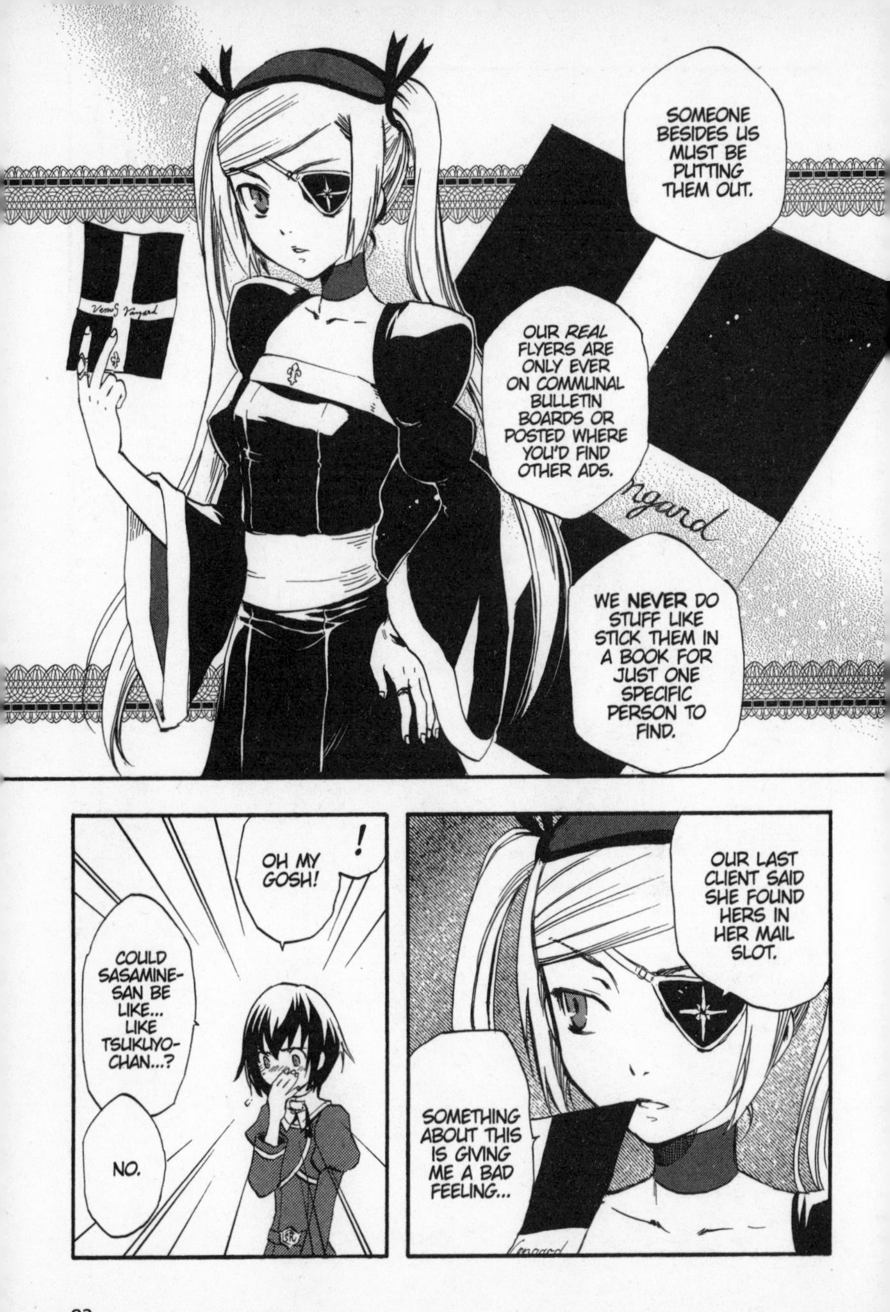
SOMEONE BESIDES US MUST BE PUTTING THEM OUT.
OUR *REAL* FLYERS ARE ONLY EVER ON COMMUNAL BULLETIN BOARDS OR POSTED WHERE YOU'D FIND OTHER ADS.
WE NEVER DO STUFF LIKE STICK THEM IN A BOOK FOR JUST ONE SPECIFIC PERSON TO FIND.
OUR LAST CLIENT SAID SHE FOUND HERS IN HER MAIL SLOT.
SOMETHING ABOUT THIS IS GIVING ME A BAD FEELING...
!
OH MY GOSH!
COULD SASAMINE-SAN BE LIKE... LIKE TSUKUYO-CHAN...?
NO.

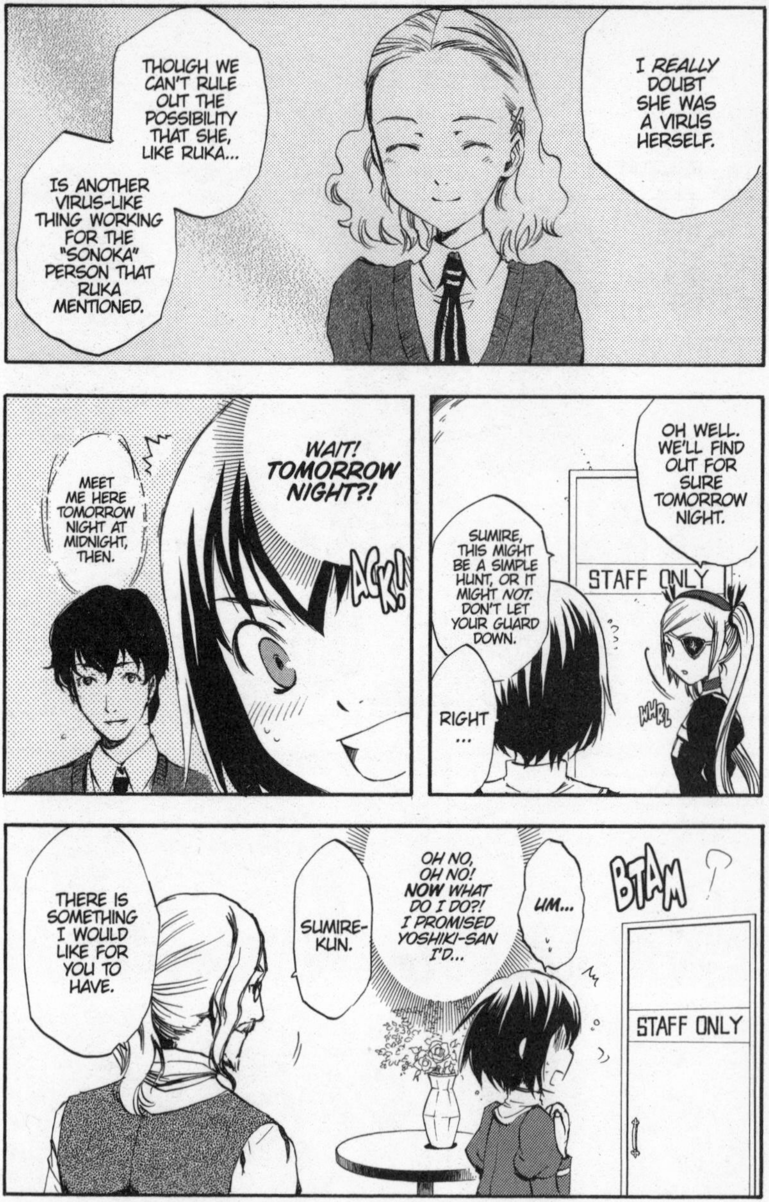
I *REALLY* DOUBT SHE WAS A VIRUS HERSELF.
THOUGH WE CAN'T RULE OUT THE POSSIBILITY THAT SHE, LIKE RUKA...
IS ANOTHER VIRUS-LIKE THING WORKING FOR THE "SONOKA" PERSON THAT RUKA MENTIONED.
OH WELL. WE'LL FIND OUT FOR SURE TOMORROW NIGHT.
STAFF ONLY
SUMIRE, THIS MIGHT BE A SIMPLE HUNT, OR IT MIGHT *NOT*. DON'T LET YOUR GUARD DOWN.
WHRL
RIGHT ...
WAIT! TOMORROW NIGHT?!
ACK!
MEET ME HERE TOMORROW NIGHT AT MIDNIGHT, THEN.
BTAM
UM...
OH NO, OH NO! **NOW** WHAT DO I DO?! I PROMISED YOSHIKI-SAN I'D...
SUMIRE-KUN.
THERE IS SOMETHING I WOULD LIKE FOR YOU TO HAVE.
STAFF ONLY

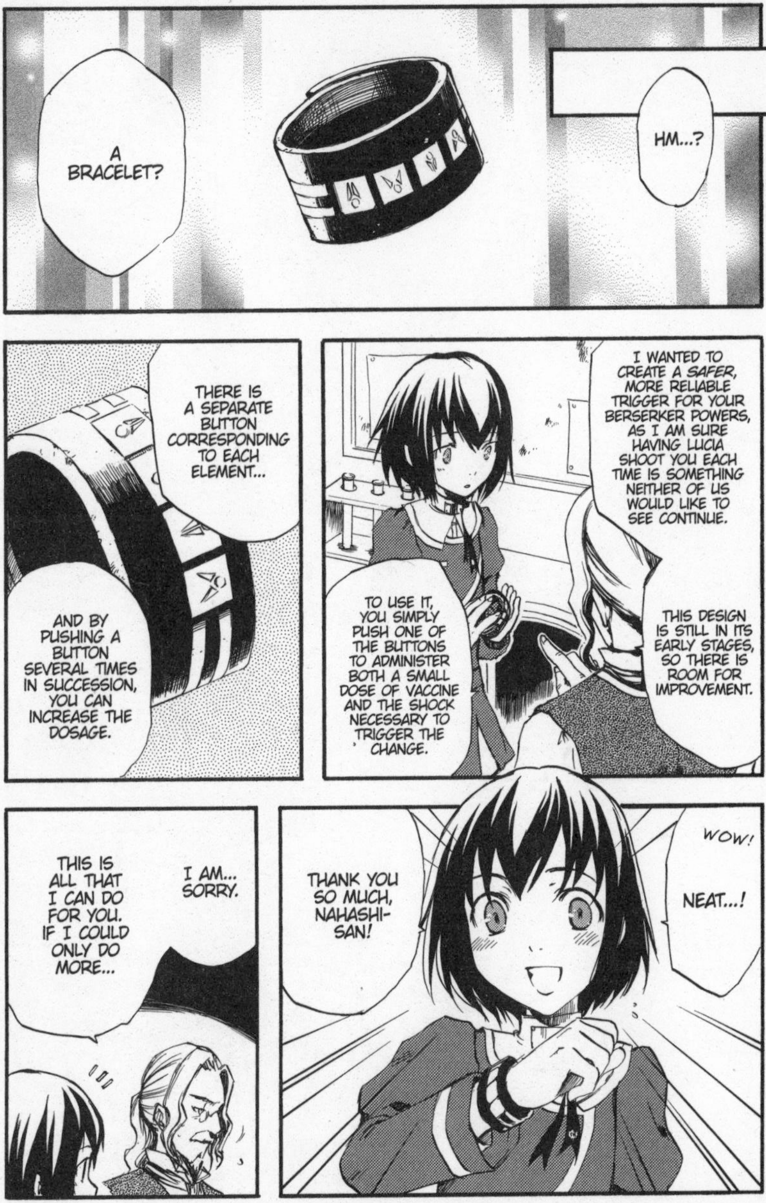
HM...?
A BRACELET?
I WANTED TO CREATE A *SAFER*, MORE RELIABLE TRIGGER FOR YOUR BERSERKER POWERS, AS I AM SURE HAVING LUCIA SHOOT YOU EACH TIME IS SOMETHING NEITHER OF US WOULD LIKE TO SEE CONTINUE.
THIS DESIGN IS STILL IN ITS EARLY STAGES, SO THERE IS ROOM FOR IMPROVEMENT.
TO USE IT, YOU SIMPLY PUSH ONE OF THE BUTTONS TO ADMINISTER BOTH A SMALL DOSE OF VACCINE AND THE SHOCK NECESSARY TO TRIGGER THE CHANGE.
THERE IS A SEPARATE BUTTON CORRESPONDING TO EACH ELEMENT...
AND BY PUSHING A BUTTON SEVERAL TIMES IN SUCCESSION, YOU CAN INCREASE THE DOSAGE.
WOW!
NEAT...!
THANK YOU SO MUCH, NAHASHI-SAN!
I AM... SORRY.
THIS IS ALL THAT I CAN DO FOR YOU. IF I COULD ONLY DO MORE...

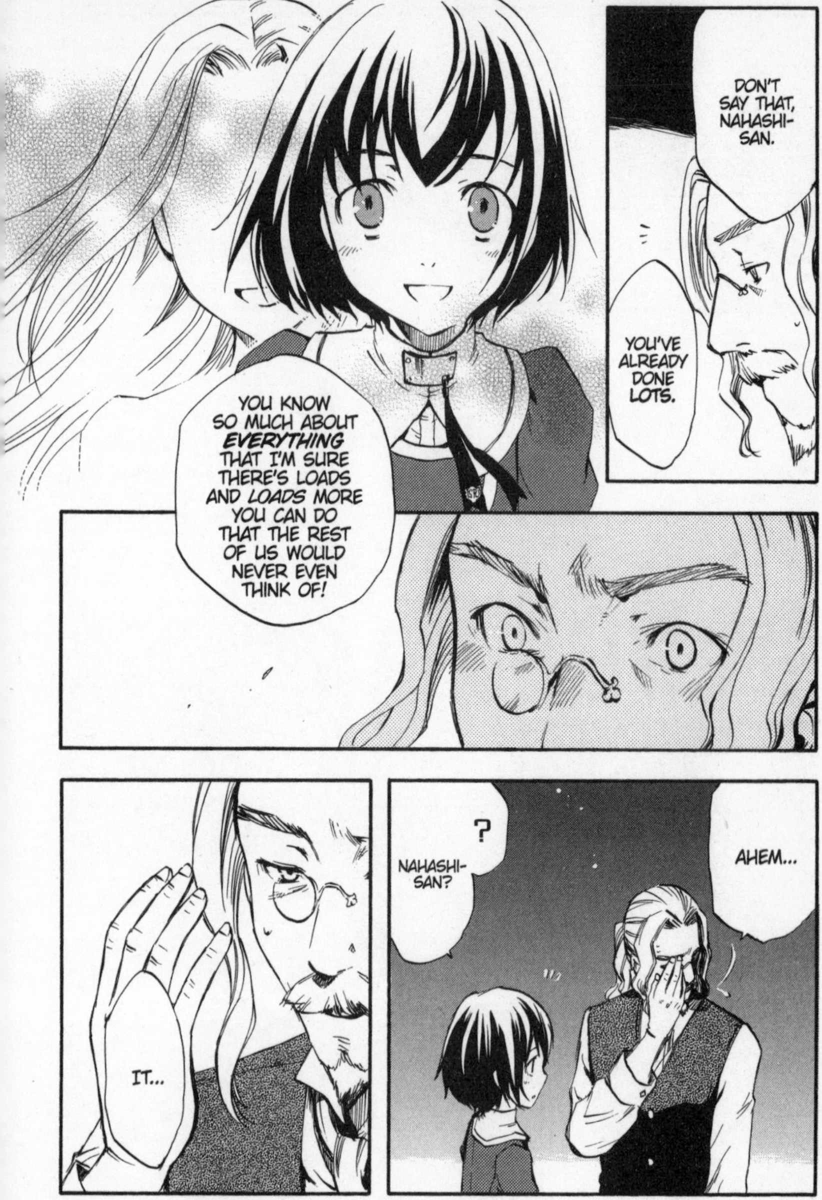
DON'T SAY THAT, NAHASHI-SAN.
YOU'VE ALREADY DONE LOTS.
YOU KNOW SO MUCH ABOUT **EVERYTHING** THAT I'M SURE THERE'S LOADS AND *LOADS* MORE YOU CAN DO THAT THE REST OF US WOULD NEVER EVEN THINK OF!
AHEM...
?
NAHASHI-SAN?
IT...

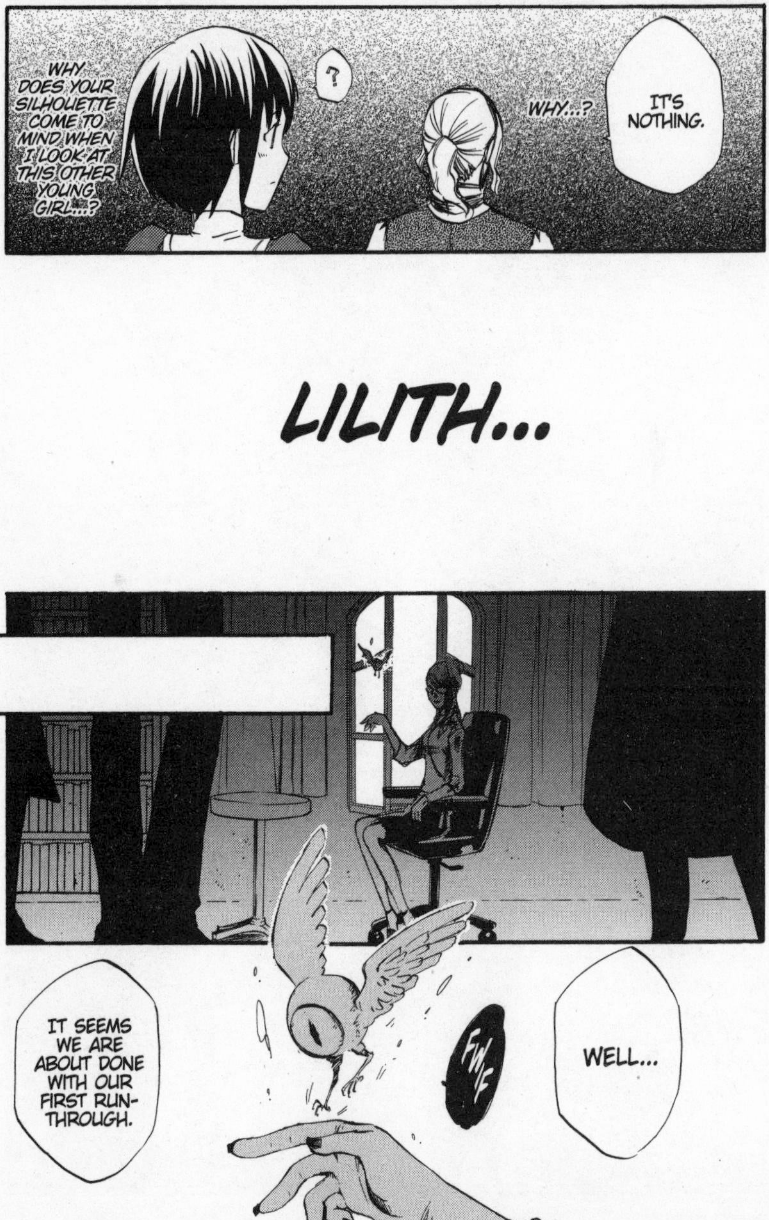
IT'S NOTHING.
WHY...?
?
WHY DOES YOUR SILHOUETTE COME TO MIND WHEN I LOOK AT THIS OTHER YOUNG GIRL...?
LILITH...
WELL...
FWF
IT SEEMS WE ARE ABOUT DONE WITH OUR FIRST RUN-THROUGH.

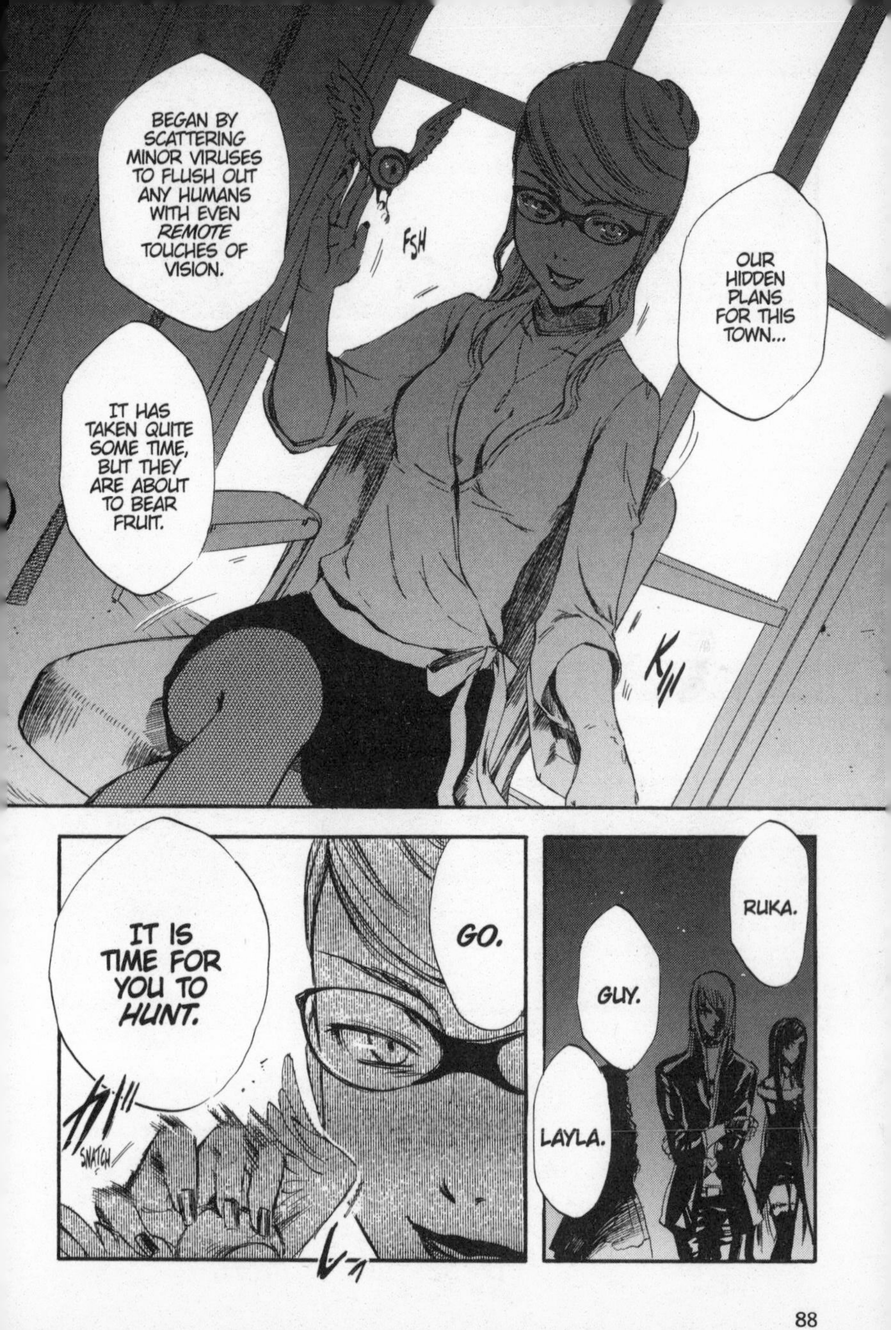
OUR HIDDEN PLANS FOR THIS TOWN...
BEGAN BY SCATTERING MINOR VIRUSES TO FLUSH OUT ANY HUMANS WITH EVEN *REMOTE* TOUCHES OF VISION.
FSH
IT HAS TAKEN QUITE SOME TIME, BUT THEY ARE ABOUT TO BEAR FRUIT.
RUKA.
GUY.
LAYLA.
GO.
IT IS TIME FOR YOU TO *HUNT.*
SNATCH

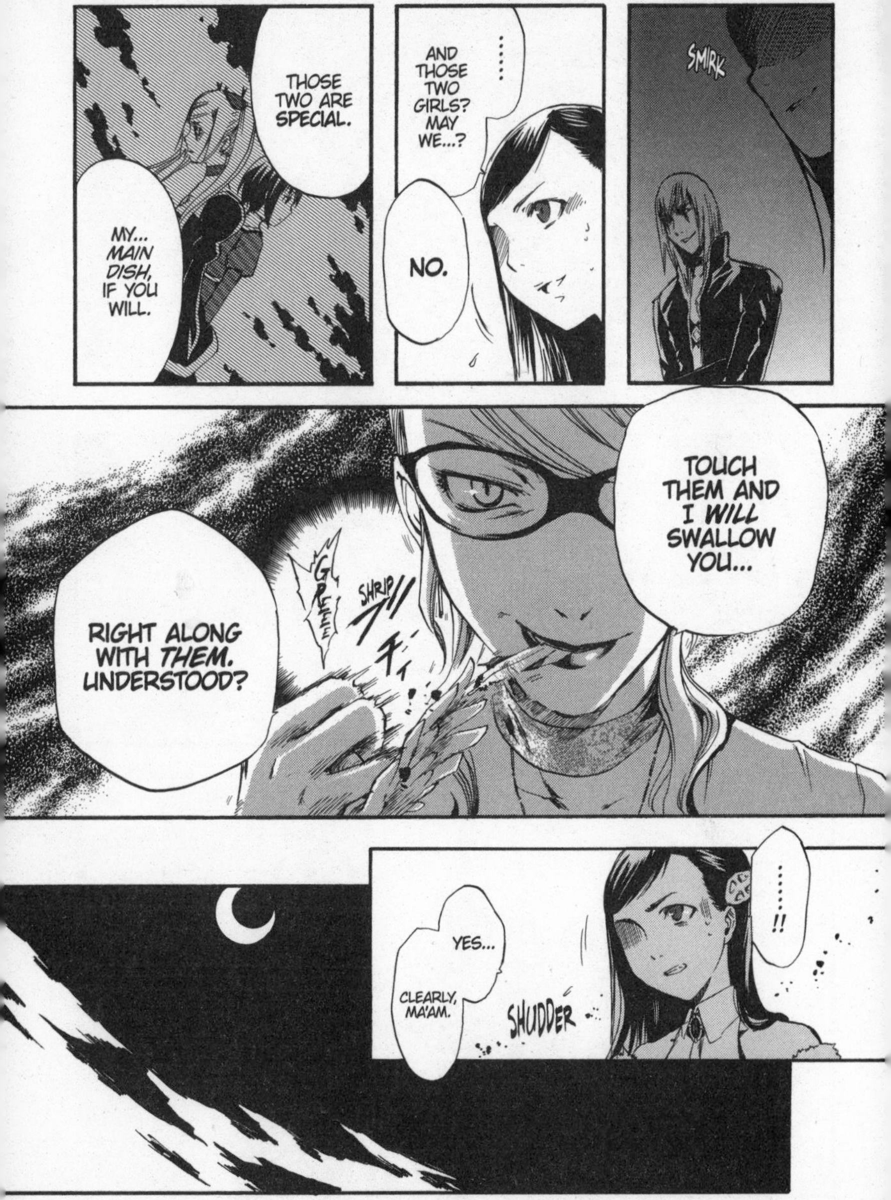
SMIRK
......
AND THOSE TWO GIRLS? MAY WE...?
NO.
THOSE TWO ARE SPECIAL.
MY... MAIN DISH, IF YOU WILL.
TOUCH THEM AND I WILL SWALLOW YOU...
SHRIP
GREEE
RIGHT ALONG WITH THEM. UNDERSTOOD?
......!!
YES...
CLEARLY, MA'AM.
SHUDDER

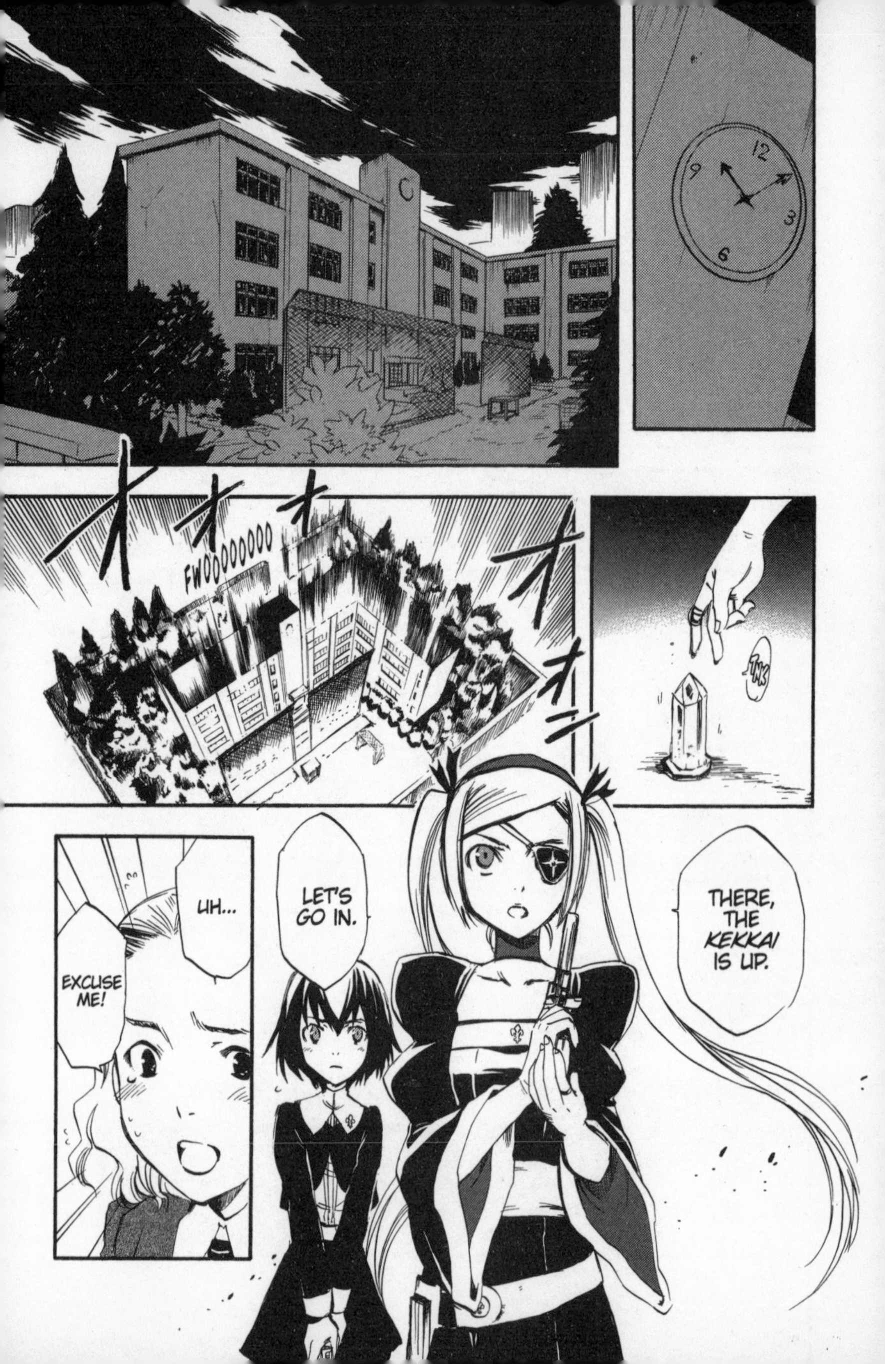
TINK
FWOOOOOOOO
THERE, THE KEKKAI IS UP.
LET'S GO IN.
UH...
EXCUSE ME!

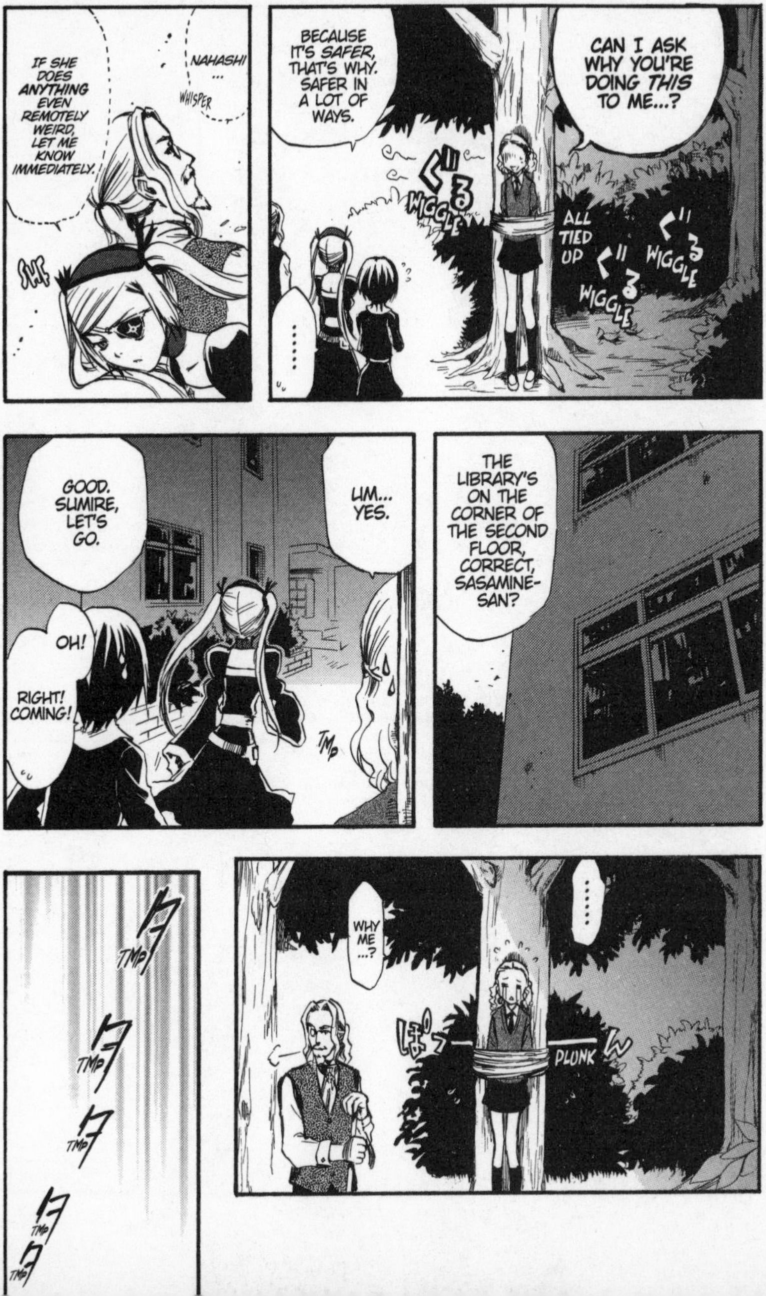
CAN I ASK WHY YOU'RE DOING THIS TO ME...?
BECAUSE IT'S SAFER, THAT'S WHY. SAFER IN A LOT OF WAYS.
ぐる
WIGGLE
ALL TIED UP
ぐる
WIGGLE
ぐる
WIGGLE
......
NAHASHI...
WHISPER
IF SHE DOES ANYTHING EVEN REMOTELY WEIRD, LET ME KNOW IMMEDIATELY.
SHF
THE LIBRARY'S ON THE CORNER OF THE SECOND FLOOR, CORRECT, SASAMINE-SAN?
UM... YES.
GOOD. SUMIRE, LET'S GO.
OH!
RIGHT! COMING!
TMP
......
WHY ME...?
PLUNK
TMP
TMP
TMP
TMP
TMP

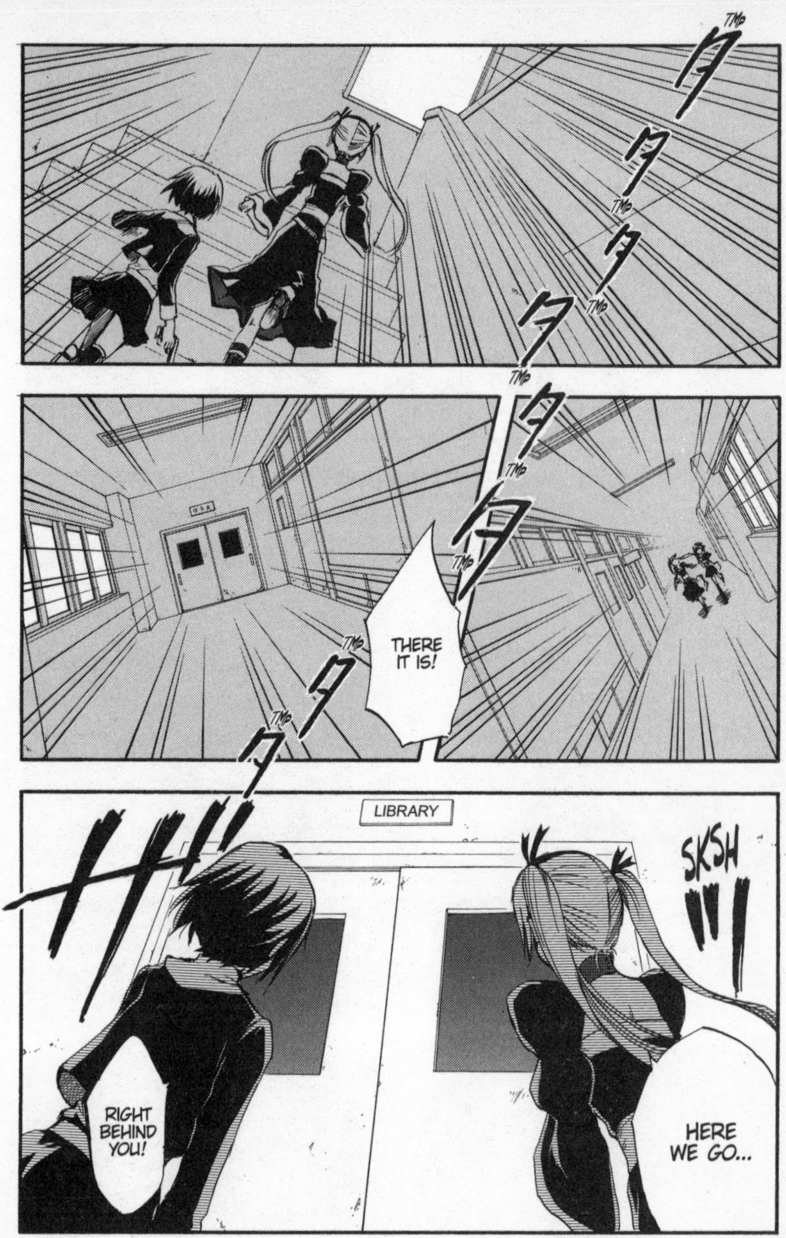
TMP
タ
TMP
タ
TMP
タ
TMP
タ
TMP
タ
THERE IT IS!
TMP
タ
TMP
タ
LIBRARY
SKSH
HERE WE GO...
RIGHT BEHIND YOU!

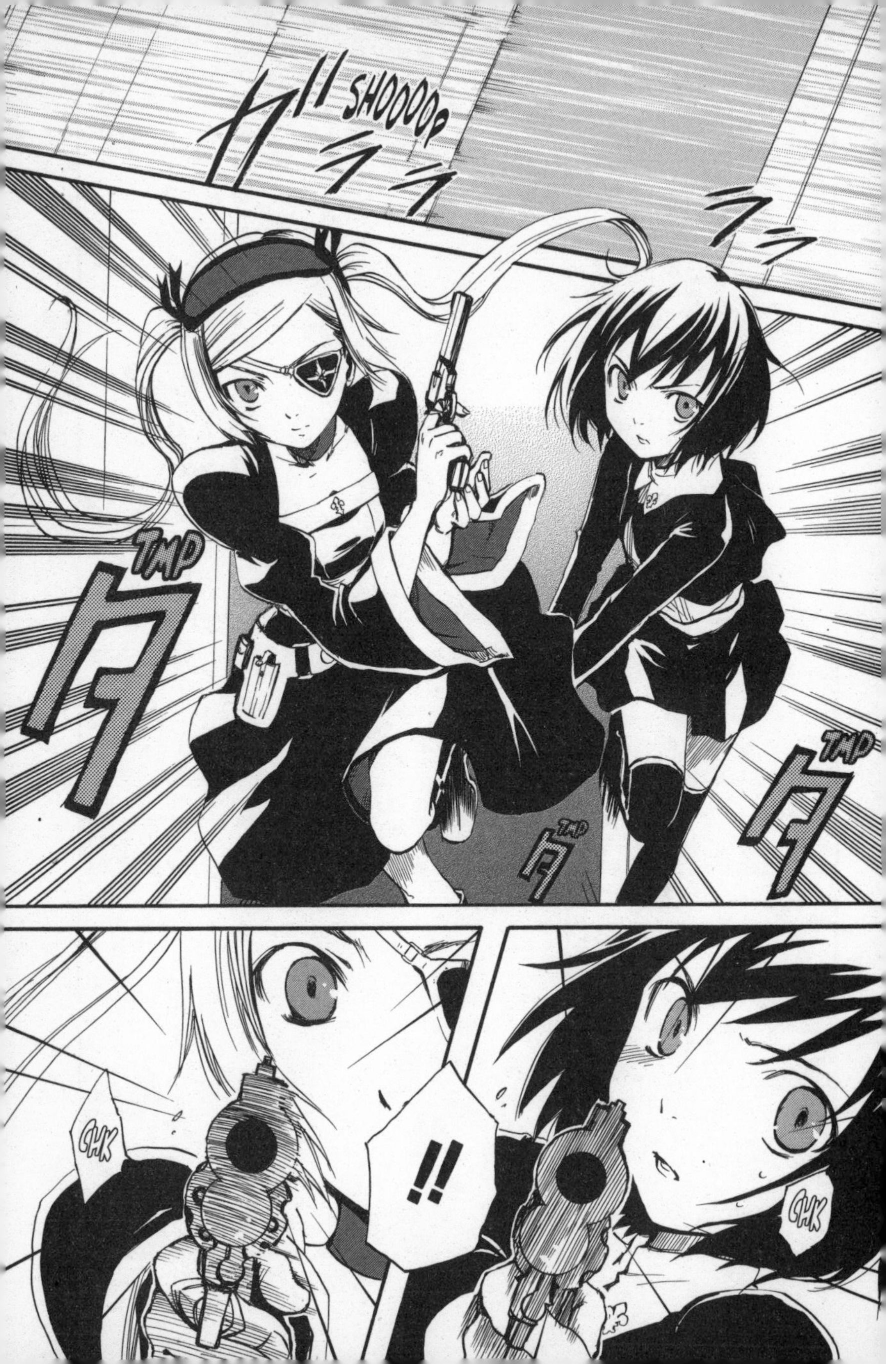
SHOOOOP
TMP
TMP
TMP
CHK
!!
CHK

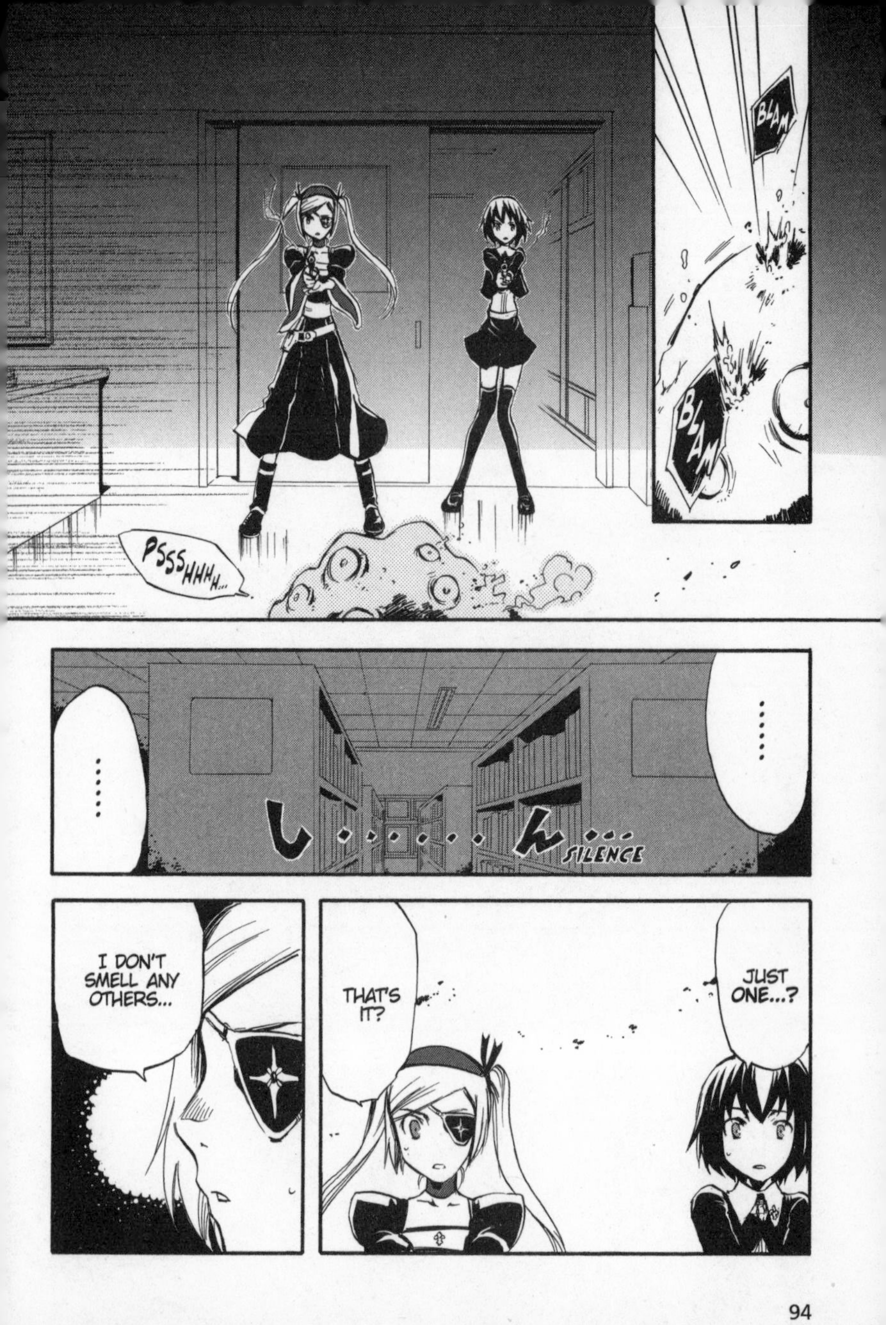
BLAM
BLAM
PSSSHHHH...
......
......
SILENCE
JUST ONE...?
THAT'S IT?
I DON'T SMELL ANY OTHERS...

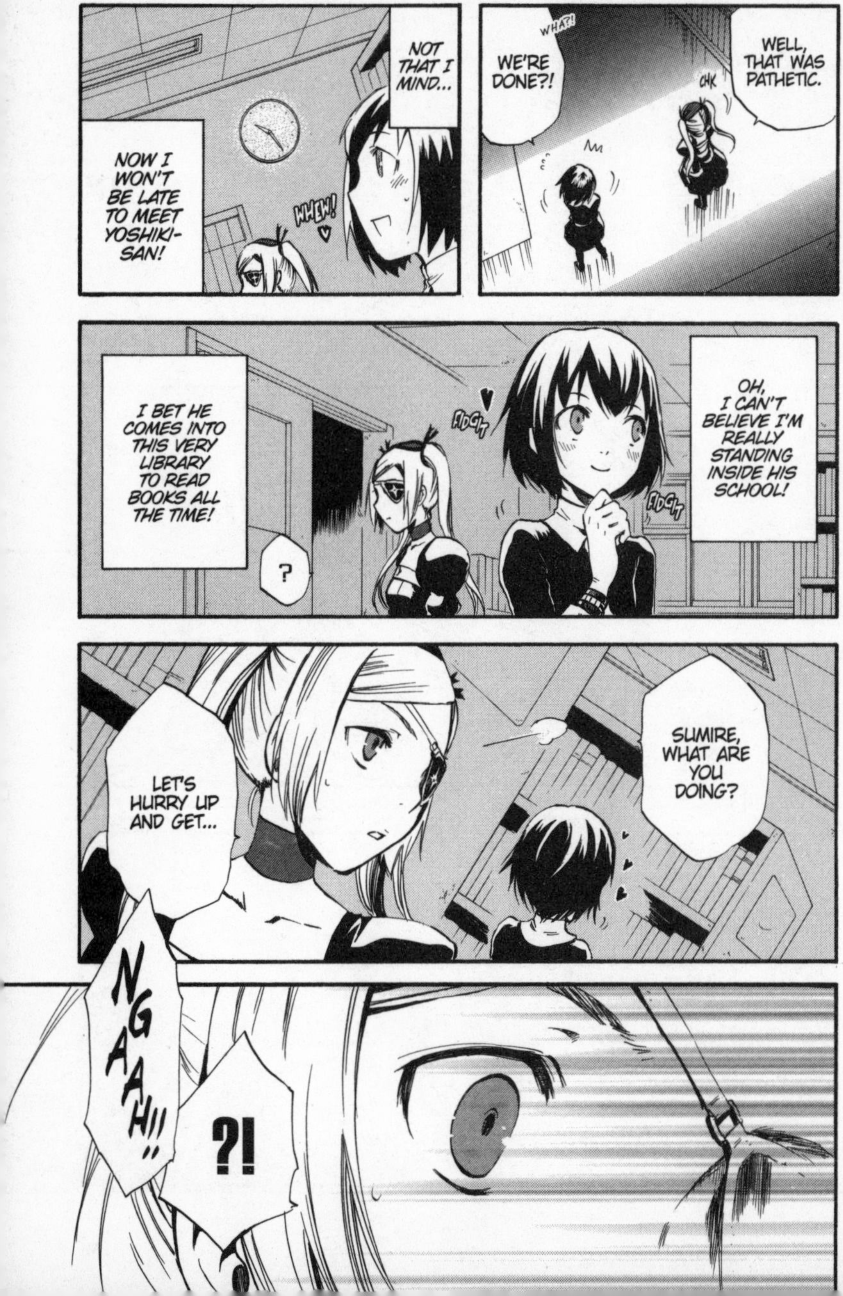
WELL, THAT WAS PATHETIC.
CHK
WHAT?!
WE'RE DONE?!
NOT THAT I MIND...
NOW I WON'T BE LATE TO MEET YOSHIKI-SAN!
WHEW!
OH, I CAN'T BELIEVE I'M REALLY STANDING INSIDE HIS SCHOOL!
FIDGIT
FIDGIT
I BET HE COMES INTO THIS VERY LIBRARY TO READ BOOKS ALL THE TIME!
?
SUMIRE, WHAT ARE YOU DOING?
LET'S HURRY UP AND GET...
?!
NGAAAH!!

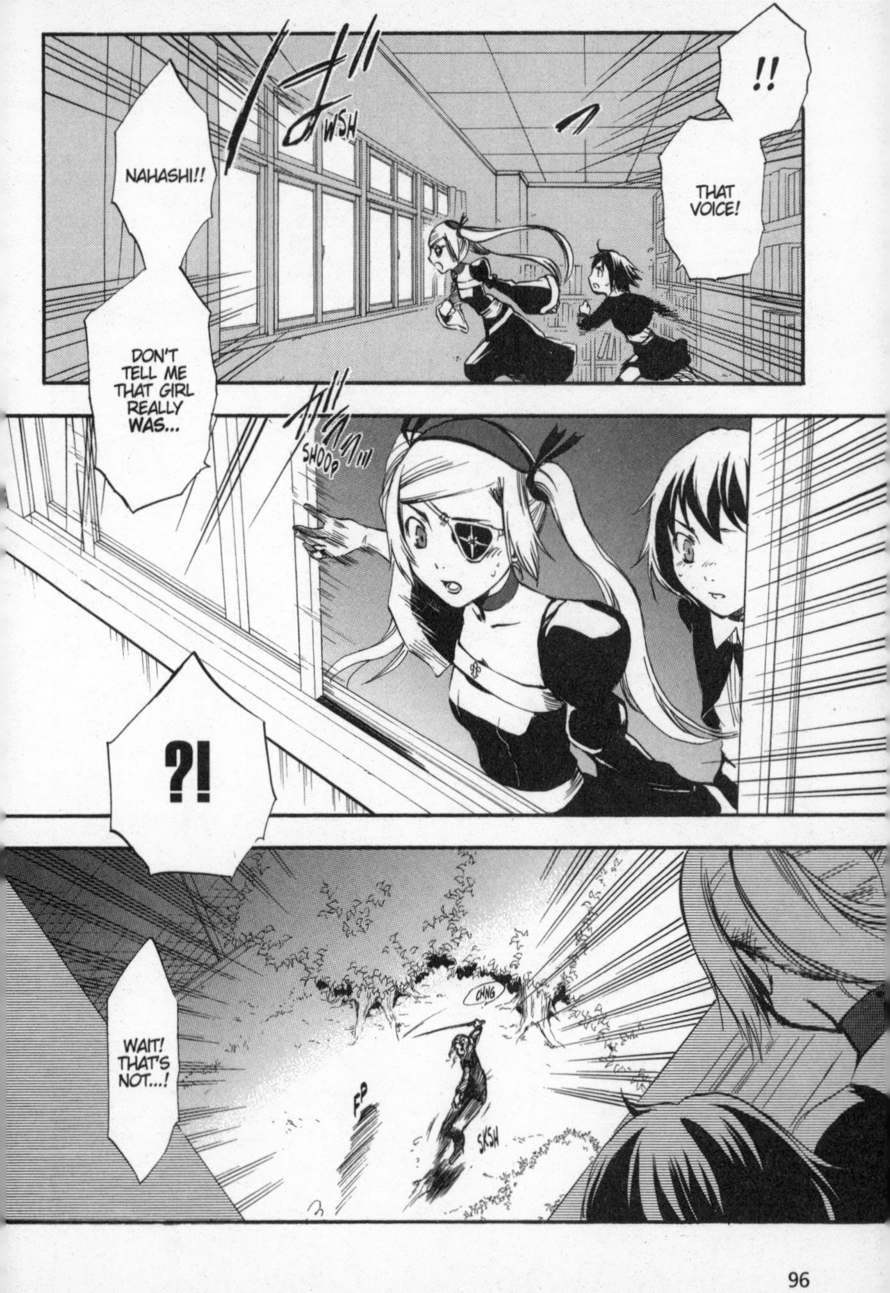
!!
THAT VOICE!
WSH
NAHASHI!!
DON'T TELL ME THAT GIRL REALLY WAS...
SHOOP
?!
CHNG
SKSH
FP
WAIT! THAT'S NOT...!

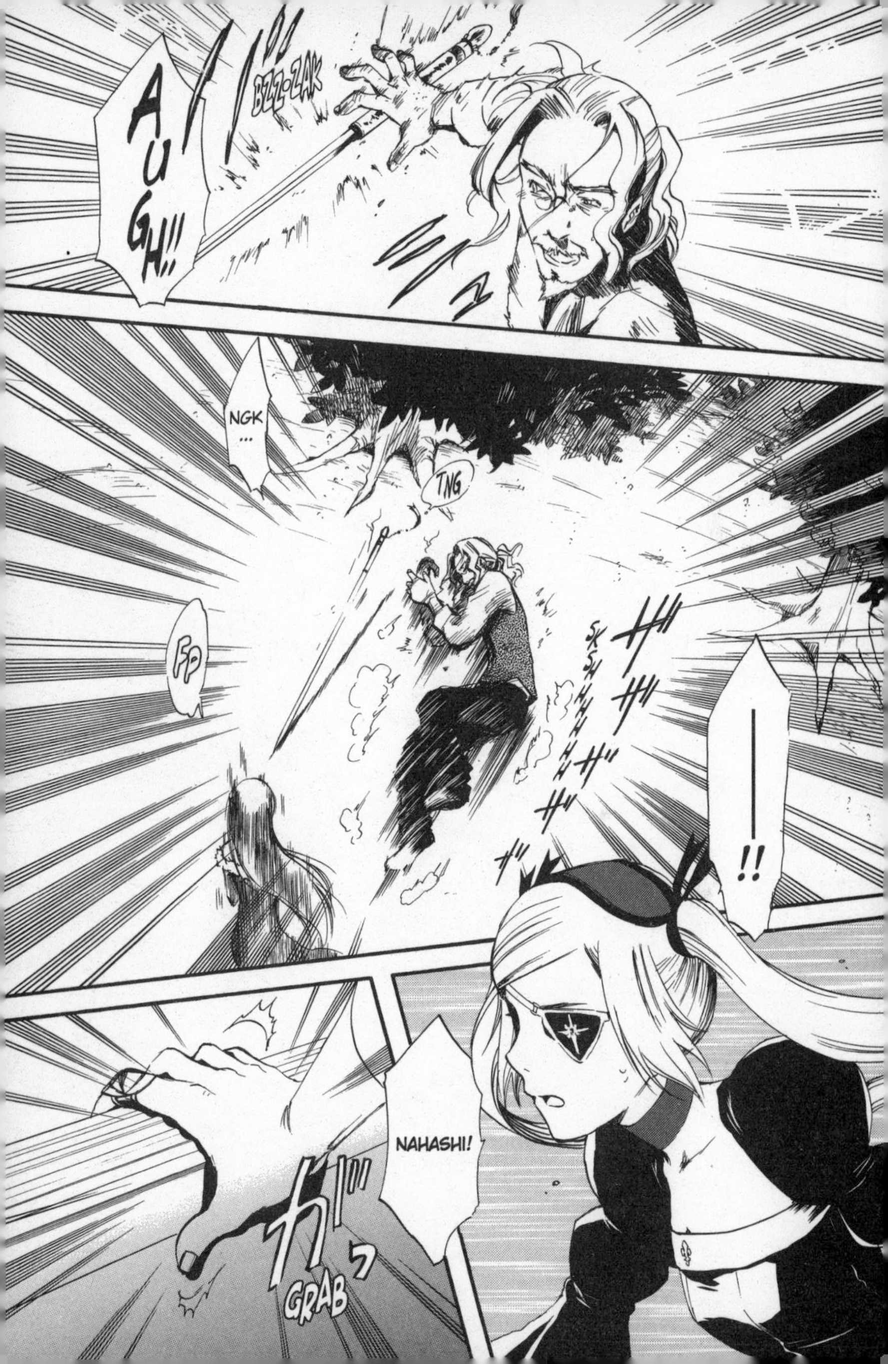
BZZ-ZAK
AUGH!!
NGK ...
TNG
SKSHHHHHH
FP
—!!
NAHASHI!
GRAB

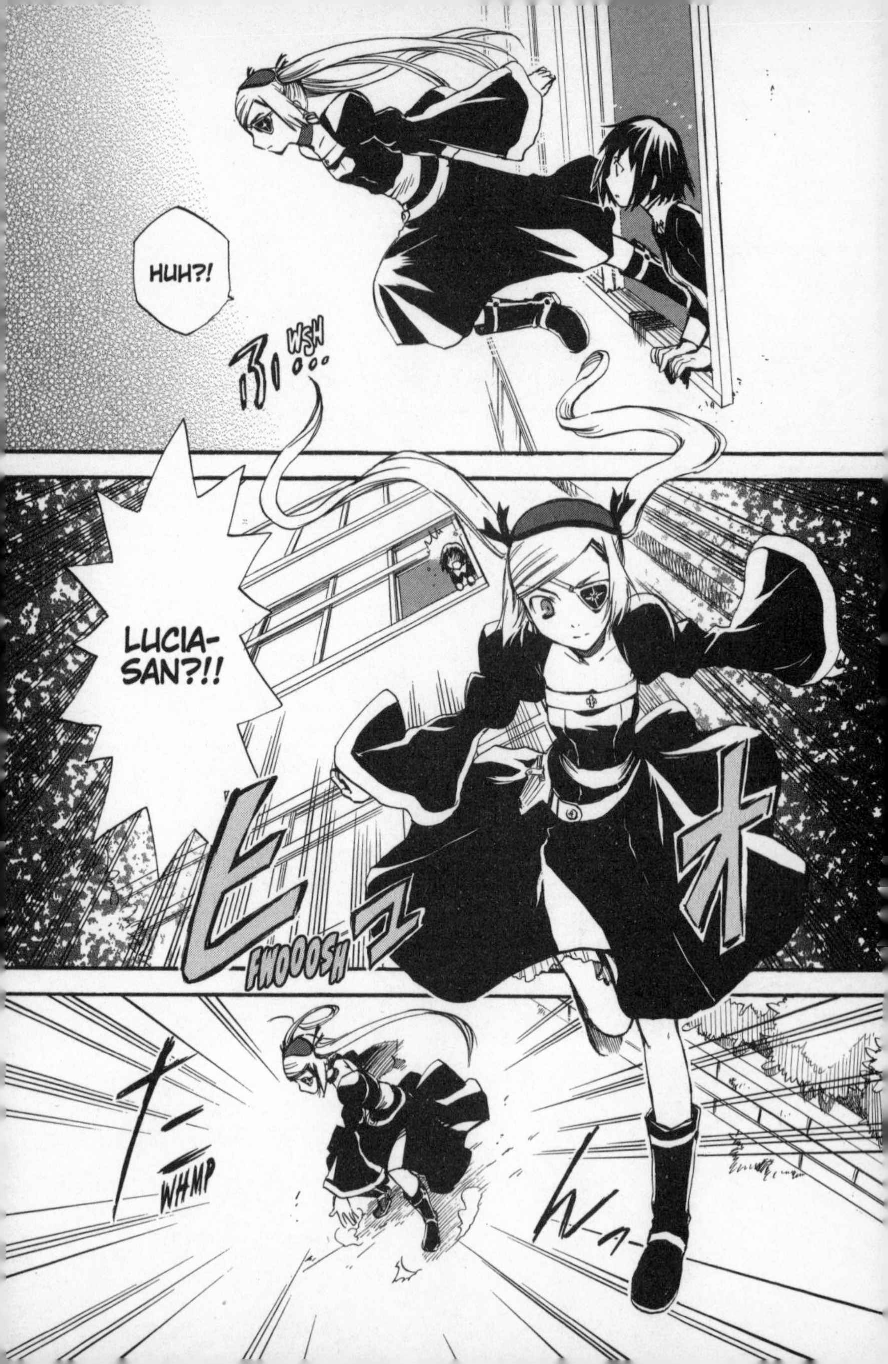
HUH?!
WSH
LUCIA-
SAN?!!
FWOOOSH
WHMP

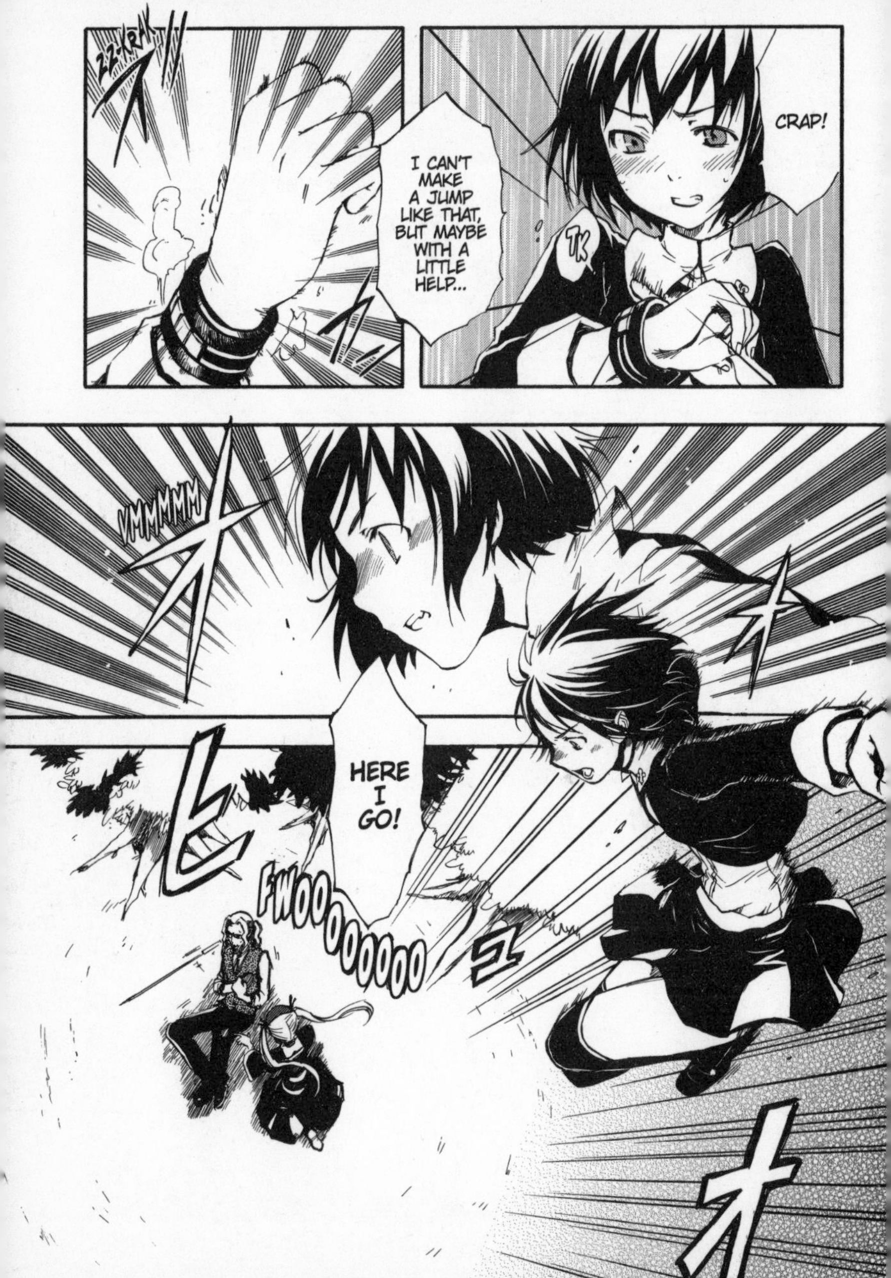
CRAP!
TK
I CAN'T MAKE A JUMP LIKE THAT, BUT MAYBE WITH A LITTLE HELP...
ZZ-KRAK
VMMMMM
HERE I GO!
FWOOOOOOOO

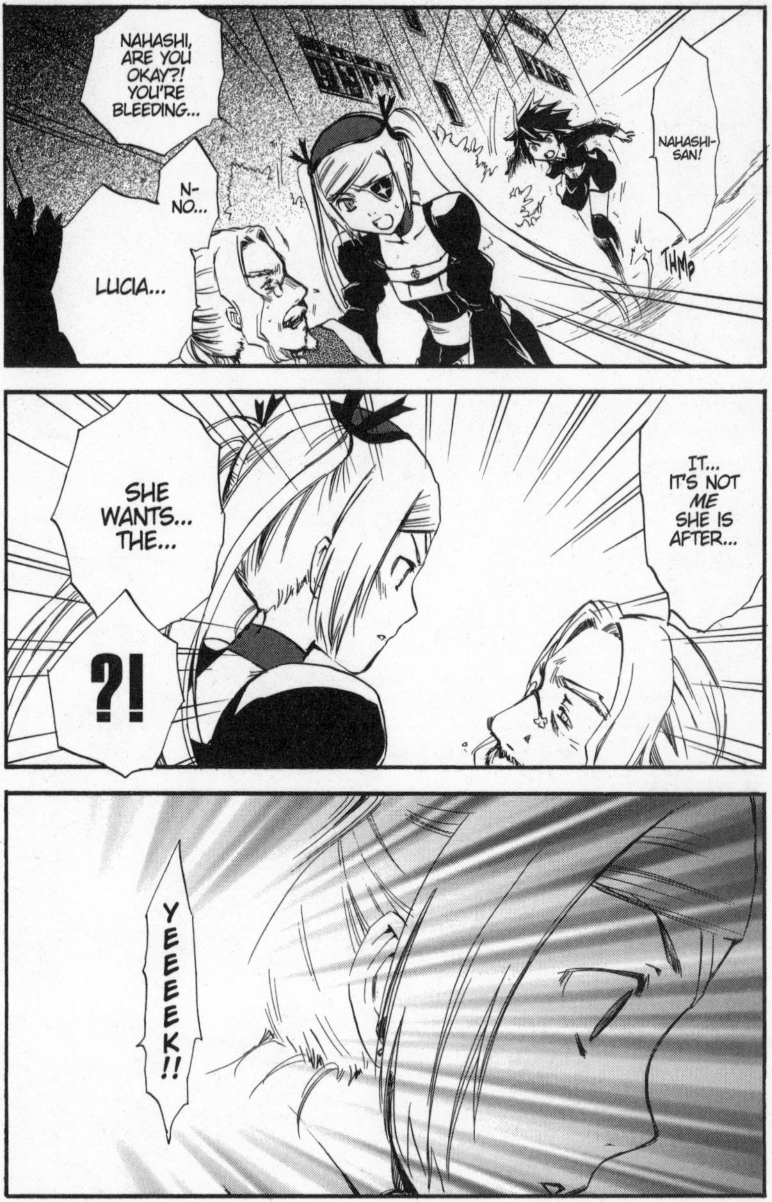
NAHASHI-SAN!
THMP
NAHASHI, ARE YOU OKAY?! YOU'RE BLEEDING...
N-NO...
LUCIA...
IT... IT'S NOT *ME* SHE IS AFTER...
SHE WANTS... THE...
?!
YEEEEEK!!

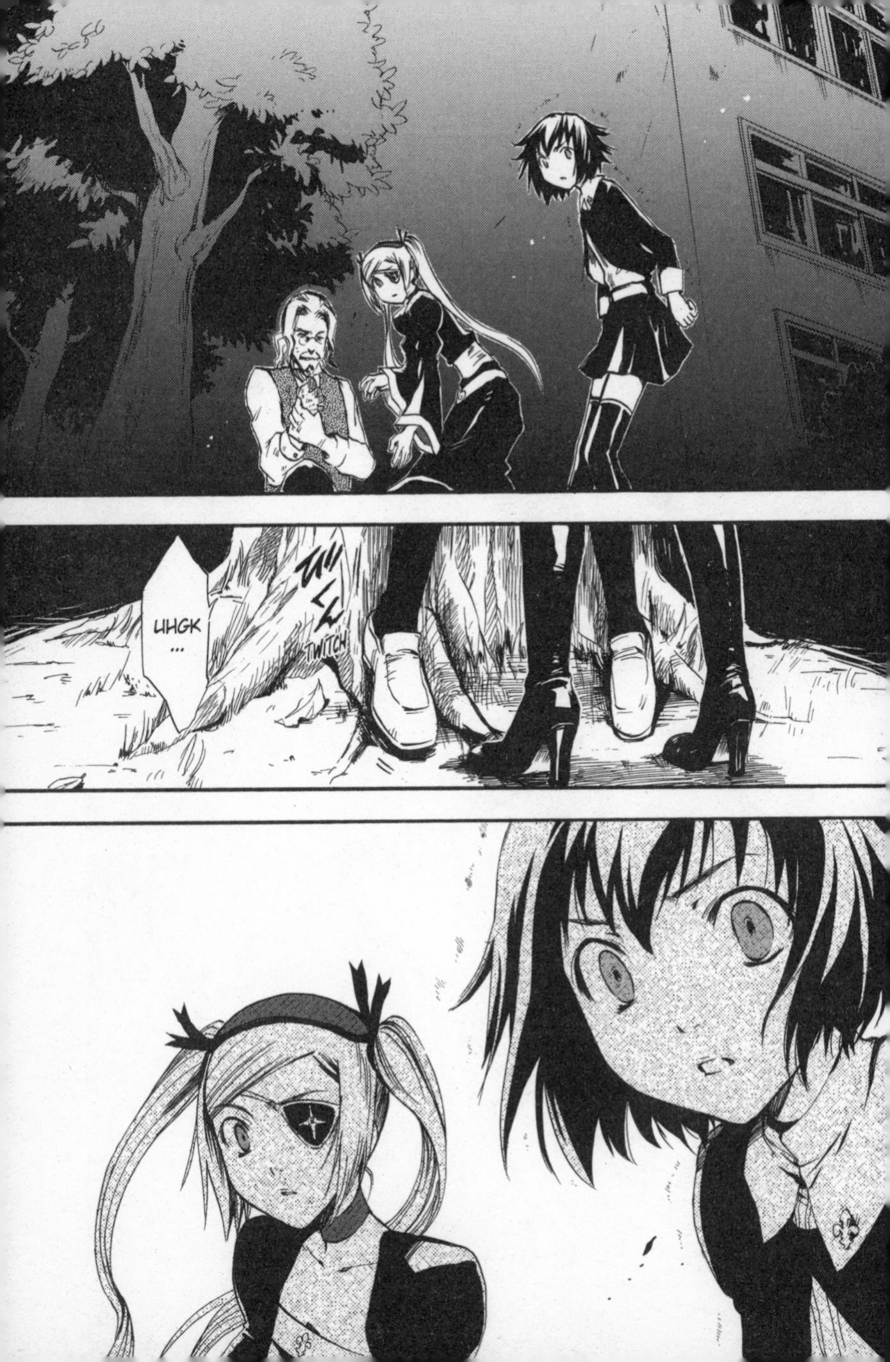
UHGK ...
TWITCH

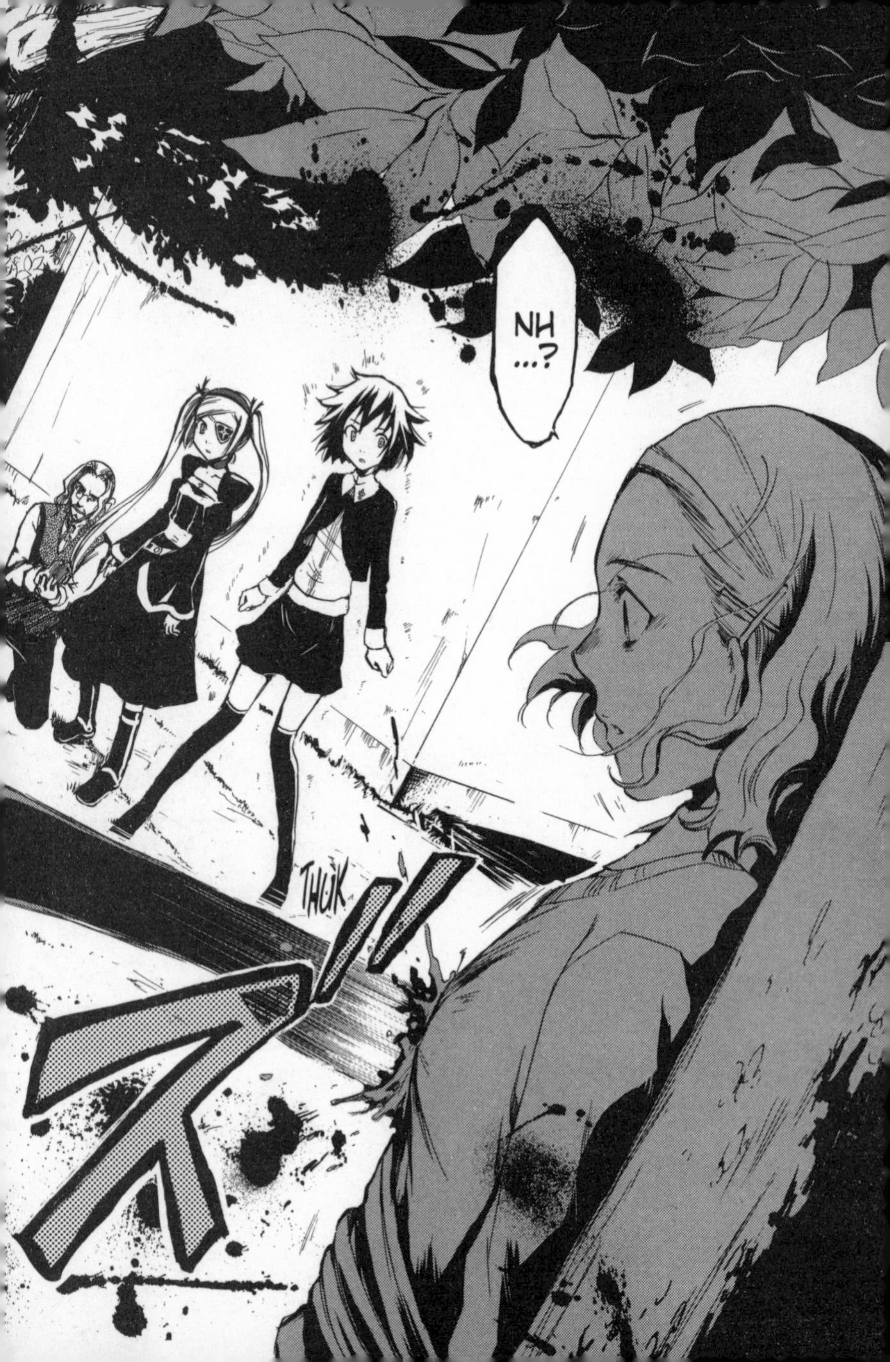
NH
...?
THUK

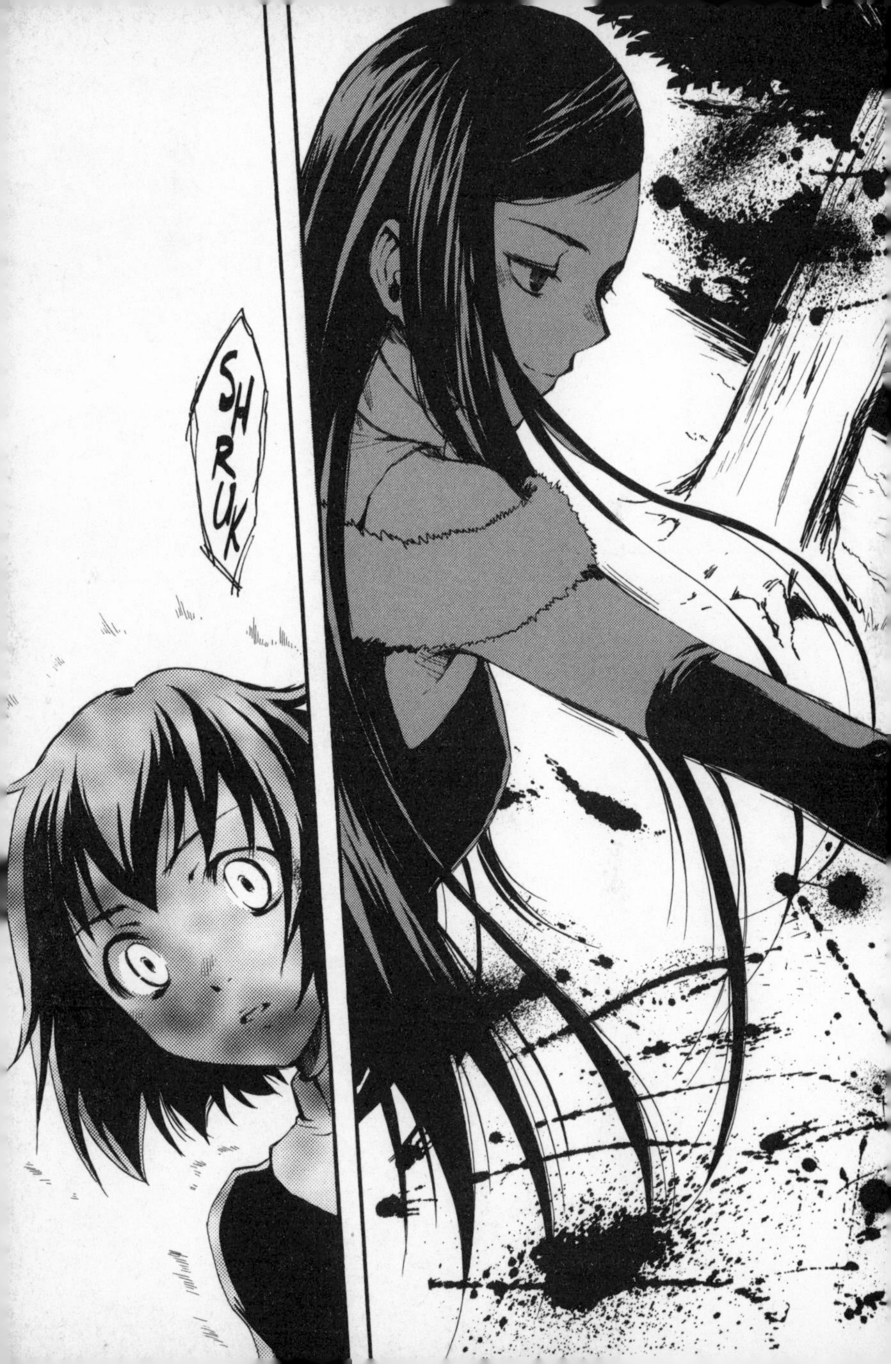
SHRUK

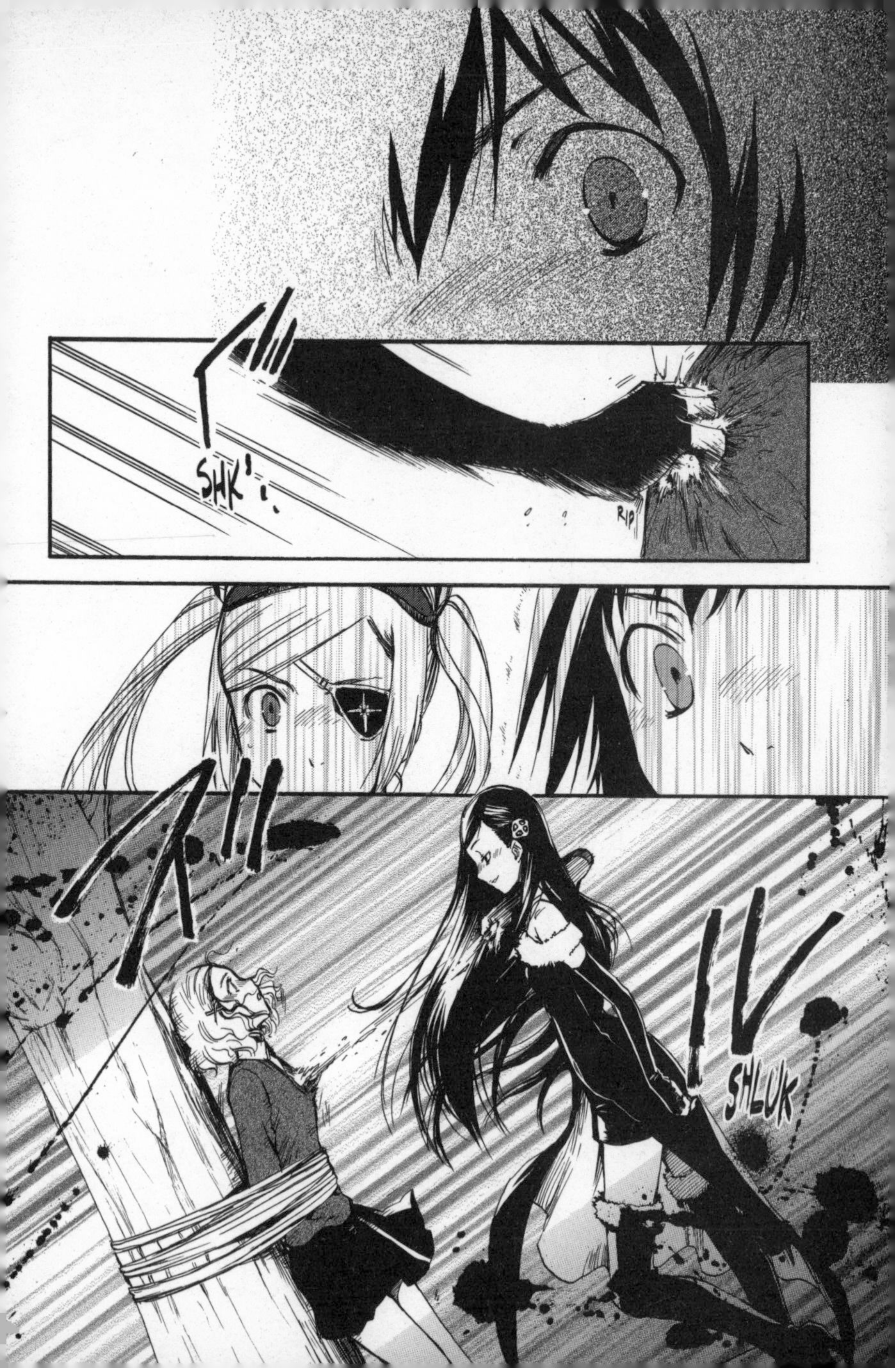
RIP
SHK
SHLUK

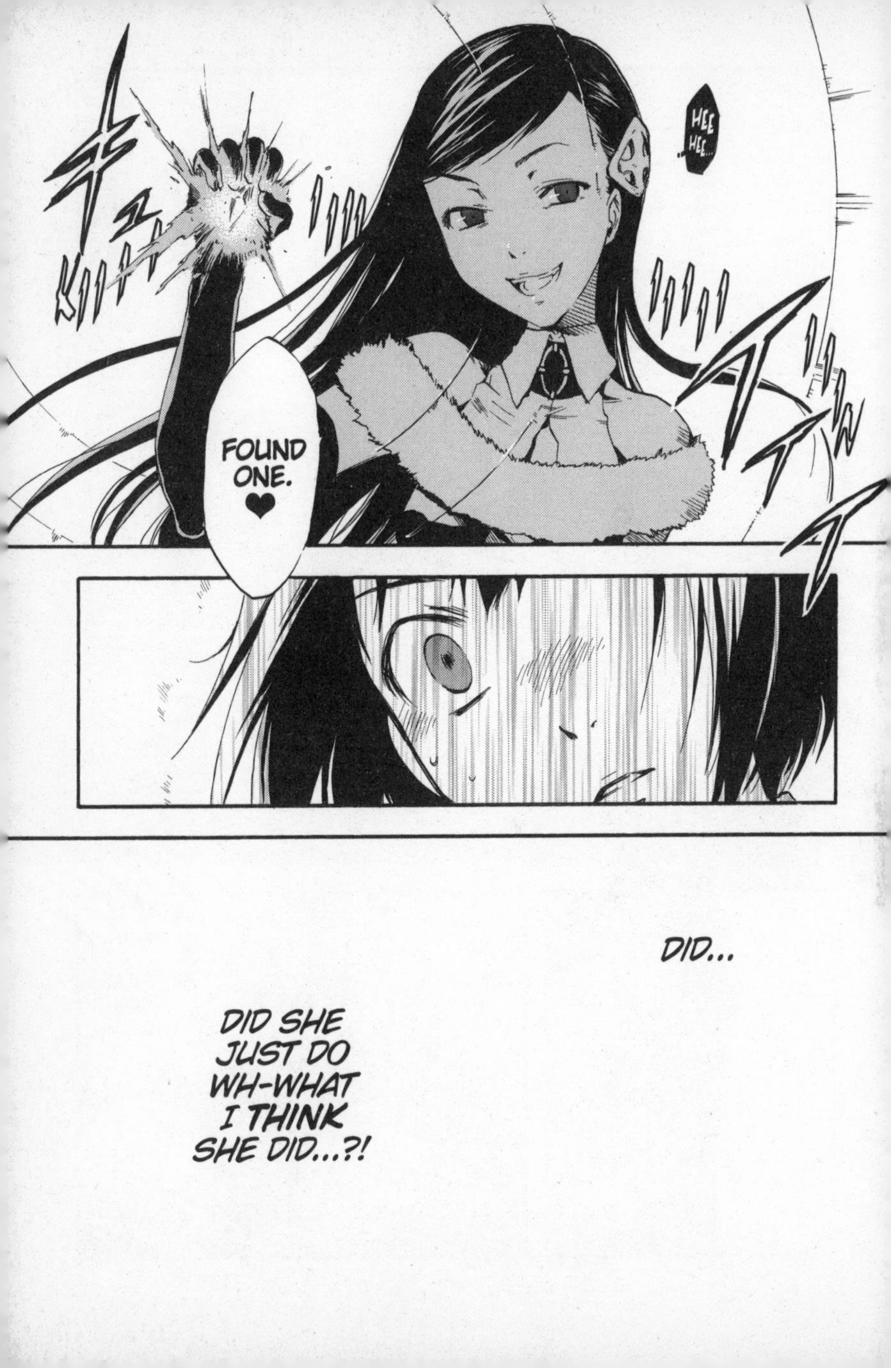
HEE HEE...
FOUND ONE. ❤
DID...
DID SHE JUST DO WH-WHAT I THINK SHE DID...?!

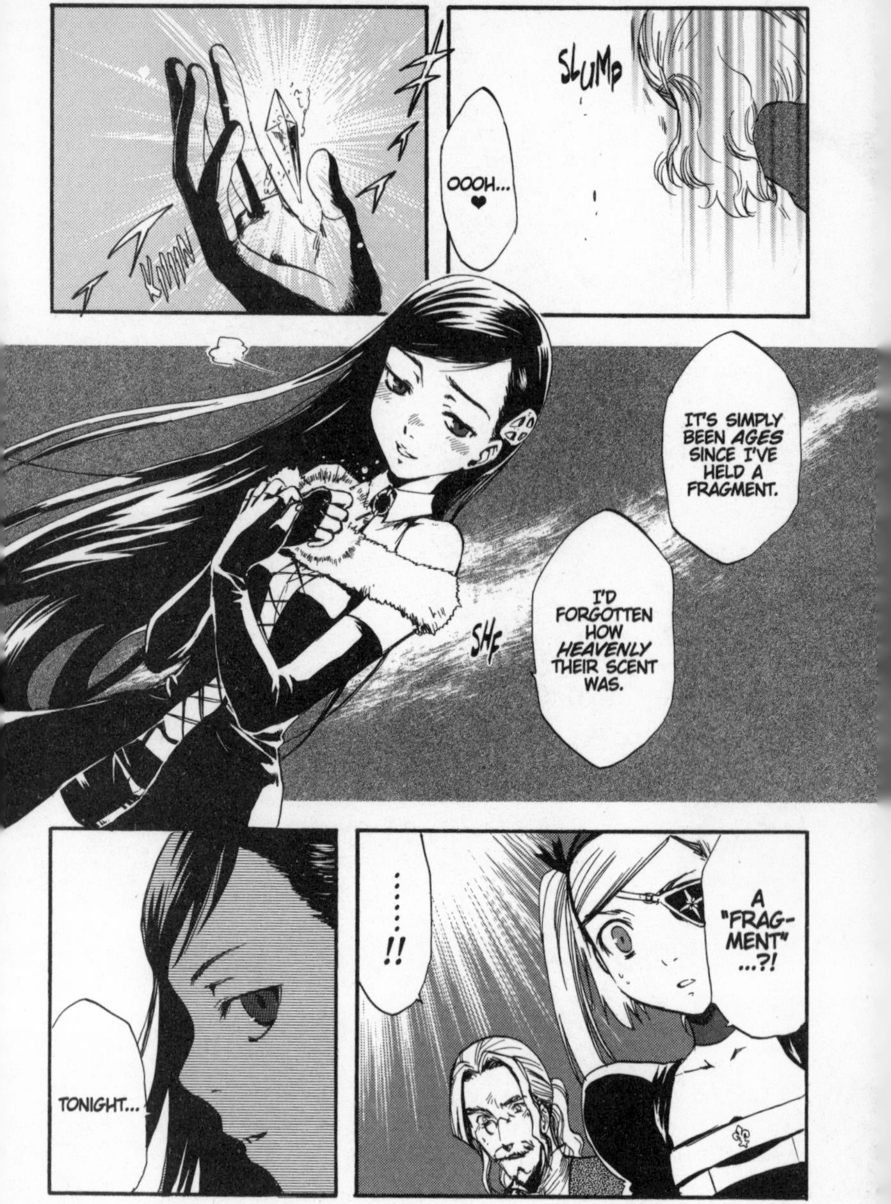
SLUMP
OOOH... ❤
IT'S SIMPLY BEEN *AGES* SINCE I'VE HELD A FRAGMENT.
I'D FORGOTTEN HOW *HEAVENLY* THEIR SCENT WAS.
SHF
A "FRAG-MENT" ...?!
......!!
TONIGHT...

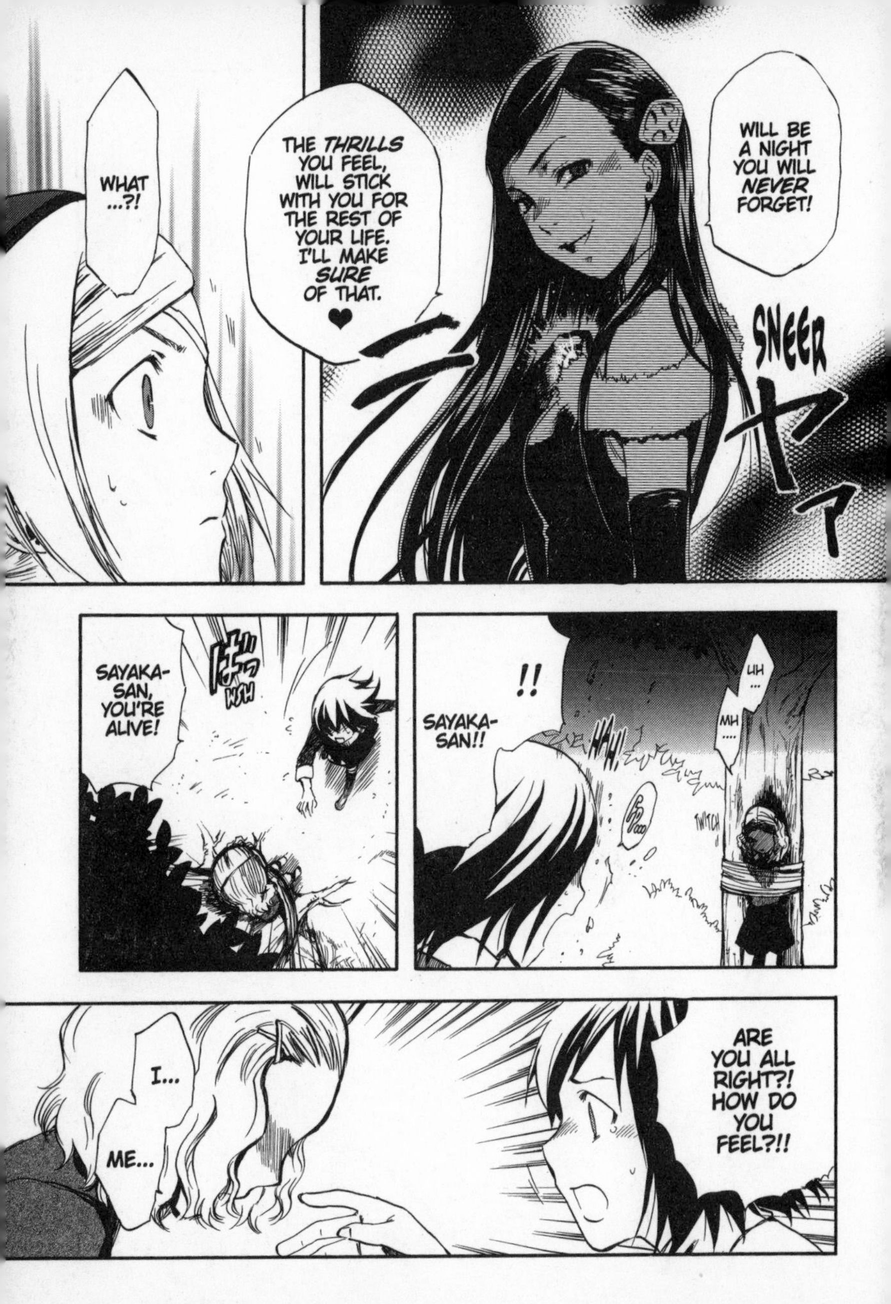
WILL BE A NIGHT YOU WILL *NEVER* FORGET!
THE *THRILLS* YOU FEEL, WILL STICK WITH YOU FOR THE REST OF YOUR LIFE. I'LL MAKE *SURE* OF THAT. ❤
SNEER
ヤァ
WHAT ...?!
UH ...
MH ....
!!
SAYAKA-SAN!!
HAH
TWITCH
ぱっ
WSH
SAYAKA-SAN, YOU'RE ALIVE!
ARE YOU ALL RIGHT?! HOW DO YOU FEEL?!!
I...
ME...

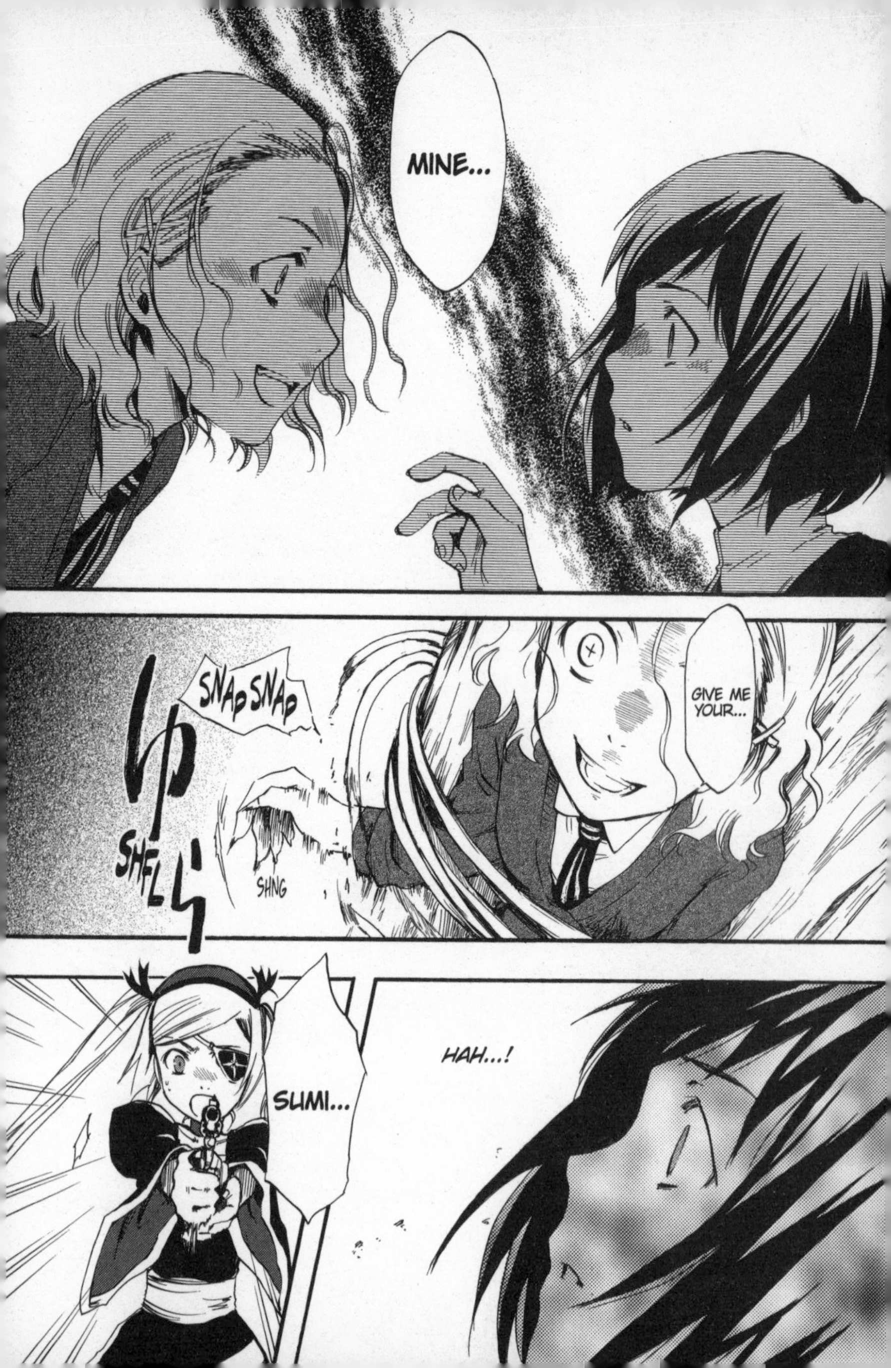
MINE...
GIVE ME YOUR...
SNAP SNAP
SHNG
ゆら
SHFL
HAH...!
SUMI...

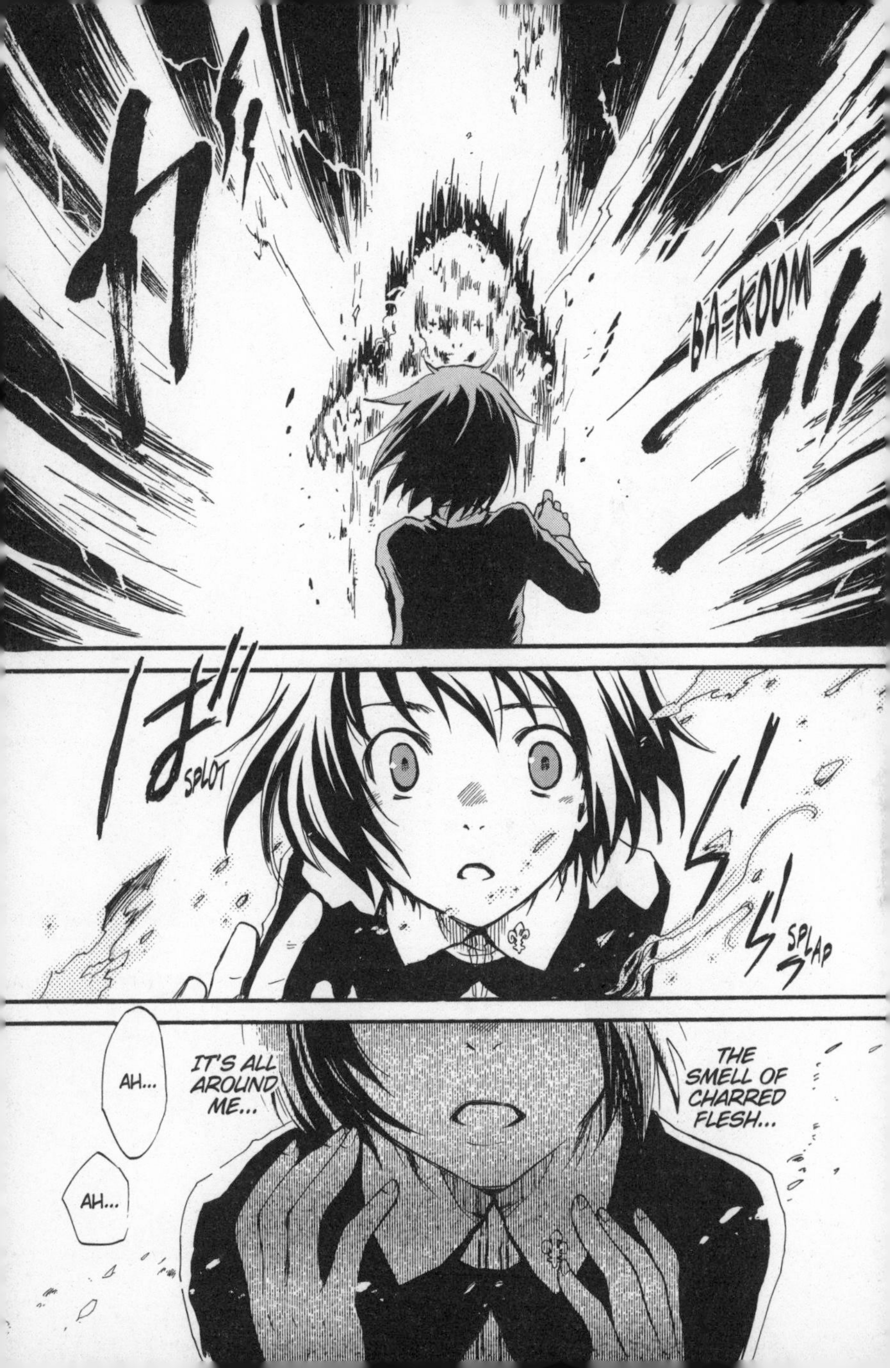
BA-KOOM
SPLAP
SPLOT
THE SMELL OF CHARRED FLESH...
IT'S ALL AROUND ME...
AH...
AH...

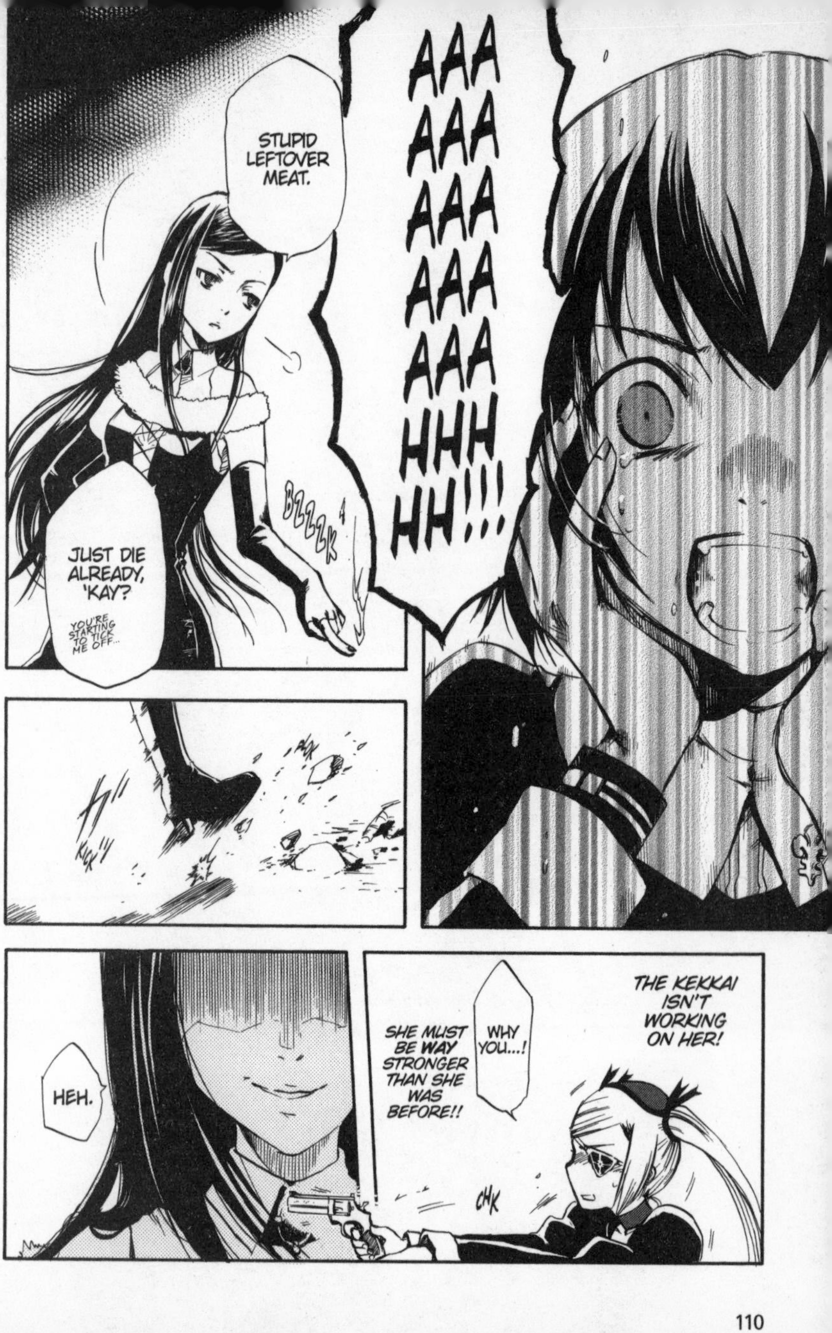
AAAAAAAAAAAAAAAAAAHHHHH!!!
STUPID LEFTOVER MEAT.
JUST DIE ALREADY, 'KAY?
YOU'RE STARTING TO TICK ME OFF...
BZZZK
KICK
THE KEKKAI ISN'T WORKING ON HER!
WHY YOU...!
SHE MUST BE WAY STRONGER THAN SHE WAS BEFORE!!
CHK
HEH.

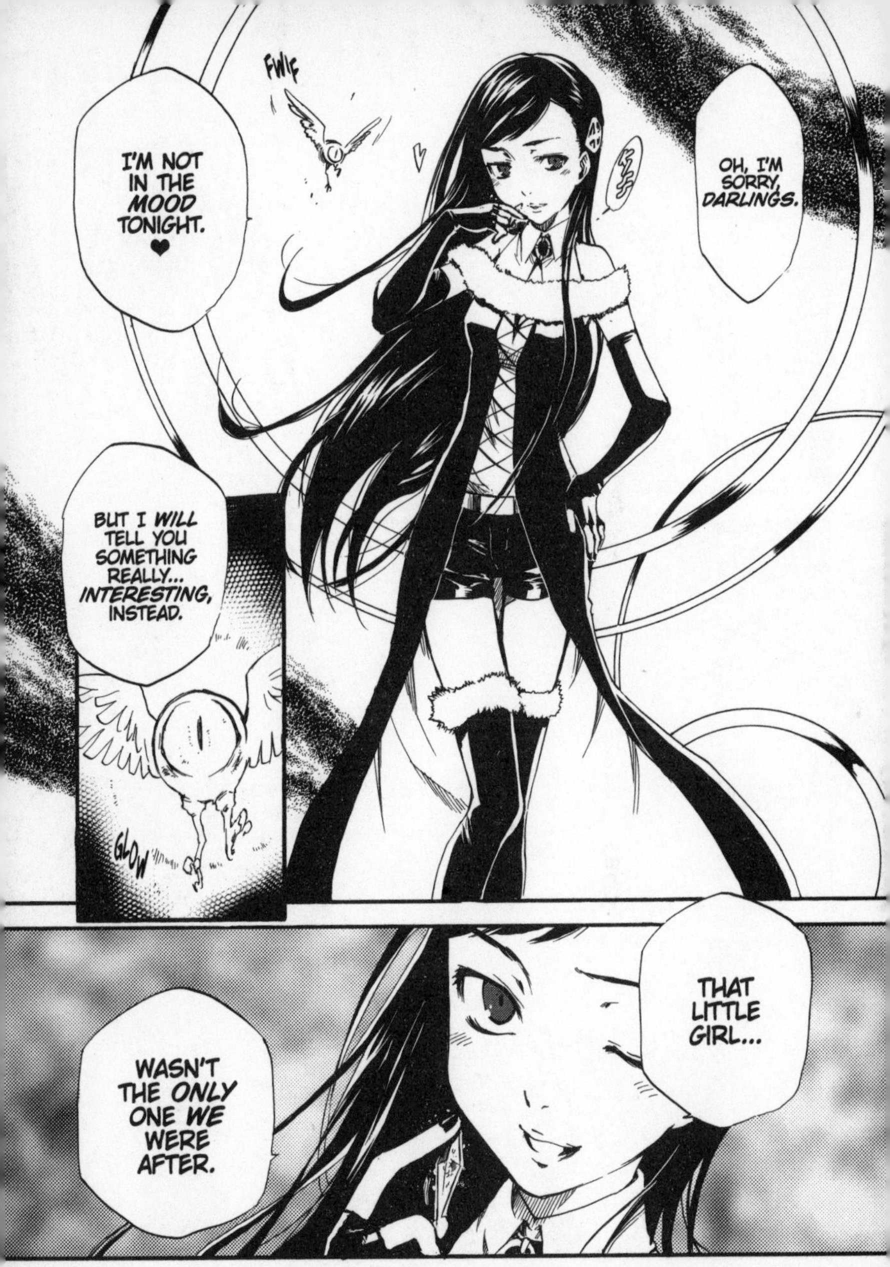
OH, I'M SORRY, DARLINGS.
FWIF
I'M NOT IN THE MOOD TONIGHT. ❤
BUT I WILL TELL YOU SOMETHING REALLY... INTERESTING, INSTEAD.
GLOW
THAT LITTLE GIRL...
WASN'T THE ONLY ONE WE WERE AFTER.

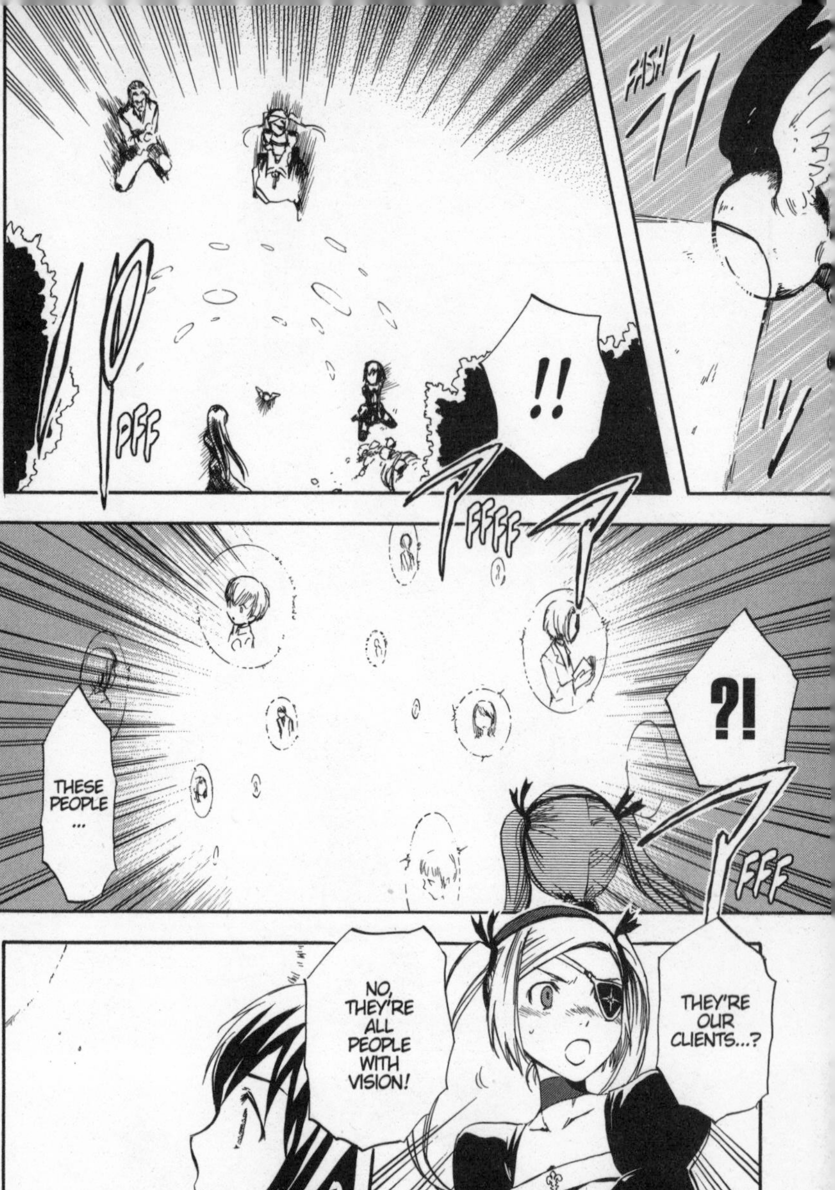
!!
PFF
FFFF
?!
FFF
THESE PEOPLE ...
THEY'RE OUR CLIENTS...?
NO, THEY'RE ALL PEOPLE WITH VISION!

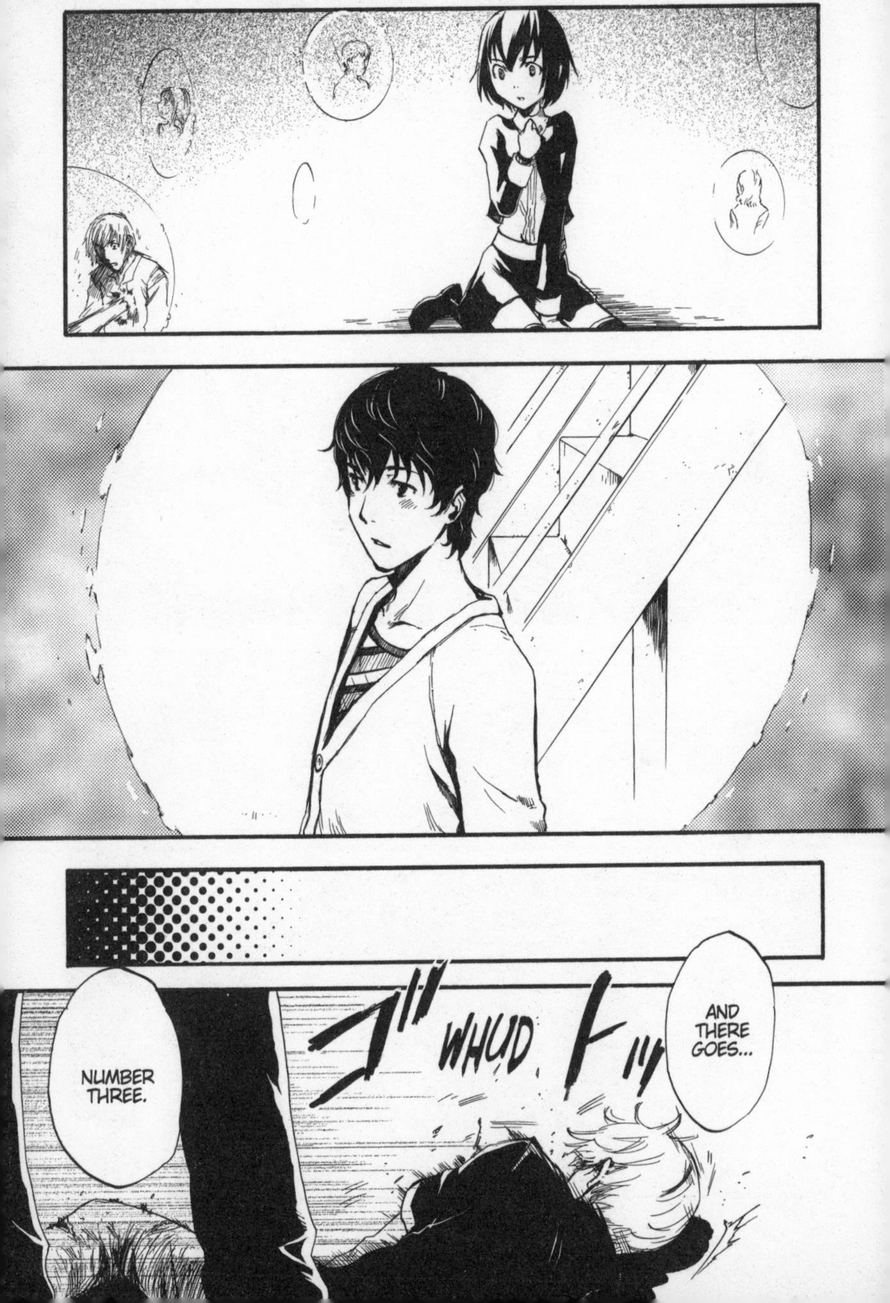
AND THERE GOES...
WHUD
NUMBER THREE.

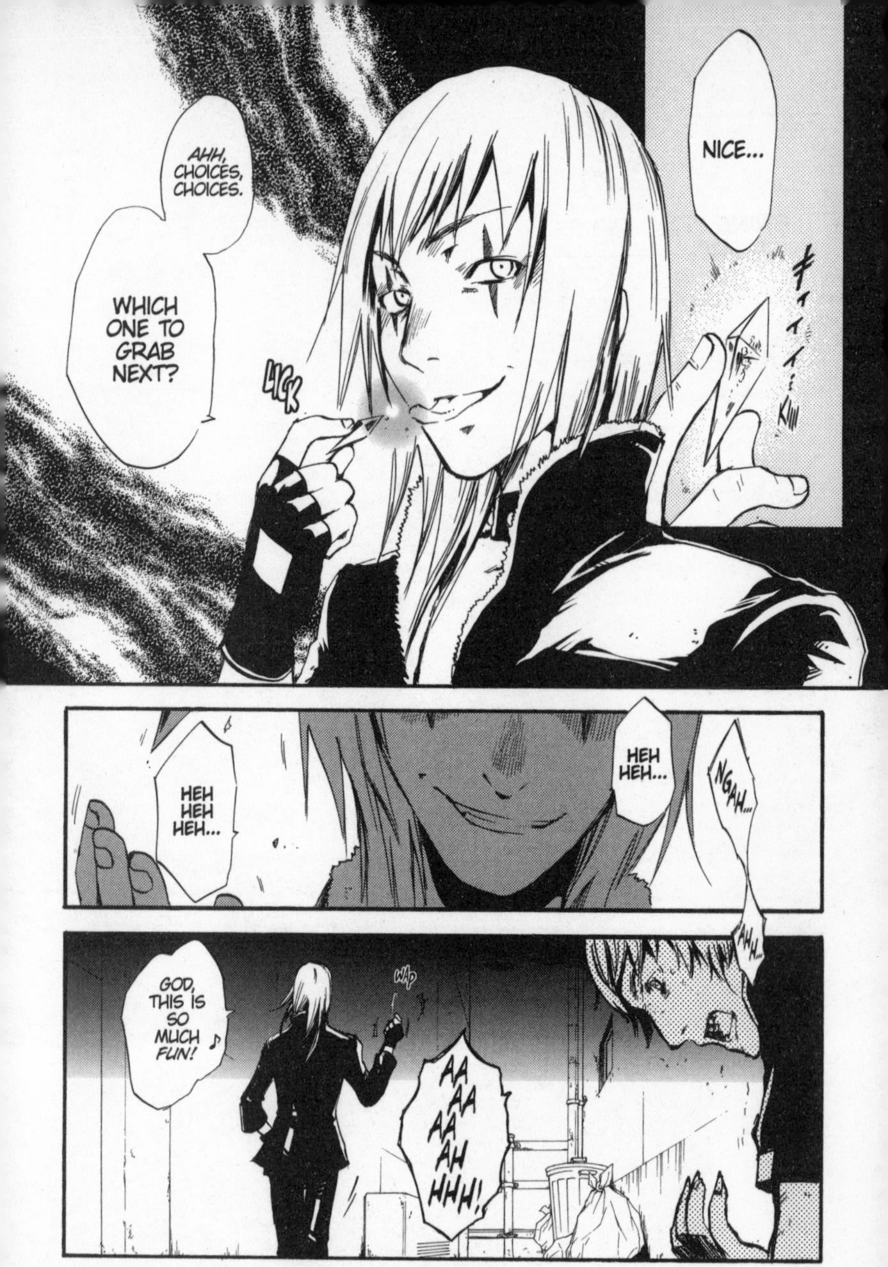
NICE...
KIIII
LICK
AHH, CHOICES, CHOICES.
WHICH ONE TO GRAB NEXT?
NGAH...
HEH HEH...
HEH HEH HEH...
AHH...
AAAAAAAHHHH!
WAP
GOD, THIS IS SO MUCH FUN! ♪

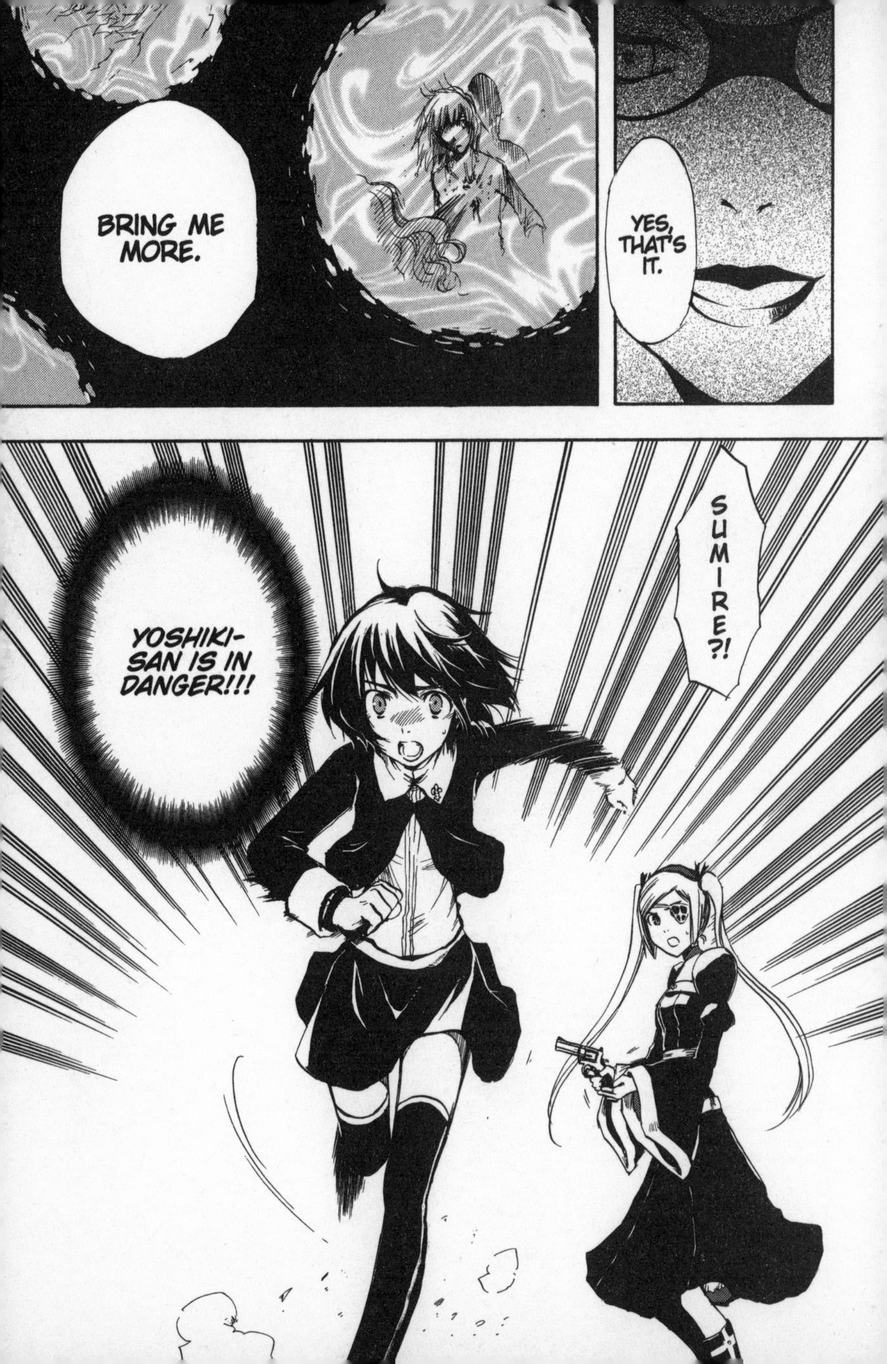
YES, THAT'S IT.
BRING ME MORE.
SUMIRE?!
YOSHIKI-SAN IS IN DANGER!!!

Jewelry
and
Clothes

Venus Vangard

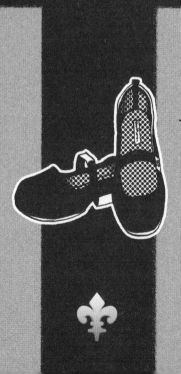

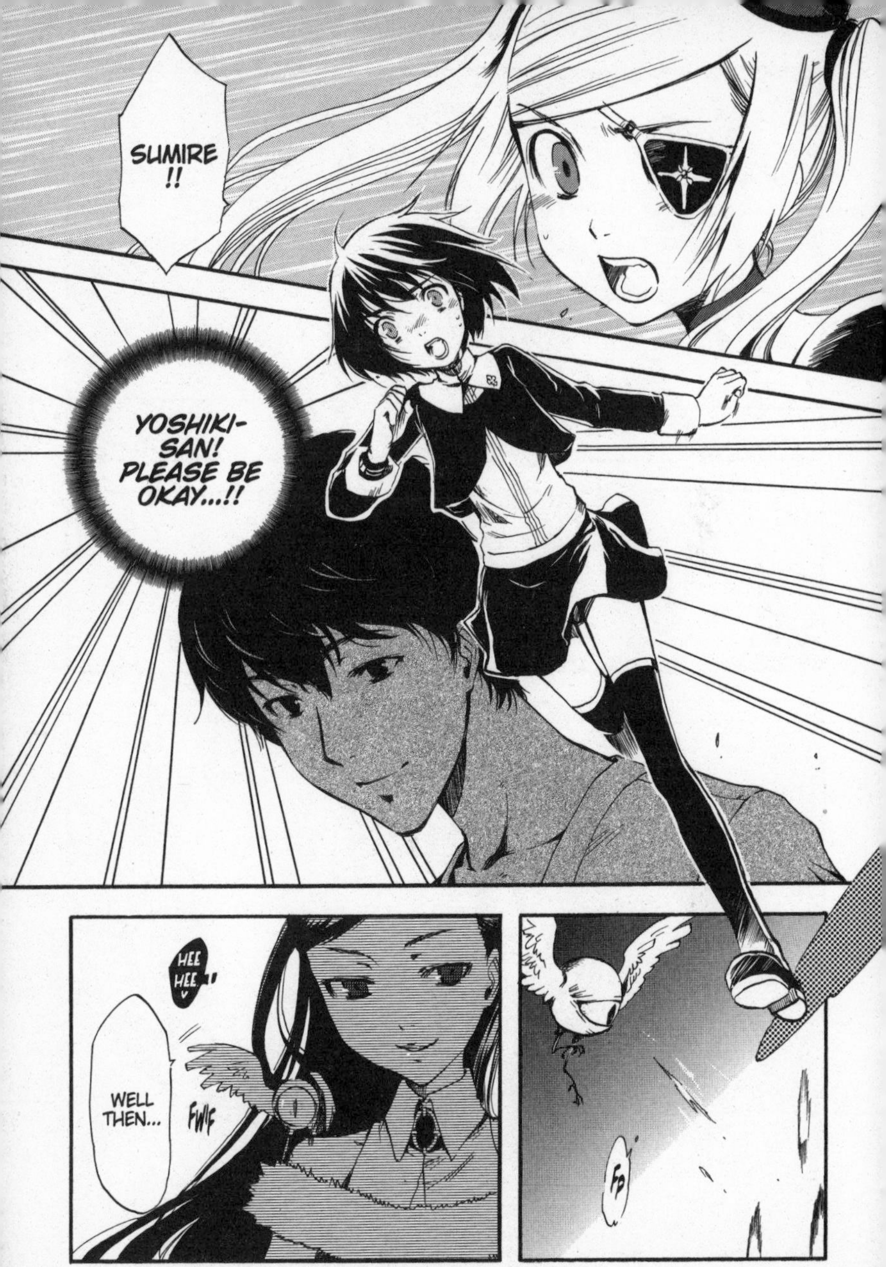
SUMIRE !!
YOSHIKI-SAN! PLEASE BE OKAY...!!
Fp
HEE HEE..!
WELL THEN...
FWIF

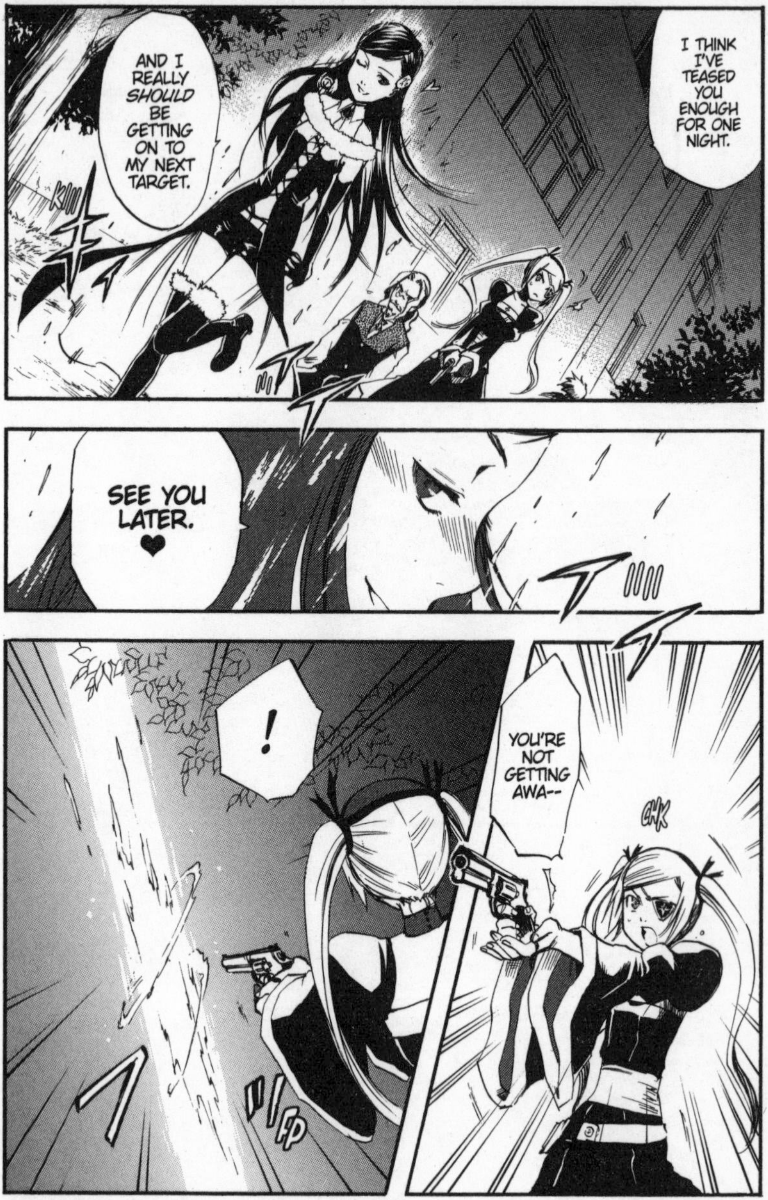
I THINK I'VE TEASED YOU ENOUGH FOR ONE NIGHT.
AND I REALLY SHOULD BE GETTING ON TO MY NEXT TARGET.
SEE YOU LATER. ❤
YOU'RE NOT GETTING AWA--
CHK
!

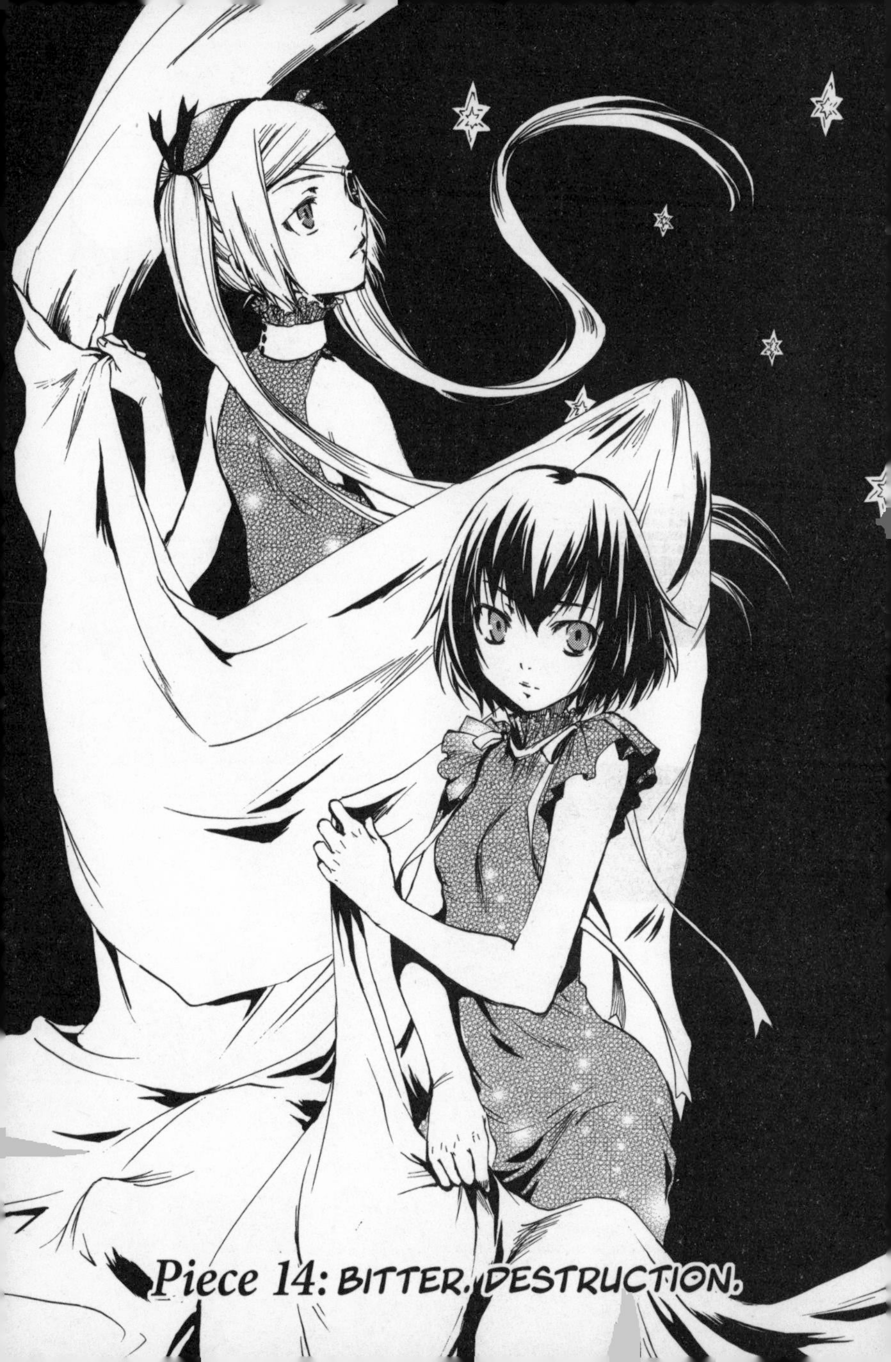
Piece 14: BITTER. DESTRUCTION.

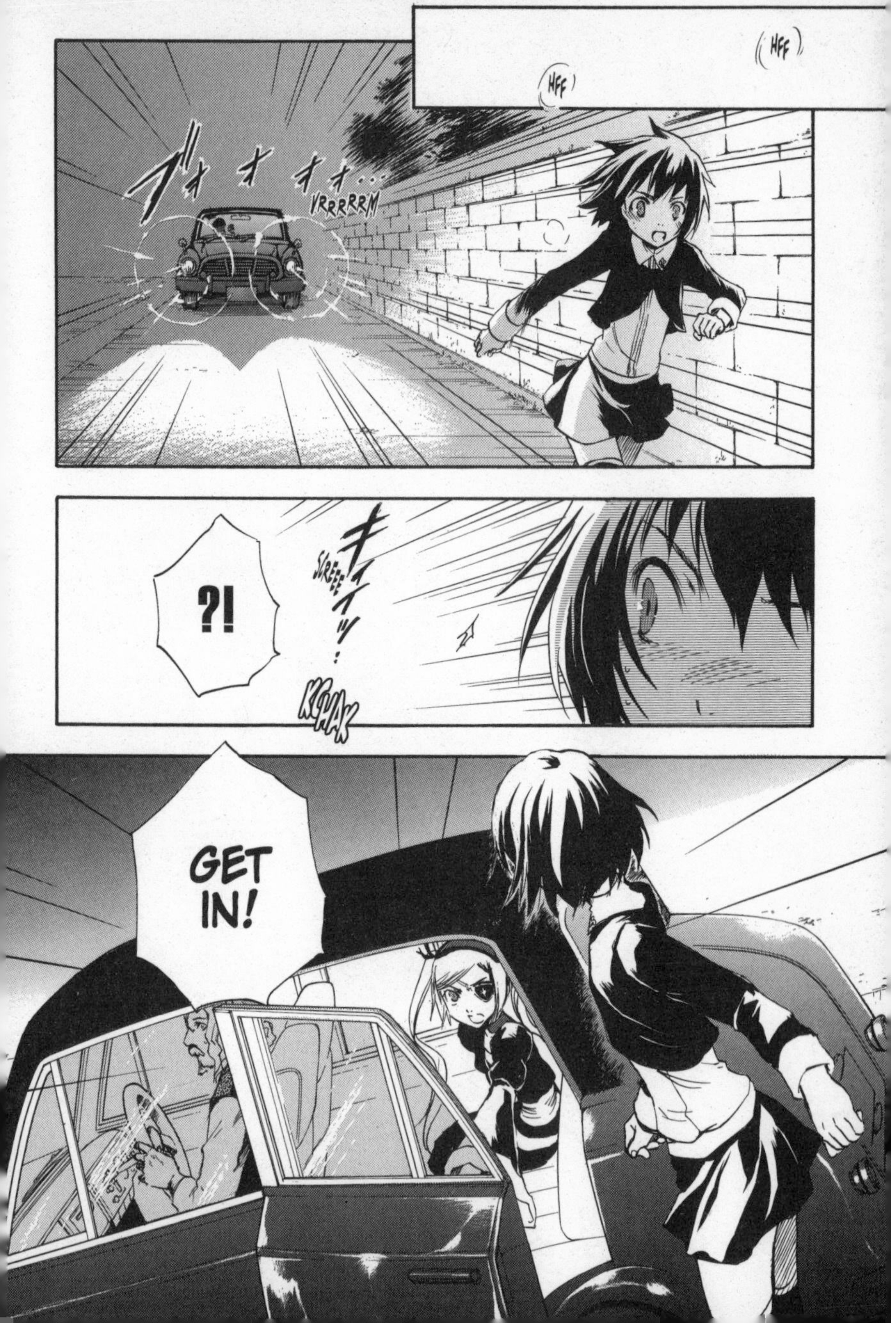
HFF
HFF
ブォォォォ…
VRRRRRM
?!
キィイッ!
SCREEE
KCHAK
GET IN!

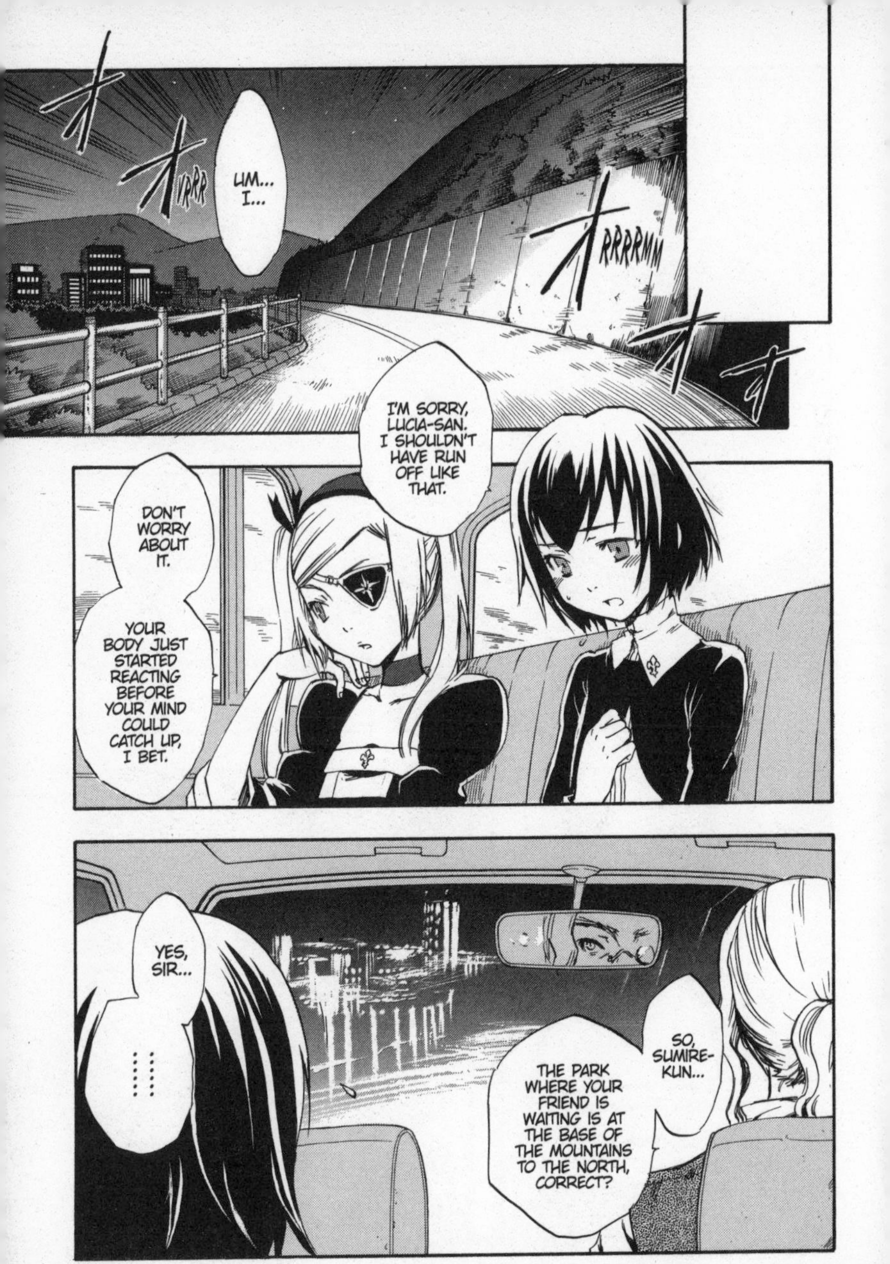
RRRRMM
VRRR
UM... I...
I'M SORRY, LUCIA-SAN. I SHOULDN'T HAVE RUN OFF LIKE THAT.
DON'T WORRY ABOUT IT.
YOUR BODY JUST STARTED REACTING BEFORE YOUR MIND COULD CATCH UP, I BET.
SO, SUMIRE-KUN...
THE PARK WHERE YOUR FRIEND IS WAITING IS AT THE BASE OF THE MOUNTAINS TO THE NORTH, CORRECT?
YES, SIR...
......

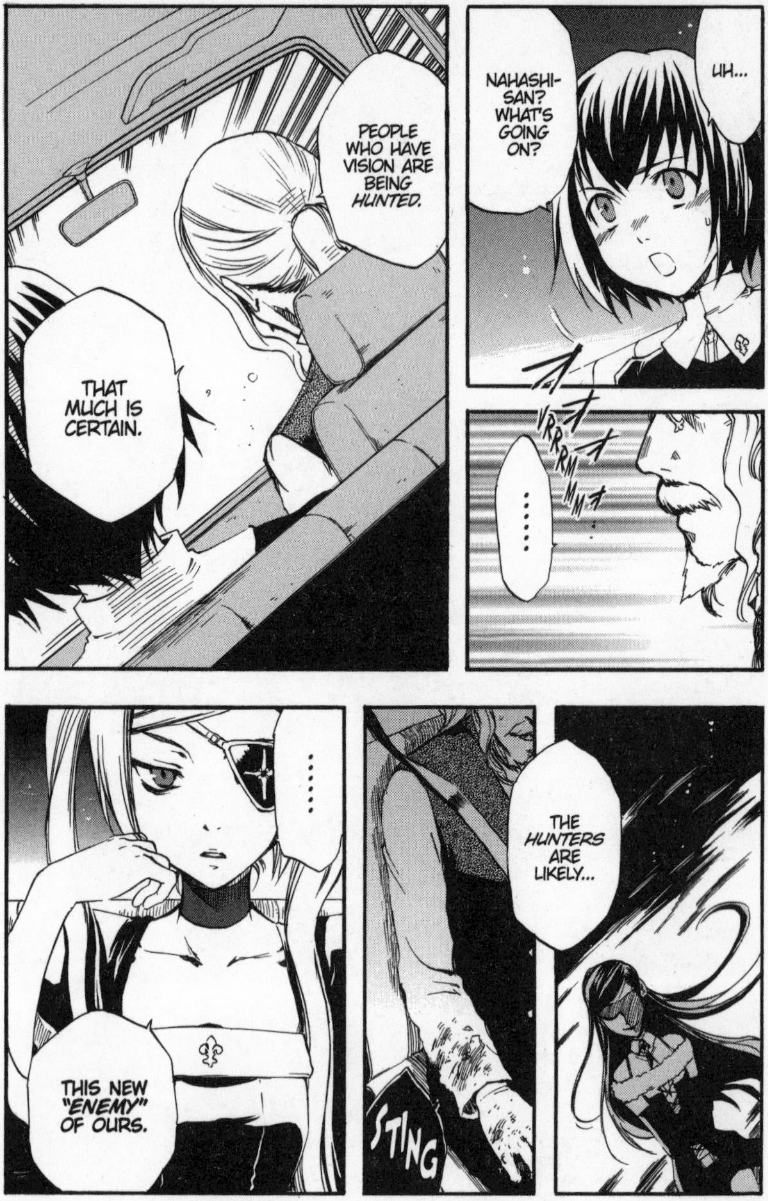
UH...
NAHASHI-SAN? WHAT'S GOING ON?
VRRRMMM
......
PEOPLE WHO HAVE VISION ARE BEING *HUNTED.*
THAT MUCH IS CERTAIN.
THE *HUNTERS* ARE LIKELY...
STING
......
THIS NEW *"ENEMY"* OF OURS.

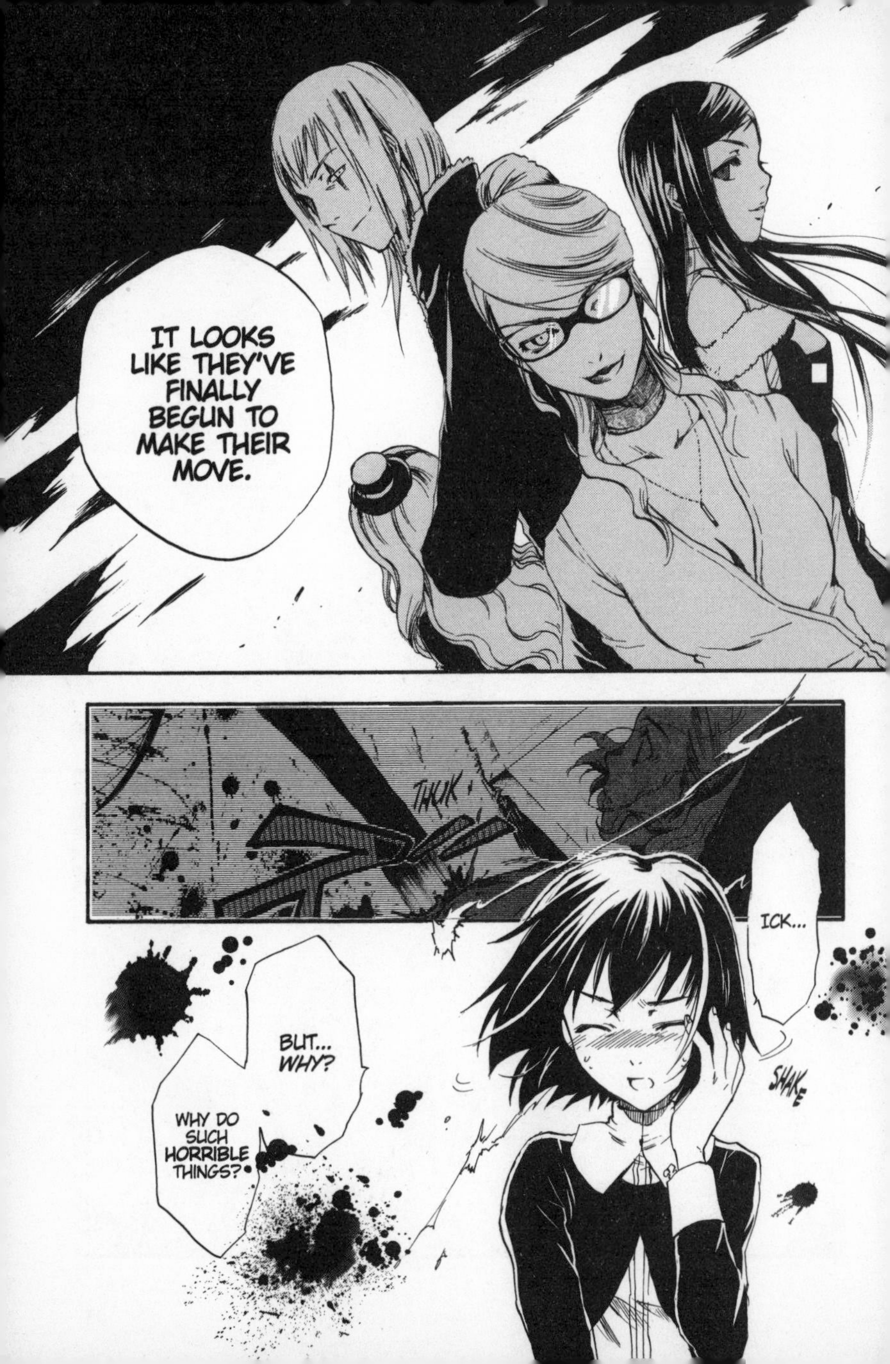
IT LOOKS LIKE THEY'VE FINALLY BEGUN TO MAKE THEIR MOVE.
THUK
ICK...
SHAKE
BUT... WHY?
WHY DO SUCH HORRIBLE THINGS?

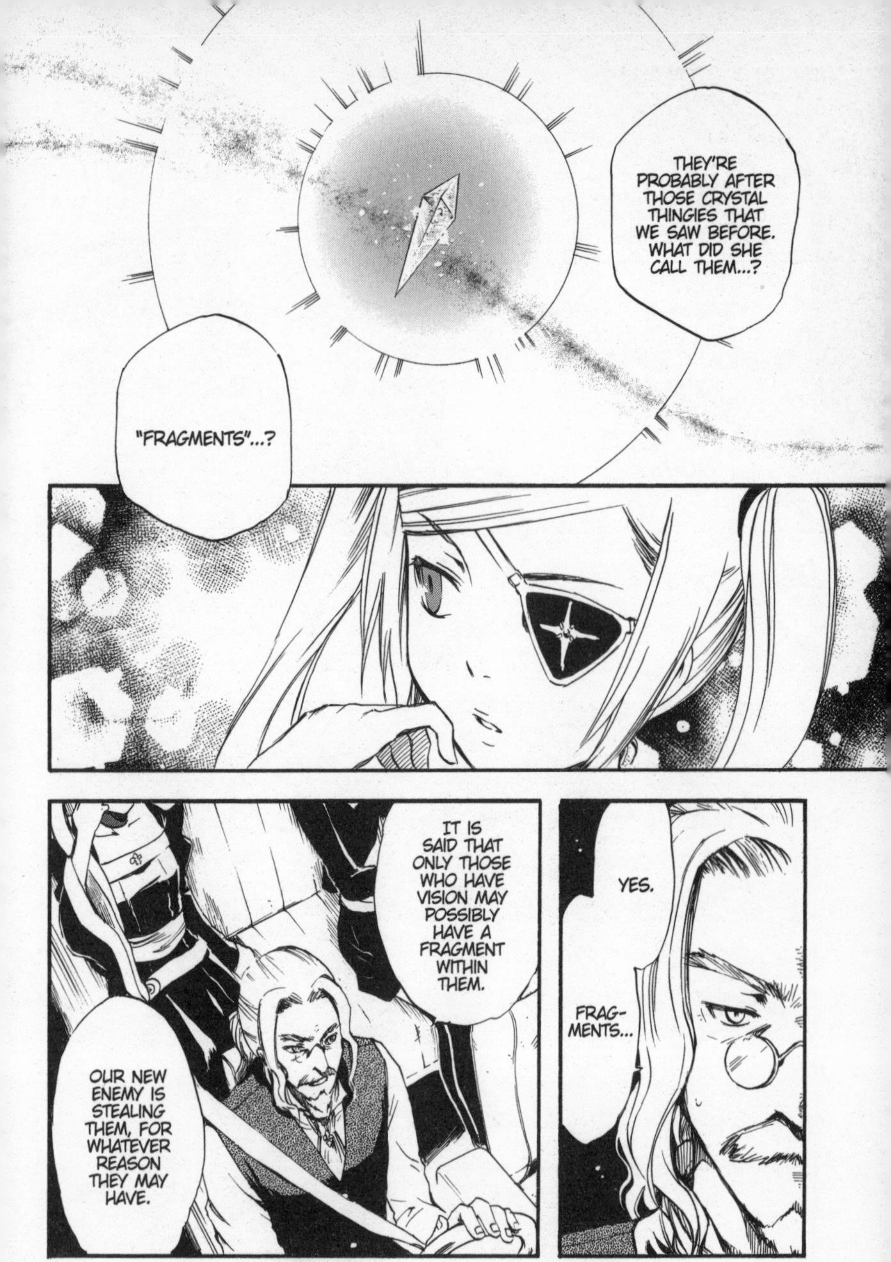
THEY'RE PROBABLY AFTER THOSE CRYSTAL THINGIES THAT WE SAW BEFORE. WHAT DID SHE CALL THEM...?
"FRAGMENTS"...?
YES.
FRAG-MENTS...
IT IS SAID THAT ONLY THOSE WHO HAVE VISION MAY POSSIBLY HAVE A FRAGMENT WITHIN THEM.
OUR NEW ENEMY IS STEALING THEM, FOR WHATEVER REASON THEY MAY HAVE.

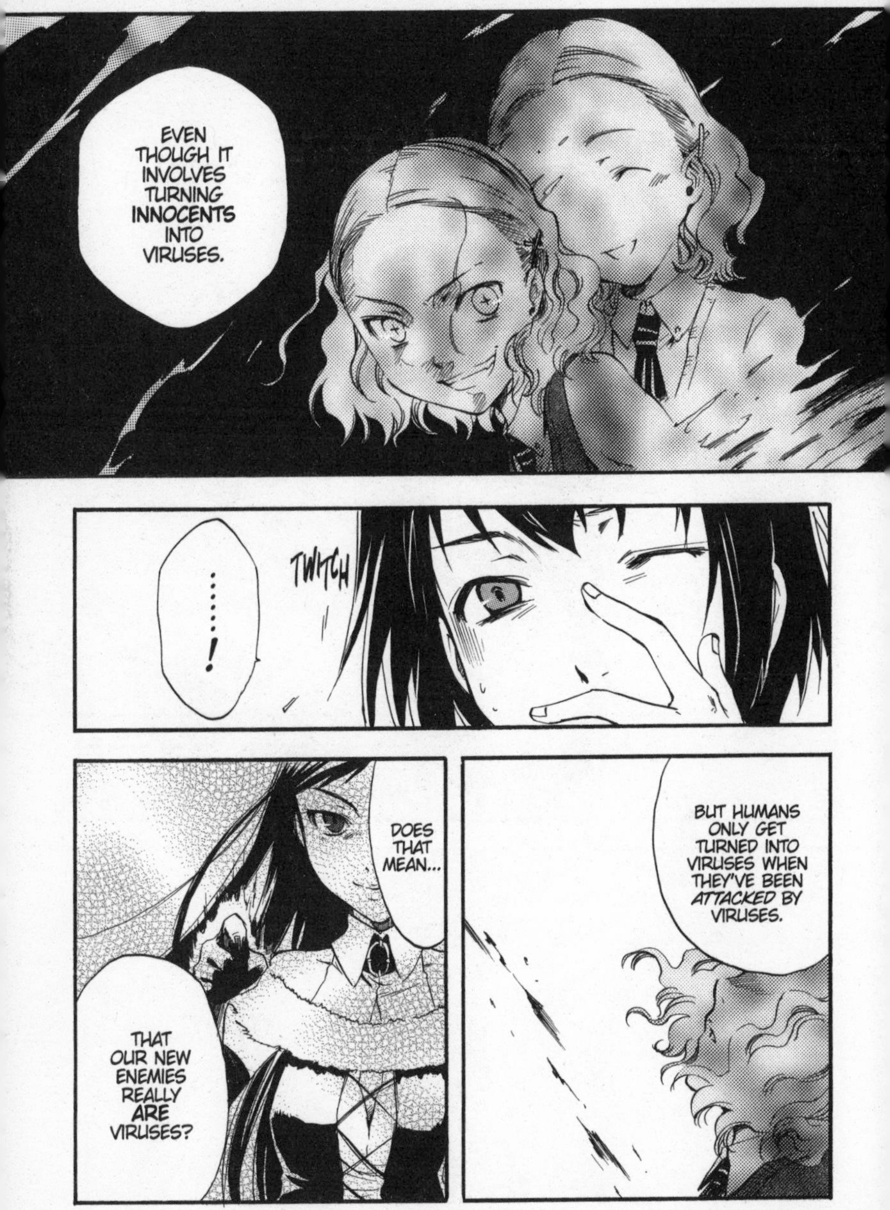
EVEN THOUGH IT INVOLVES TURNING INNOCENTS INTO VIRUSES.
TWITCH
......!
BUT HUMANS ONLY GET TURNED INTO VIRUSES WHEN THEY'VE BEEN *ATTACKED* BY VIRUSES.
DOES THAT MEAN...
THAT OUR NEW ENEMIES REALLY **ARE** VIRUSES?

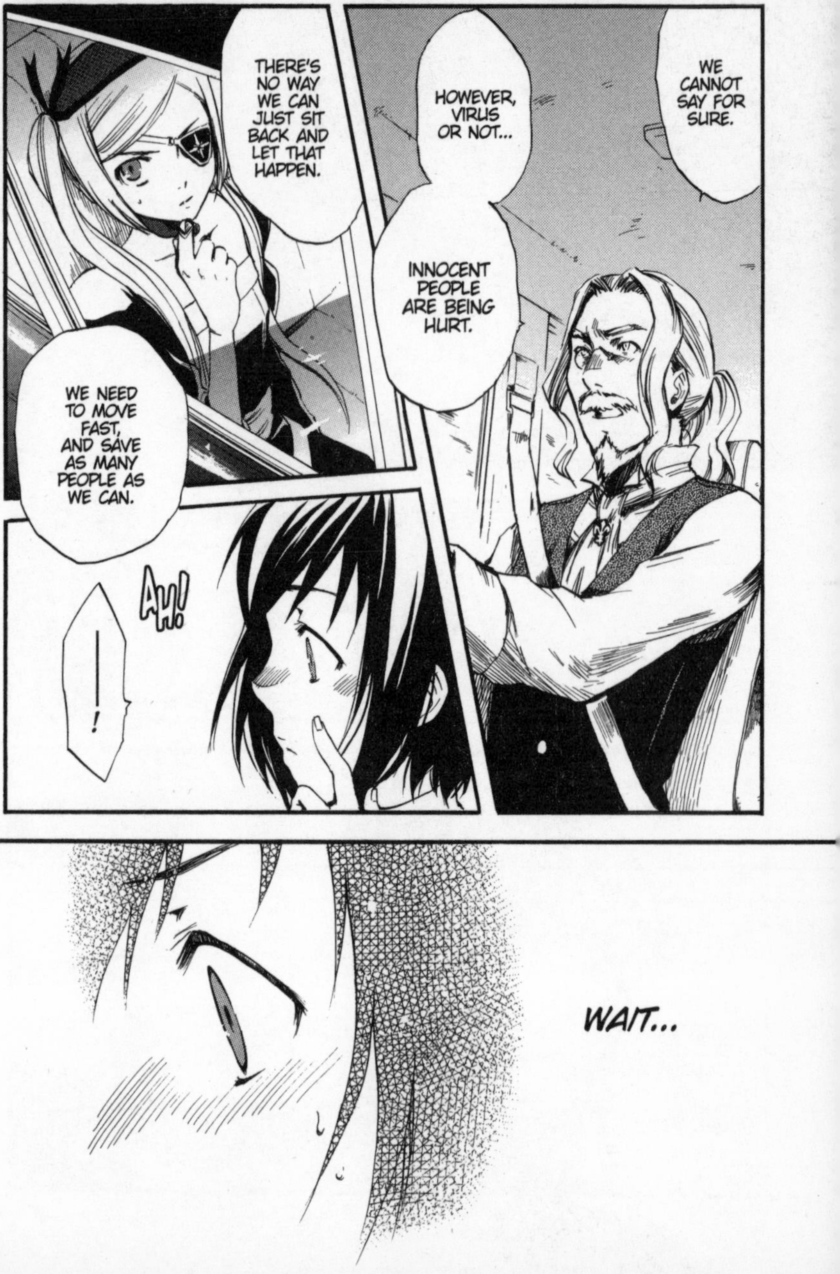
WE CANNOT SAY FOR SURE.
HOWEVER, VIRUS OR NOT...
INNOCENT PEOPLE ARE BEING HURT.
THERE'S NO WAY WE CAN JUST SIT BACK AND LET THAT HAPPEN.
WE NEED TO MOVE FAST, AND SAVE AS MANY PEOPLE AS WE CAN.
AH!
—!
WAIT...

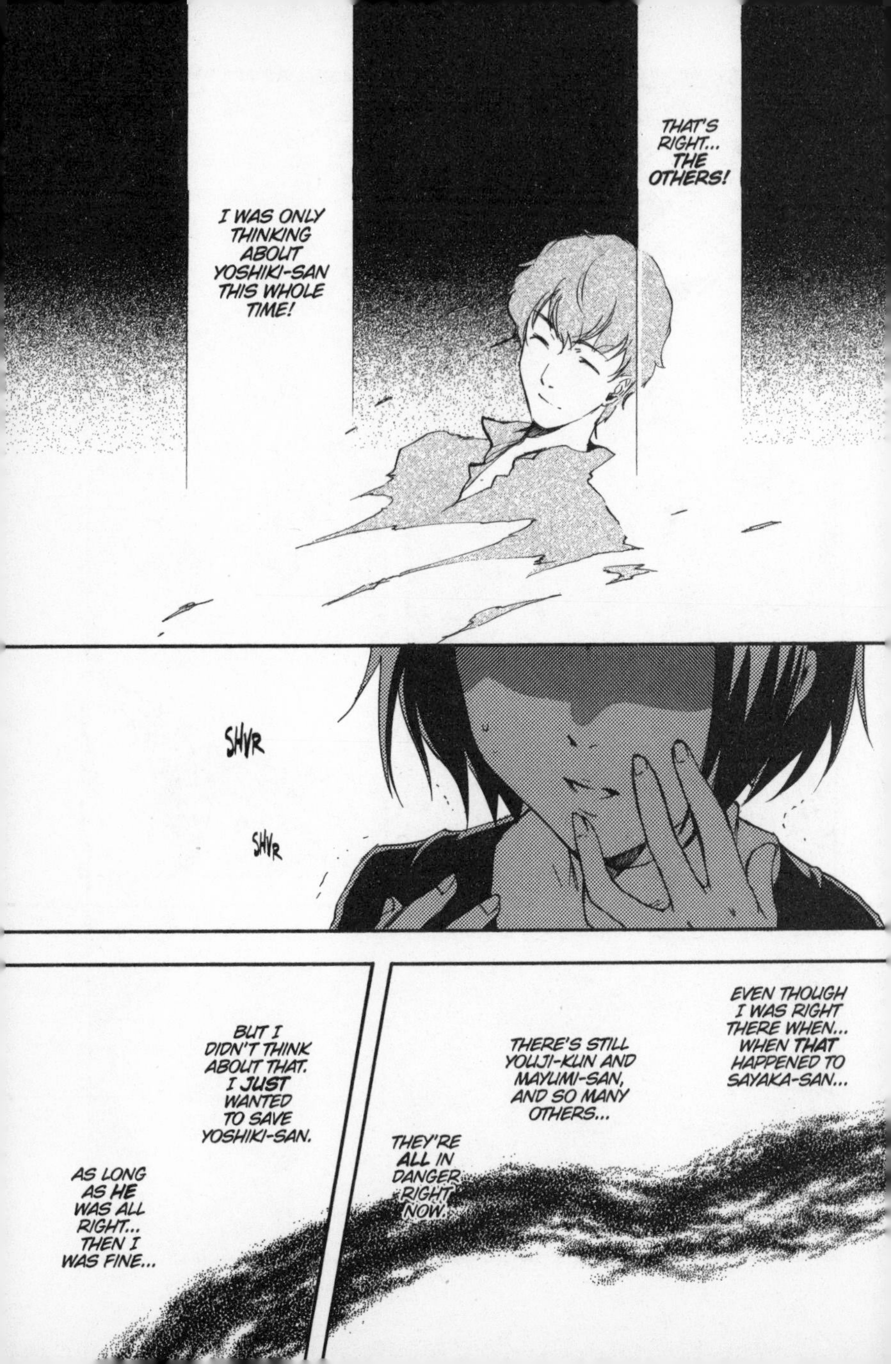
THAT'S RIGHT... THE OTHERS!
I WAS ONLY THINKING ABOUT YOSHIKI-SAN THIS WHOLE TIME!
SHVR
SHVR
EVEN THOUGH I WAS RIGHT THERE WHEN... WHEN THAT HAPPENED TO SAYAKA-SAN...
THERE'S STILL YOUJI-KUN AND MAYUMI-SAN, AND SO MANY OTHERS...
THEY'RE ALL IN DANGER RIGHT NOW.
BUT I DIDN'T THINK ABOUT THAT. I JUST WANTED TO SAVE YOSHIKI-SAN.
AS LONG AS HE WAS ALL RIGHT... THEN I WAS FINE...

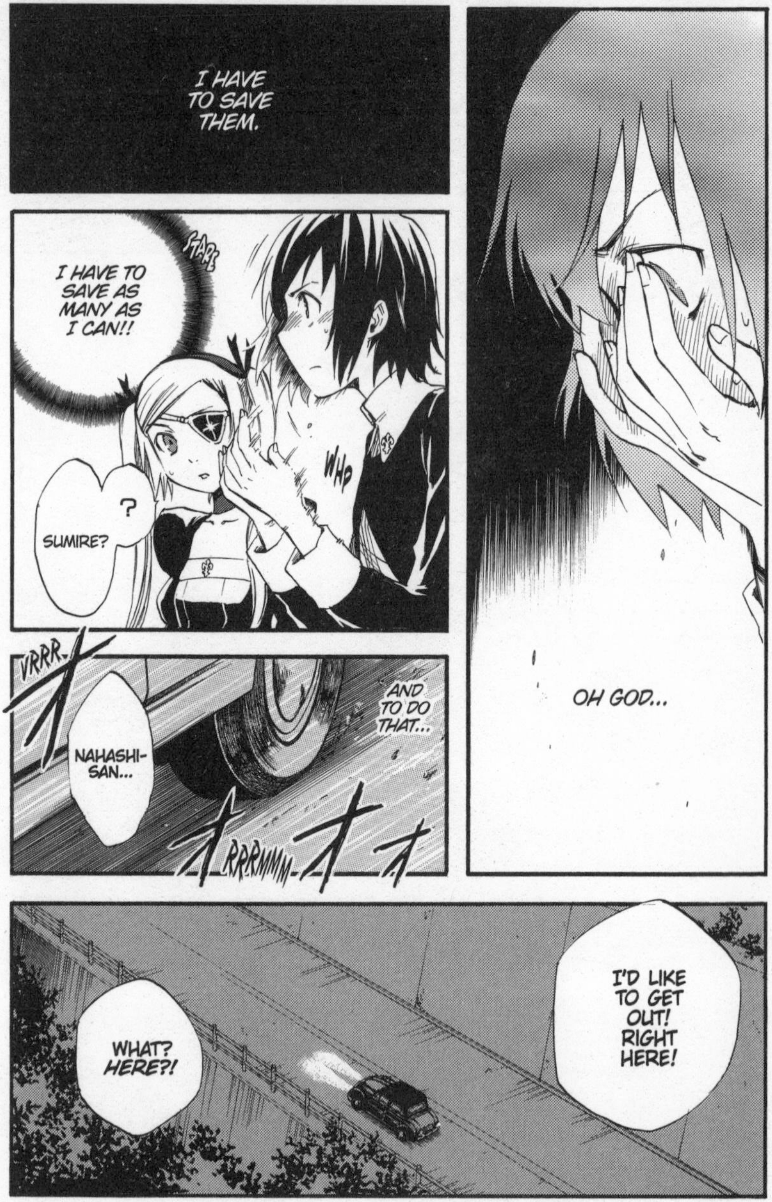
OH GOD...
I HAVE TO SAVE THEM.
STARE
I HAVE TO SAVE AS MANY AS I CAN!!
WHP
?
SUMIRE?
AND TO DO THAT...
NAHASHI-SAN...
VRRR
RRRMMM
I'D LIKE TO GET OUT! RIGHT HERE!
WHAT? HERE?!

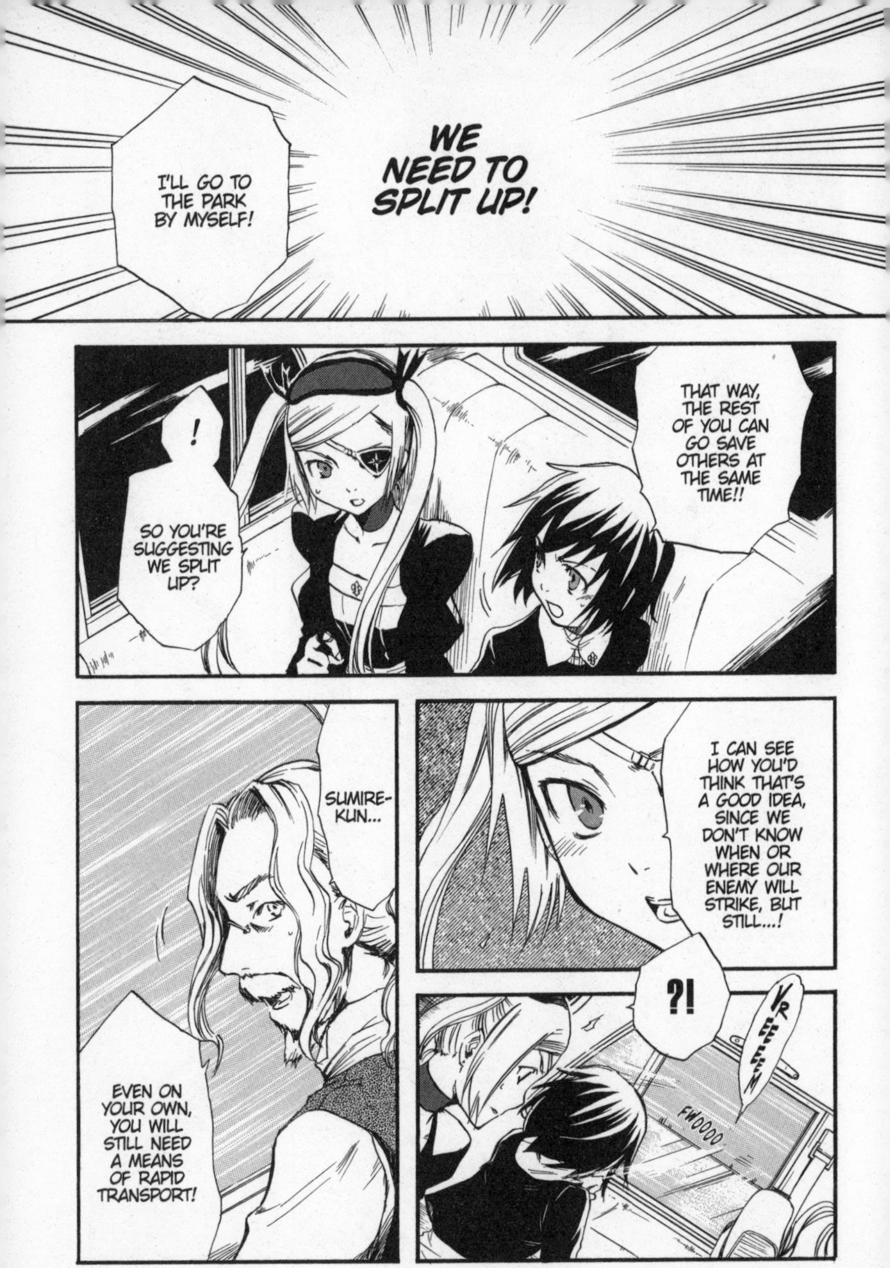
WE NEED TO SPLIT UP!
I'LL GO TO THE PARK BY MYSELF!
THAT WAY, THE REST OF YOU CAN GO SAVE OTHERS AT THE SAME TIME!!
!
SO YOU'RE SUGGESTING WE SPLIT UP?
I CAN SEE HOW YOU'D THINK THAT'S A GOOD IDEA, SINCE WE DON'T KNOW WHEN OR WHERE OUR ENEMY WILL STRIKE, BUT STILL...!
?!
VREEEEEM
FWOOOO
SUMIRE-KUN...
EVEN ON YOUR OWN, YOU WILL STILL NEED A MEANS OF RAPID TRANSPORT!

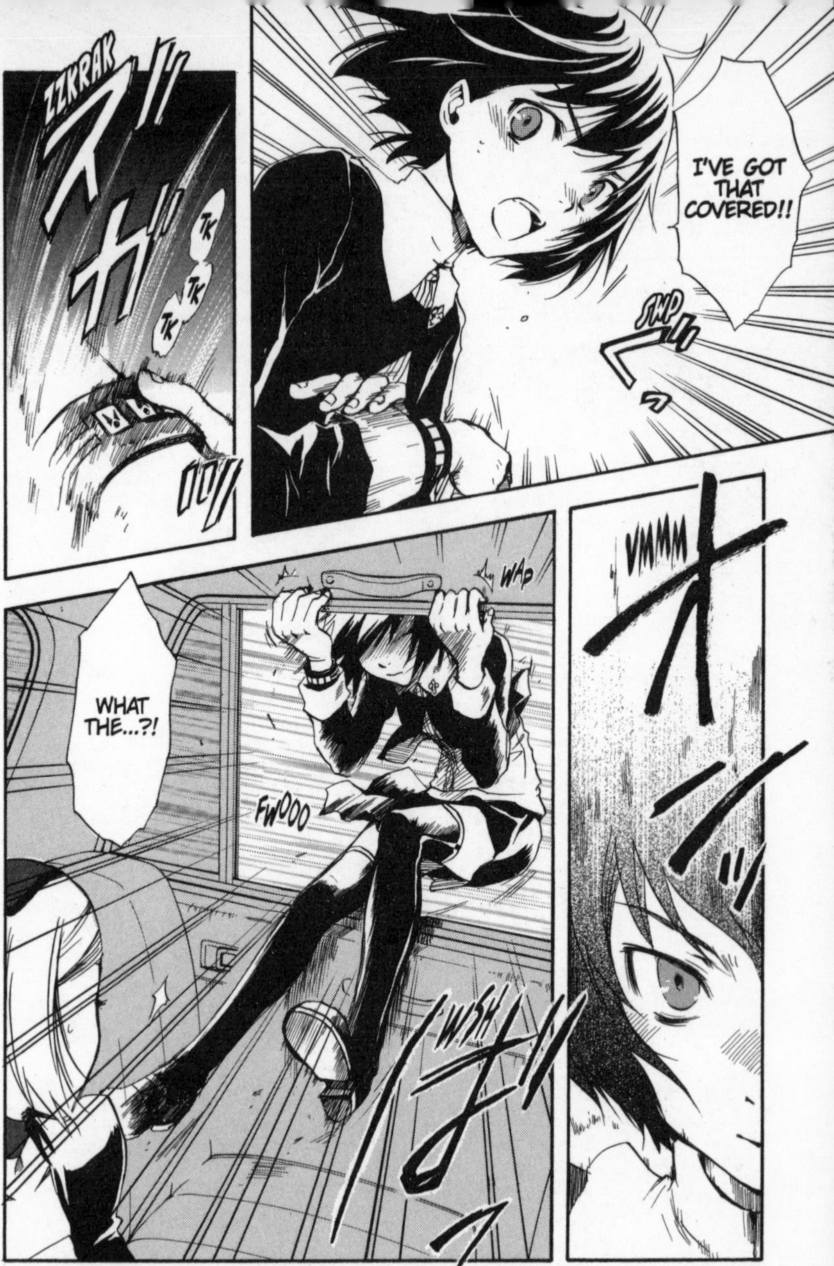
I'VE GOT THAT COVERED!!
SWP
ZZKRAK
TK TK TK TK
VMMM
WAP
WHAT THE...?!
FWOOO
FWISH

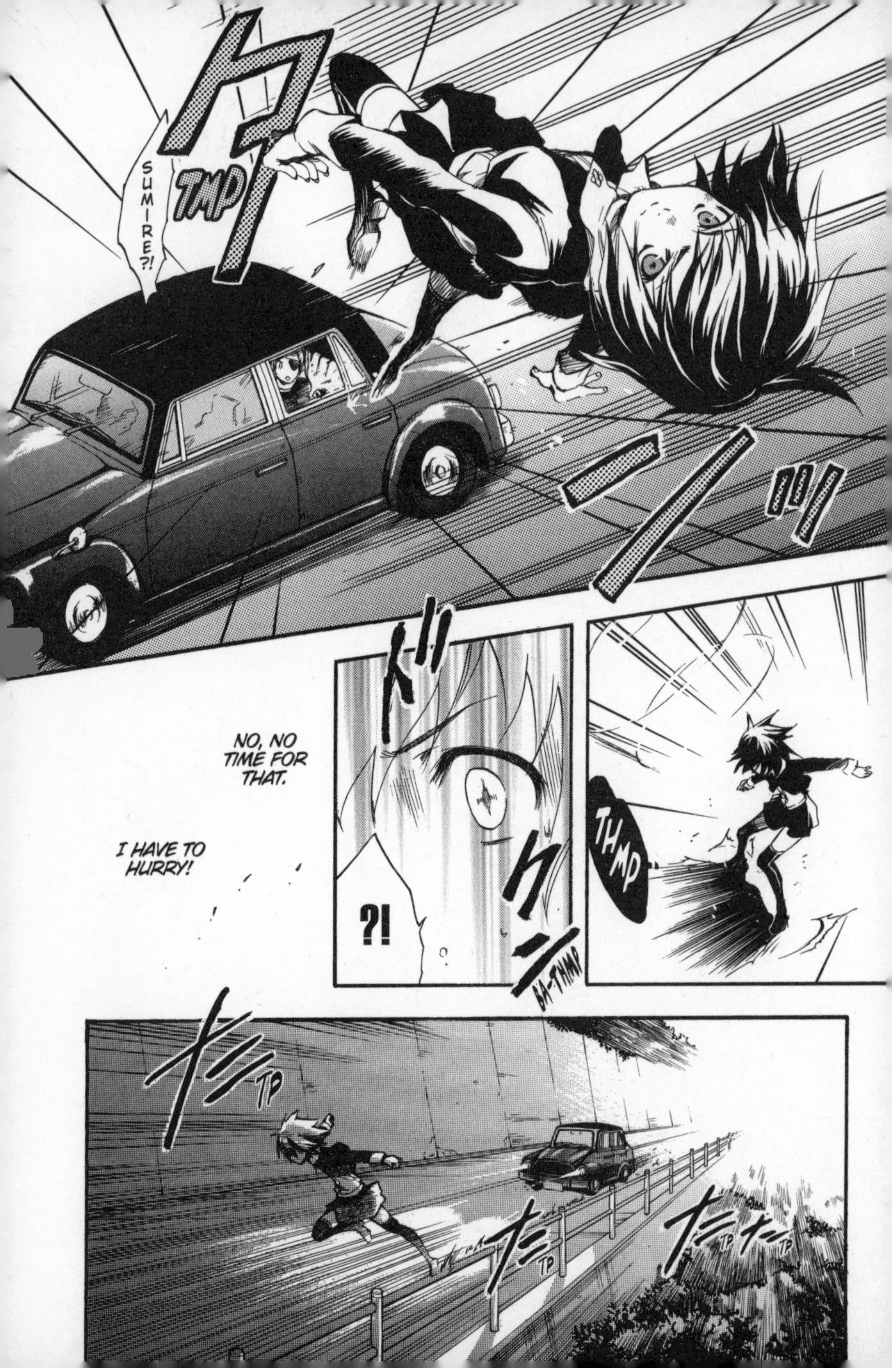
SUMIRE?!
TMP
THMP
?!
BA-THMP
NO, NO TIME FOR THAT.
I HAVE TO HURRY!
TP
TP
TP
TP

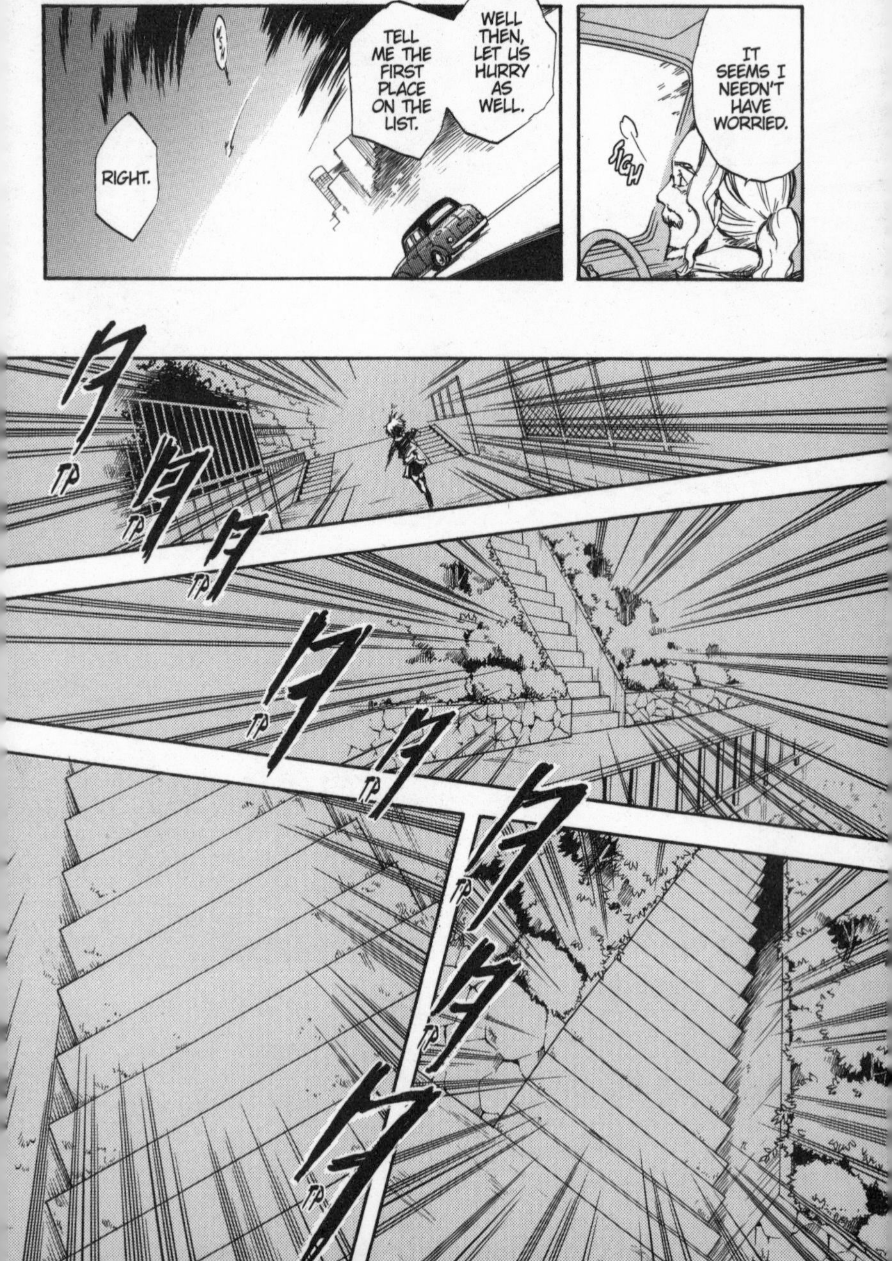
IT SEEMS I NEEDN'T HAVE WORRIED.
SIGH
WELL THEN, LET US HURRY AS WELL.
TELL ME THE FIRST PLACE ON THE LIST.
RIGHT.
TP
TP
TP
TP
TP
TP
TP
TP

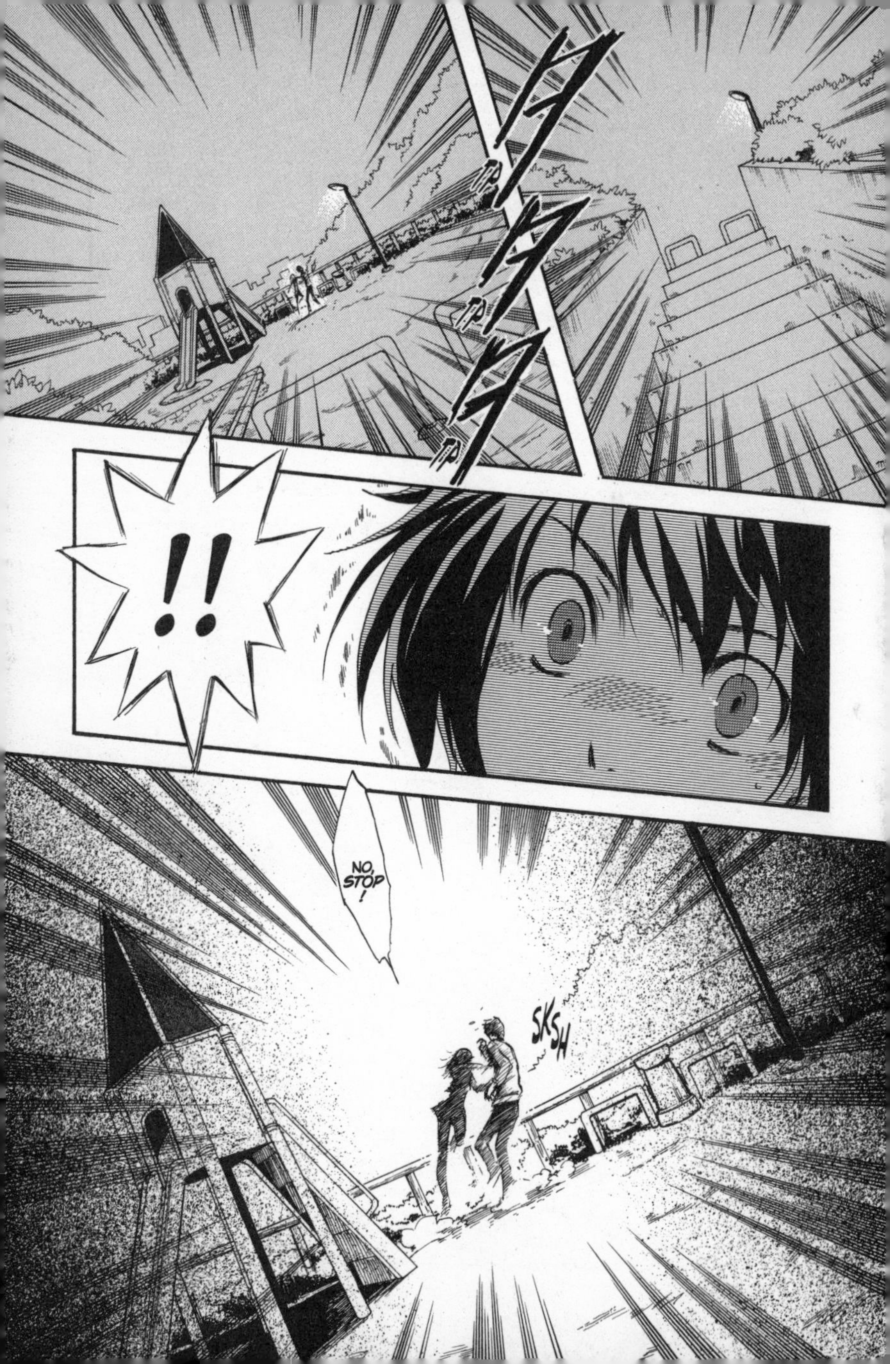
tp tp tp
!!
NO, STOP!
SKSH

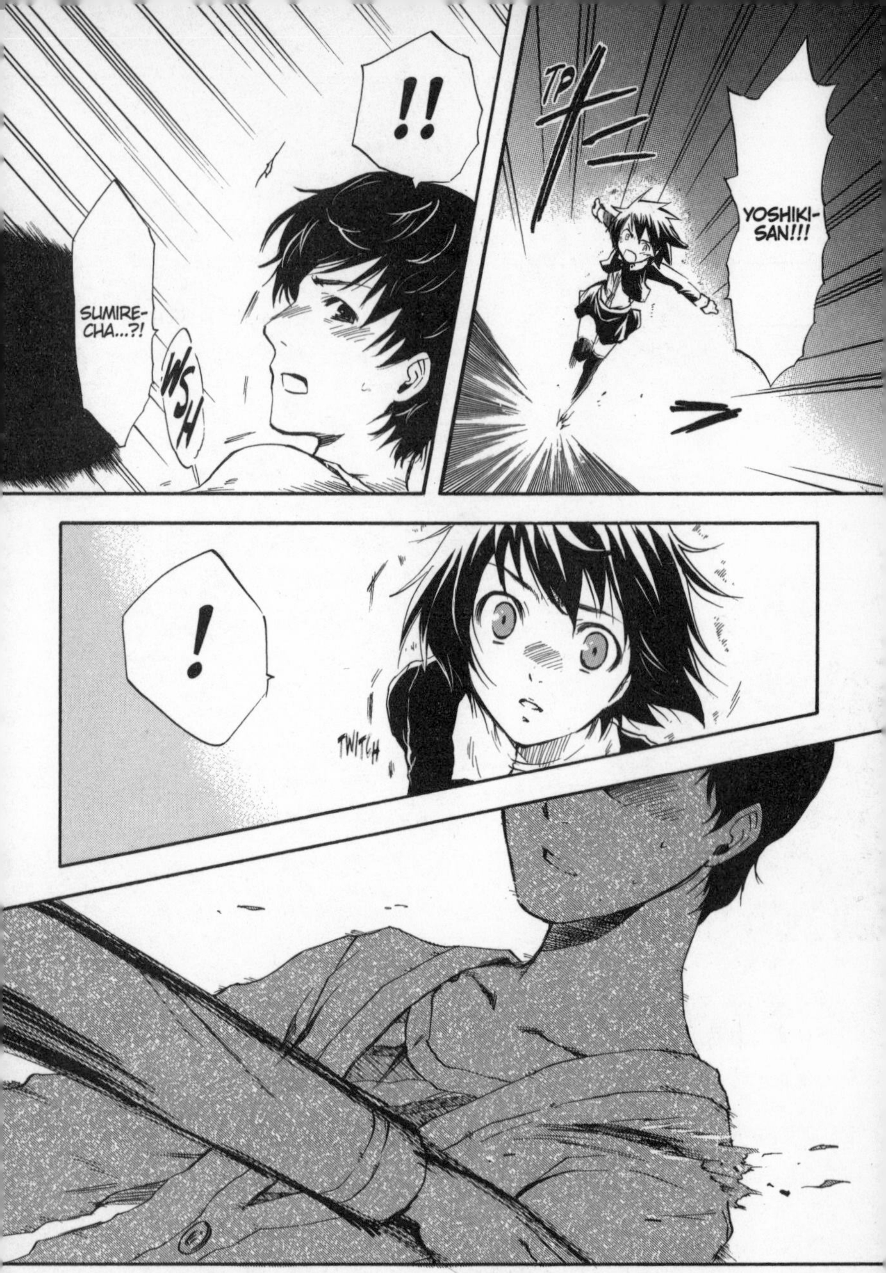
YOSHIKI-SAN!!!
TP
!!
SUMIRE-CHA...?!
WSH
!
TWITCH

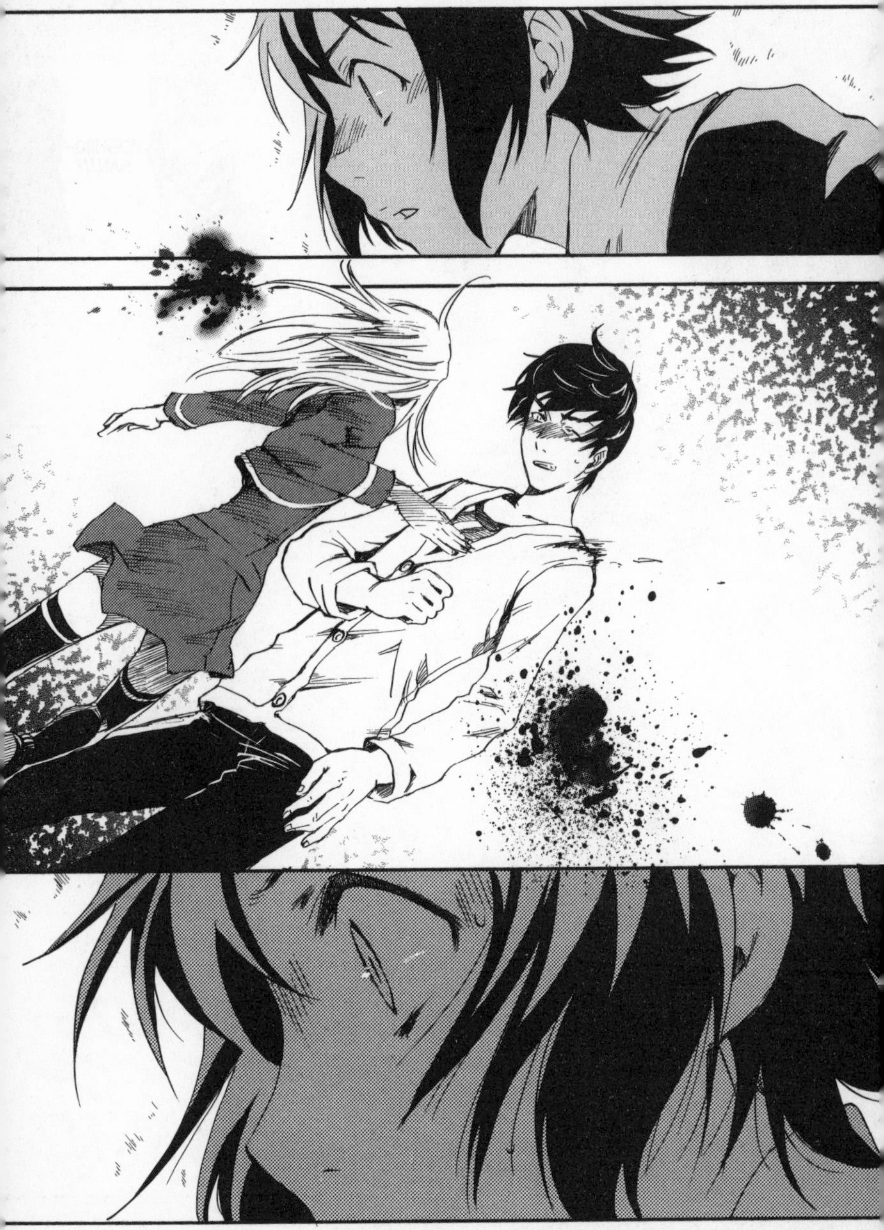

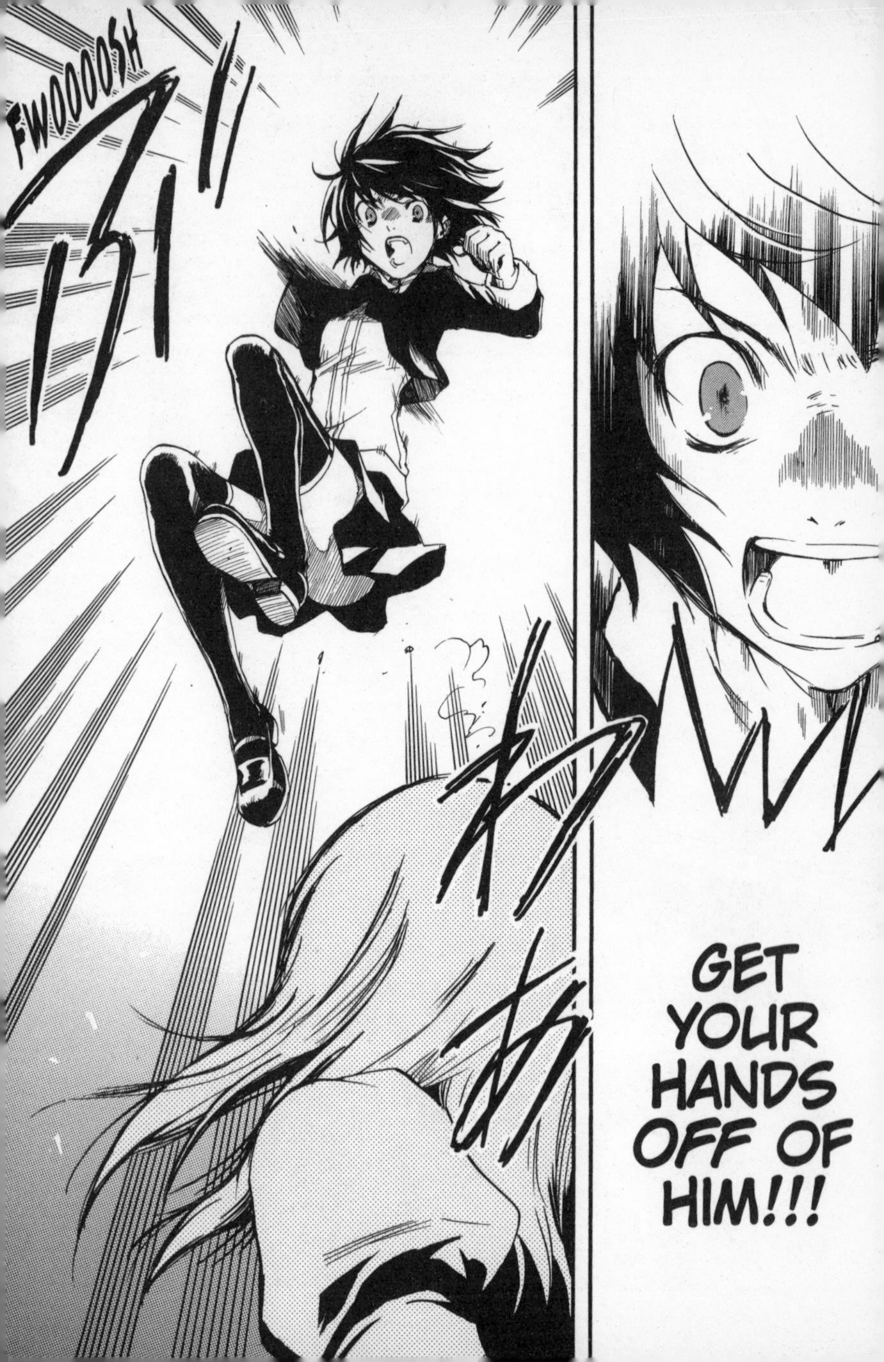
GET YOUR HANDS OFF OF HIM!!!
FWOOOOSH

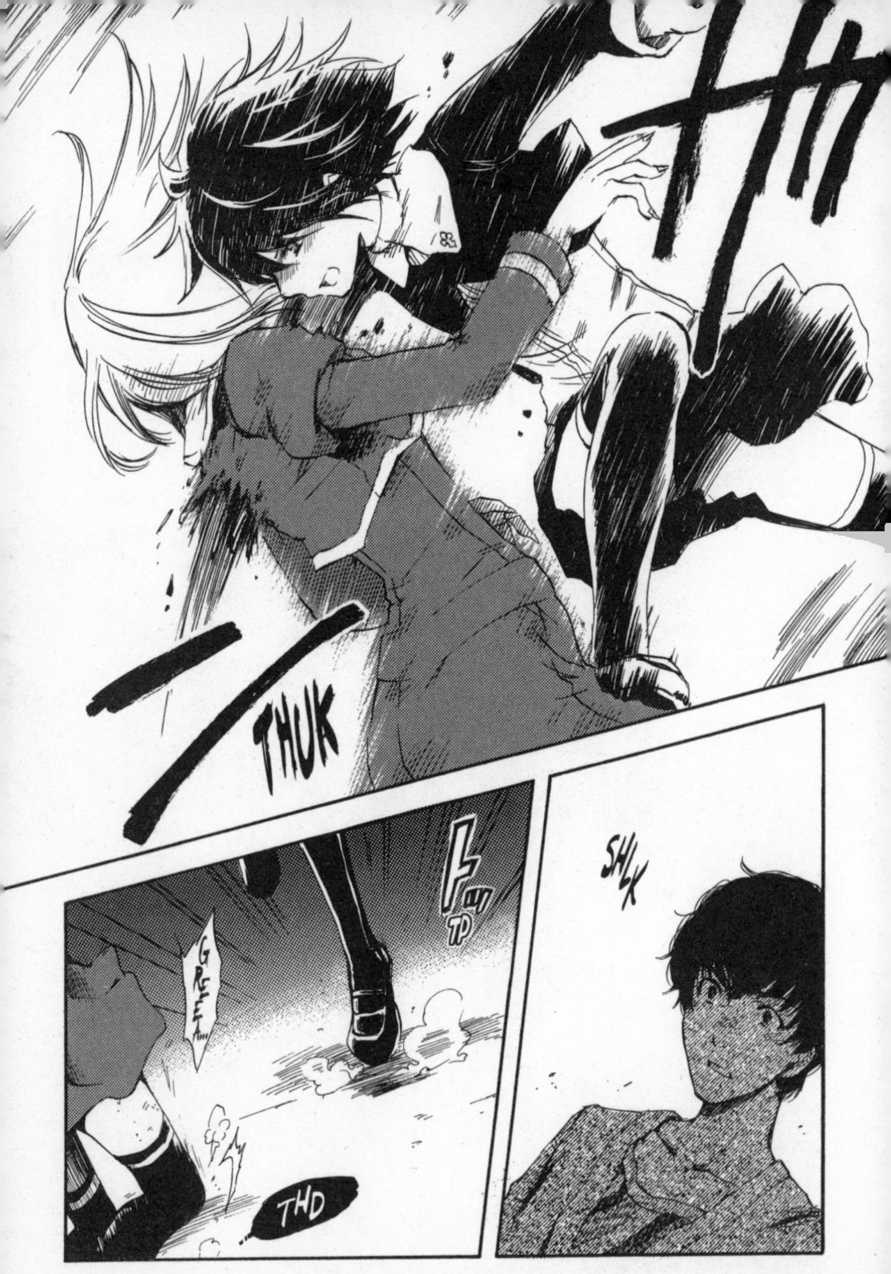
THUK
SHLK
TP
GREEEA...
THD

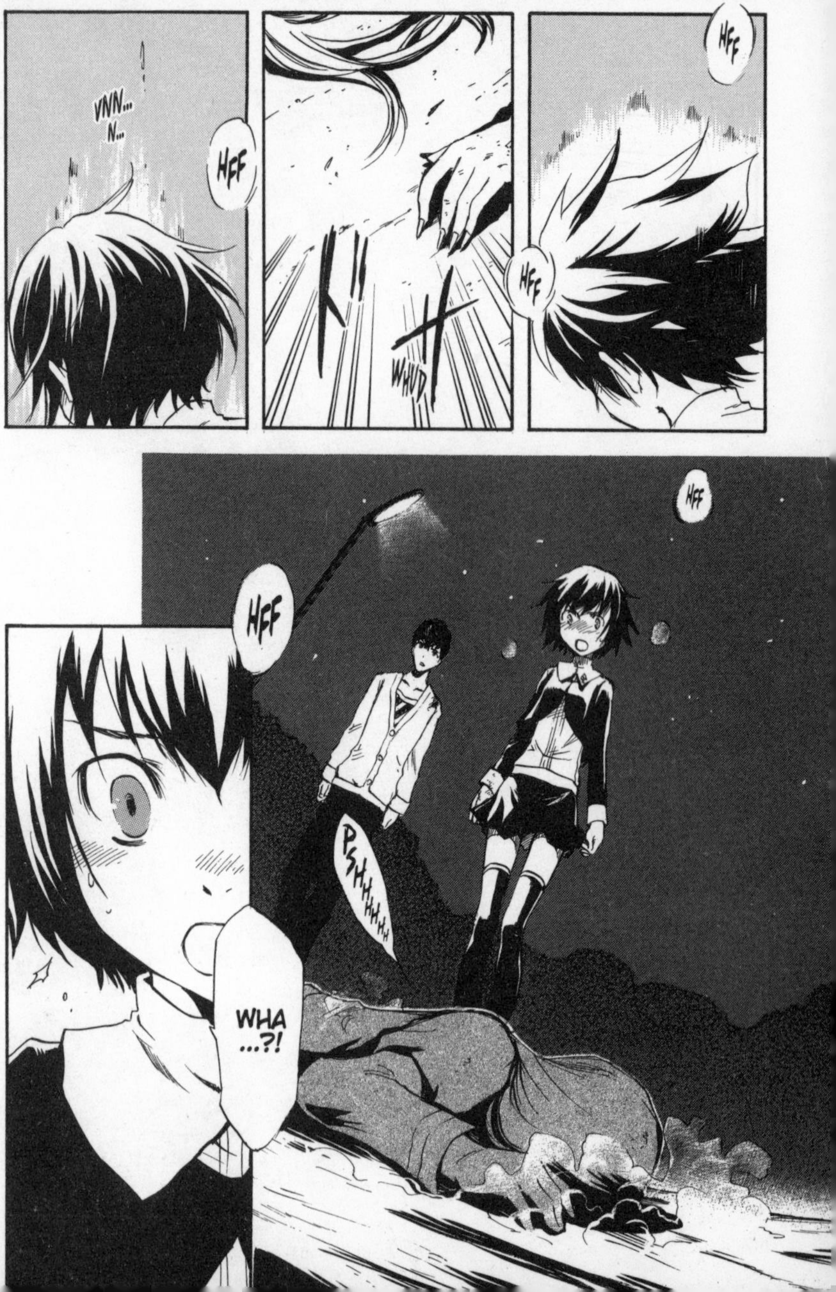
HFF
HFF
WHUD
VNN... N...
HFF
HFF
HFF
PSHHHHHH
WHA ...?!

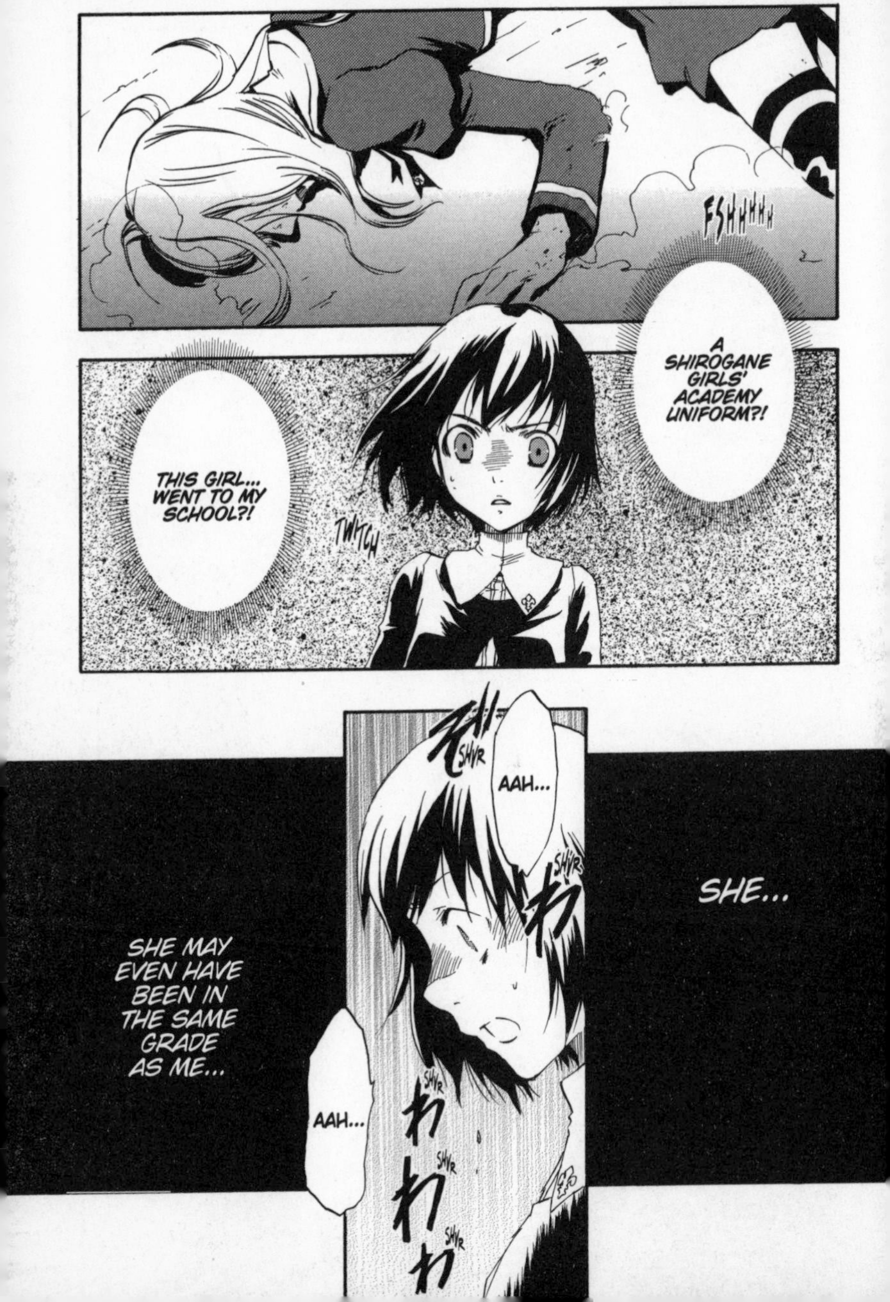
FSHHHHH
A SHIROGANE GIRLS' ACADEMY UNIFORM?!
TWITCH
THIS GIRL... WENT TO MY SCHOOL?!
SHE...
SHIVR
AAH...
SHIVR
SHE MAY EVEN HAVE BEEN IN THE SAME GRADE AS ME...
AAH...
SHIVR
SHIVR
SHIVR

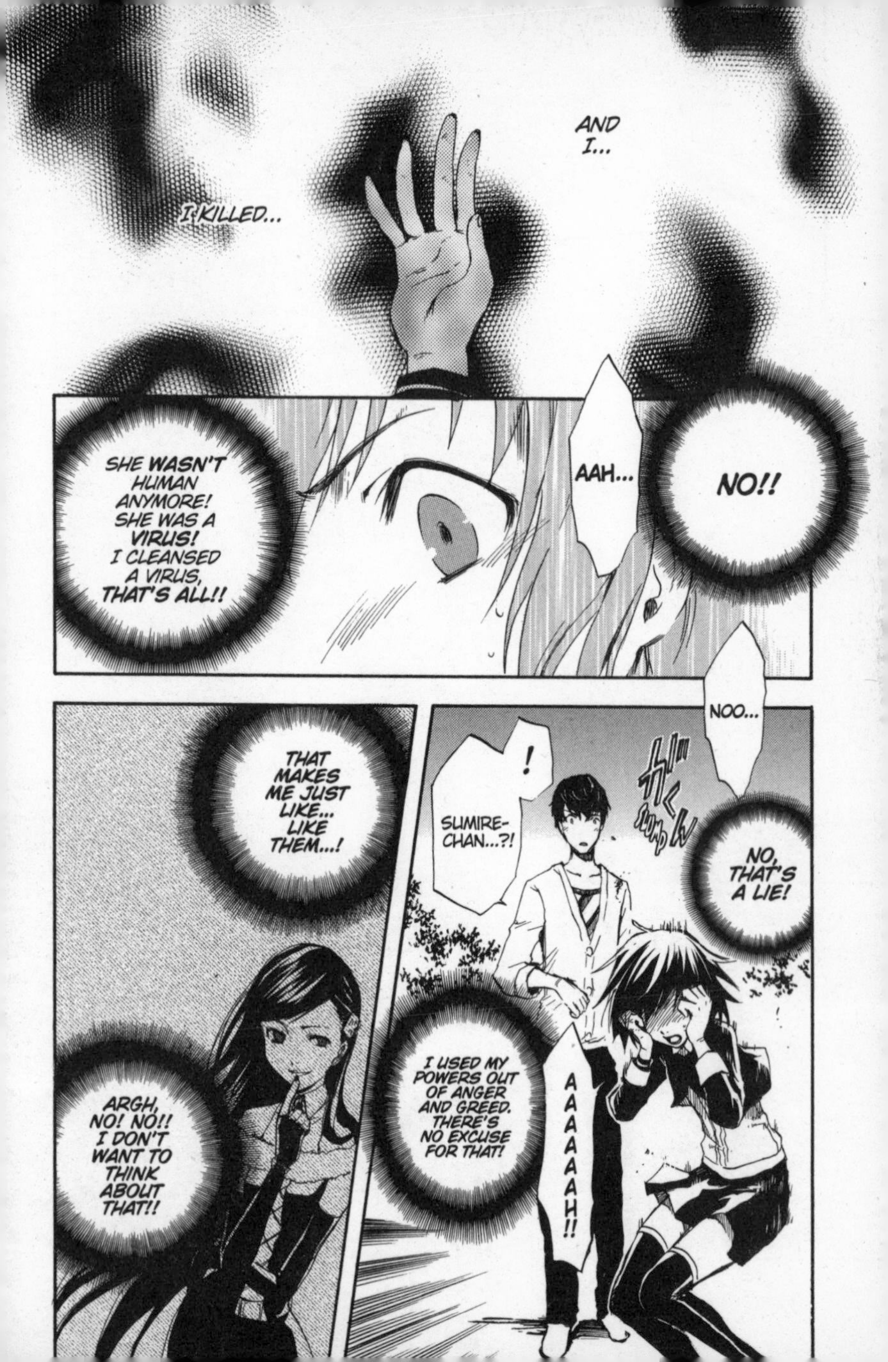
AND I...
I KILLED...
NO!!
AAH...
SHE WASN'T HUMAN ANYMORE! SHE WAS A VIRUS! I CLEANSED A VIRUS, THAT'S ALL!!
NOO...
!
SUMIRE-CHAN...?!
NO, THAT'S A LIE!
I USED MY POWERS OUT OF ANGER AND GREED. THERE'S NO EXCUSE FOR THAT!
AAAAAAAAAH!!
THAT MAKES ME JUST LIKE... LIKE THEM...!
ARGH, NO! NO!! I DON'T WANT TO THINK ABOUT THAT!!

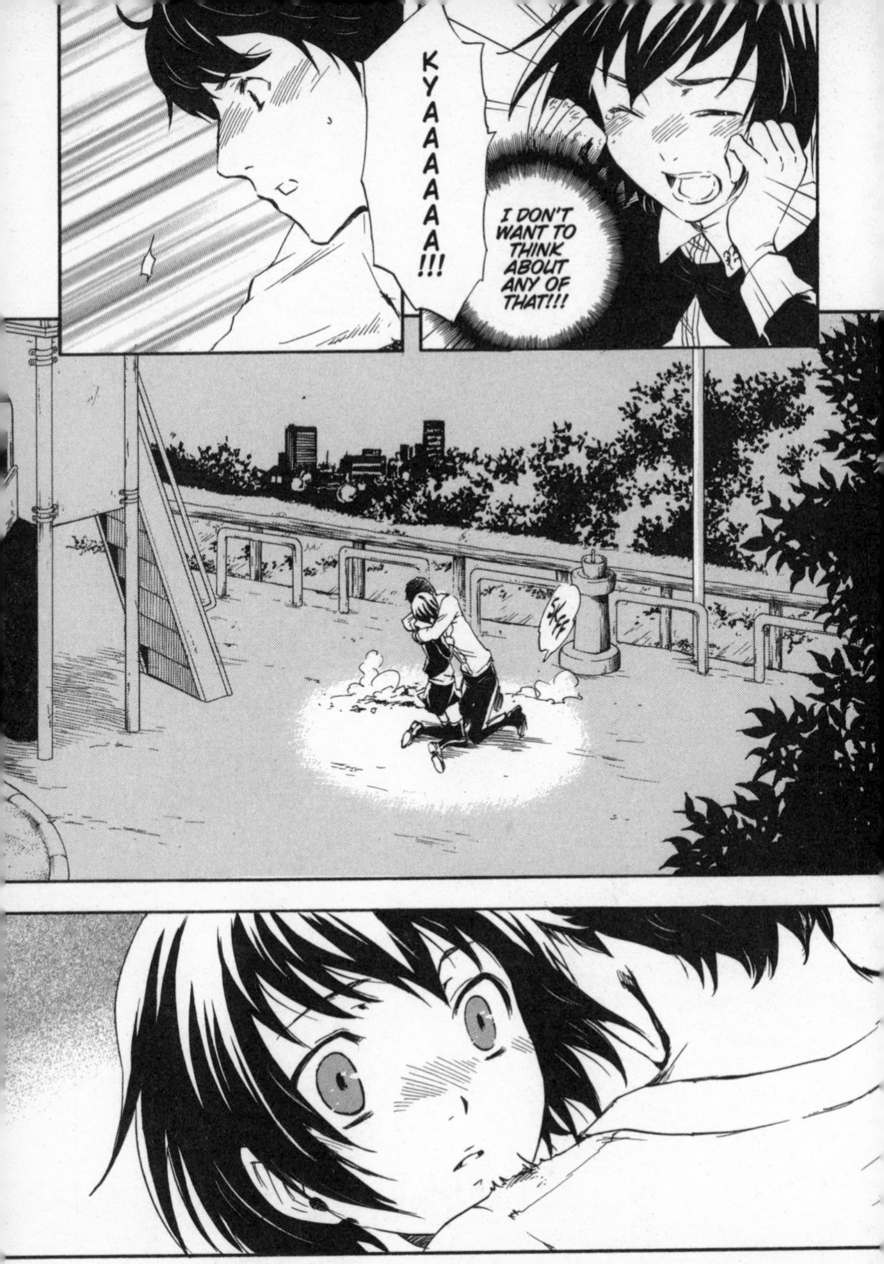
I DON'T WANT TO THINK ABOUT ANY OF THAT!!!
KYAAAAAAA!!!
SKFF

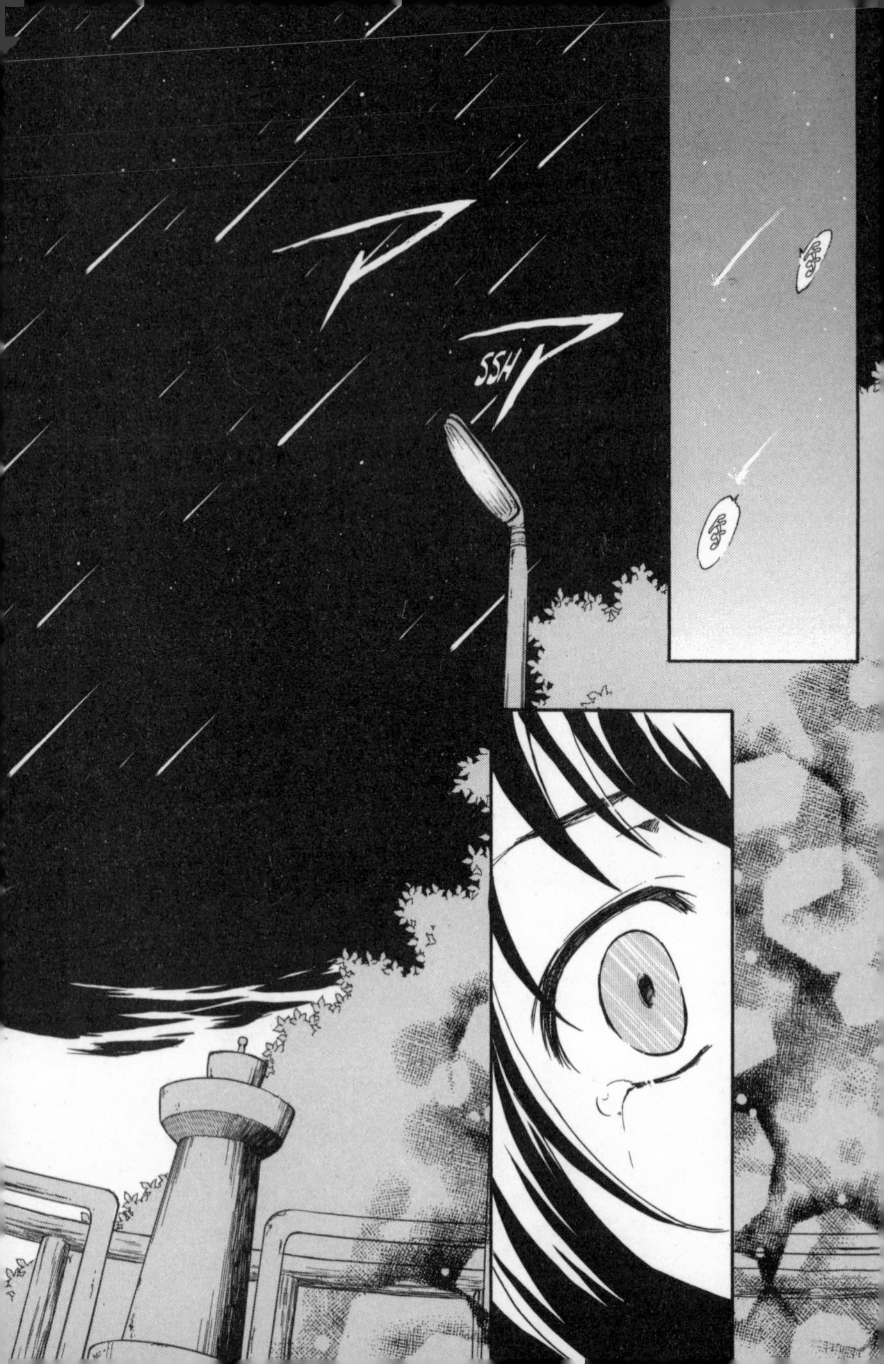
SSH

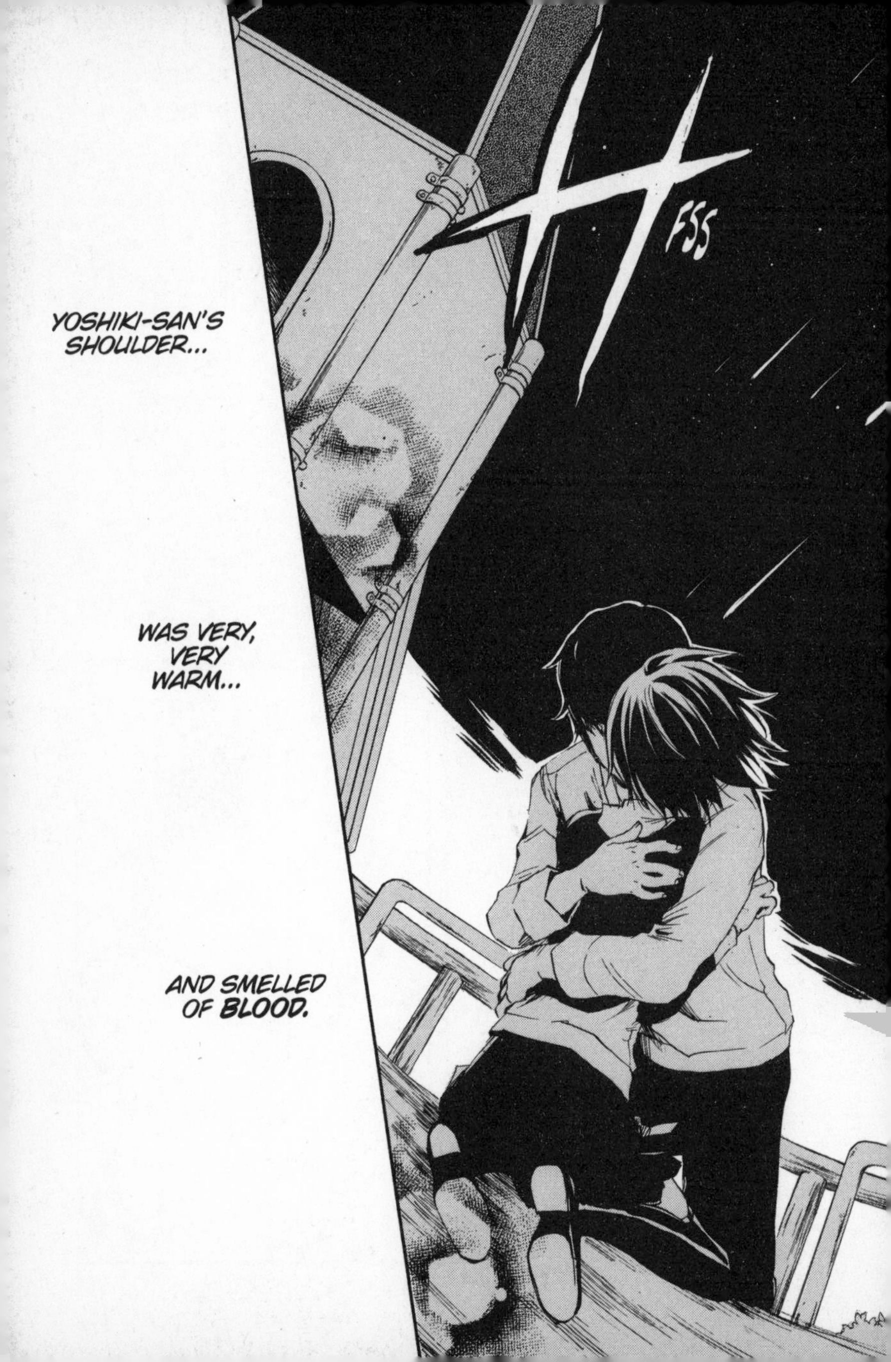
FSS
YOSHIKI-SAN'S SHOULDER...
WAS VERY, VERY WARM...
AND SMELLED OF BLOOD.

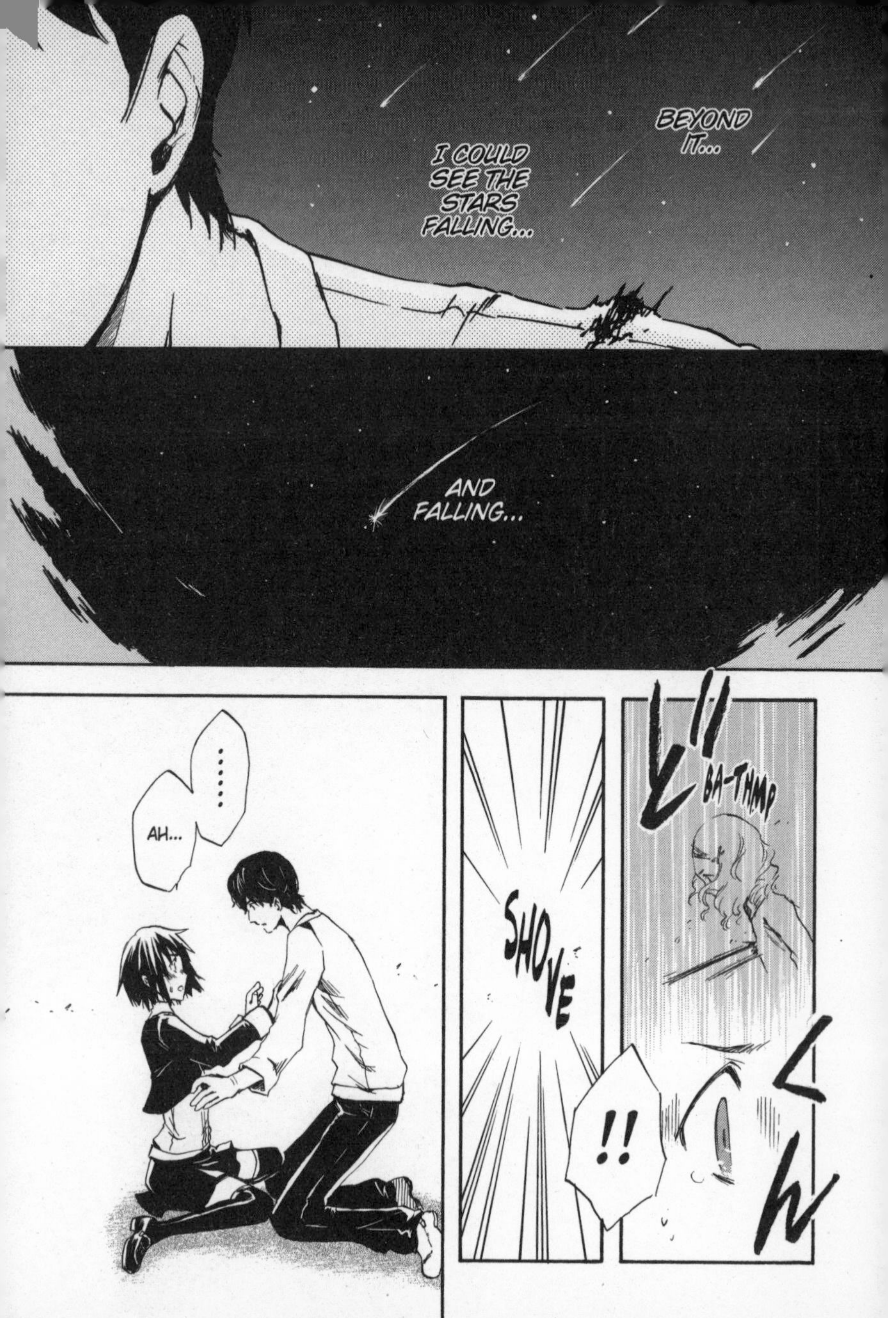
BEYOND IT...
I COULD SEE THE STARS FALLING...
AND FALLING...
BA-THMP
!!
SHOVE
......
AH...

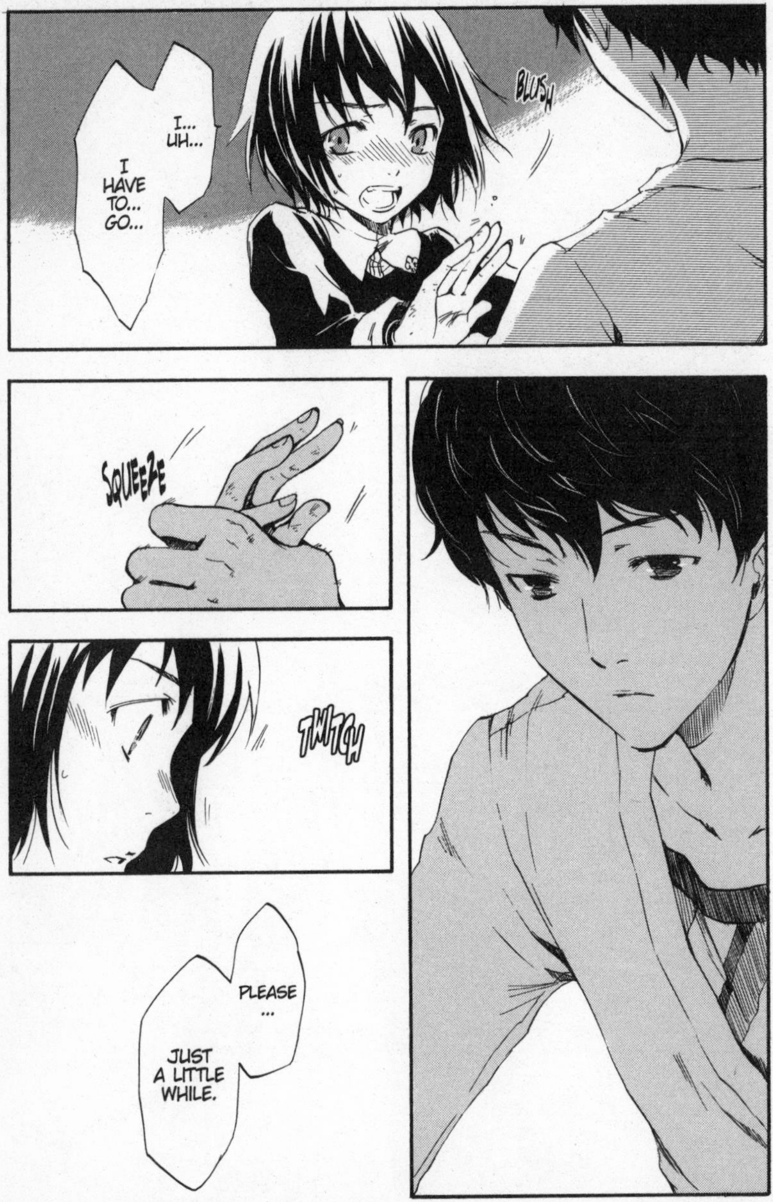
BLUSH
I... UH...
I HAVE TO... GO...
SQUEEZE
TWITCH
PLEASE ... JUST A LITTLE WHILE.

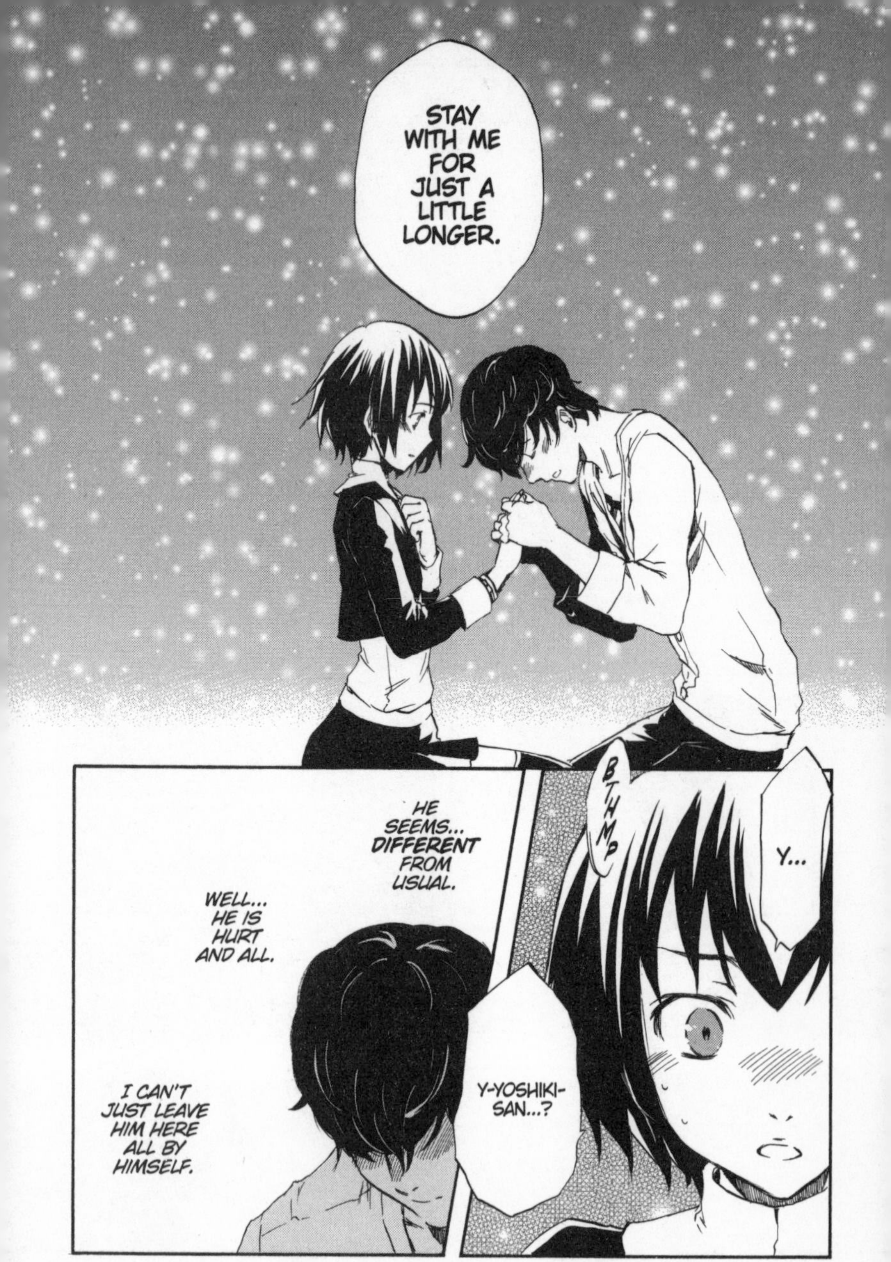
STAY WITH ME FOR JUST A LITTLE LONGER.
Y...
BTHMP
Y-YOSHIKI-SAN...?
HE SEEMS... DIFFERENT FROM USUAL.
WELL... HE IS HURT AND ALL.
I CAN'T JUST LEAVE HIM HERE ALL BY HIMSELF.

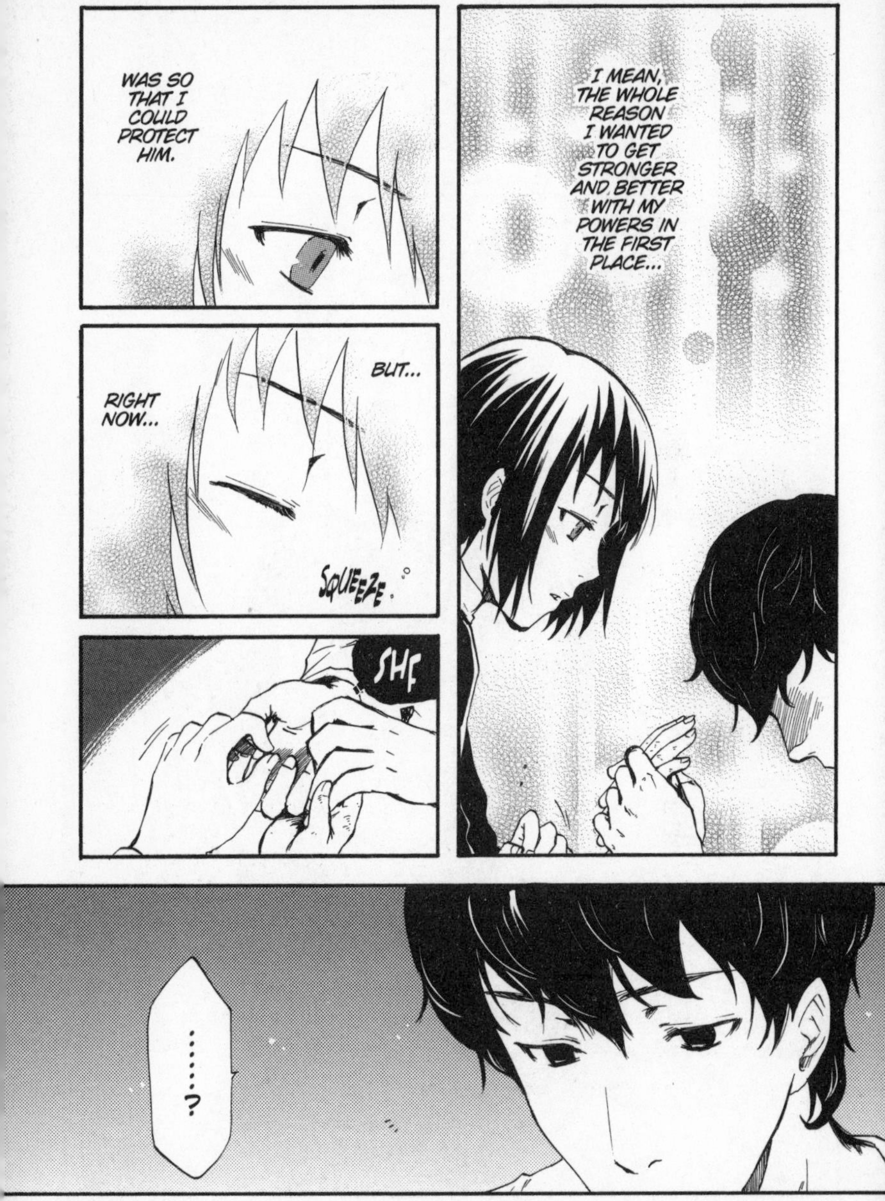
I MEAN, THE WHOLE REASON I WANTED TO GET STRONGER AND BETTER WITH MY POWERS IN THE FIRST PLACE...
WAS SO THAT I COULD PROTECT HIM.
BUT...
RIGHT NOW...
SQUEEZE
SHF
......?

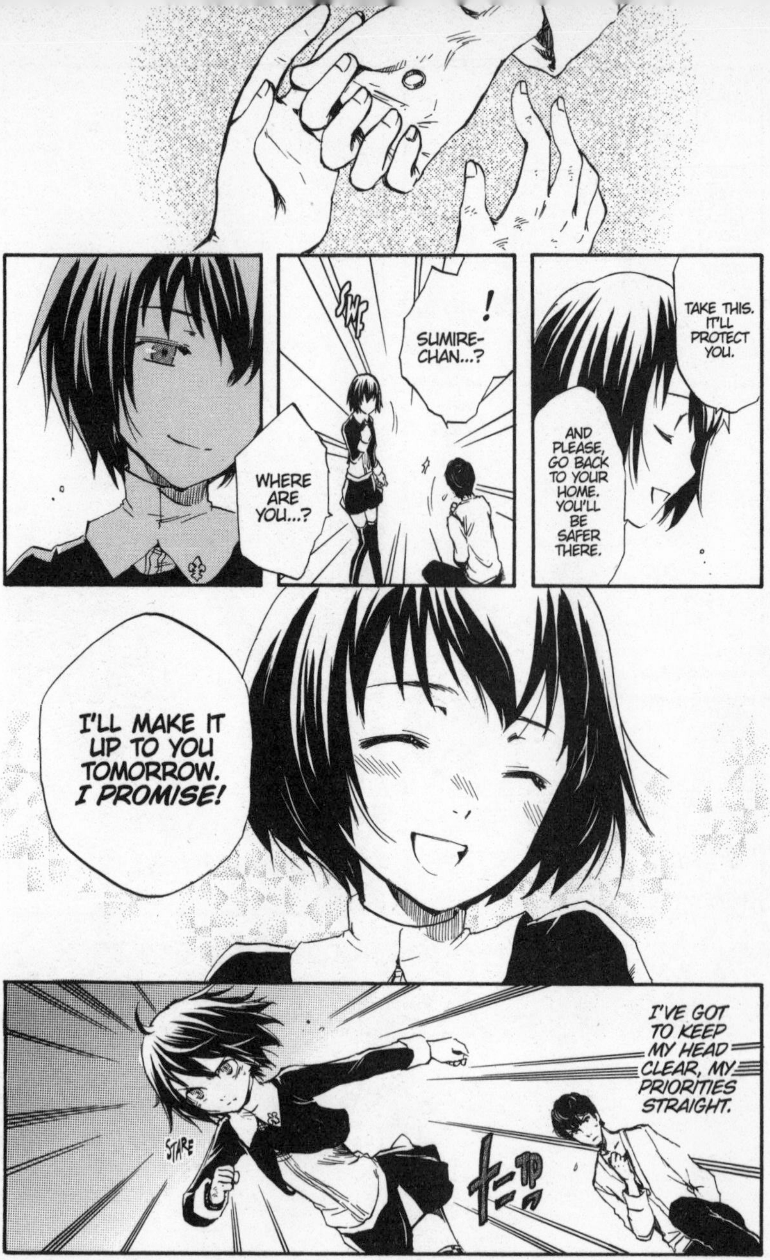
TAKE THIS. IT'LL PROTECT YOU.
AND PLEASE, GO BACK TO YOUR HOME. YOU'LL BE SAFER THERE.
!
SUMIRE-CHAN...?
WHERE ARE YOU...?
I'LL MAKE IT UP TO YOU TOMORROW. I PROMISE!
I'VE GOT TO KEEP MY HEAD CLEAR, MY PRIORITIES STRAIGHT.
STARE

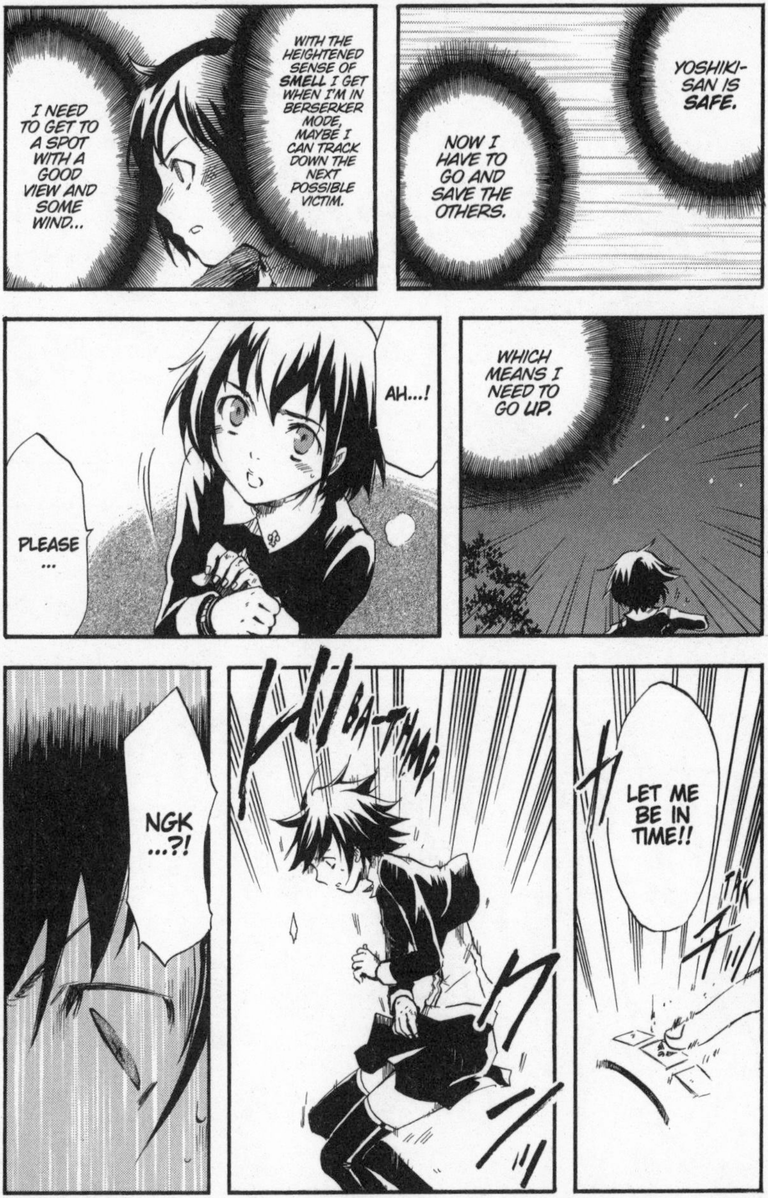
YOSHIKI-SAN IS SAFE.
NOW I HAVE TO GO AND SAVE THE OTHERS.
WITH THE HEIGHTENED SENSE OF SMELL I GET WHEN I'M IN BERSERKER MODE, MAYBE I CAN TRACK DOWN THE NEXT POSSIBLE VICTIM.
I NEED TO GET TO A SPOT WITH A GOOD VIEW AND SOME WIND...
WHICH MEANS I NEED TO GO UP.
AH...!
PLEASE ...
LET ME BE IN TIME!!
TAK
BA-THMP
NGK ...?!

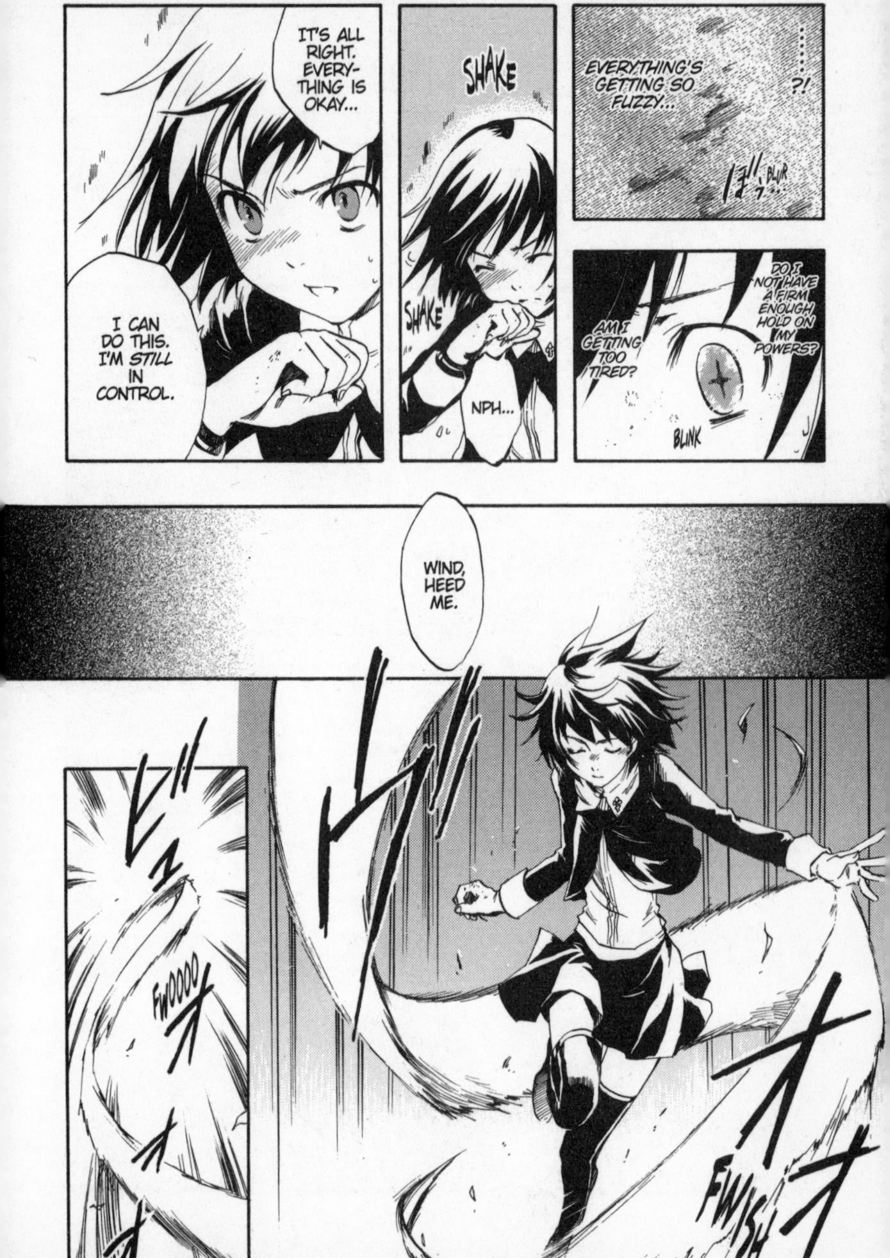
......?!
EVERYTHING'S GETTING SO FUZZY...
BLUR...
DO I NOT HAVE A FIRM ENOUGH HOLD ON MY POWERS?
AM I GETTING TOO TIRED?
BLINK
SHAKE
SHAKE
NPH...
IT'S ALL RIGHT. EVERYTHING IS OKAY...
I CAN DO THIS. I'M STILL IN CONTROL.
WIND, HEED ME.
FWISH
FWOOOO

WOOOOOOO

YES, THAT'S IT.
MORE.

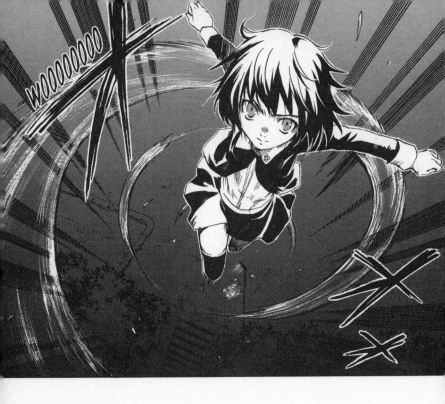

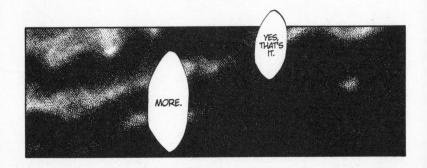

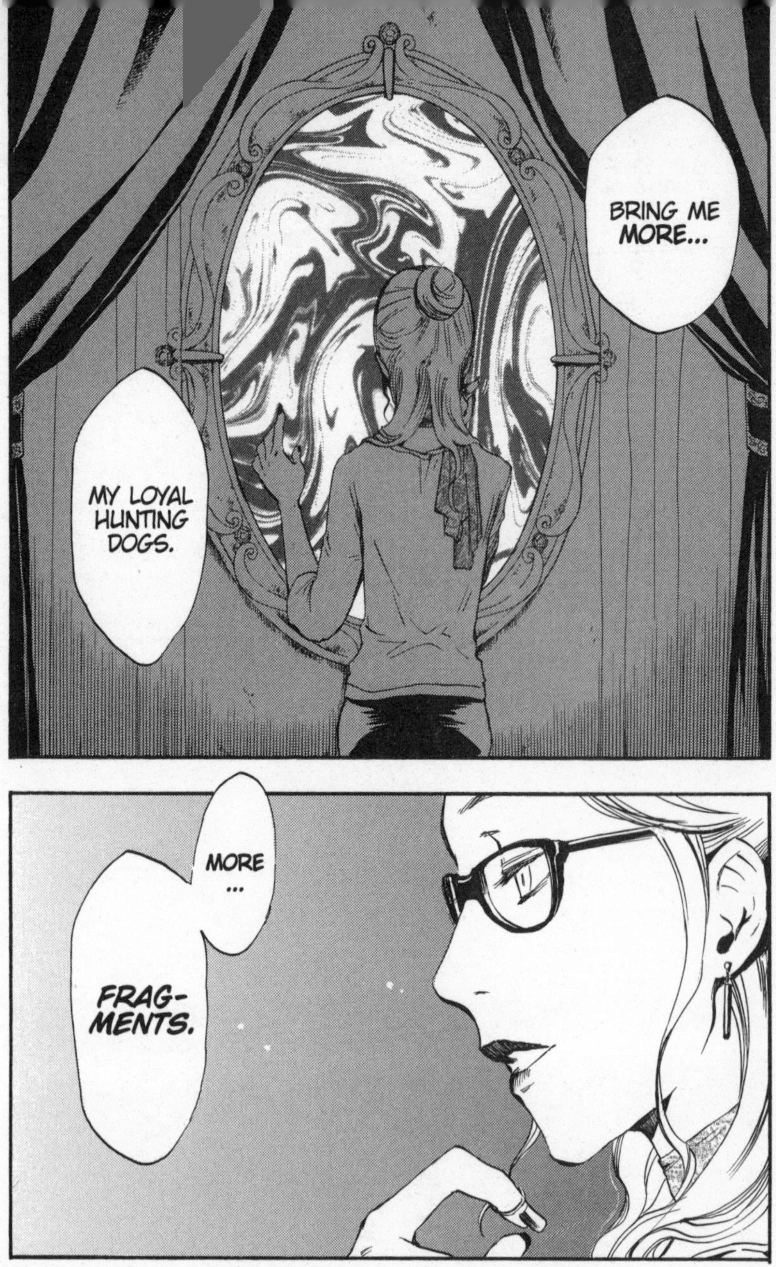
BRING ME MORE...
MY LOYAL HUNTING DOGS.
MORE ...
FRAG-MENTS.

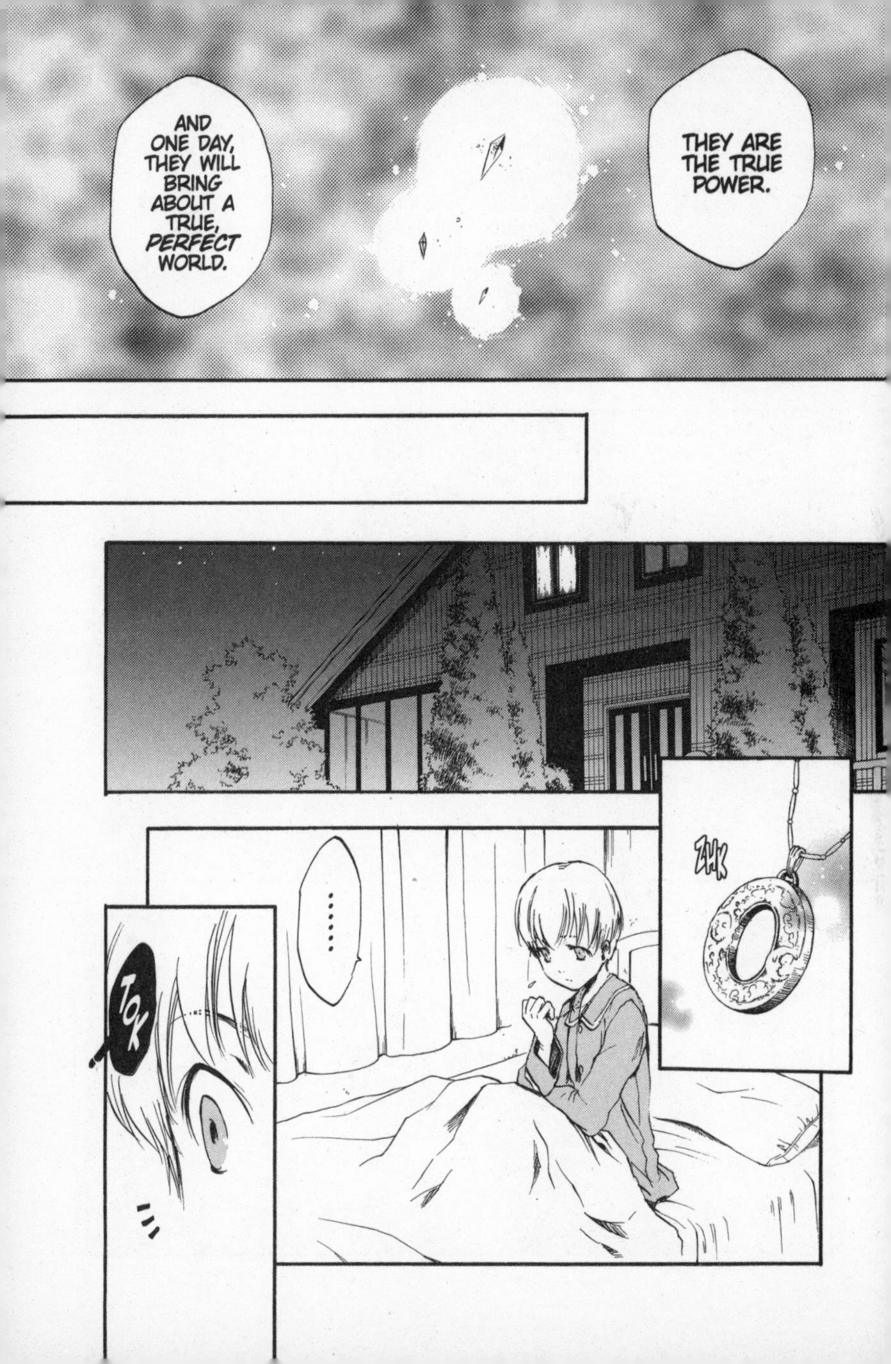
THEY ARE THE TRUE POWER.
AND ONE DAY, THEY WILL BRING ABOUT A TRUE, PERFECT WORLD.
ZHK
......
TOK

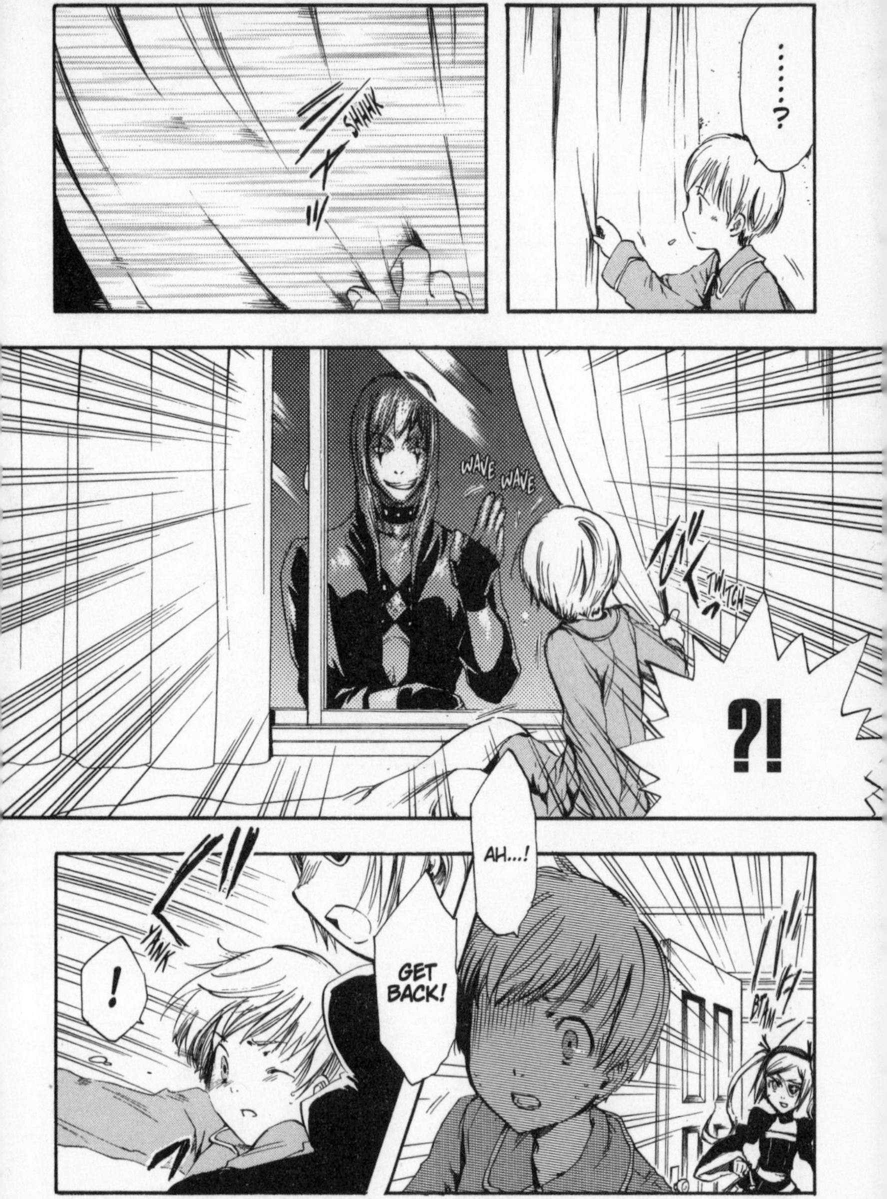

……っ?
SHHHK
WAVE WAVE
TWITCH
?!
AH...!
YANK
BTAM
!
GET BACK!

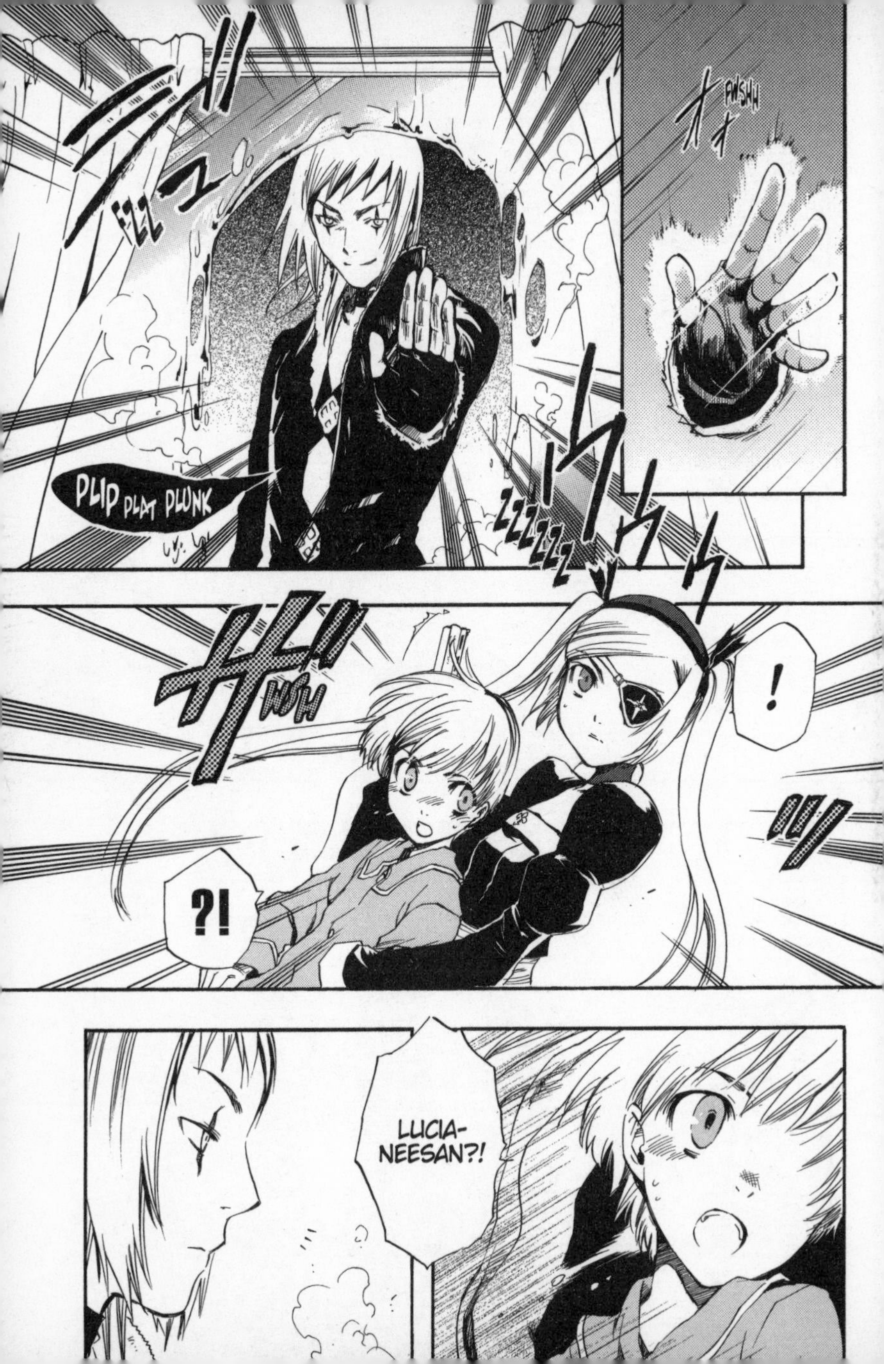
FWSHH
FZZZ
PLIP PLAT PLUNK
ZZZZZZZ
!
WSH
?!
LUCIA-NEESAN?!

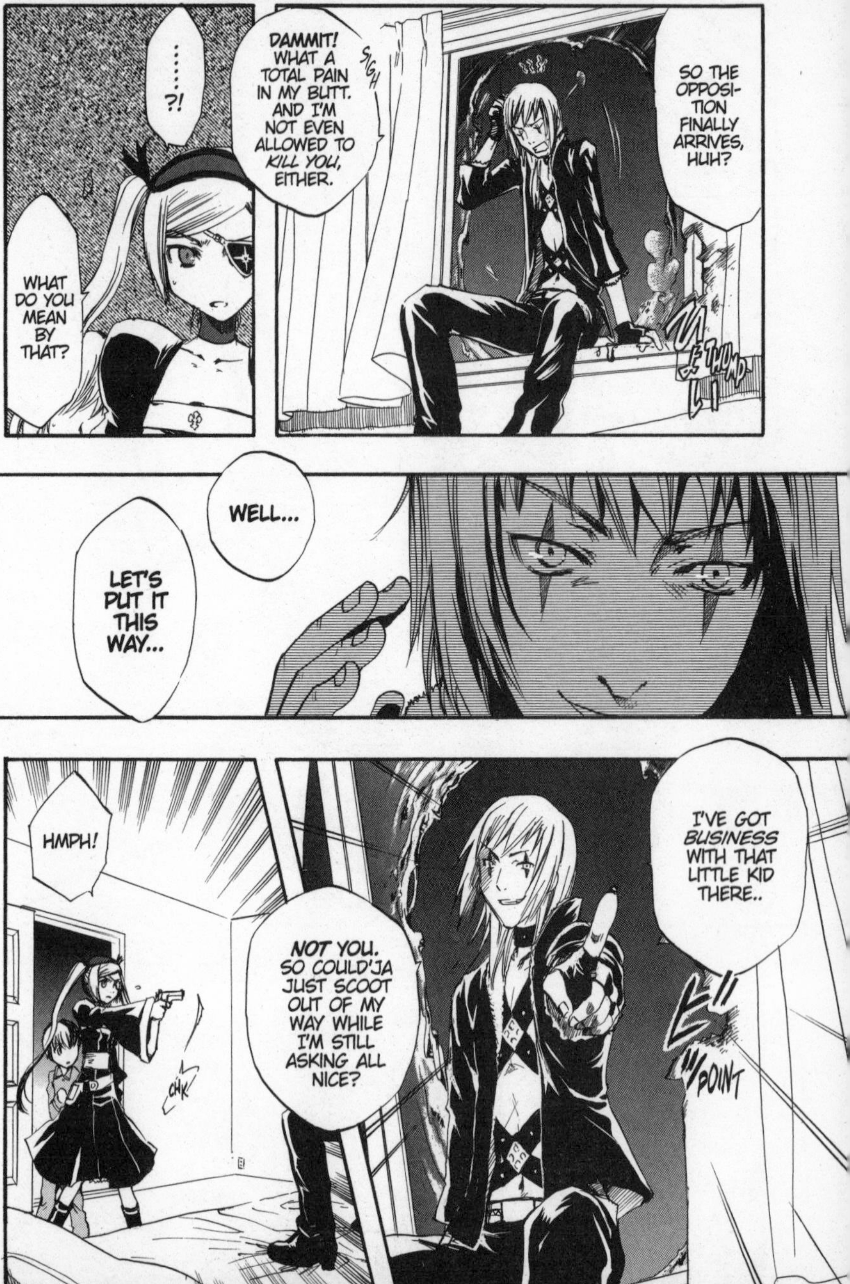
SO THE OPPOSITION FINALLY ARRIVES, HUH?
THUMP
SIGH
DAMMIT! WHAT A TOTAL PAIN IN MY BUTT. AND I'M NOT EVEN ALLOWED TO *KILL YOU*, EITHER.
......?!
WHAT DO YOU MEAN BY THAT?
WELL...
LET'S PUT IT THIS WAY...
I'VE GOT *BUSINESS* WITH THAT LITTLE KID THERE..
POINT
NOT YOU. SO COULD'JA JUST SCOOT OUT OF MY WAY WHILE I'M STILL ASKING ALL NICE?
HMPH!
CHK

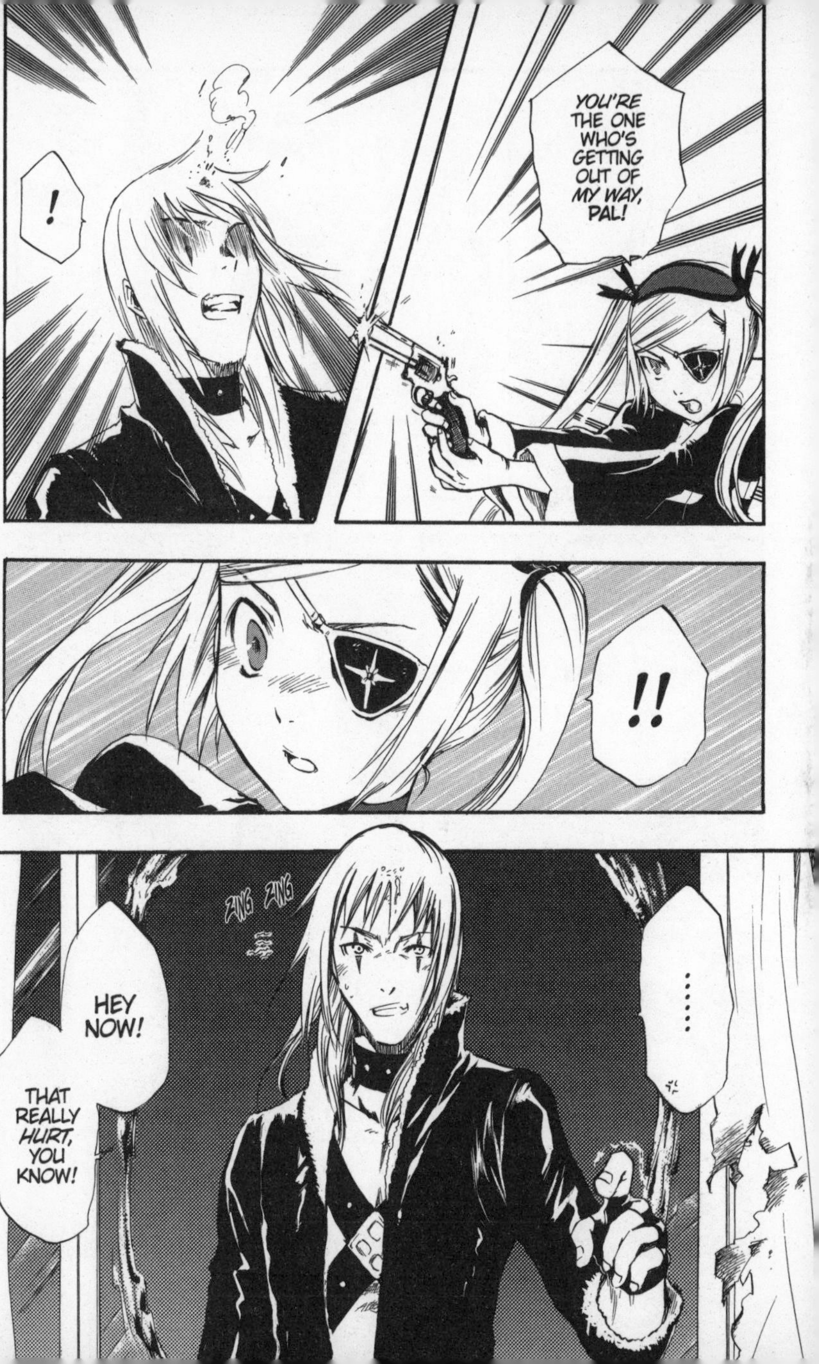
YOU'RE THE ONE WHO'S GETTING OUT OF MY WAY, PAL!
!
!!
......
ZING ZING
HEY NOW!
THAT REALLY HURT, YOU KNOW!

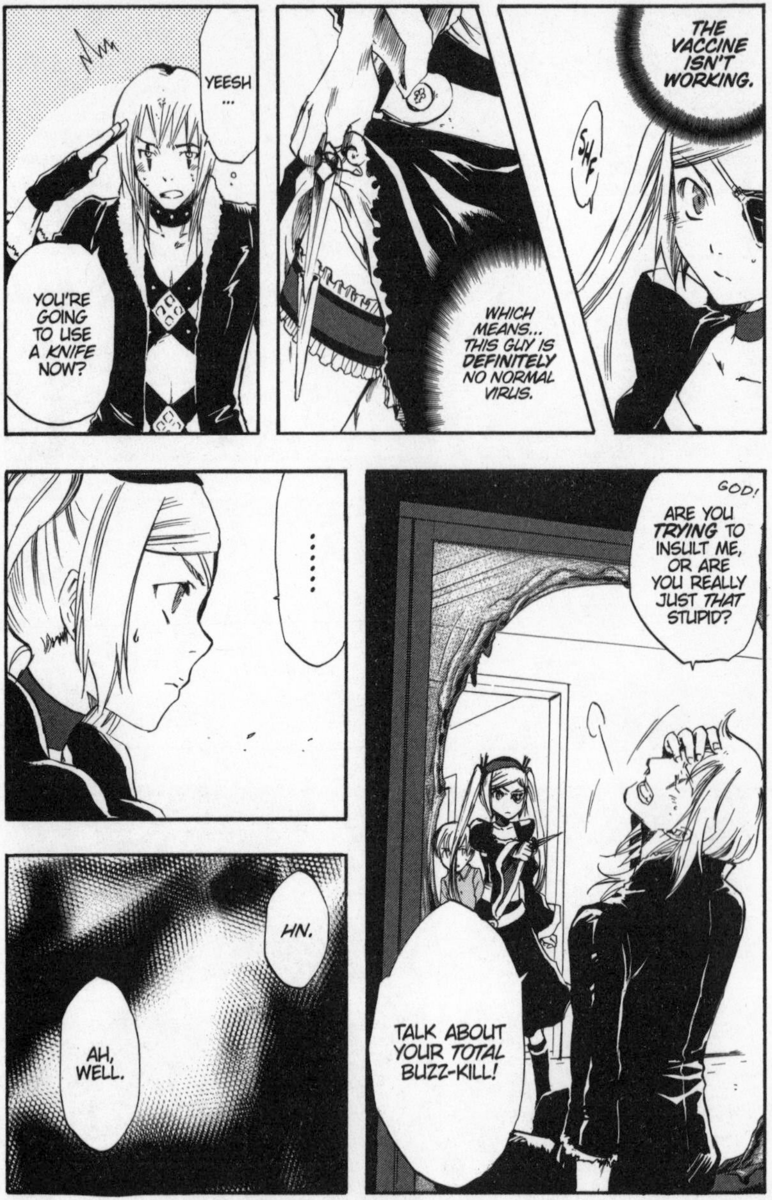
THE VACCINE ISN'T WORKING.
SHE
WHICH MEANS... THIS GUY IS DEFINITELY NO NORMAL VIRUS.
YEESH ...
YOU'RE GOING TO USE A KNIFE NOW?
GOD!
ARE YOU TRYING TO INSULT ME, OR ARE YOU REALLY JUST THAT STUPID?
TALK ABOUT YOUR TOTAL BUZZ-KILL!
......
HN.
AH, WELL.

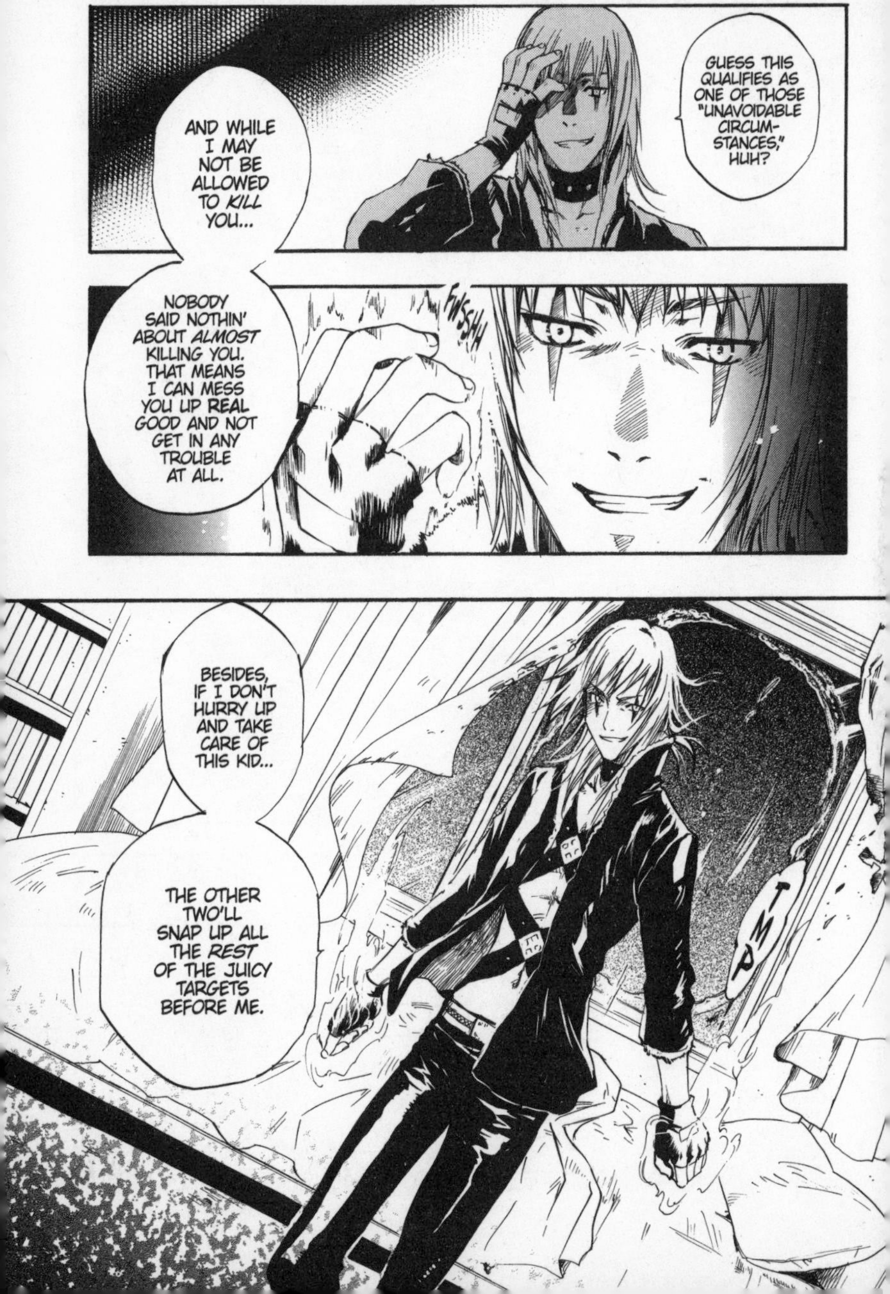
GUESS THIS QUALIFIES AS ONE OF THOSE "UNAVOIDABLE CIRCUM-STANCES," HUH?
AND WHILE I MAY NOT BE ALLOWED TO *KILL* YOU...
FWSSHH
NOBODY SAID NOTHIN' ABOUT *ALMOST* KILLING YOU. THAT MEANS I CAN MESS YOU UP REAL GOOD AND NOT GET IN ANY TROUBLE AT ALL.
BESIDES, IF I DON'T HURRY UP AND TAKE CARE OF THIS KID...
THE OTHER TWO'LL SNAP UP ALL THE *REST* OF THE JUICY TARGETS BEFORE ME.
TMP

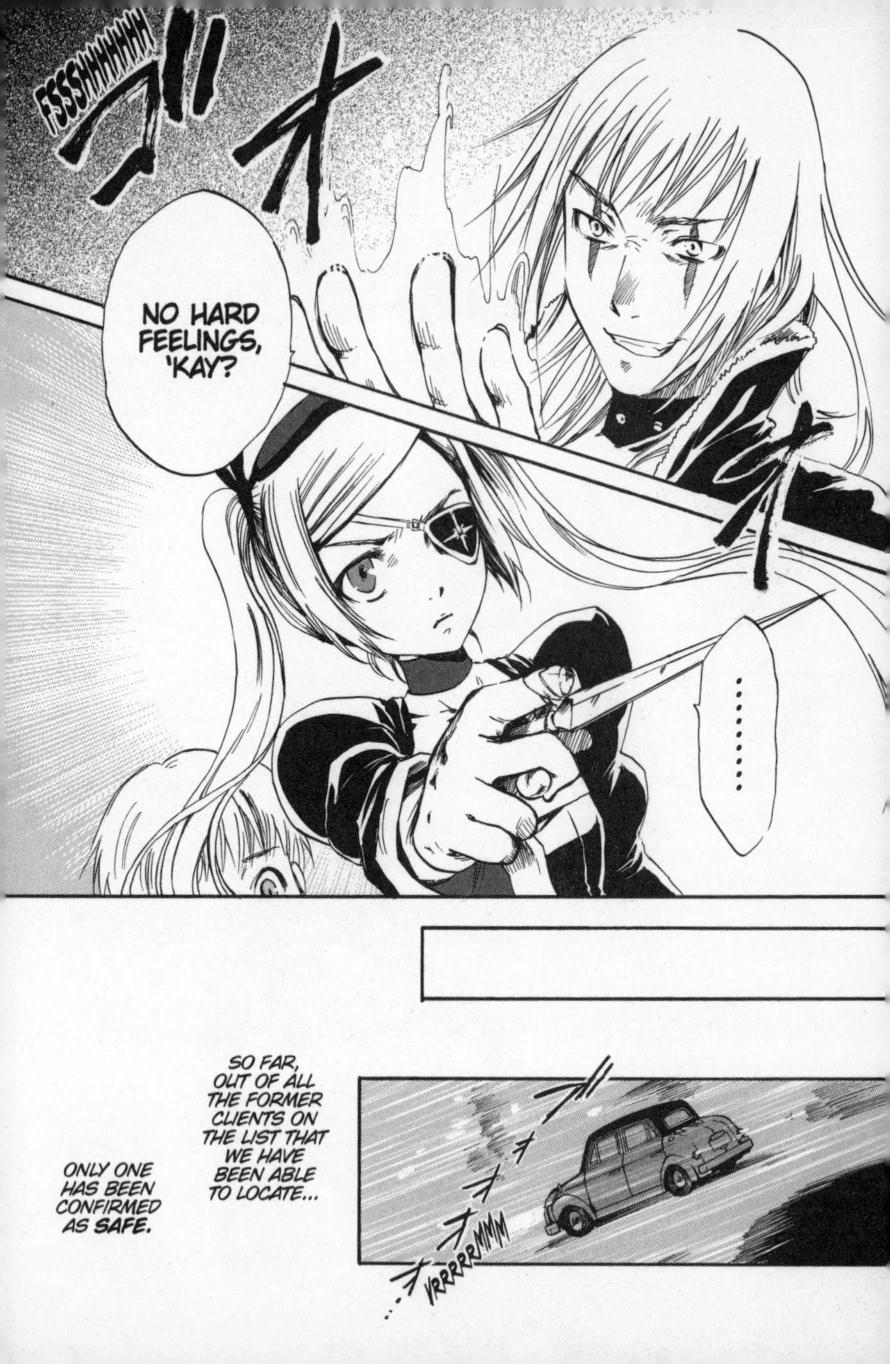
FSSSHHHHHH
NO HARD FEELINGS, 'KAY?
....
SO FAR, OUT OF ALL THE FORMER CLIENTS ON THE LIST THAT WE HAVE BEEN ABLE TO LOCATE...
ONLY ONE HAS BEEN CONFIRMED AS SAFE.
VRRRRRMMMM

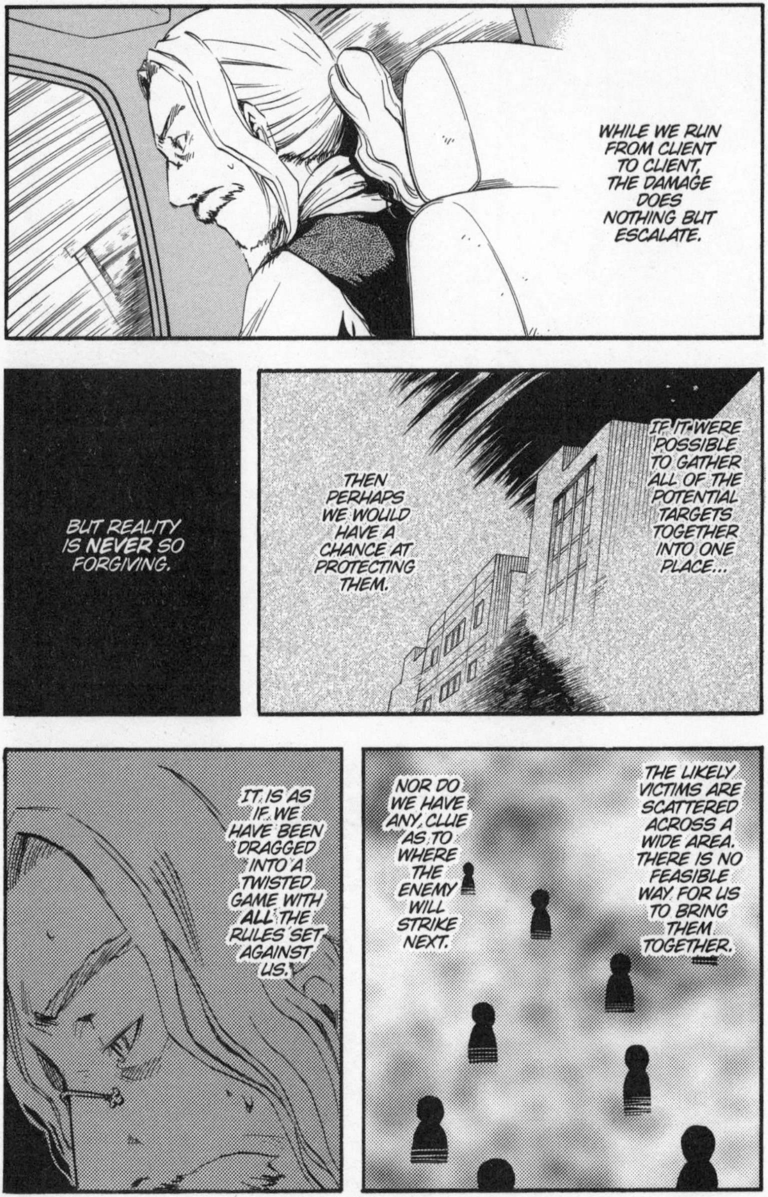
WHILE WE RUN FROM CLIENT TO CLIENT, THE DAMAGE DOES NOTHING BUT ESCALATE.
IF IT WERE POSSIBLE TO GATHER ALL OF THE POTENTIAL TARGETS TOGETHER INTO ONE PLACE...
THEN PERHAPS WE WOULD HAVE A CHANCE AT PROTECTING THEM.
BUT REALITY IS **NEVER** SO FORGIVING.
THE LIKELY VICTIMS ARE SCATTERED ACROSS A WIDE AREA. THERE IS NO FEASIBLE WAY FOR US TO BRING THEM TOGETHER.
NOR DO WE HAVE ANY CLUE AS TO WHERE THE ENEMY WILL STRIKE NEXT.
IT IS AS IF WE HAVE BEEN DRAGGED INTO A TWISTED GAME WITH **ALL** THE RULES SET AGAINST US.

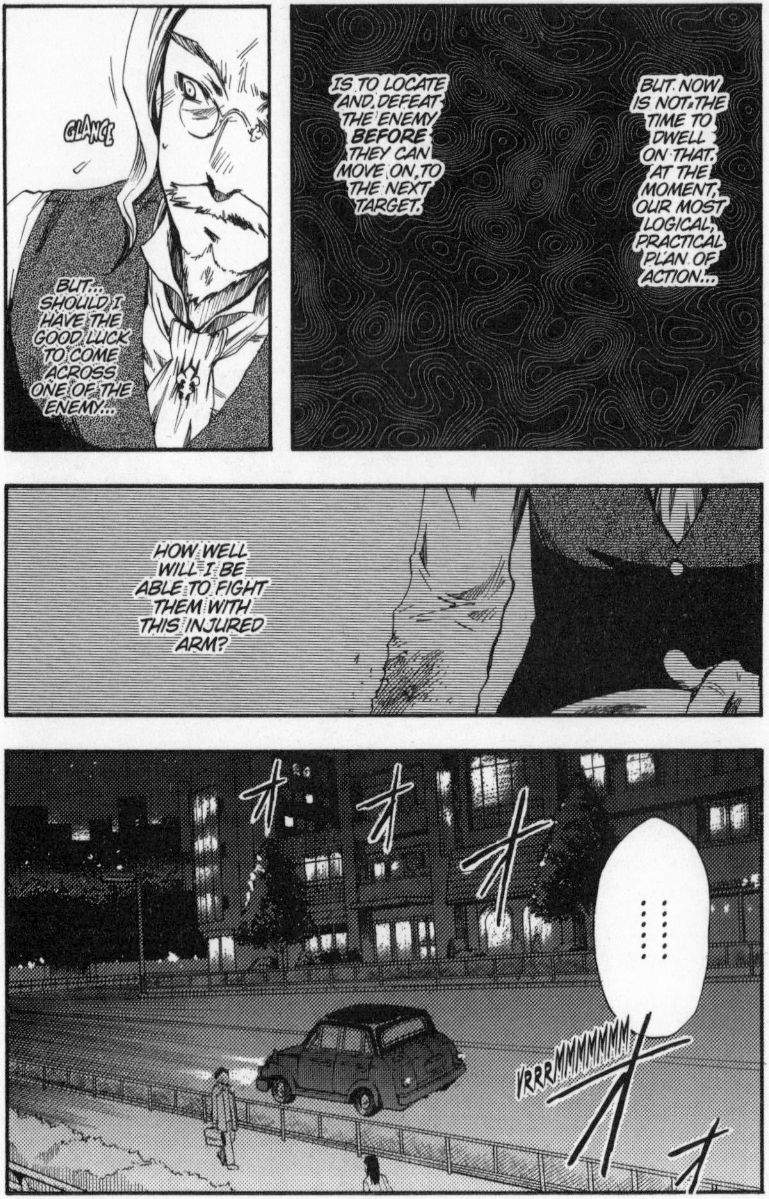
BUT NOW IS NOT THE TIME TO DWELL ON THAT. AT THE MOMENT, OUR MOST LOGICAL, PRACTICAL PLAN OF ACTION...
IS TO LOCATE AND DEFEAT THE ENEMY **BEFORE** THEY CAN MOVE ON TO THE NEXT TARGET.
GLANCE
BUT... SHOULD I HAVE THE GOOD LUCK TO COME ACROSS ONE OF THE ENEMY...
HOW WELL WILL I BE ABLE TO FIGHT THEM WITH THIS INJURED ARM?
......
VRRRMMMMMMM

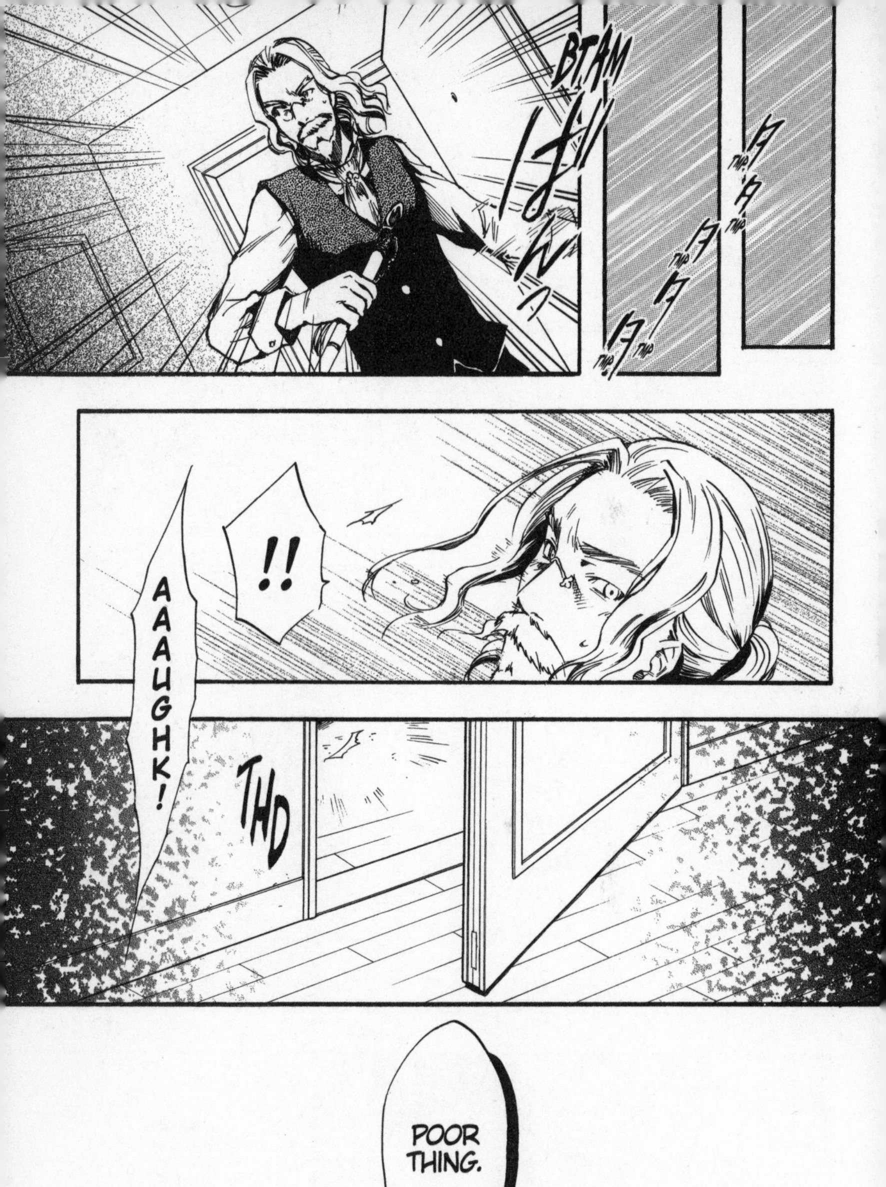
TMP! TMP! TMP! TMP! TMP!
BTAM
!!
AAAUGHK!
THD
POOR THING.

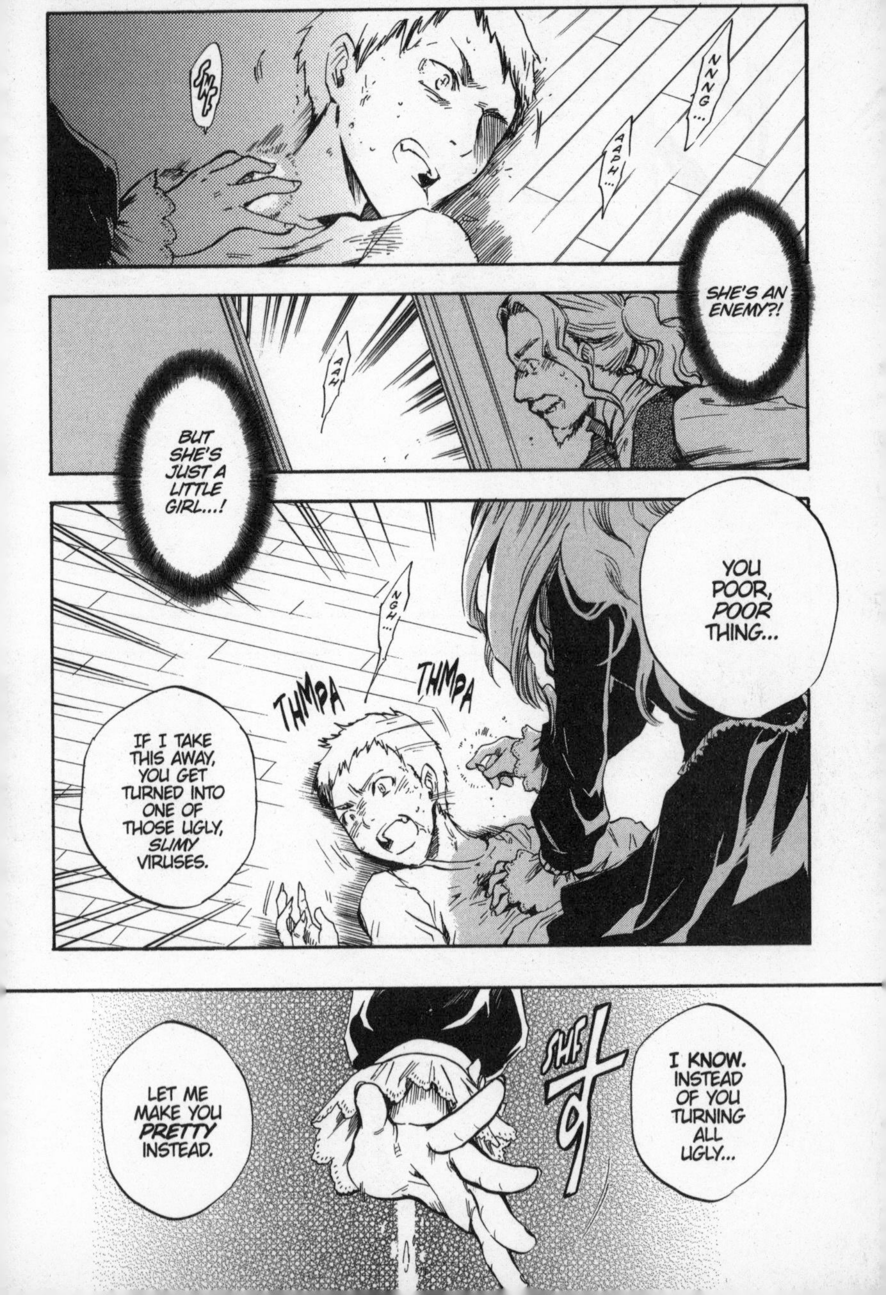
NNNG...
AAPH...
SHE'S AN ENEMY?!
AAH
BUT SHE'S JUST A LITTLE GIRL...!
YOU POOR, POOR THING...
NGH...
THMPA
THMPA
IF I TAKE THIS AWAY, YOU GET TURNED INTO ONE OF THOSE UGLY, SLIMY VIRUSES.
I KNOW. INSTEAD OF YOU TURNING ALL UGLY...
LET ME MAKE YOU PRETTY INSTEAD.

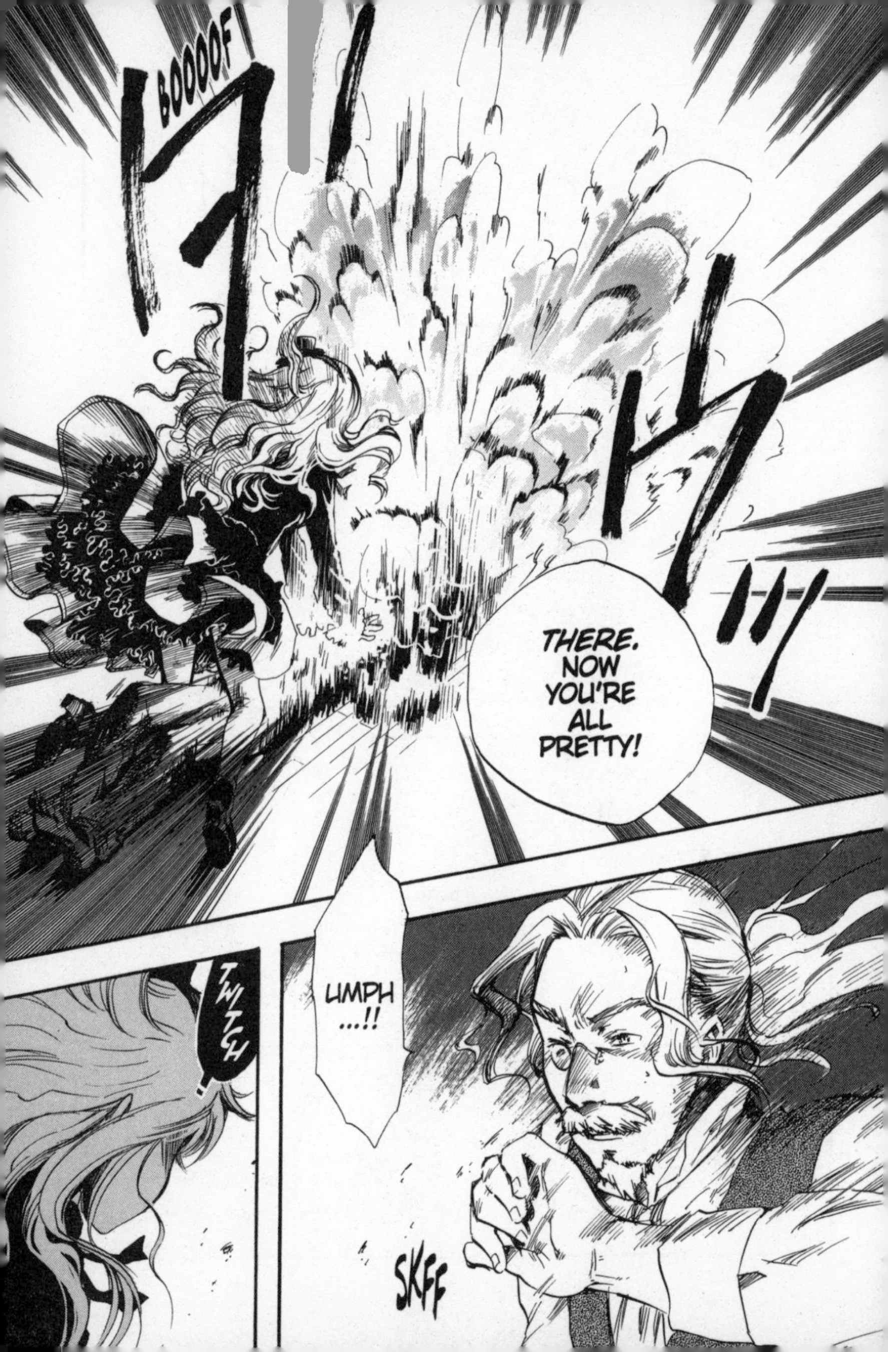
BOOOF
THERE. NOW YOU'RE ALL PRETTY!
UMPH ...!!
SKFF
TWITCH

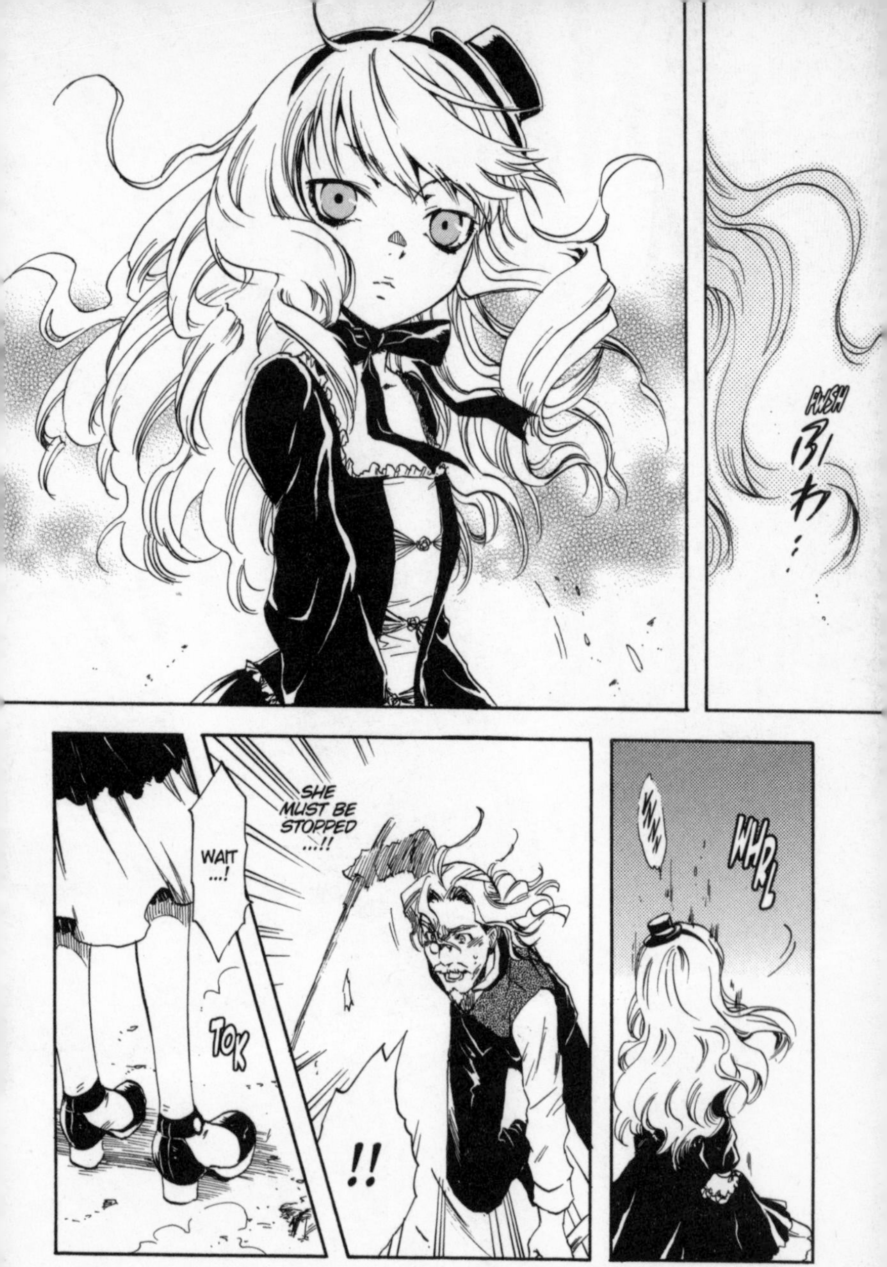
RWSH
ふわ…
VNNN
WHRL
SHE MUST BE STOPPED ...!!
!!
WAIT ...!
TOK

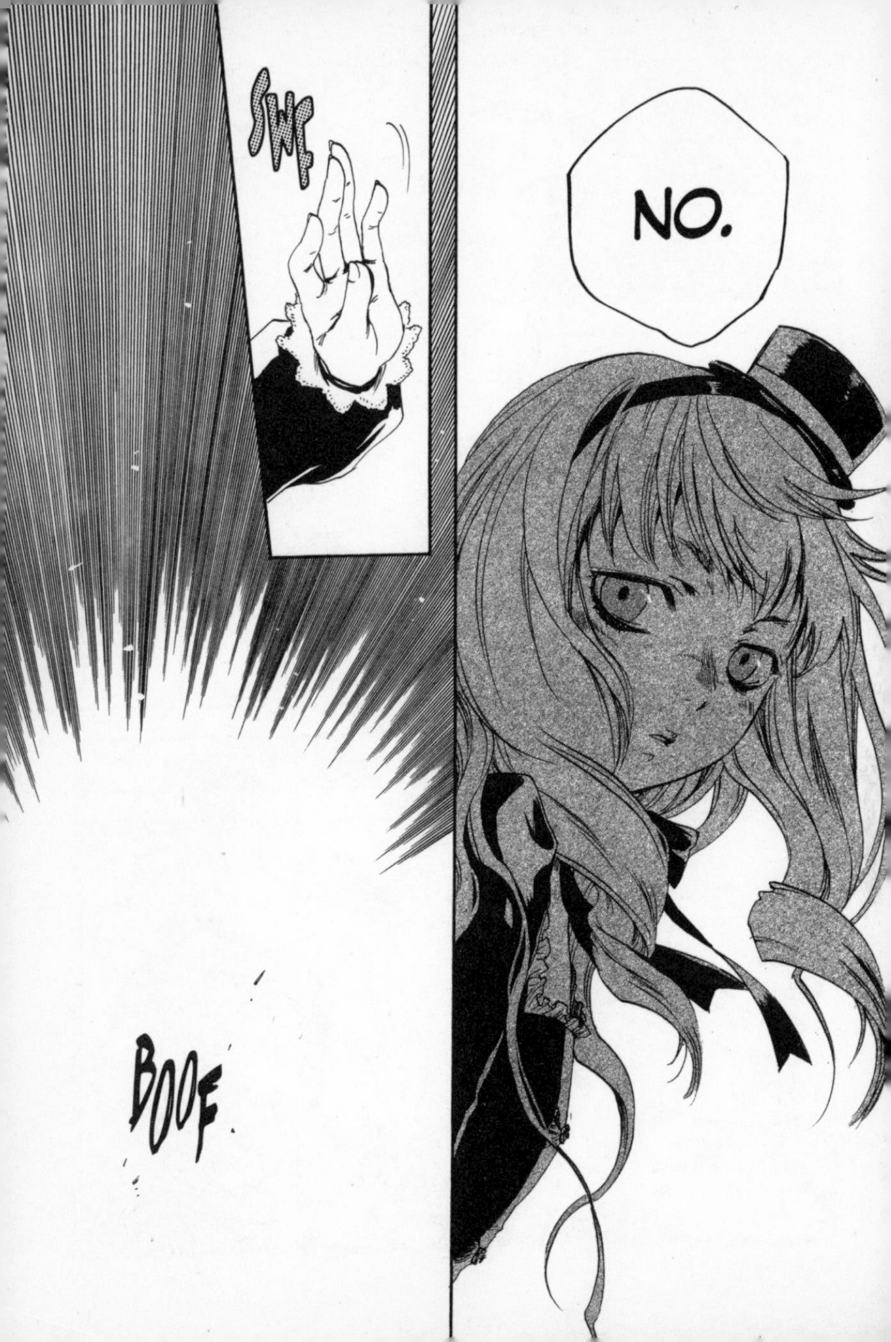
NO.
SWF
BOOF

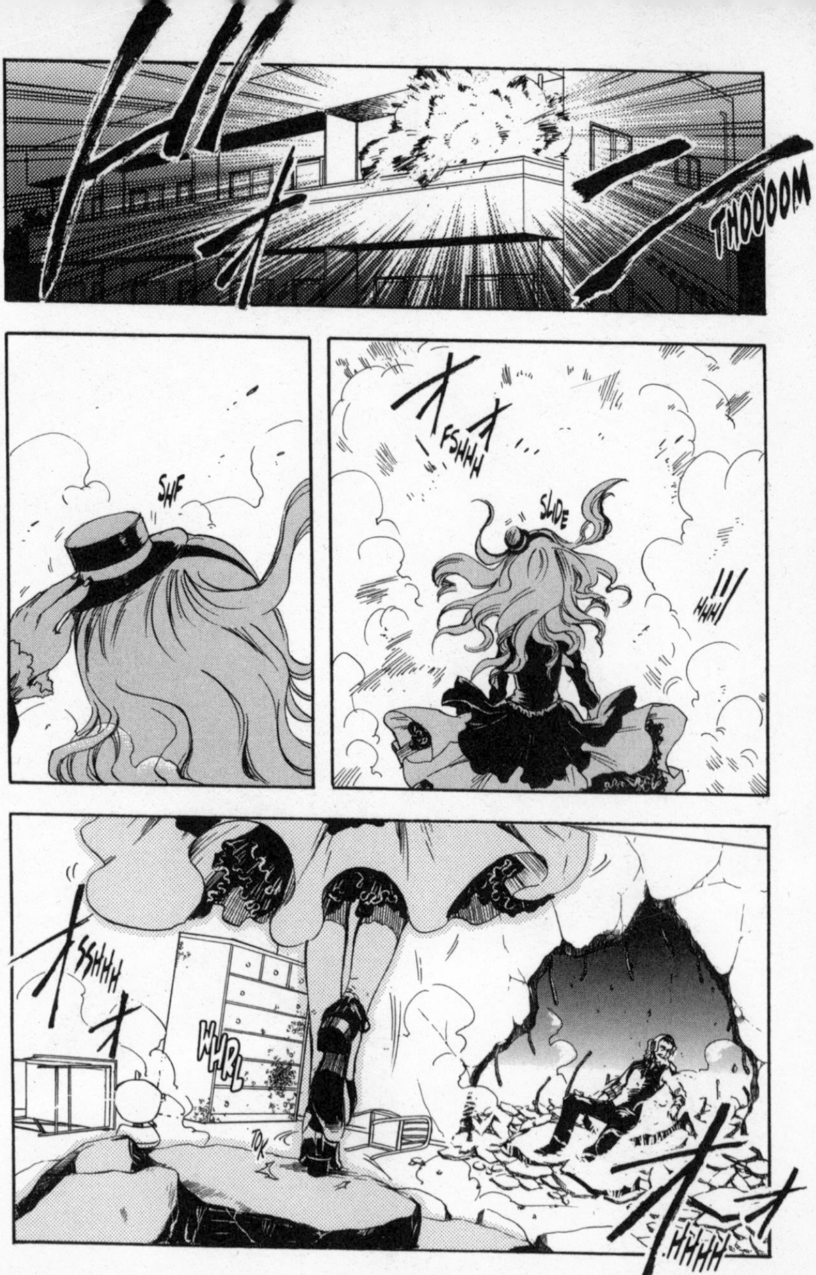
THOOOOM
FSHHH
SLIDE
HHH
SHF
HHHH
WHRL
TOK
SSHHH

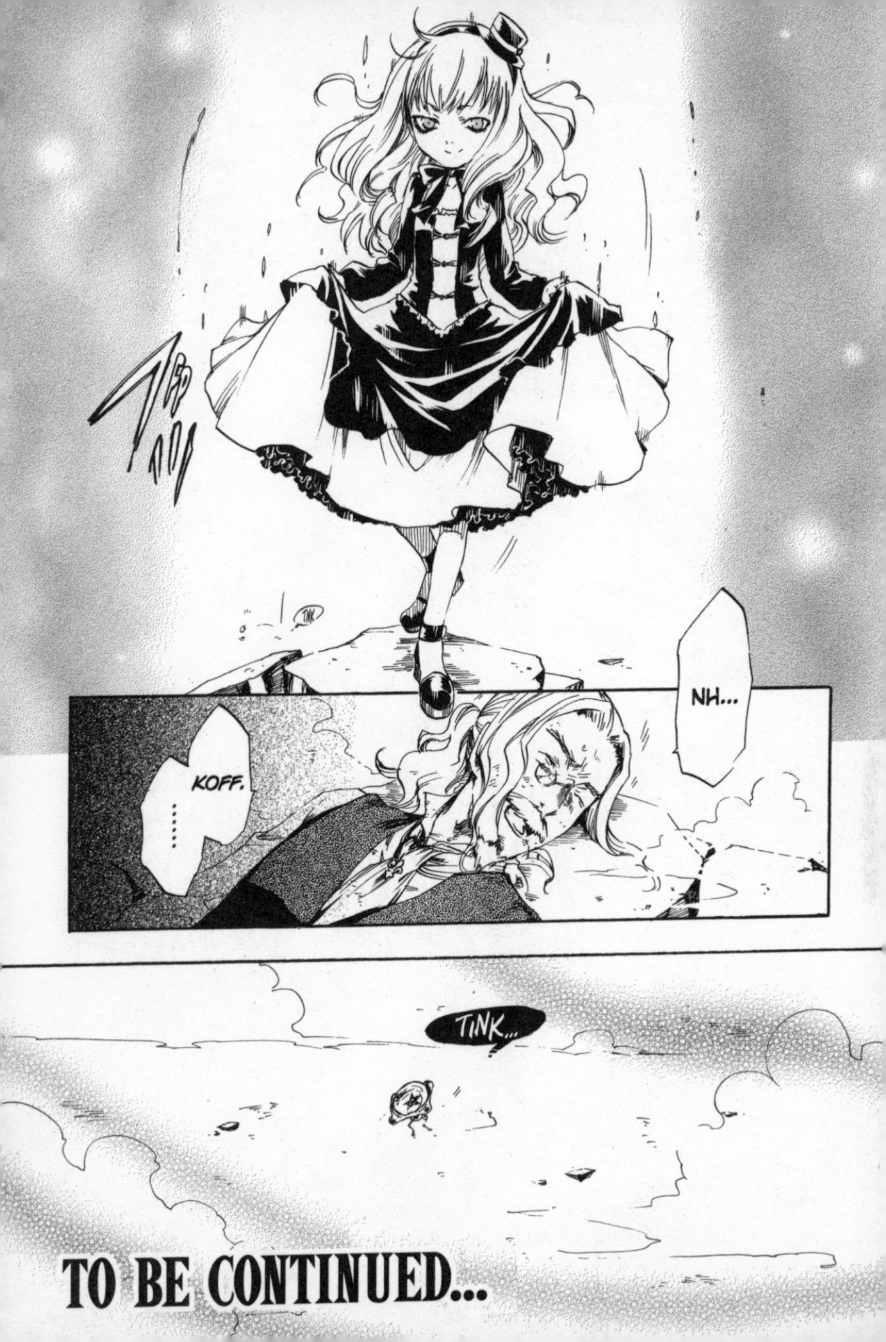
TINK
NH...
KOFF.
......
TINK...
TO BE CONTINUED...

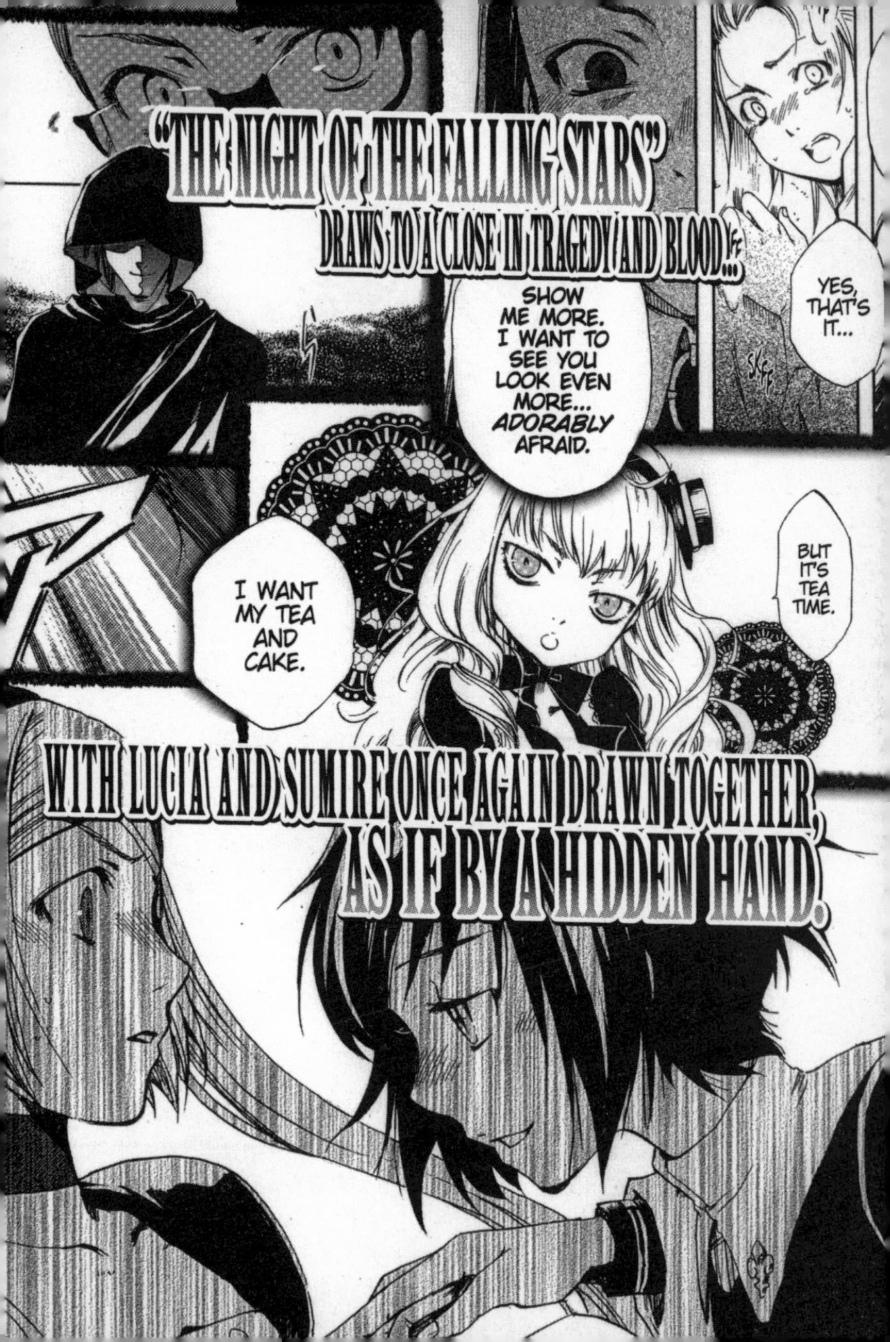
"THE NIGHT OF THE FALLING STARS"
DRAWS TO A CLOSE IN TRAGEDY AND BLOOD!!...
YES, THAT'S IT...
SKFF
SHOW ME MORE. I WANT TO SEE YOU LOOK EVEN MORE... *ADORABLY* AFRAID.
BUT IT'S TEA TIME.
I WANT MY TEA AND CAKE.
WITH LUCIA AND SUMIRE ONCE AGAIN DRAWN TOGETHER,
AS IF BY A HIDDEN HAND.

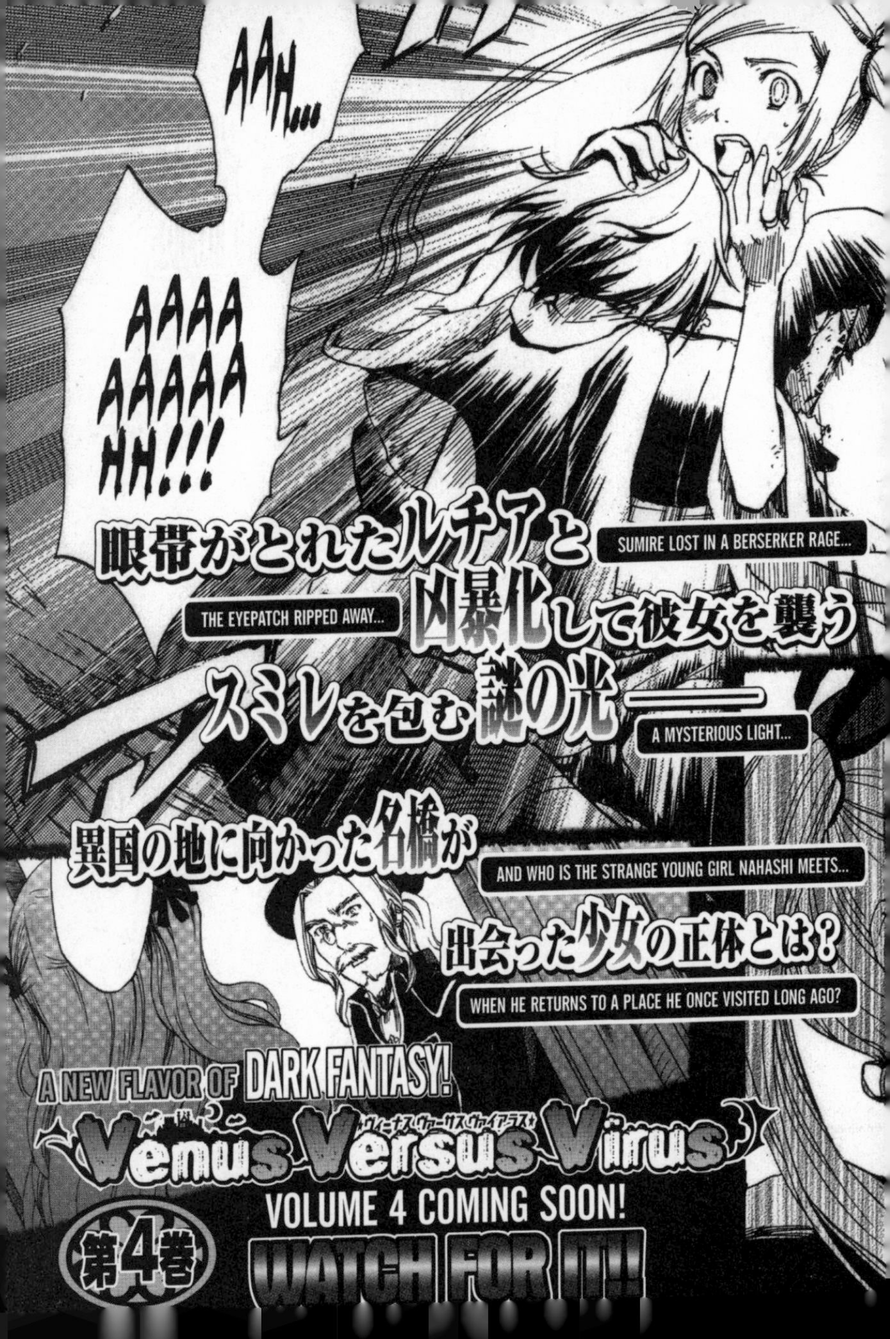
AAH...
AAAA AAAAA HH!!!
眼帯がとれたルチアと
SUMIRE LOST IN A BERSERKER RAGE...
THE EYEPATCH RIPPED AWAY...
凶暴化して彼女を襲う
スミレを包む謎の光——
A MYSTERIOUS LIGHT...
異国の地に向かった名橋が
AND WHO IS THE STRANGE YOUNG GIRL NAHASHI MEETS...
出会った少女の正体とは？
WHEN HE RETURNS TO A PLACE HE ONCE VISITED LONG AGO?
A NEW FLAVOR OF DARK FANTASY!
ヴィーナス ヴァーサス ヴァイアラス
Venus Versus Virus
VOLUME 4 COMING SOON!
第4巻
WATCH FOR IT!!

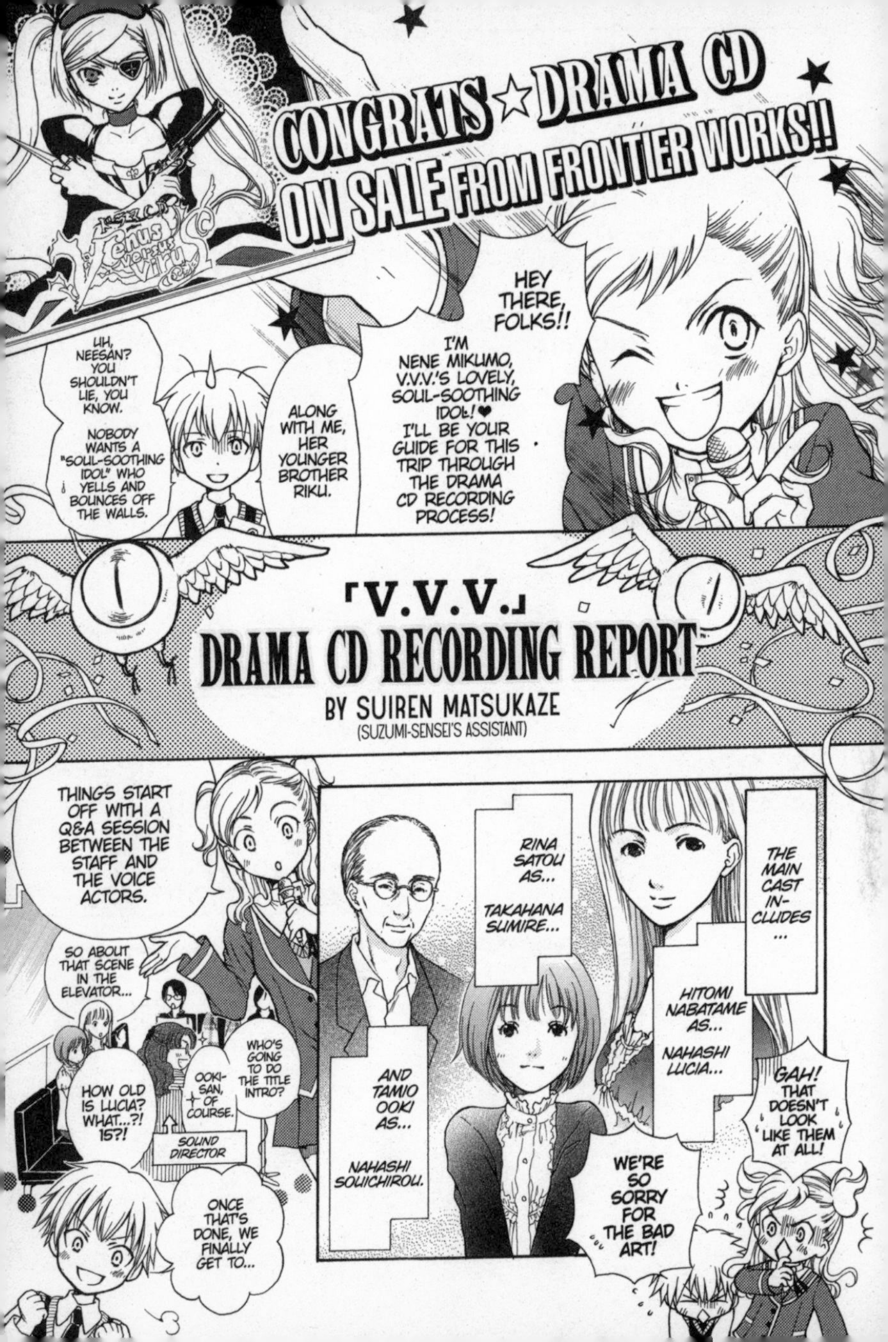
CONGRATS☆DRAMA CD
ON SALE FROM FRONTIER WORKS!!
HEY THERE, FOLKS!!
I'M NENE MIKUMO, V.V.V.'S LOVELY, SOUL-SOOTHING IDOL!❤ I'LL BE YOUR GUIDE FOR THIS TRIP THROUGH THE DRAMA CD RECORDING PROCESS!
ALONG WITH ME, HER YOUNGER BROTHER RIKU.
UH, NEESAN? YOU SHOULDN'T LIE, YOU KNOW.
NOBODY WANTS A "SOUL-SOOTHING IDOL" WHO YELLS AND BOUNCES OFF THE WALLS.
「V.V.V.」
DRAMA CD RECORDING REPORT
BY SUIREN MATSUKAZE
(SUZUMI-SENSEI'S ASSISTANT)
THE MAIN CAST IN-CLUDES ...
RINA SATOU AS...
TAKAHANA SUMIRE...
HITOMI NABATAME AS...
NAHASHI LUCIA...
AND TAMIO OOKI AS...
NAHASHI SOUICHIROU.
GAH! THAT DOESN'T LOOK LIKE THEM AT ALL!
WE'RE SO SORRY FOR THE BAD ART!
THINGS START OFF WITH A Q&A SESSION BETWEEN THE STAFF AND THE VOICE ACTORS.
SO ABOUT THAT SCENE IN THE ELEVATOR...
WHO'S GOING TO DO THE TITLE INTRO?
OOKI-SAN, OF COURSE.
HOW OLD IS LUCIA? WHAT...?! 15?!
SOUND DIRECTOR
ONCE THAT'S DONE, WE FINALLY GET TO...

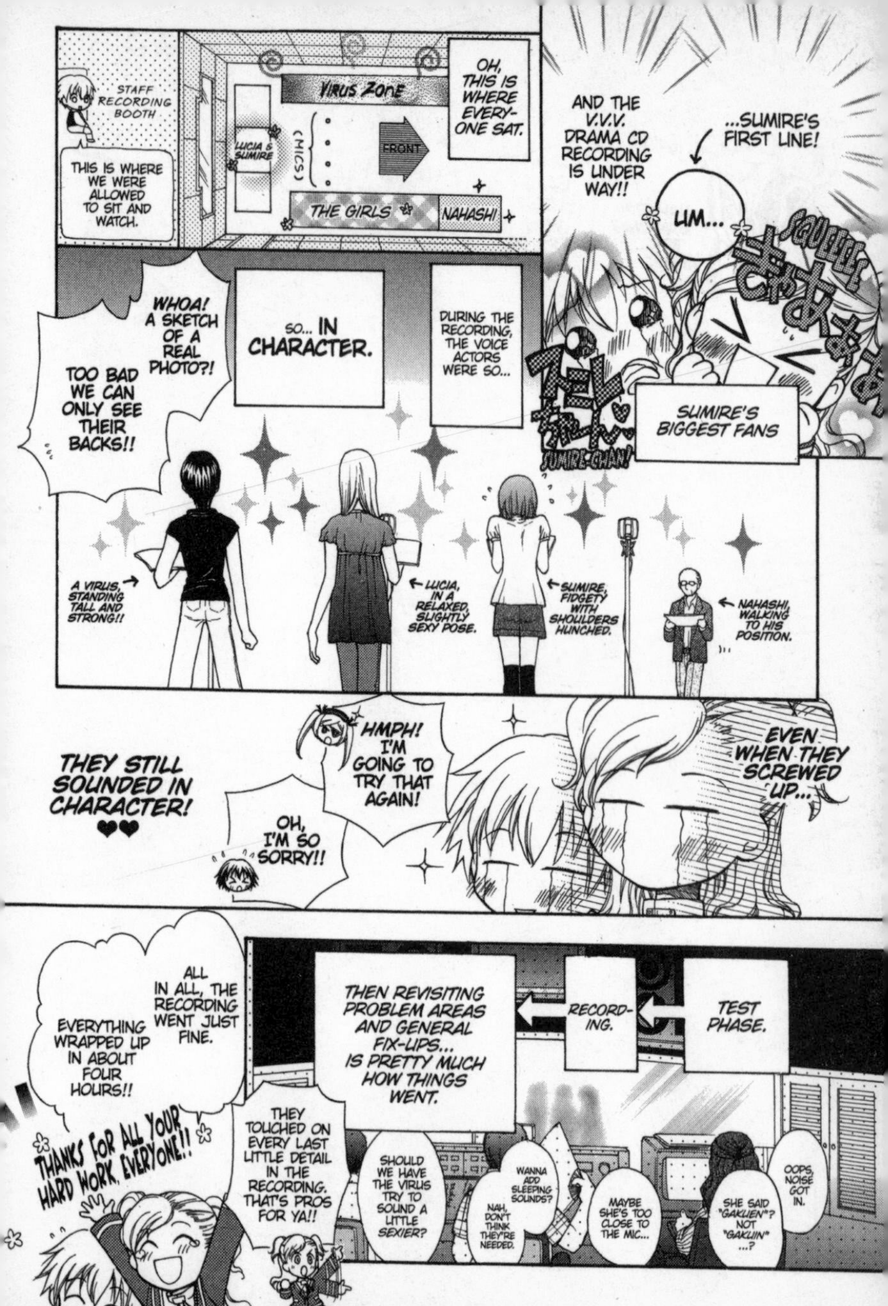
AND THE V.V.V. DRAMA CD RECORDING IS UNDER WAY!!
...SUMIRE'S FIRST LINE!
UM...
きゃあああ
スミレちゃん♥
SUMIRE-CHAN!
SUMIRE'S BIGGEST FANS
OH, THIS IS WHERE EVERYONE SAT.
VIRUS ZONE
FRONT
(MICS)
LUCIA & SUMIRE
THE GIRLS
NAHASHI
STAFF RECORDING BOOTH
THIS IS WHERE WE WERE ALLOWED TO SIT AND WATCH.
DURING THE RECORDING, THE VOICE ACTORS WERE SO...
SO... IN CHARACTER.
WHOA! A SKETCH OF A REAL PHOTO?!
TOO BAD WE CAN ONLY SEE THEIR BACKS!!
NAHASHI, WALKING TO HIS POSITION.
SUMIRE, FIDGETY WITH SHOULDERS HUNCHED.
LUCIA, IN A RELAXED, SLIGHTLY SEXY POSE.
A VIRUS, STANDING TALL AND STRONG!!
EVEN WHEN THEY SCREWED UP...
HMPH! I'M GOING TO TRY THAT AGAIN!
OH, I'M SO SORRY!!
THEY STILL SOUNDED IN CHARACTER! ❤❤
TEST PHASE.
RECORDING.
THEN REVISITING PROBLEM AREAS AND GENERAL FIX-UPS... IS PRETTY MUCH HOW THINGS WENT.
ALL IN ALL, THE RECORDING WENT JUST FINE.
EVERYTHING WRAPPED UP IN ABOUT FOUR HOURS!!
OOPS, NOISE GOT IN.
SHE SAID "GAKUEN"? NOT "GAKUIN"...?
MAYBE SHE'S TOO CLOSE TO THE MIC...
WANNA ADD SLEEPING SOUNDS?
NAH, DON'T THINK THEY'RE NEEDED.
SHOULD WE HAVE THE VIRUS TRY TO SOUND A LITTLE SEXIER?
THEY TOUCHED ON EVERY LAST LITTLE DETAIL IN THE RECORDING. THAT'S PROS FOR YA!!
THANKS FOR ALL YOUR HARD WORK, EVERYONE!!

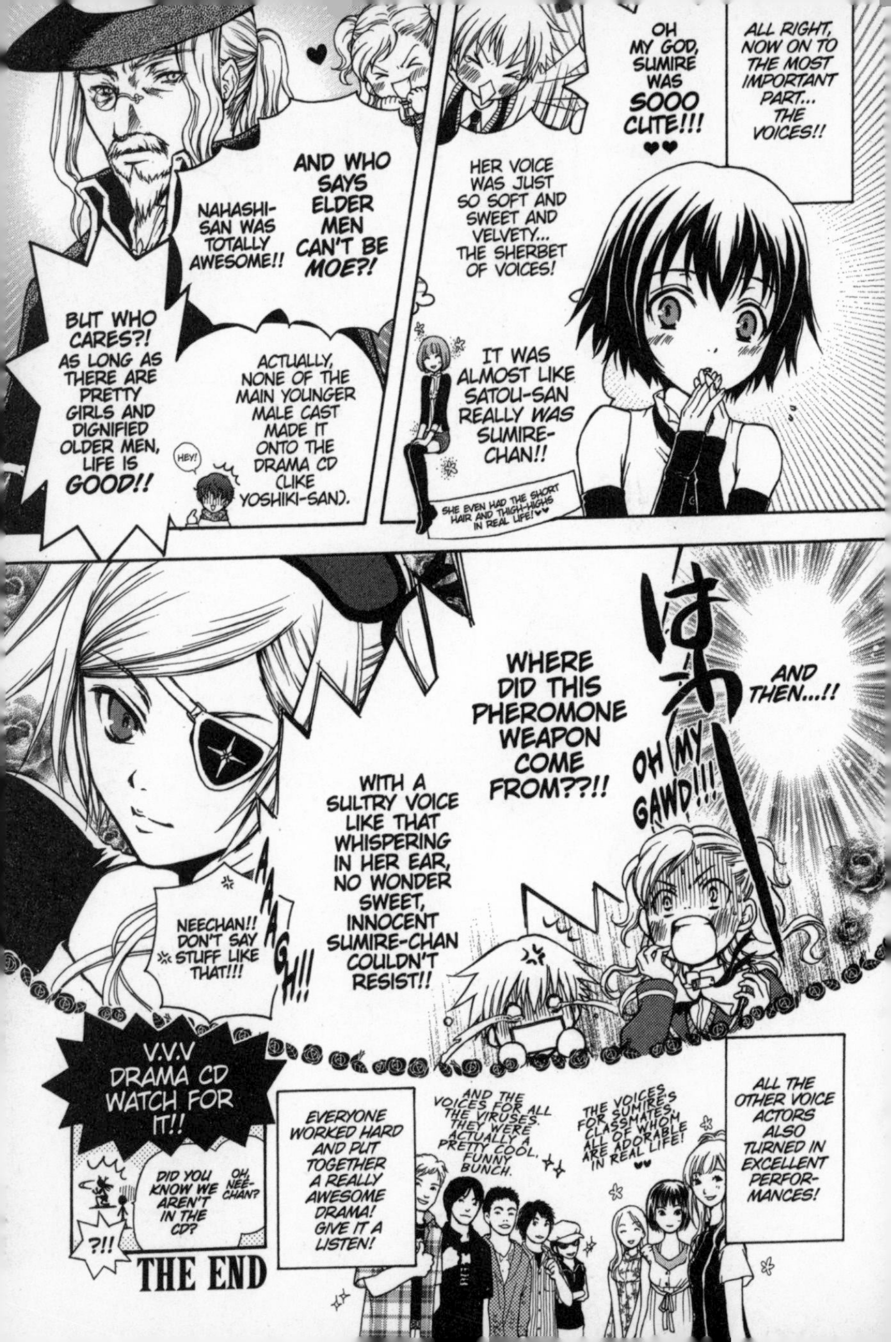
ALL RIGHT, NOW ON TO THE MOST IMPORTANT PART... THE VOICES!!
OH MY GOD, SUMIRE WAS SOOO CUTE!!! ♥♥
HER VOICE WAS JUST SO SOFT AND SWEET AND VELVETY... THE SHERBET OF VOICES!
IT WAS ALMOST LIKE SATOU-SAN REALLY WAS SUMIRE-CHAN!!
SHE EVEN HAD THE SHORT HAIR AND THIGH-HIGHS IN REAL LIFE! ♥♥
AND WHO SAYS ELDER MEN CAN'T BE MOE?!
NAHASHI-SAN WAS TOTALLY AWESOME!!
ACTUALLY, NONE OF THE MAIN YOUNGER MALE CAST MADE IT ONTO THE DRAMA CD (LIKE YOSHIKI-SAN).
HEY!
BUT WHO CARES?! AS LONG AS THERE ARE PRETTY GIRLS AND DIGNIFIED OLDER MEN, LIFE IS GOOD!!
AND THEN...!!
OH MY GAWD!!!
WHERE DID THIS PHEROMONE WEAPON COME FROM??!!
WITH A SULTRY VOICE LIKE THAT WHISPERING IN HER EAR, NO WONDER SWEET, INNOCENT SUMIRE-CHAN COULDN'T RESIST!!
AAAGH!!
NEECHAN!! DON'T SAY STUFF LIKE THAT!!!
ALL THE OTHER VOICE ACTORS ALSO TURNED IN EXCELLENT PERFORMANCES!
THE VOICES FOR SUMIRE'S CLASSMATES, ALL OF WHOM ARE ADORABLE IN REAL LIFE! ♥♥
AND THE VOICES FOR ALL THE VIRUSES. THEY WERE ACTUALLY A PRETTY COOL, FUNNY BUNCH.
EVERYONE WORKED HARD AND PUT TOGETHER A REALLY AWESOME DRAMA! GIVE IT A LISTEN!
V.V.V DRAMA CD WATCH FOR IT!!
OH, NEE-CHAN?
DID YOU KNOW WE AREN'T IN THE CD?
?!!
THE END

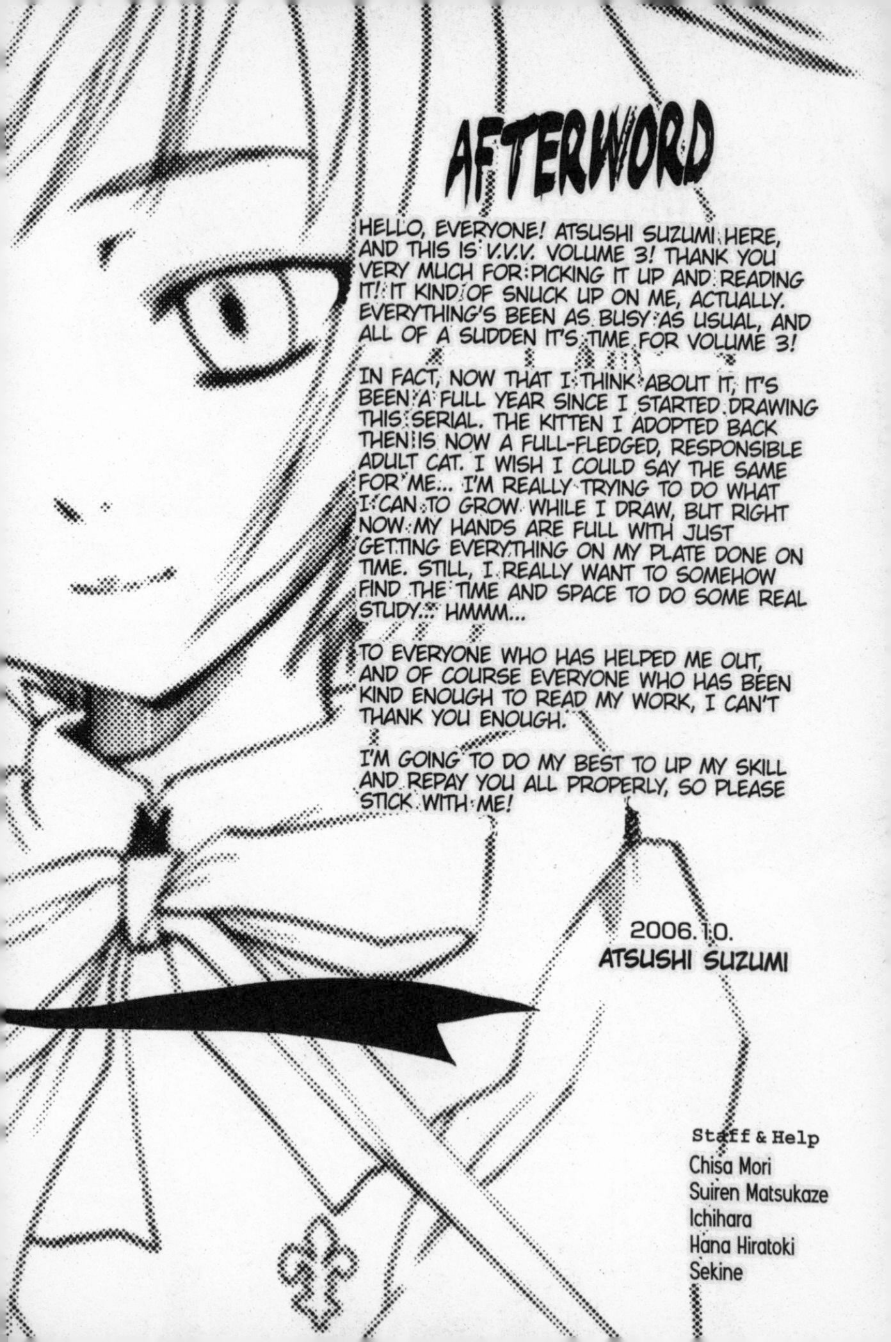

AFTERWORD

HELLO, EVERYONE! ATSUSHI SUZUMI HERE, AND THIS IS *V.V.V.* VOLUME 3! THANK YOU VERY MUCH FOR PICKING IT UP AND READING IT! IT KIND OF SNUCK UP ON ME, ACTUALLY. EVERYTHING'S BEEN AS BUSY AS USUAL, AND ALL OF A SUDDEN IT'S TIME FOR VOLUME 3!

IN FACT, NOW THAT I THINK ABOUT IT, IT'S BEEN A FULL YEAR SINCE I STARTED DRAWING THIS SERIAL. THE KITTEN I ADOPTED BACK THEN IS NOW A FULL-FLEDGED, RESPONSIBLE ADULT CAT. I WISH I COULD SAY THE SAME FOR ME... I'M REALLY TRYING TO DO WHAT I CAN TO GROW WHILE I DRAW, BUT RIGHT NOW MY HANDS ARE FULL WITH JUST GETTING EVERYTHING ON MY PLATE DONE ON TIME. STILL, I REALLY WANT TO SOMEHOW FIND THE TIME AND SPACE TO DO SOME REAL STUDY... HMMM...

TO EVERYONE WHO HAS HELPED ME OUT, AND OF COURSE EVERYONE WHO HAS BEEN KIND ENOUGH TO READ MY WORK, I CAN'T THANK YOU ENOUGH.

I'M GOING TO DO MY BEST TO UP MY SKILL AND REPAY YOU ALL PROPERLY, SO PLEASE STICK WITH ME!

2006.10.

ATSUSHI SUZUMI

Staff & Help

Chisa Mori

Suiren Matsukaze

Ichihara

Hana Hiratoki

Sekine

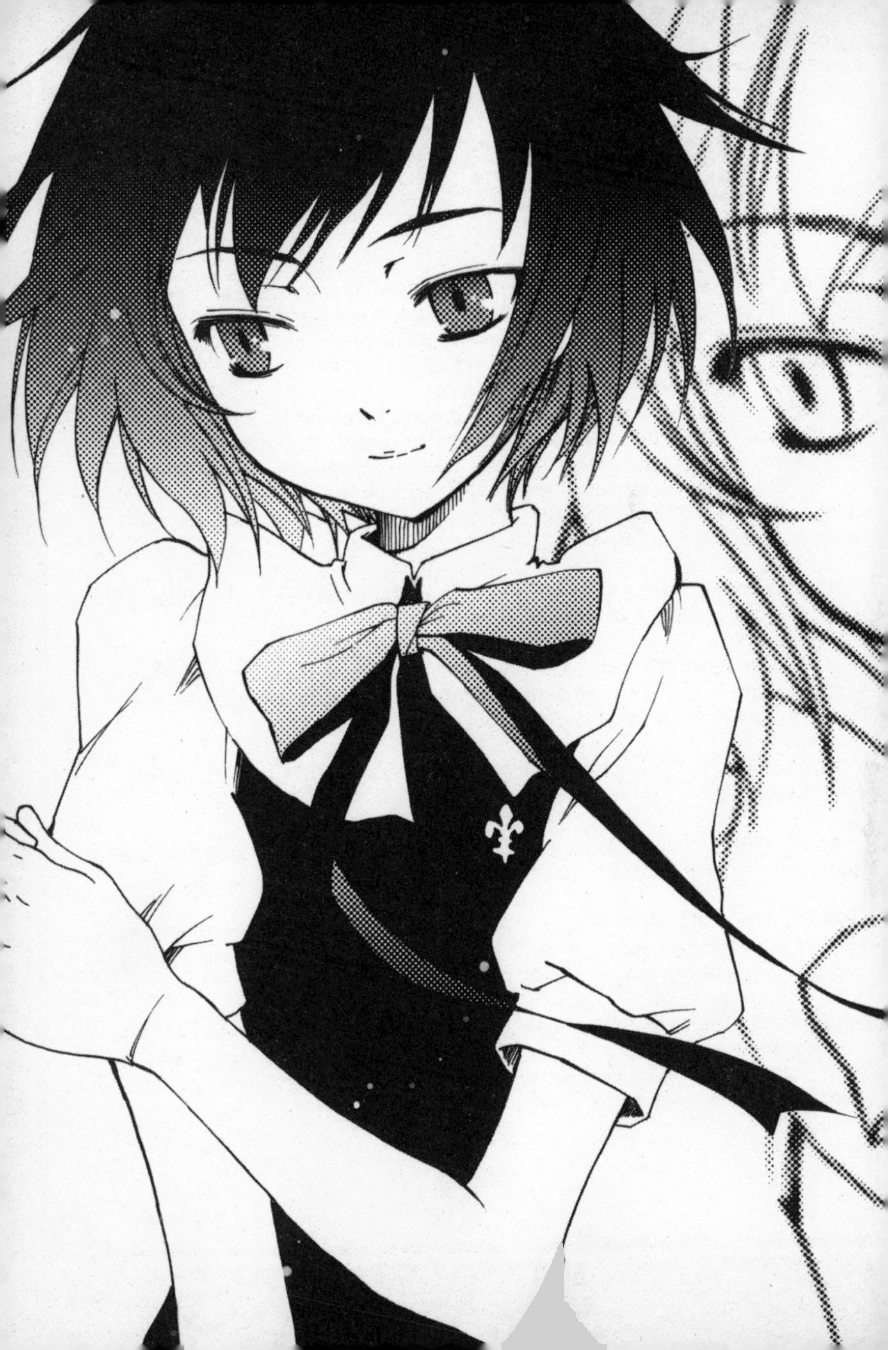

JAPANESE HONORIFICS GUIDE

To ensure that all character relationships appear as they were originally intended, all character names have been kept in their original Japanese name order with family name first and given name second. For copyright reasons, creator names appear in standard English name order.

In addition to preserving the original Japanese name order, Seven Seas is committed to ensuring that honorifics—polite speech that indicates a person's status or relationship towards another individual—are retained within this book. Politeness is an integral facet of Japanese culture and we believe that maintaining honorifics in our translations helps bring out the same character nuances as seen in the original work.

The following are some of the more common honorifics you may come across while reading this and other books:

-san – The most common of all honorifics, it is an all-purpose suffix that can be used in any situation where politeness is expected. Generally seen as the equivalent to Mr., Miss, Ms., Mrs., etc.

-sama – This suffix is one level higher than "-san" and is used to confer great respect upon an individual.

-dono – Stemming from the word "tono," meaning "lord," "-dono" signifies an even higher level than "-sama," and confers the utmost respect.

-kun – This suffix is commonly used at the end of boys' names to express either familiarity or endearment. It can also be used when addressing someone younger than oneself or of a lower status.

-chan – Another common honorific. This suffix is mainly used to express endearment towards girls, but can also be used when referring to little boys or even pets. Couples are also known to use the term amongst each other to convey a sense of cuteness and intimacy.

Sempai – This title is used towards one's senior or "superior" in a particular group or organization. "Sempai" is most often used in a school setting, where underclassmen refer to upperclassmen as "sempai," though it is also commonly said by employees when addressing fellow employees who hold seniority in the workplace.

Kouhai – This is the exact opposite of "sempai," and is used to refer to underclassmen in school, junior employees at the workplace, etc.

Sensei – Literally meaning "one who has come before," this title is used for teachers, doctors, or masters of any profession or art.

Oniisan – This title literally means "big brother." First and foremost, it is used by younger siblings towards older male siblings. It can be used by itself or attached to a person's name as a suffix (niisan). It is often used by a younger person toward an older person unrelated by blood, but as a sign of respect. Other forms include the informal "oniichan" and the more respectful "oniisama."

Oneesan – This title is the opposite of "oniisan" and means "big sister." Other forms include the informal "oneechan" and the more respectful "oneesama."

⚜ TRANSLATION NOTES ⚜

8.3 A "kekkai" is a magical barrier or ward.

75.3 The original joke here is a word-pun. Sumire is trying to say "mochiron desu" ("of course"), but is stuttering on the "mo" part. In Japanese, "momo" means "peach," so Yoshiki thinks for a moment that she's saying "peach peach."

87.2 In the first printings of Venus Versus Virus Vol. 1 & 2, we incorrectly spelled Lilith's name as "Lillith." We admit this as an error and have corrected the spelling for Vol. 3.

174.5 "Gakuen" is a general word for "school." "Gakuin" is the word for "academy."

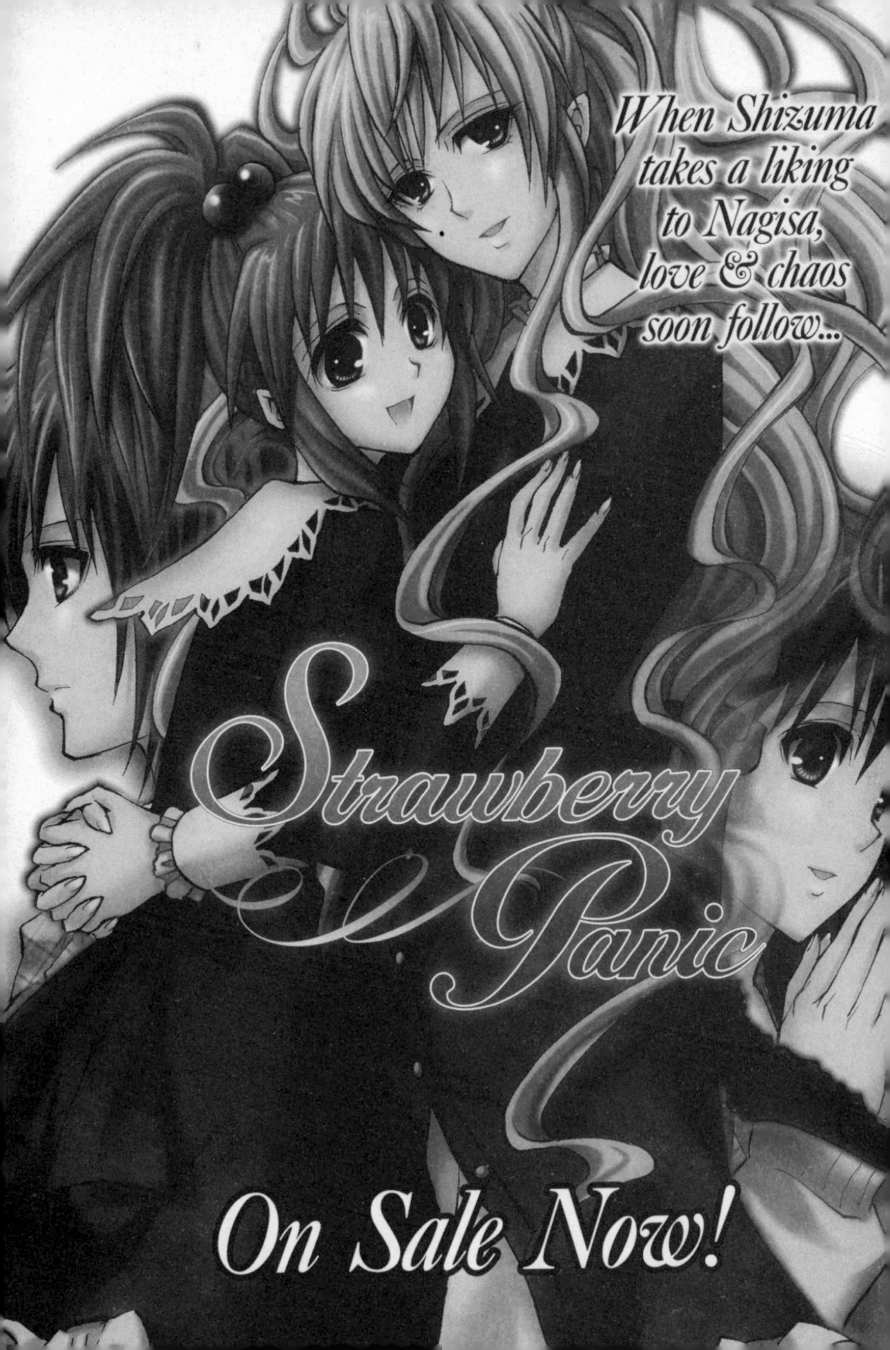

When Shizuma takes a liking to Nagisa, love & chaos soon follow...
Strawberry Panic
On Sale Now!

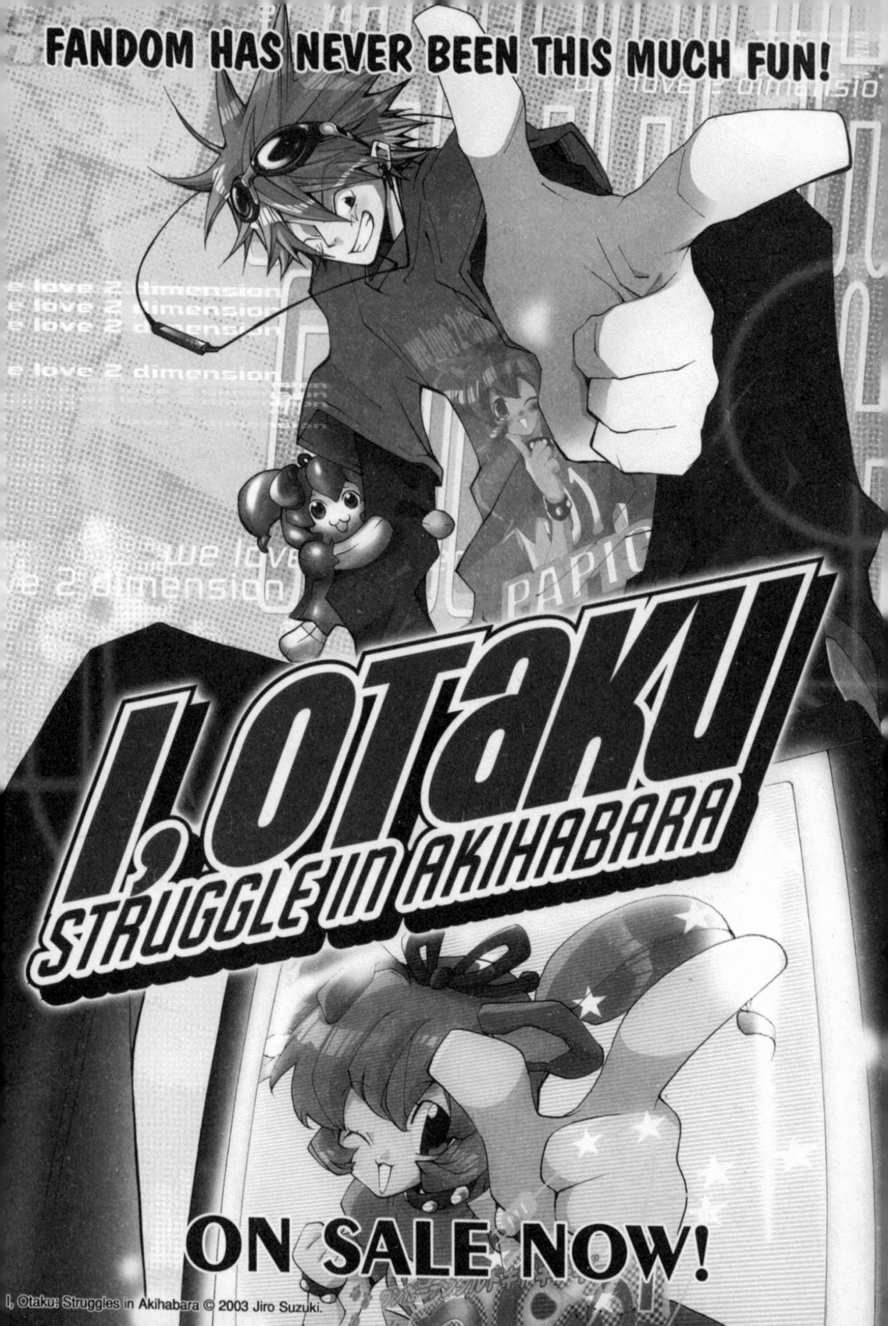
FANDOM HAS NEVER BEEN THIS MUCH FUN!
I, OTAKU
STRUGGLE IN AKIHABARA
ON SALE NOW!

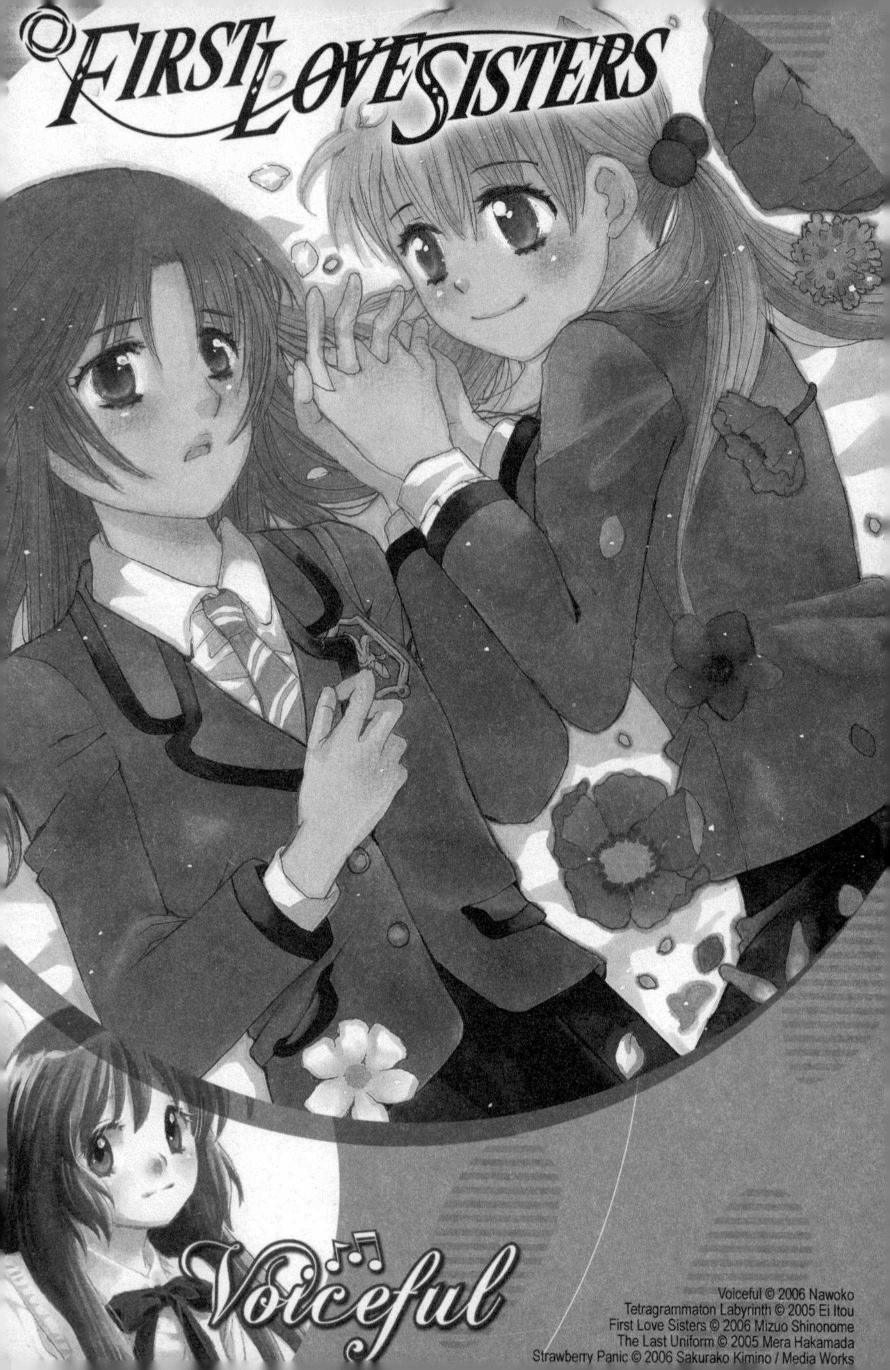
FIRST LOVE SISTERS
Voiceful

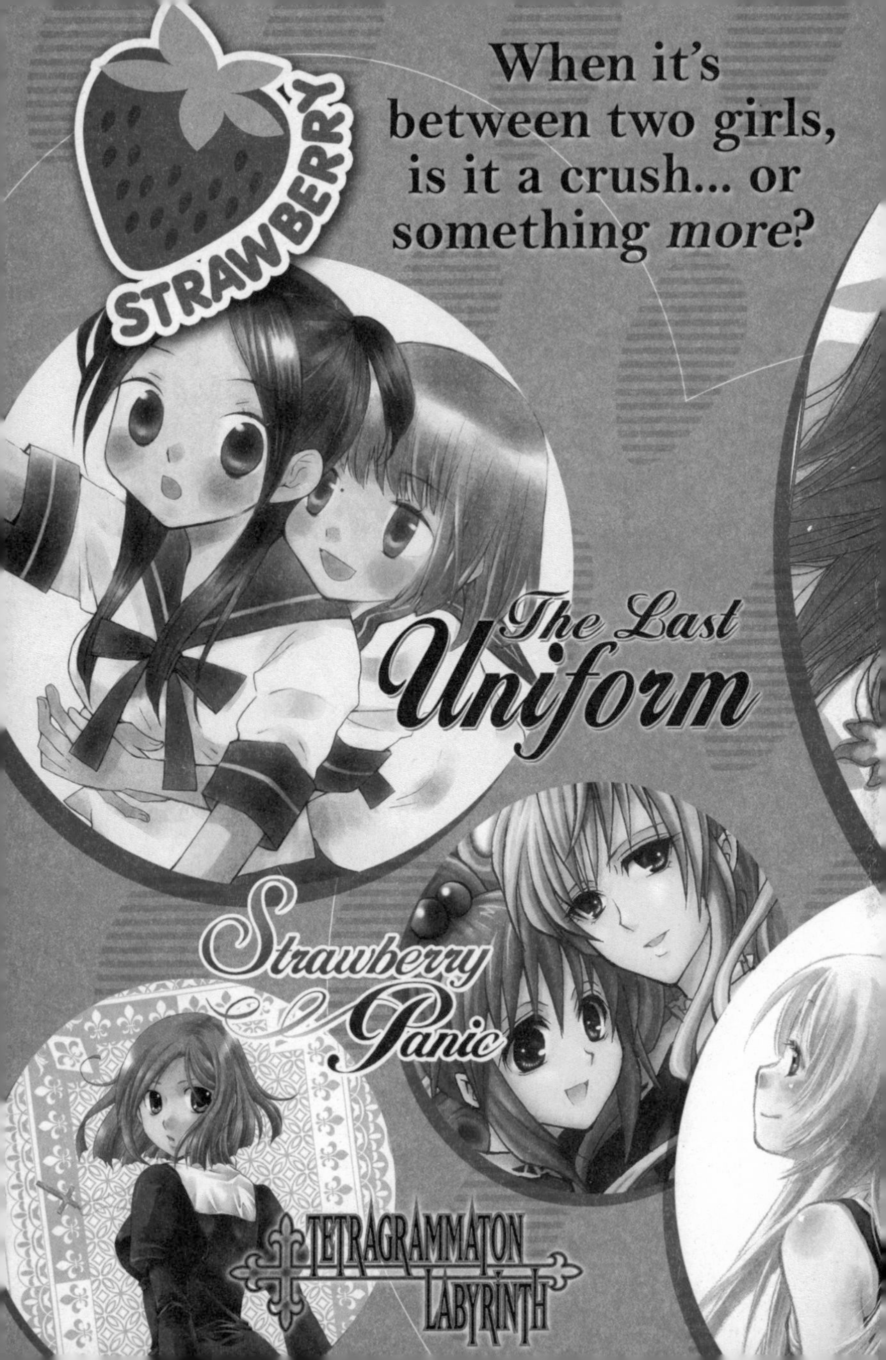
STRAWBERRY
When it's between two girls, is it a crush... or something *more*?
The Last Uniform
Strawberry Panic
TETRAGRAMMATON LABYRINTH

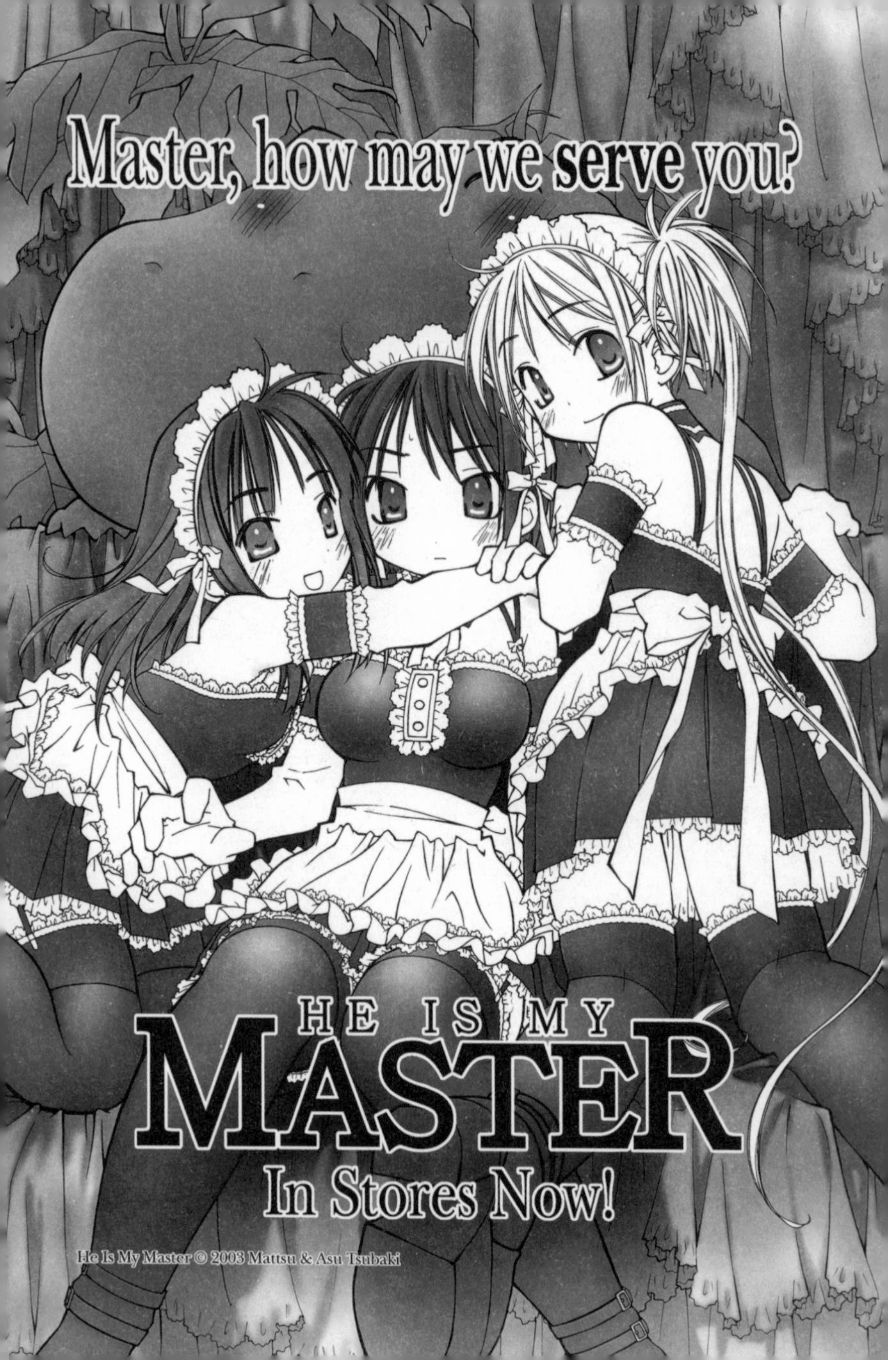
Master, how may we serve you?
HE IS MY
MASTER
In Stores Now!
He Is My Master © 2003 Mattsu & Asu Tsubaki

Amazing Agent
LUNA

volume 4

Amazing Agent Luna © 2005 Seven Seas Entertainment, LLC, and Nunzio DeFilippis & Christina Weir.

Volume 1 - 3
In Stores Now!

Luna: the perfect secret agent. A girl grown in a lab from the finest genetic material, she has been trained since birth to be the U.S. government's ultimate espionage weapon. But now she is given an assignment that will test her abilities to the max - *high school!*

story **Nunzio DeFilippis** & **Christina Weir** • *art* **Shiei**

visit www.gomanga.com

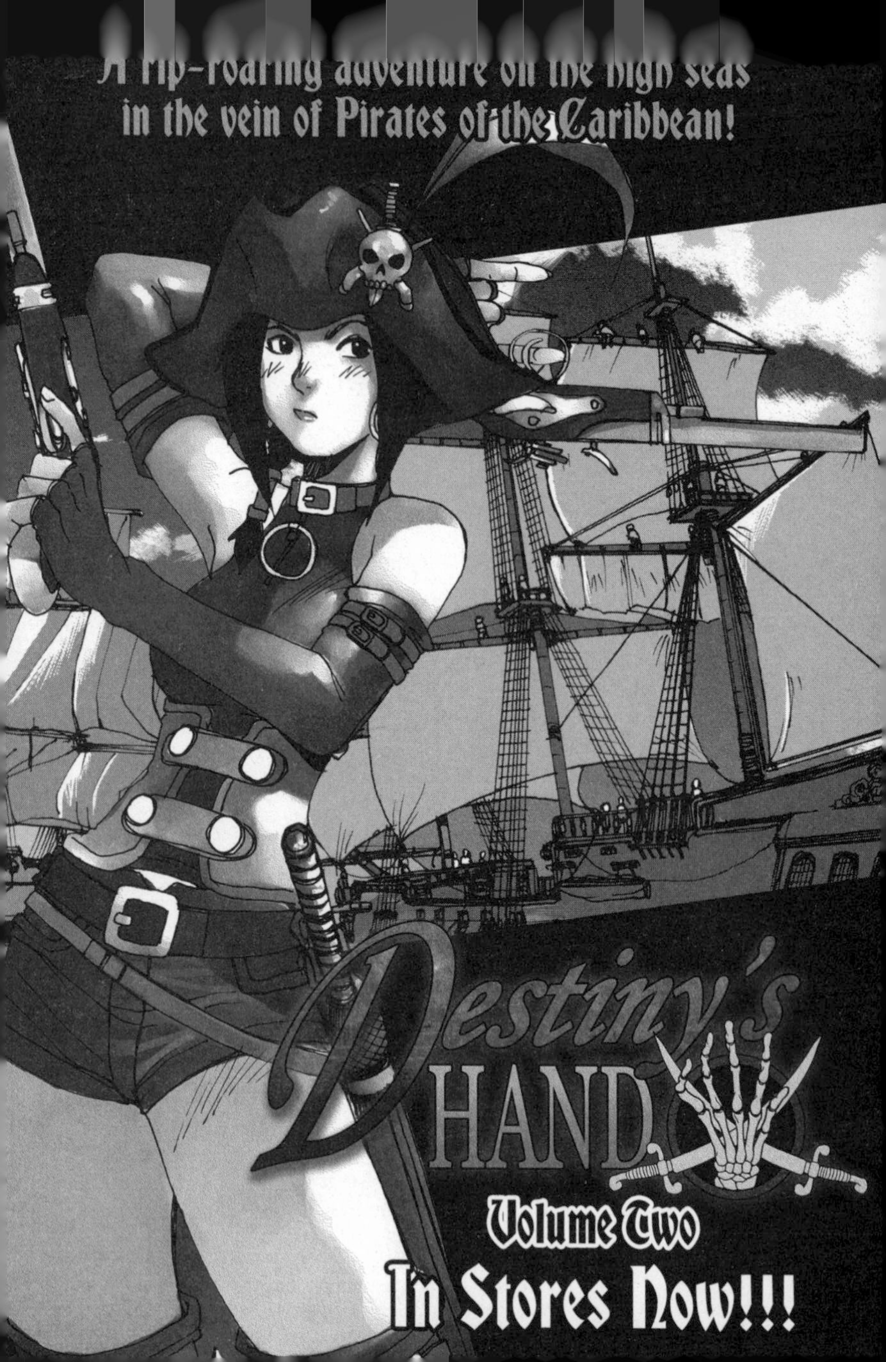
A rip-roaring adventure on the high seas
in the vein of Pirates of the Caribbean!
Destiny's
HAND
Volume Two
In Stores Now!!!

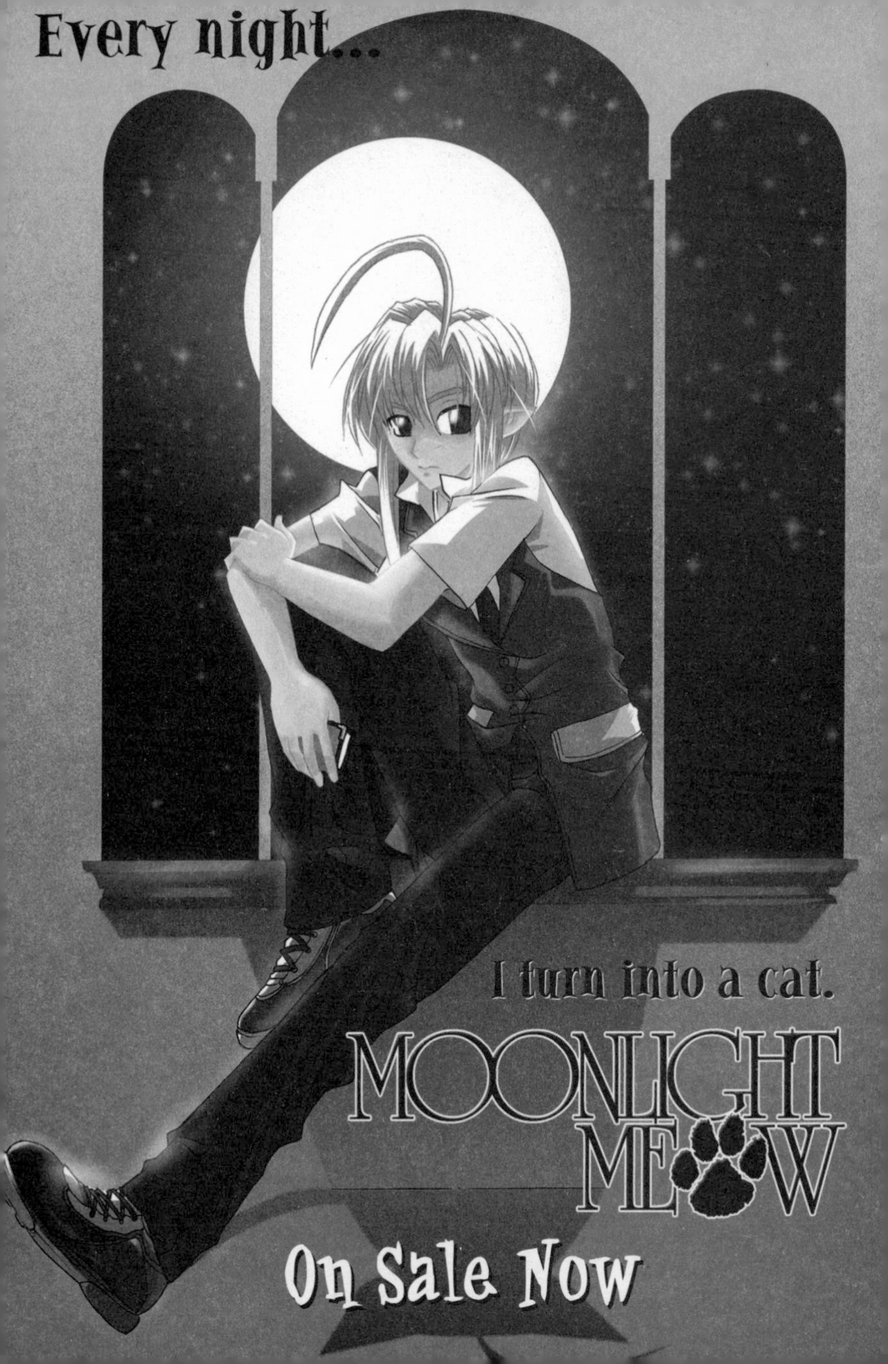

Every night...
I turn into a cat.
MOONLIGHT MEOW
On Sale Now

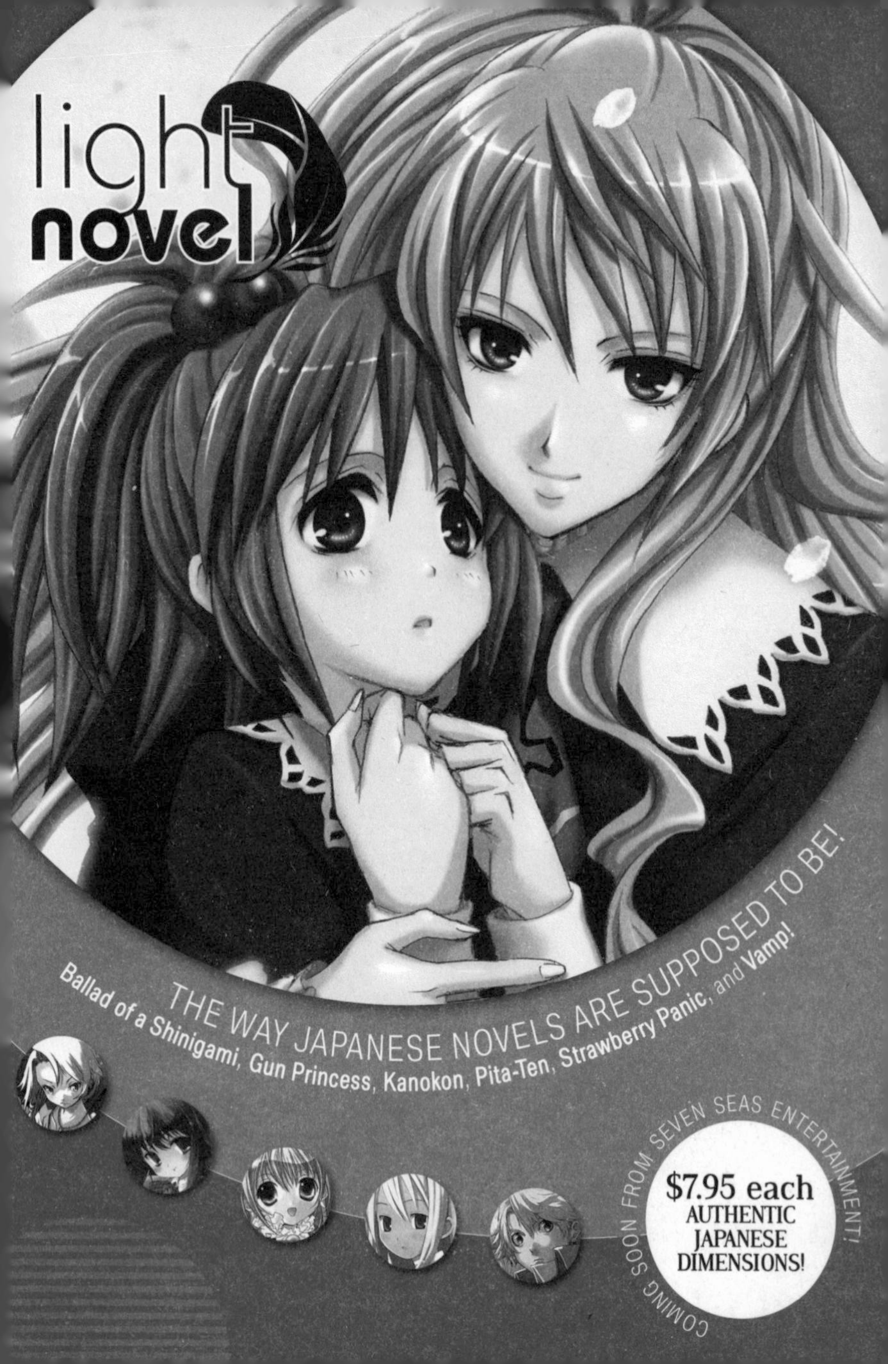
light novel
THE WAY JAPANESE NOVELS ARE SUPPOSED TO BE!
Ballad of a Shinigami, Gun Princess, Kanokon, Pita-Ten, Strawberry Panic, and Vamp!
COMING SOON FROM SEVEN SEAS ENTERTAINMENT!
$7.95 each
AUTHENTIC JAPANESE DIMENSIONS!

VOLUME 3

story & art by **Atsushi Suzumi**

STAFF CREDITS

translation	**Adrienne Beck**
adaptation	**Janet Houck**
retouch & lettering	**Roland Amago**
design	**Roland Amago**
layout	**Bambi Eloriaga**
copy editor	**Lori Smith**
editor	**Adam Arnold**

publisher **Seven Seas Entertainment**

VENUS VERSUS VIRUS VOL. 3
© ATSUSHI SUZUMI 2006
First published in 2006 by Media Works Inc., Tokyo, Japan
English translation rights arranged with Media Works, Inc.

Visit us online at www.gomanga.com

ISBN: 978-1-933164-90-8

Printed in Canada

First printing: March 2008

10 9 8 7 6 5 4 3 2 1

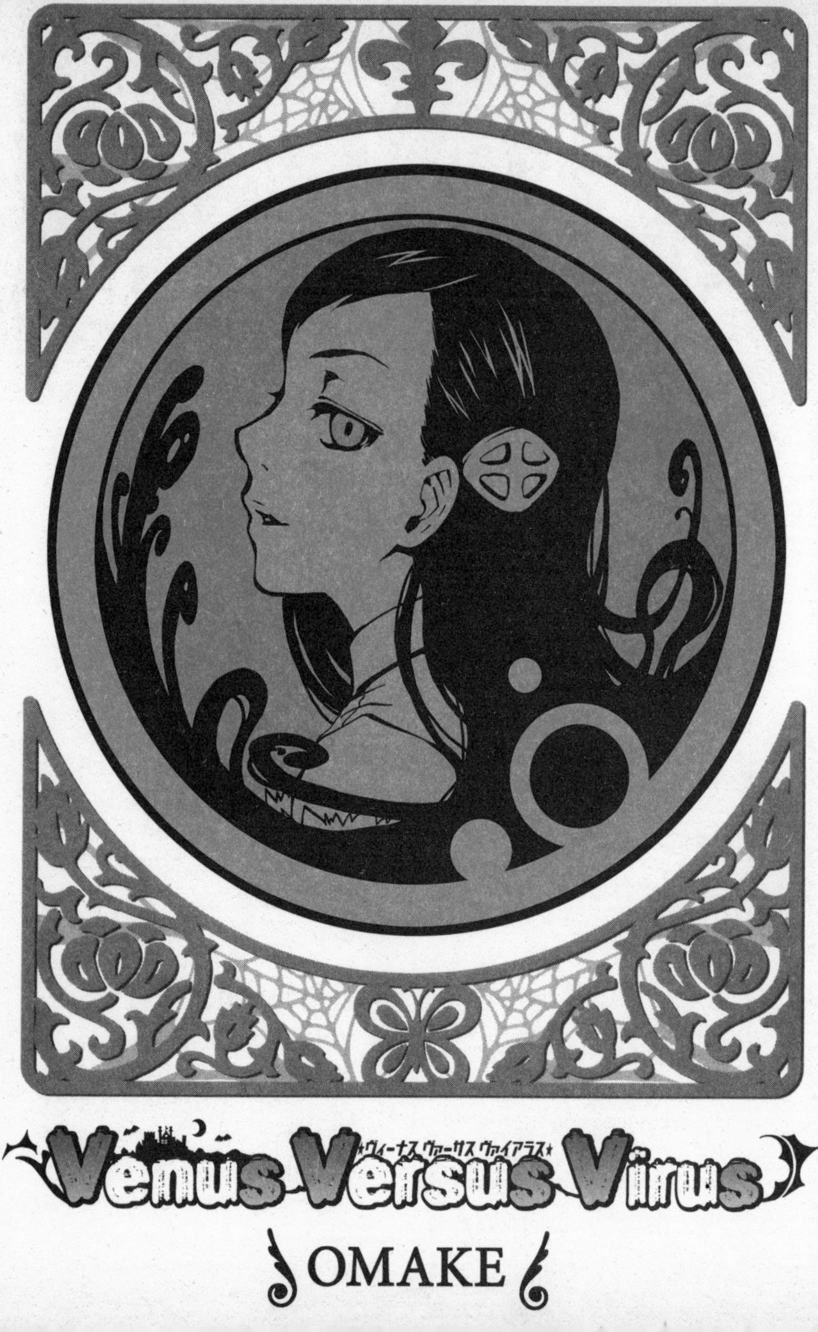

Venus Versus Virus

ヴィーナス ヴァーサス ヴァイアラス

OMAKE

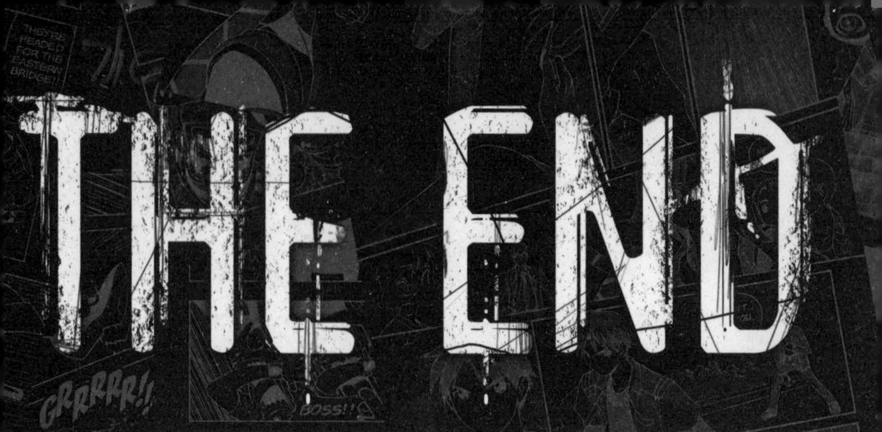
THE END
THEY'RE HEADED FOR THE EASTERN BRIDGE!!
BOSS!!

YOU'RE READING THE WRONG WAY

This is the last page of
Venus Versus Virus Volume 3.

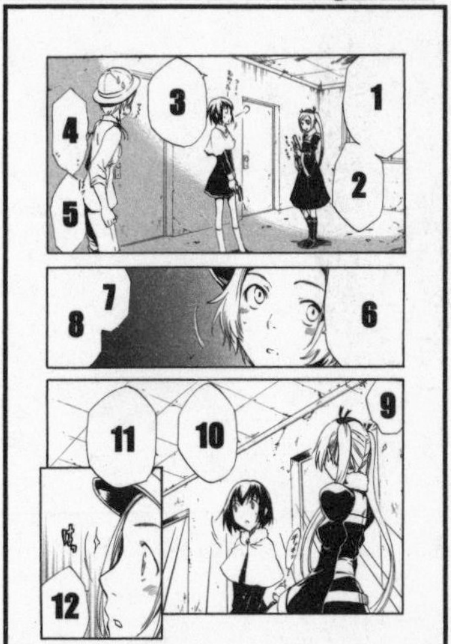
1
2
3
4
5
6
7
8
9
10
11
12

This book reads from right to left, Japanese style. To read from the beginning, flip the book over to the other side, start with the top right panel, and take it from there.

If this is your first time reading manga, just follow the diagram. It may seem backwards at first, but you'll get used to it! Have fun!